Daughters of Ireland

BY JANET TODD

Mary Wollstonecraft: A Revolutionary Life

Women's Friendship in Literature

Sensibility

Feminist Literary History

The Sign of Angellica: Women, Writing and Fiction 1660–1800

Gender, Art and Death

The Secret Life of Aphra Behn

Daughters of Ireland

THE REBELLIOUS
KINGSBOROUGH SISTERS
AND THE MAKING OF
A MODERN NATION

JANET TODD

BALLANTINE BOOKS

NEW YORK

A BALLANTINE BOOK
Published by The Random House Publishing Group
Copyright © 2003 by Janet Todd

www.ballantinebooks.com

Library of Congress Cataloging-in-Publication Data
Todd, Janet M., 1942–
Daughters of Ireland : the rebellious Kingsborough sisters and
the making of a modern nation / Janet Todd.—1st ed.
p. cm.
ISBN 0-345-44764-6

1. Moore, Margaret King, 1772–1835. 2. King, Mary Elizabeth, d. 1819. 3. Kingston,
Robert King, Earl of, 1754–1799—Family. 4. Wollstonecraft, Mary, 1759–1797—Friends
and associates. 5. Women and literature—Ireland—History—19th century. 6. Ireland—
History—Rebellion of 1798—Biography. 7. Women revolutionaries—Ireland—
Biography. 8. Authors, Irish—19th century—Biography. 9. Cork (Ireland : County)—
Biography. 10. Mitchelstown (Ireland)—Biography. I. Title.

PR5101.M343Z89 2004
941.507'092'2—dc22
[B]   2003062764

Manufactured in the United States of America

First Edition: February 2004

10   9   8   7   6   5   4   3   2   1

Book design by Shubhani Sarkar

Contents

List of Illustrations

Acknowledgments

WHILE TAKING TOTAL RESPONSIBILITY FOR ERRORS IN MY account, I wish to thank many people for most generous help. The descendants of Robert Edward King—the late Barclay King-Tenison, Earl of Kingston, and Colonel A. L. King-Harman—were helpful with both suggestions and documents. So was the descendant of Margaret King, Andrea Dazzi, with his wife, Cristina, in San Marcello, to whom I am also grateful for kind hospitality. I owe a great debt to many distinguished Irish historians. Kevin Whelan allowed me access to his research on the Irish Union; Sir Richard Aylmer and Anthony Malcomson were both extremely generous with suggestions and documents, especially concerning Lady Moira; Anthony Malcomson, in addition, kindly inspected for me the letters in the possession of Lady Georgina Forbes. Brian MacDermot sent me a volume of correspondence of his medical ancestor and Bill Power gave me an enlightening tour of Mitchelstown and the remnants of the castle; the Munster Women's Collective and the Eighteenth-Century Ireland Society invited me to talk at Cork University and Maynooth College at just the right moments in my research. Bruce Barker-Benfield, Marilyn Butler, Claire Connolly, Judy Corbalis, Seamus Cullen, Elizabeth Denlinger, David Fleming, Elizabeth M. Kirwan, Rolf Loeber, Willy Maley, Alison McCann, John Mullins, Jim Nash, Clarissa Campbell Orr, Brendan Pendred, Elizabeth Spearing, Claire Tomalin, Stephen Wagner and Penny Woods have all pointed me in useful directions.

I am grateful to the following libraries for allowing me access to their special collections and for giving me permission to draw upon unpublished material: The Carl H. Pforzheimer Collection of Shelley and His

Circle, The New York Public Library, Astor, Lenox and Tilden Foundations; Cambridge University Library; the Bodleian Library, Oxford; the British Library; the Dublin National Library; the National Archives of Ireland; the Public Record Office of Northern Ireland; the Cork City Library and Cork Archives, Cork; the West Sussex Records Office; the Historical Manuscripts Commission, Chancery Lane, London; and the Public Record Office, Kew. I am indebted to most helpful librarians in each of these institutions.

I would like to thank Colonel King-Harman for permission to reproduce the portraits of Caroline, Lady Kingsborough, and Robert, Lord Kingsborough, as well as the letter from Lord Kingsborough to Colonel Henry Fitzgerald, now in the Public Record Office of Northern Ireland. I would also like to thank Eton College for permission to reproduce the portrait of George King, and the Walker Art Gallery of Liverpool for similar permission for the portrait of Mary Wollstonecraft.

My main debts are to my research assistant, Antje Blank, who has immeasurably helped this project with her care and enthusiasm, and to the University of Glasgow, which has generously supported it.

Chronology

1759	APR. 27	Mary Wollstonecraft born in London
1760	OCT. 25	George III succeeds to British throne
1761	OCT.	Beginning of Whiteboy activism in Munster, Ireland
1766	MAR. 15	Catholic priest Nicholas Sheehy executed at Clonmel, convicted of instigating Whiteboy violence and murder
1769	DEC. 5	Robert King, Lord Kingsborough, marries Caroline Fitzgerald in Dublin
1770		George King, later 3rd Earl of Kingston, born in London
c. 1771		Margaret King born in Dublin
1772	DEC. 15	Lord and Lady Kingsborough leave Ireland for the Grand Tour
1773	DEC. 16	"Boston tea party": colonial protest against British taxation
1775	APR. 19	Beginning of American War of Independence
	SEPT. 25	Lord and Lady Kingsborough arrive back in Dublin
	OCT. 12	James Butler, Catholic Archbishop of Cashel, orders his clergy to denounce Whiteboyism from pulpit
1776	JUNE 20	Arthur Young begins tour of Ireland
1777	SEPT.	Arthur Young hired by Kingsboroughs at Mitchelstown
1778	AUG. 11	Catholic Relief Act allows Catholics to take out leases and inherit in same manner as Protestants
1779		Arthur Young dismissed by Lord Kingsborough
1780	JUNE 2–9	Anti-Catholic Gordon Riots in London
		Arthur Young's *A Tour in Ireland 1776–1779* published in London
c. 1780		Mary King born
1781	OCT. 19	British surrender at Yorktown signals end of American War of Independence
1782	MAY 4	Catholic Relief Act allows Catholics to purchase land except within parliamentary boroughs
	JUNE 21	British act for repeal of Declaratory Act (passed Apr. 7, 1720, it had asserted British Parliament's right to legislate for Ireland)
		Beginning of "Grattan's Parliament"
1783	APR. 17	British Renunciation Act asserts Irish Parliament's exclusive right to legislate for Ireland

	DEC. 19	William Pitt appointed Prime Minister of Great Britain
		Robert, Lord Kingsborough, takes one of Co. Cork parliamentary seats in fiercely contested election
1785		Anti-tithe Rightboy campaign in Co. Cork
1786	OCT.	Wollstonecraft as governess to Kingsborough daughters
		Wollstonecraft's *Thoughts on the Education of Daughters* published by Joseph Johnson in London
		Joseph Cooper Walker, *Historical Memoirs of the Irish Bards* published in Dublin
1787	MAR. 26	Tumultuous Risings Act to curb rioting and hindering of tithe-collection
	JULY	Wollstonecraft dismissed by Lady Kingsborough
1788	NOV. 5	George III becomes insane
		Wollstonecraft's *Mary: A Fiction* and *Original Stories from Real Life* published by Johnson in London
1789	MAR. 10	George III declared sane
	JUNE 20	John Fitzgibbon, later Earl of Clare, becomes Lord Chancellor of Ireland
	JULY 14	Fall of Bastille in Paris
		Charlotte Brooke, *Reliques of Irish Poetry* published in Dublin
1790	JAN. 5	Earl of Westmoreland sworn in as Lord Lieutenant of Ireland
	FEB. 15	Robert, Lord Kingsborough, becomes Joint Governor of Co. Cork
	JUNE/JULY	Robert, Lord Kingsborough, loses his parliamentary seat in Co. Cork but is returned in by-election the following year
	NOV. 1	Edmund Burke, *Reflections on the Revolution in France* published in London
	NOV. 29	Wollstonecraft's response, *A Vindication of the Rights of Men,* published anonymously
1791	MAR. 13	Thomas Paine, *Rights of Man,* pt. 1, published in London
	SEPT. 12	Stephen Moore, 2nd Earl of Mount Cashell, marries Margaret King
	OCT. 14	Society of United Irishmen founded in Belfast
	NOV. 9	Dublin Society of United Irishmen meets
1792	JAN. 4	*Northern Star,* organ of United Irishmen in Belfast, first published
	JAN.	Wollstonecraft's *A Vindication of the Rights of Woman* published by Johnson
	FEB. 16	Thomas Paine, *Rights of Man,* pt. 2, published in London
	FEB. 20	Petition of Catholic Committee for parliamentary franchise rejected by Irish House of Commons
	DEC. 27	Lord Edward Fitzgerald marries Pamela, "Mademoiselle Egalité"
1793	JAN. 21	Louis XVI executed in Paris
	FEB. 1	France declares war on England
	FEB. 25	Act to prevent importation of arms and ammunition and their movement without license passed by Irish House of Commons
	FEB. 25	First Foot Guards, among them Col. Henry Fitzgerald, embark for Continent

	APR. 9	Catholic Relief Act extending parliamentary franchise to some Catholics and allowing them to hold civil and military office
		Militia Act establishing militia of ca. 15,000 soldiers
	AUG. 16	Convention Act prohibiting political assemblies for the purpose of preparing petitions to Parliament
1794	JAN. 29	Opening of trial of Archibald Hamilton Rowan, secretary of Dublin Society of United Irishmen, on charges of distributing seditious material, defense led by John Philpot Curran
	MAY 2	Rowan flees to France where he makes acquaintance of Wollstonecraft
	MAY 23	United Irishmen outlawed
	JULY 11	Duke of Portland joins Pitt's cabinet in London
	JULY 27–28	Death of Robespierre and fall of the Jacobin faction in Paris
	SEPT. 8	British army in Flanders, commanded by Duke of York, defeated at Hondschoote by French republican forces
	NOV. 5	Treason Trials end in London with the acquittal of Thomas Hardy, Thomas Holcroft, John Horne Tooke and John Thelwall
	DEC. 2	Duke of York recalled
1795	JAN. 4	Earl Fitzwilliam sworn in as Lord Lieutenant
	JAN. 23	French republican forces capture icebound Dutch fleet, Prince of Orange capitulates
	FEB. 12	Grattan introduces bill for further relief of Catholics
	FEB. 23	Fitzwilliam dismissed
	MAR. 31	Earl Camden sworn in as Lord Lieutenant
	MAY 5	Irish House of Commons rejects Grattan's Catholic Relief Bill
	MAY	First Foot Guards, among them Col. Henry Fitzgerald, return to London
	SEPT. 21	"Battle of the Diamond" in Co. Armagh between Peep O'Day Boys and Defenders results in foundation of Orange Order
	OCT.	Mary Wollstonecraft attempts suicide for second time, jumping from Putney Bridge, London
	OCT. 29	George III on way to open London Parliament is attacked by crowds demanding food and peace
	NOV.	Passing of Treason Practices Act and Seditious Meetings Act in British House of Commons limiting rights of popular protest
1796	MAR. 24	Insurrection Act in Ireland
	AUG.	Arthur O'Connor and Gen. Lazare Hoche meet secretly in France to discuss French support for United Irish rising
	OCT. 17	Irish House of Commons rejects Grattan's motion to admit Catholics to Parliament
	OCT. 26	Habeas Corpus suspended in Ireland (continued by successive acts)
	DEC. 22–27	French ships, carrying invasion troops and Wolfe Tone, arrive in Bantry Bay to assist Irish insurgents; bad weather scatters fleet and prevents landing
1797	JUNE 4	Orange Lodge formed in Dublin
	AUG. 30	Mary Wollstonecraft Godwin born
	SEPT. 10	Mary Wollstonecraft dies of septicemia following childbirth
	SEPT. 23	Newspaper advertisements beginning to appear announcing the elopement of Mary King

	SEPT. 28	Announcement in *The Times* of Mary King's return to her family
	OCT. 1	Duel fought between Col. Henry Fitzgerald and Col. Robert Edward King
	OCT. 5	Robert King, Lord Kingsborough, threatens Col. Henry Fitzgerald in a letter
	NOV. 8	Edward, 1st Earl of Kingston, dies; Robert becomes second Earl
	NOV. 10	Sir Ralph Abercromby appointed Commander-in-Chief in Ireland
	DEC.	Col. Henry Fitzgerald shot by Robert King, 2nd Earl of Kingston, at Kilworth Inn
1798	MAR. 12	Arrest of sixteen executive members of United Irish committee meeting at Oliver Bond's house, Dublin
	APR. 25	Abercromby succeeded by Gen. Gerard Lake as Commander-in-Chief in Ireland
	MAY 17	Meeting of United Irish executive postpones rising from May 18 to 23
	MAY 18	Trial and acquittal of Robert King, 2nd Earl of Kingston, before the Irish House of Lords
	MAY 19	Lord Edward Fitzgerald is wounded in arrest at Nicholas Murphy's house
	MAY 23	Irish Rebellion begins
	MAY 27	Battle of Oulart Hill; detachment of North Cork militia almost annihilated
	MAY 29	Viscount Castlereagh appointed Chief Secretary
	MAY 30	Wexford town occupied by rebels
	JUNE 2	George King, Lord Kingsborough, taken hostage by Wexford rebels
	JUNE 4	Lord Edward Fitzgerald dies from wounds
	JUNE 5	Rebels defeated at New Ross; massacre of Protestants at Scullabogue
	JUNE 20	Marquis Cornwallis replaces Lord Camden as Lord Lieutenant
	JUNE 21	Gen. Lake's forces defeat rebels at Vinegar Hill; Wexford subsequently recaptured; George, Lord Kingsborough, freed
	AUG. 1	Battle of Nile; French fleet destroyed by British navy under command of Admiral Horatio Nelson
	AUG. 22	French troops led by Gen. Humbert land at Killala to invade Ireland
	AUG. 27	Government forces, under command of Gen. Lake, routed by Gen. Humbert at Castlebar
	SEPT. 8	Humbert surrenders
	OCT. 12	Further French troops land in County Donegal, among them Wolfe Tone; they are defeated; Wolfe Tone captured
	NOV. 10	Wolfe Tone sentenced to death by court-martial in Dublin; tries to commit suicide; dies Nov. 19
1799	JAN. 23	George Ponsonby's motion in favor of continued legislative independence for Ireland rejected
	JAN. 31	Pitt's speech in British House of Commons supporting a Union
	APR.	Robert, 2nd Earl of Kingston, dies
	NOV. 9–10	18–19 *Brumaire:* Napoleon Bonaparte becomes first consul of France

Margaret Moore, Countess of Mount Cashell, *A Few Words in Favour of Ireland* and *Reply to a Ministerial Pamphlet* published in Dublin

1800	MAR. 25	Suppression of Rebellion Act empowering Lord Lieutenant to authorize court-martial trials
	APR. 9	Leading United Irishmen, among them Thomas Addis Emmet, Arthur O'Connor and Thomas Russell, imprisoned at Fort George, Scotland (until June 30, 1802)
	JULY 2	British Act of Union
	AUG. 1	Irish Act of Union

Margaret Moore, Countess of Mount Cashell, *A Hint to the Inhabitants of Ireland by a Native* published in Dublin

Maria Edgeworth, *Castle Rackrent* published

1801	JAN. 1	Union of Great Britain and Ireland comes into force. Dublin parliament dissolved
	FEB. 3	Pitt resigns as Prime Minister over disagreement with George III concerning Catholic emancipation

Sir Richard Musgrave's *Memoirs of the Different Rebellions in Ireland* published in Dublin

1803	JULY 23	Robert Emmet's rising in Dublin
	SEPT. 20	Robert Emmet executed after conviction of high treason
1804	MAY 18	Napoleon Bonaparte proclaimed Emperor
1805		Margaret Moore separates from her husband Stephen, 2nd Earl of Mount Cashell
1811	FEB. 5	Prince of Wales becomes Regent following George III's insanity
1814	JULY 28	Mary Wollstonecraft Godwin elopes with Percy Bysshe Shelley
		Margaret Moore, now calling herself Mrs. Mason, settles in Pisa with her lover George Tighe
1815	JUNE 18	Napoleon Bonaparte defeated at Waterloo; he abdicates
1819		Mary King dies
1820		George III dies, George IV succeeds
1821	AUG. 12– SEPT. 3	George IV visits Ireland, is greeted on arrival by George, 3rd Earl of Kingston
1822	OCT. 27	Stephen, 2nd Earl of Mount Cashell, dies
		Castlereagh, now Marquis of Londonderry, commits suicide
1823	JAN. 13	Caroline King, mother of Mary, Margaret and George, dies
1826		George Tighe marries Margaret Moore, "Mrs. Mason"
1827		Sir Jonah Barrington's *Personal Sketches of His Own Time* published in London
1831		Thomas Moore's *Life and Death of Lord Edward Fitzgerald* published in London
1833		George King, 3rd Earl of Kingston, pronounced insane
1835	JAN.	Margaret, "Mrs. Mason," dies
1839		George King, 3rd Earl of Kingston, dies

The Kingston Family

SIR WILLIAM FENTON *m.* MARGARET FITZGIBBON,
HEIRESS OF WHITE KNIGHT

KATHERINE FENTON *m.* SIR JOHN KING,
1ST BARON
KINGSTON, *d. 1676*

ROBERT, 2ND BARON KINGSTON

JOHN, 3RD BARON *m.* MARGARET O'CAHAN
KINGSTON, *d. 1728*

JAMES, 4TH BARON *m.* (1ST) ELIZABETH FREKE
KINGSTON, *d. 1761*
m. (2ND)
ISABELLA OGLE

GEORGE

RICHARD FITZGERALD *m.* (1ST) MARGARET
m. (2ND) MARY MERCER

HENRY FITZGER-
ALD,
d. 1797

GERALD HENRY,
d. 1845
m. (1ST) ISABELLA STAPLES

MARGARET
m. JOHN JOCELYN

2 DAUGHTERS

GEORGE,
3RD EARL OF
KINGSTON, *d. 1839*
m. HELENA MOORE

MARGARET, *m.* (1ST) STEPHEN,
d. 1835   2ND EARL OF
MOUNT CASHELL,
m. (2ND) WILLIAM TIGHE

ROBERT EDWARD,
1ST VISCOUNT
LORTON,
d. 1854

EDWARD

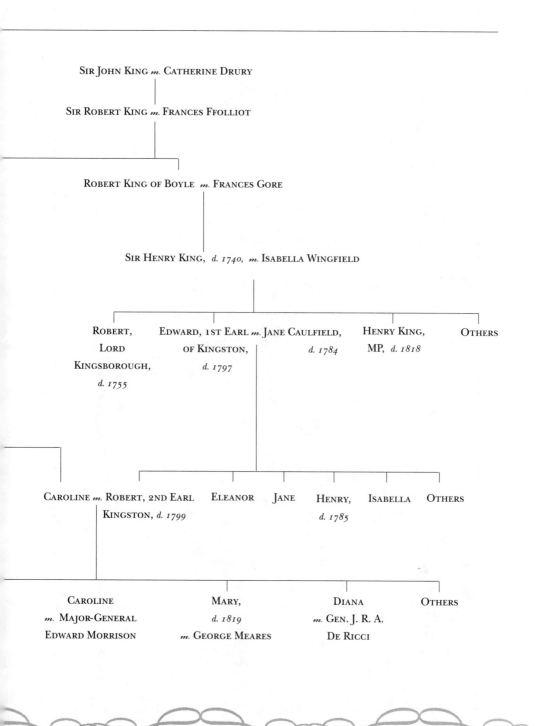

SIR JOHN KING *m.* CATHERINE DRURY

SIR ROBERT KING *m.* FRANCES FFOLLIOT

ROBERT KING OF BOYLE *m.* FRANCES GORE

SIR HENRY KING, *d. 1740, m.* ISABELLA WINGFIELD

ROBERT,   EDWARD, 1ST EARL *m.* JANE CAULFIELD,   HENRY KING,   OTHERS
LORD   OF KINGSTON,   *d. 1784*   MP, *d. 1818*
KINGSBOROUGH,   *d. 1797*
d. 1755

CAROLINE *m.* ROBERT, 2ND EARL   ELEANOR   JANE   HENRY,   ISABELLA   OTHERS
         KINGSTON, *d. 1799*   *d. 1785*

CAROLINE   MARY,   DIANA   OTHERS
m. MAJOR-GENERAL   *d. 1819*   *m.* GEN. J. R. A.
EDWARD MORRISON   *m.* GEORGE MEARES   DE RICCI

Ireland in 1798

N

ULSTER
Belfast
Lough Neagh
Ballynahinch
R. Bann

Killala Bay
Killala
Sligo
Castlebar   Boyle

CONNAUGHT
Roscommon   Longford
Edgeworthstown
Mearescourt
Maynooth
Celbridge   R. Liffey   Dublin
Shannon

LEINSTER
Wicklow

R. Nore
Oulart Hill
Limerick   Enniscorthy   Vinegar Hill
Tipperary   New Ross   Scullabogue
MUNSTER   R. Funcheon   Wexford
Mitchelstown   Waterford
Kilworth
Fermoy
KERRY   R. Blackwater
Cork

Bantry Bay

0   10   20   30   40   50 miles
0   10   20   30   40   50   60   70   80   90   100 km

Daughters of Ireland

The Price of a Bride

The spirit of collateral calculation . . .

—HORACE WALPOLE

IN MAY 1798 AN EARL WAS TRIED BEFORE HIS PEERS FOR THE murder of his wife's cousin. The trial of Robert, Earl of Kingston, before the Irish House of Lords proved an extraordinary event in the King family, already torn apart by political difference and personal conflict. It also impinged on a crucial period in Irish and Anglo-Irish history: the Rebellion of 1798.

Robert and his wife, Caroline, were heirs of a dynasty. Long before 1798 their ancestors the Fitzgeralds had become notorious for combining murder, money, feuding and revolt. Through the generations they mingled old Celtic and English blood, becoming a fairly typical, ethnically diverse Anglo-Irish clan. They were especially proud of being descended from the White Knight, who derived his glamorous name from the color of his armor—or from the white scarf with which the English monarch

Edward III bandaged his battle wound. The Knight established his castle at Mitchelstown in County Cork.

In the 1650s the Fitzgerald heiress brought the White Knight's inheritance of castle and fertile lands into the hands of the Kings, a Yorkshire family of civil servants whose grateful English sovereigns had rewarded them with Irish property at Boyle in County Roscommon. By this marriage the Kings became masters of thousands of acres in southern and midland Ireland. They liked the glamour of the White Knight and used him in family portraits as they moved up the ranks to become the Barons Kingston.

By the time of James, 4th Baron Kingston, in the eighteenth century, the King estates had been divided, and it became a dream of successive generations to unite them. But it was not one that James could realize, since at his death in 1761 he left only a married daughter, Margaret, to inherit his lands—as a woman she could not accede to his title. She had married rather beneath her: a country gentleman, Richard Fitzgerald of Mount Ophaley, County Kildare, a vain but attractive militia colonel with a modest civil pension of £200. When the marriage had occurred, however, the baron had had a son living and not much value was placed on the daughter—in the marriage market wealth far outweighed rank. With this young man's death, the family hopes had now to settle on Margaret's only child, Caroline, who became heiress of over seventy-five thousand acres of Cork and Limerick stretching across twenty miles. It was one of the largest fortunes in Ireland and she was one of the most sought-after girls.

Anxious about such wealth remaining in women's hands, James worked out a will that would ensure his estates traveled to Caroline and onward to the goal: a son in the bloodline. Through Caroline, too, the King lands in Counties Roscommon and Cork might once more be united; then her son could inherit all and give the family huge political and social prominence across the island. Caroline's father, Richard Fitzgerald, must of course be compensated, so James's will stipulated that if her mother was dead, Caroline at twenty-one would inherit all the land of

the White Knight, but Richard, her father, should receive an income of
£2,000 as long as his daughter remained unmarried. However things
were arranged and sweetened, the daughter would always be a great deal
wealthier than her father. She might also remain wealthier than her eldest son, since he could not inherit until she relinquished the property.

In 1763, before her child was ten, Margaret died. Given her great
riches and the danger of fortune hunters, Caroline was made a ward in
chancery during her minority. Her father, Richard, was her guardian.

Three years after his wife's death Richard married again. His new
spouse was a pleasant, sociable lady who brought him a modest fortune
but not one on the scale of his first wife's. Soon they were parents of
three daughters. Each would require a decent portion if she was to marry
within her rank and keep up socially with her rich half sister. For the
moment, as guardian of Caroline, Richard had access to the Mitchelstown rents but even with this goldmine he never quite had enough ready
cash for his needs.

Caroline had a strange status, favored heiress and stepchild in a new
family. It cannot have been easy for any of them. They lived at Richard's
estate, Kilminchy Castle, in Maryborough, Queen's County (Laois), and
kept a house in fashionable Merrion Square in Dublin. Earlier in the
century the premier duke of Ireland, the Duke of Leinster, had built a
large, rather forbidding country mansion in an undeveloped suburb of
the city on the edge of Molesworth Fields, south of the Liffey. Rightly he
assumed it would turn into a townhouse when his status attracted fashionable people to move close by. Merrion Square grew up around him
and some of the newer inhabitants were Richard, his wife, their children
and Caroline.

Occasionally they also visited Mitchelstown, and Caroline must always
have known that she alone owned the castle, not her father. Where
middle-class girls grew up assuming they would marry and place the
dowry from their parents into the hands of a husband, an aristocratic
heiress such as Caroline knew her importance from birth as carrier and
holder of estates.

Yet father and daughter got on reasonably well. Richard did not overburden the girl with learning but ensured she had the proper ladylike accomplishments of French and music. He could also be indulgent and he bought Caroline the sort of present every little girl wants: a pony called Button.

Inevitably there was a buzz of activity around the rich child. Someone must secure her in marriage before she had a mind of her own or, as one guardian of an heiress expressed it, "before she was aware of what man or money was." It was common to arrange marriages on the basis of barter, and young women usually had little say in a matter that fathers had agreed. Caroline's interest would be represented mainly in the discussion of jointure (money to support her if her husband predeceased her) and pin money (her annual allowance). Her grandfather Baron Kingston's will ensured that the estates would always be vested in her and not simply be merged with those of a husband. If he died before she did, she would continue to hold them before leaving them to her eldest son.

As far as birth was concerned, the major claimant for the rich prize was William, son of the Duke and Duchess of Leinster, the Duchess being one of the five lively daughters of the English Duke of Richmond. It was impossible to marry higher in Ireland and the Leinsters had immense political and social prestige.* But the Duke and Duchess had had a superfluity of children and consequently their great state was not supported by great riches. Also there were other Kings waiting in the wings with more zeal and assiduity than the Leinsters could muster.

These Kings, holders of the Roscommon lands at Boyle, had the advantage of being blessed by the dead Baron Kingston, who had favored an alliance of the two branches of his wealthy family. Like the Mitchels-

---

* In the matter of names and titles I have put clarity before accuracy. Aristocrats change titles as they move through life but, except in one or two exceptional cases, I have remained with a single title, thus sometimes anticipating, sometimes ignoring an elevation. To avoid confusion over the many families of Fitzgeralds or Geraldines, I have called the wife and children of the Earl of Kildare, later 1st Duke of Leinster, the Leinsters throughout, while retaining the name Fitzgeralds for the relatives of Richard Fitzgerald. I have treated the Rawdon-Hastings similarly and called them the Moiras, while the Moores become the Mount Cashells, and the Boyles the Shannons.

town Kings, the Boyle Kings had gone some way up the social scale and were now Viscounts Kingsborough.

The present holder of the title was Edward, an ambitious, brooding, rather humorless man, who had succeeded his notoriously rakish and charming brother some years before. He was determined to avoid his brother's mistakes and make a respectable mark on the world. He would begin by resurrecting the defunct King title of Baron Kingston; he would then top it with an earldom. He felt he had the property to back his claims: he had inherited King House, big but unfashionably in the middle of Boyle town, and he was now reconstructing another mansion at nearby Rockingham that had a properly large demesne. This opulence was augmented by a further inheritance from his brother, a good solid townhouse in Dublin, 15–16 Henrietta Street, the grandest of the twenty-one terraced dwellings built in the 1720s and '30s away from the old city center. After he had achieved the proper honors, Edward would combine his titles and Boyle lands with the great Mitchelstown estates now vested in young Caroline. His instrument in this ambitious plan must be his eldest son, Robert, an unprepossessing youth now being educated expensively in England at Eton College.

Over the next years Edward kept an eye on Caroline, as well as on the opposition from the powerful Leinsters. He encouraged his own young daughters to write to the girl and swap stories about ponies. At the same time he set about a letter-writing campaign to capture the earldom of Kingston for his family and raise their social position.

In the mid-eighteenth century Ireland was ruled from Dublin under the British crown. The executive was usually drawn from the great Irish families, while ultimate authority lay in the crown-appointed Viceroy or Lord Lieutenant in Dublin Castle, seat of British power in Ireland. As the main instrument for rewards and favors, including titles and honors, the Lord Lieutenant was the most important personage to impress.

Despite his wealth, position and desire to please, Edward was never quite in favor with Dublin Castle or with the new young Hanoverian king George III in England, but he was persistent. He began by insisting on

reviving the family name of Kingston and in June 1764 the Lord Lieutenant relayed to him that the King had agreed to create him Baron Kingston. At once the Rockingham mansion was named Kingston Hall. But, despite being entertained at Boyle, the Lord Lieutenant was unwilling to raise his host further. Edward was undeterred and wrote directly to ask for an earldom. It was refused.

In 1765 a new Lord Lieutenant, Lord Townshend, arrived in Dublin. At once Edward approached him but, despite high hopes, he had a distressing audience. It left him fearing the great man doubted his "Attachment to the House of Hanover" and "His Majesty's sacred Person." Profusely he expressed his loyalty to the crown.

He then started lobbying a neighbor in Henrietta Street, the Speaker of the Irish House of Commons, John Ponsonby, asking him to mediate with Townshend on his behalf. The Speaker did so and made Edward understand that the Lord Lieutenant was now sympathetic. Thus emboldened, Edward entertained Lord Townshend at dinner in King House.

In August 1768 he got his wish and became Earl of Kingston. Deeply grateful, he took his seat in the Irish House of Lords, knowing that his elevation had given him a better chance of gaining his second aim: the capturing of the Mitchelstown heiress. His new title allowed his son to take his old one and become Lord Kingsborough, a better-sounding name than plain Robert or Robin King. William, the Leinster candidate, still overtopped him in rank, since, on the death of his eldest brother, the young man had become Marquess of Kildare and heir to a dukedom.

Even before the Kingston title had been secured negotiations had been opened for the potential uniting of Caroline and Robert—or rather the Roscommon and Cork estates of Boyle and Mitchelstown. Robert was still away at school at Eton; his absence was an advantage, since an adolescent boy would not help in the wooing. He could be fetched home when needed.

The first necessity was to secure Colonel Richard Fitzgerald, Caroline's father. Edward had been courting him for some years and in 1763, the year Richard's wealthy wife died, Edward had provided him with a

parliamentary seat in which he had an interest at Boyle. This was a consistent kindness, since seats were much sought after and Richard had little political aptitude—once elected, he seldom attended Parliament. Despite receiving this patronage, Richard still insisted on being wooed for his consent to the marriage, since he had debts and a family of little girls. Edward understood his anxieties for he too had a family and large debts.

Meanwhile the Leinsters were advancing, trusting in their status to secure the prize. Unhappily for them William, their candidate, was far from Ireland on the grand Continental tour he had begun after his years at Eton. It was the custom for the British and Irish aristocracy to send young heirs on a European trip to educate and refine them and to acquire the southern artifacts to adorn their new mansions. Especially in need of refinement, young William was visiting Italy, France and Austria, supposedly learning military arts, sometimes being painfully homesick and sometimes enjoying the sexual freedom the Continent allowed. While he was away his mother and aunts, particularly Lady Holland in London—mother of the future politician Charles James Fox—looked out for his interests, and both wrote to him as soon as Caroline Fitzgerald, "Miss F," came on the market.

Like the other Leinster sons, William was devoted to his mother, and family letters of sentimental attachment flowed between him and the Duchess. Her favorite was the younger Edward, a glamorous and affectionate boy, and for him she reserved her greatest outpourings of love. But she was properly attached to all her children although, like his siblings, she could not avoid regarding William as dull. Since he felt ready for marriage and wanted to settle down and at the same time help the chaotic finances of his extravagant and huge family—the Duchess bore the Duke seventeen children, of whom eleven survived to maturity—it did not take much to interest him in Caroline Fitzgerald and her vast Mitchelstown estates. It helped that the girl was also reputed a beauty.

In July 1767 William wrote from Florence to his mother, authorizing his family to begin negotiating for a bride, though at that point he did not even know her age. Three months later he was more urgent: "I believe to make up for my travelling expenses (that causes me more uneasiness than one can imagine) you must marry me to Miss FitzGerald as soon as I return; so I beg you'll make Cecilia and Emily [his young aunt and sister] pay their court to her whenever they see her." His keenness was not *entirely* financial: "I like the description that Cecilia sent me very well, and I think there is no time to lose, as I hear they want to marry Master King to her directly, and it would be a thousand pities that poor William should lose so good a match. (I am in earnest.)" Later he told his mother, "I hope you'll make the young ladies be civil to Miss FitzGerald upon all occasions, as I wish I was married to her and settled." He thought it would be a good idea to get her to their grand house of Carton so they could impress and work on her there.

The gossip about Caroline and "Master King" had come from his aunt Lady Holland, who was more concerned with the competition than her sister—and perhaps, since she had been with William on part of his travels, more aware of his limitations as a suitor.

Despite his thoughts running continually on the rich "Miss F," William made no arrangements for returning from Italy to woo Caroline. He was an anxious youth; he knew he disappointed his demanding mother and might have been afraid to appear too eager in an affair in which he could fail. In Ireland little progress was being made, and Lady Holland rather wondered at her sister's backwardness; surely the Leinsters should be maneuvering in earnest by now. On 1 April 1768 she reminded them that her own lord was "wild" about the idea, implying that they might themselves show more enthusiasm. She herself was "most exceedingly for the match because William himself is," but the matter rested in the hands of the Duke and Duchess, who would need to bustle if they were to outwit the Kings. Only they could know "how far it may be necessary to hasten it immediately." Meanwhile she had been investigating. A friend of William's told her "how likely it was [Caroline] might already be engaged to the Kings who would take certain measures to secure her in their family." Yet there was hope, since Robert, "Master King," was

"very young" and another Etonian declared "he never saw an uglier little monkey in his life, and that he acts quite like a child." But, she added, "for all that unless the Duke of Leinster outbids him, I fear he will get Miss from the Marquess."

Still the Duchess did not press forward, remarking to her sister Holland that surely Caroline Fitzgerald was too young to marry. Lady Holland tartly replied that their own mother had been thirteen when she married their father, who had then been sent on his travels until their mother matured. The marriage was extremely happy and fertile.

Stirred at last, the Leinsters urged William to terminate his tour, return to Ireland and catch Caroline. He was pessimistic but agreed: "I approve much of your scheme of finishing my travels at once, and if Miss FitzGerald and I can agree, I should look upon myself as the happiest of beings. But I am afraid the chance is but small as I hear the Kingstons are determined to have her." Yet even now he did not hurry and two months later he was still writing from Turin, urging others to do his wooing: "if we could but make ourselves sure of Miss FitzGerald, we shall be very happy and content. But I can't say I flatter myself too much, for fear of disappointment." His mother continued her encouragement by scoffing at "the little King."

Then William had the disheartening news that the boy had become Lord Kingsborough through his father's assiduity. In Vienna, he heard something even more disturbing: that the "little King" had actually married Caroline. He now might need to save face, so he started by writing cautiously of the rumor:

> There surely must be something in it, as I have even heard of it from some of the Irish officers here, so I doubt by a thing being so universal must have some foundation. I should not be so very desirous were it not in a letter of Emily's some time ago that you also seem to wish it. . . . If I could but have the good luck to please [the young lady] . . . it would then be in my power to render my dear brothers and sisters more happy. And surely by that means I should be the happiest of mortals.

Otherways money would not avail with me. Nor would it with any disagreeable person.

He had talked himself around and now urged his mother to try for a match at once: "Worst come to worst, the being refused would be better than never having proposed."

Meanwhile the "Kingstons" were indeed "determined to have her." Edward, Earl of Kingston, had by now proposed marriage in earnest—to Richard rather than his daughter Caroline—and begun detailed negotiations over money and property. The marriage would unite the old King estates, Boyle and Rockingham, with the southern Mitchelstown ones, and cut a swath of ownerships through Roscommon and Sligo to the north down to Cork and Tipperary in the south. The children, Robert and Caroline, were young but the deed must be done quickly with so many eager young men sniffing around.

The approach, less tentative than the Leinsters', appealed directly to Richard Fitzgerald's pocket. There was no discussion of compatible or incompatible temperaments; the transaction was between two men with an interest in money. Richard would lose a lot by the marriage but more if his daughter married imprudently. Caroline, though only fifteen, was known to resent her stepmother and might welcome translation to another household with the status of a married woman, and they hoped she would see the quick match as an escape from home. The domestic tension was used by the Earl of Kingston in his courting of Richard, whose life must be more peaceful without the child they all depended on.

While domestically appealing, it was obviously not in Richard Fitzgerald's financial interest that his wealthy daughter should go entirely out of his control. Both men knew that, besides the annual income of £2,000 that came to him as his first wife's widower, he could help himself to a great deal more from the Mitchelstown estate while Caroline remained

an unmarried child. He would lose this power on her marriage. Consequently Edward had to offer sweeteners.

So he proposed a onetime gift of £12,000; he did not call it payment for Caroline, but the meaning was clear. With this money Richard could settle his debts. Edward was candid: "if your Daughter shall live to the age of 21 years My Family will gain far more than the £12,000 by the Marriage." This was true, for the rent roll of the Mitchelstown estates was £42,000 a year. The sum of £12,000 would be returned to Edward if Caroline died before her majority and the Kings failed to reap the expected advantages. The Earl apologized for this proviso, but his own estate had been much reduced through family squabbles; otherwise it would have been a "free gift." He would further undertake that Robert would, when he came of age and into control of his wife's funds, allow his father-in-law to keep the rents from the estates that he had been collecting between the old Baron Kingston's death and Caroline's wedding. He would merely have to pay the charges. From now onward he would relay to the young couple £6,000 a year from the Mitchelstown rents.

When he had gained agreement in principle, Edward praised Richard's "very noble & generous conduct." Caroline was, of course, richer and more favored than her half sisters, but Richard should now "be enabled to make a reasonable provision" for these girls, especially as they were expected to keep up good relations with Caroline. This could happen if they made a "decent appearance in the World that the Brors & Sisters of Lady K ought." "[A]s far as fortune can administer to happiness your Daughters will be abundant," he insisted, but not of course on the scale of their half sister Caroline. *She* had everything—money, youth and looks—and the Earl admitted that he had "procured for [his son] one of the prettiest Heiress's in the British Dominions." He made no claims for the appearance of the childish "Robin."

The Earl of Kingston's boasted "Liberality" appears less generous when the letter containing the offer is read beside another written to his son four years after the wedding. This asks Robert to reimburse him for

the £12,000, now starkly called "the money I have been out of pocket in bringing about your marriage." In other words, while the father was profusely thanked for his generosity by Richard, the son was paying for it. Or rather, since the money was ultimately Caroline's, the heiress was paying for her own sale. Meekly Robert agreed to reimburse his father when Caroline and he came of age. It is unclear whether Caroline knew of these dealings in herself.

Financial maneuvering was usual in the aristocracy and would not have detracted from the wedding festivities when on 5 December 1769 the sixteen-year-old Robert King, Lord Kingsborough, married the fifteen-year-old Caroline Fitzgerald in St. Michan's Church, Dublin. The ceremony was performed by the Bishop of Limerick and recorded in the Prerogative Court of the Archbishop of Armagh rather than the local diocesan courts, as befitted the marriage of so much money. After it the young people "set out with a splendid retinue" for Boyle. The *Hibernian Chronicle* recorded the union of estates:

> married . . . Lord Kingsborough . . . to Miss Fitzgerald, a Lady of every accomplishment, and the greatest fortune in his Majesty's Dominions or perhaps in Europe, daughter of Colonel Fitzgerald and Granddaughter to the late Lord Kingston, by the union of this amiable couple, the extensive possessions of her grandfather in the counties of Cork, Limerick, Tipperary, and Kerry, are once more united with perhaps one of the most considerable in this kingdom.

No one spoke of love. Robert married because he was told to and was not popular at school, Caroline because she was told to, to get away from home and have her own household. She might well have preferred the Marquess of Kildare, since she had a sense of status and would have appreciated being a duchess in time. They might even have made a happy couple, for William was a formal young man who liked ceremony and magnificence.

But he did not pine for his lost bride. When his father died, leaving greater debts than the family anticipated, William was even more in need of an heiress. In Paris in 1774 he at last met one who would have him, the short, painfully shy and blushing Emilia, only daughter of Lord St. George and heiress of extensive property in and around Dublin. His initial response was matter-of-fact: "she is very quiet and don't seem riotously disposed. In short, if her fortune is what they say, I think [the wedding] is very likely to take place." More experienced with whores than well-brought-up girls, William, now Duke of Leinster, yet managed his courtship, married the heiress and substantially reduced his family debts. He became fond of his awkward wife and their six girls but never succeeded in impressing his mother and siblings, and he continued to be regarded by all of them as dreary and stolid. So perhaps, despite his grand living, he would not have appealed to the sprightly and spoiled Caroline. Conscious of his own mediocrity, he would have smarted under her tongue as much as Robert was about to do.

. C H A P T E R   2 .

Married Life

They lived in the usual fashionable style,
and seldom saw each other.

—MARY WOLLSTONECRAFT, *MARY, A FICTION*

THE TEENAGERS CAROLINE AND ROBERT, VISCOUNT AND VIS-
countess Kingsborough, began married life on Caroline's £6,000 a year
and Robert's allowance, not princely but enough for a fine standard of
living with servants, retainers, houses, carriages, visits and travel. (For
comparison, John Trusler in *The Economist* [1774] gives £370 16s as a
yearly income that would be needed to support a household with two servants.) With the expectation of a great deal more money when Caroline
came of age and Robert succeeded his father as Earl of Kingston, the
pair could also borrow lavishly.

The young couple emerge clearly from their letters. In one written
to Robert's sister Jane before the wedding Caroline mimicked conventional adult phrases, writing of flowers, balls and even the weather in the
way demanded of a young lady. But the child peeps through when she
speaks of a girlfriend having a horse "very near as good as Button for I

will not allow it to be quite as good" and when she makes a smudge where she is unsure whether to write "lye" or "ly" for *lie*. Robert's first writing is juvenile in mode and penmanship but his spelling and grammar are correct; Lady Holland described the style of her own young son: "His letters are quite a schoolboy's. He is well, hopes we are, and compliments everybody. Adieu. Yours most sincerely." In time Robert's letters would become freer and more fluent, if never full, and his penmanship would move toward his wife's more adult hand. Later still he would adopt the imperious writing of the grandee and dash off sentences with an assurance neither Caroline nor Edward ever achieved.

After the wedding the couple briefly visited Mitchelstown, then settled in with Robert's parents, Edward and Jane. Payment for their upkeep came from Caroline's fortune. As their first home, Edward had offered them King House in Boyle, as well as the large Dublin townhouse on the south side of Henrietta Street. Caroline thought Boyle unfashionable and preferred Kingston Hall, still being fitted out and not proposed.* Henrietta Street, with its plain façade and ornate interior, was more appealing, and this they accepted. Edward offered the furniture, which was left in the house.

Caroline actually believed she required "intirely new" things and looked forward to choosing them. In recent years furniture had become a luxurious consumer item and fashionable people changed it as they changed their style of dress: it was as important to have the latest brocades on one's chairs as on one's back. Even as a young girl Caroline was aware of fashion and she was probably yearning for the elegant carved rich woods and the French upholstered gilt look now coming into vogue. In Henrietta Street they would have grand neighbors to keep up with: apart from helpful Speaker Ponsonby on the north side, the street housed on the south his son-in-law, the formidable Earl of Shannon from Castlemartyr, the greatest political power in Cork. Unhappily for young

---

* No one much seemed to want King House, and in 1775 Edward sold it to the War Office for £3,000; it became an infantry barracks and a recruiting center. It then fell into ruins but has recently been handsomely restored as a museum.

Caroline, Edward had a numerous family and he expected Robert and his wife to share the house—and its original furnishings—with them.

After marriage Caroline retained her governess and, since Robert was not to return to Eton, Edward engaged Mr. Tickell to aid his son. Tickell had already been a tutor to aristocracy as well as acting as Robert's housemaster at school. He was a gentlemanly man, like his inferiors and superiors not above a little fluttering on the lottery, and he would act as both mentor and secretary. Robert welcomed the arrangement; he liked Tickell, who stayed with him for some years after he had outgrown a tutor. Evidently Tickell was a man of tact, for it cannot have been easy to retain the respect or trust of this privileged couple. When he wrote letters to Edward he called Robert his "young friend" and when he sent a congratulatory note on yet another happy birth for Edward's wife, Jane, he suggested it be held back if "unseasonable." He kept Edward in gossip, commenting on the unpopularity of the present Lord Lieutenant, for instance, and he criticized lords who patronized gentlemen, then cavalierly dismissed them, thereby delicately informing Lord Kingston of his duty.

Tickell had much to teach Robert. The boy emerged from Eton with little except some knowledge of the classics, a subject revived in the eighteenth century to provide an education in manly Roman virtue for rulers of the growing British Empire. Another rationale for such a restricted curriculum was that it developed skills in debating, necessary for the ruling class, which depended on rhetoric to shine in Parliament. The progressive middle and entrepreneurial classes deplored the emphasis and obtained a more useful modern scientific and technological education for their sons. Other critics were contemptuous of a training that used words trivially and let repartee replace wisdom. But the aristocracy did not set up for wisdom, only style. Judging from reports, young Robert had not yet mastered the art of polite conversation and witty speech. He was ill at ease with himself and happier out of doors than in a drawing room.

Almost at once there was bad feeling between Caroline and her mother-in-law, Jane. Caroline accused Jane of being rude to her and of sowing bad feeling between her and her new husband by questioning

her about Robert's movements when she knew perfectly well what they were. On the other side Jane found the rich child pert and insolent. She had a silly way of speaking, a little lisp, noticeable because she liked talking so much. A babyish drawl was quite the mode over in England among the aristocrats who surrounded the celebrated Duchess Georgiana, but in Caroline, the less charismatic teenager, it irritated the in-laws.

It was also clear from the start that the married pair were not pleased with each other. Caroline was bossy and bullying, and Robert shrank from her public rudeness and private taunts. She found him childish, boring and gauche. He started to confide in his mother, who felt upset for her eldest son. She showed her resentment and Caroline thought herself ill used and took refuge in ailments. No one was surprised: delicacy went with rank and, whether they regarded her as a hypochondriac or not, it was essential to keep the potential mother of sons in the best condition. Richard Lovell Edgeworth, an inquisitive Anglo-Irish gentleman, noticed that where the middling class drank whiskey punch and were intemperate and the lower orders "drink as much whiskey as they can get and are notwithstanding strong and healthy," the upper classes "who drink wine and eat luxuriously are on the contrary afflicted with all the demons of disease."

One remedy for the rich was expensive travel. So with a large retinue of servants, as well as Mr. Tickell and the governess, the family, young and old, left for England. They would visit the resort of Scarborough on the bracing North Sea coast. Sea bathing and the drinking of small quantities of salt water had become fashionable for the wealthy invalid. They would then proceed to London.

Often when such young people married they were kept apart until they achieved some maturity. The Duke and Duchess of Richmond, parents of the Duchess of Leinster, had been so unaware of each other that when the young man returned from his tour he did not recognize his wife; happily he found the grown woman most attractive. According to the German Prince Pückler-Muskau, who wrote a description of the Kings after he had taken a tour of England and Ireland, "The tutor and governess received the strictest injunction to watch the young couple most narrowly, and to prevent every possibility of a tête-à-tête. But 'somehow or other,' as my informant said, three years afterwards they found means to elude their vigilance."

In fact copulation had occurred more quickly than that. Their first child was born in London probably late in 1770 and was named after King George III, who graciously agreed to be the godfather. The baby was christened at St. Luke's, Chelsea. As a friend remarked after the birth, the combined ages of father, mother and child amounted to only thirty-two. Presumably Caroline had discovered some longings in herself and perhaps some charms in the reputedly ugly Robert. In the only portrait of him he appears elaborately dressed in blue waistcoat, fur-edged silver topcoat and romantic cape, his hair curled, his brows black, and his blue eyes straightforward and frank. He had been mocked as small; here he seems delicate. In her portrait Caroline looks altogether larger, a voluptuous young woman with thick brown hair and commanding manner.

Neither was a loving parent. Back in Ireland they deposited baby George with Edward and Jane in Boyle. They had not seen him for nearly three months when Robert wrote to his father thanking him for a good account of their child. They themselves settled in the Henrietta Street house in Dublin.

By July 1771 Caroline was pregnant again and Robert was impressed with the changing female shape: "Caroline is very well and grown very Big, I think she is as Big as she was of George, She and I were at Church last Sunday, and I am afraid she will be there again next, I should be very glad she was brought to bed, we have been so long expecting." This time her labor was difficult, more so than with George, and Caroline was ill for some time after the birth; perhaps the circumstance prevented her from warming much to the new child. The baby born at Henrietta Street was their first girl; they called her Margaret Jane, after their two mothers.

The young couple were not the only inhabitants of the house. Robert's mother, Jane, was often there and she had made it a practice to lie in at this address when her time came. Also her children, Nelly, Jane and young Henry, felt at home there. Henry was a welcome inhabitant:

he and baby George played amicably together, managing to avoid the colds that afflicted the two Janes. Caroline enjoyed seeing the boys so companionable: "They agree extremely well, indeed they have both such good tempers it would be impossible for them not to do so." She also came to like thirteen-year-old Nelly, who preferred the Dublin life of balls and parties to days of fishing and dining at home at Kingston. But Caroline rather resented Jane and her mother, who took over the house and made it feel too small. In the tense atmosphere generated between the women Caroline lost a bracelet and blamed everyone until she found it again. The whole King clan was relieved when she and Robert paid a visit to her father in Kilminchy; it did not improve her mood, however, and she was openly rude to Robert in front of her stepmother.

Part of the tension over the bracelet arose from the fact that a young noble couple had to be formally presented at the Castle. For this public ceremony Caroline wanted to be glamorous and she expected to wear her best jewelry. Meanwhile Edward was urging Robert to get on with the ceremony because he wanted his son to second an invitation to Lord Townshend to visit Boyle during the winter. Although pressed on all sides, the young man put off the event as long as he could and Caroline grew cross: "I believe he will be very much rejoiced when it is over, as he don't seem to enjoy the thought of going at all," she reported. She was right: Robert still felt the awkward Eton schoolboy, enjoying his morning readings with Tickell and having no stomach for adult socializing and wheeling and dealing. Indeed, many more polished people found the crowded, formal Castle events a trial. The social commentator Mrs. Delany described an amazing "hurly-burly" of "squarking, shrieking, all sorts of noises; some ladies lost their lappets, others were trod upon."

Finally Robert was persuaded and at the end of November 1771 he recorded that he and Caroline had been presented at the vice-regal court:

I told you in my last that I was to be introduced at the Castle; that operation is now over, which I am very glad of; but before that I underwent

at least as disagreeable an one, which is this; the Minister and Church Wardens wrote to me begging I would collect at a Charity Sermon at St Michans, and My Mama & I thought I cou'd not send an excuse, I put in three Guineas.

Himself so ill at ease, he was bemused by his new wife's sociability: "this place is more disagreeable than ever, not a day passes that I do not pay some visits, My Mama, sisters & Caroline have been at home but one night since we came," he told his father. His boyhood had been interrupted and he resented it. He took as many trips to the country alone as he could.

Back in Boyle in the summer with little George he confided to his mother how much he regretted his marriage and how "brutal" Caroline was being to him. She sympathized, for she too found Caroline's behavior intolerable. In Boyle he had time to note his son's development: he wrote to Edward that George had got another tooth and asked him to send some lemons to make jelly for the little boy. Then Caroline arrived and her constant bad temper set all in disorder. But there was no escaping: marriage was for life. Or rather, there was one escape, in porter— strong beer mainly imported from England—which he began to drink copiously. Edward noticed and upbraided him, making him more miserable. He turned again to his mother; she took his part, consoled him and alienated him further from Caroline.

Soon they were back in Dublin with Jane and the girls and there were more severe irruptions. Little George in particular delighted his grandmother. She was still bearing children and had much advice to give her young daughter-in-law on the raising of the heir. But Caroline did not want it and tempers grew frayed. Her visiting stepmother and father witnessed some of the outbursts, no doubt grateful that they were no longer hosting this difficult young woman. "[S]ince I came to Town . . . She has been very rude & improper to my Mother for her care of George, & cou'd not govern herself before a parcel of Strangers, & particularly before the Coll: & Mrs Fitzgerald last Monday," Robert reported to his father; he added, "Car-

oline has been quiet these two days past, & I am in hopes is sorry for what She has done." Happily her father and stepmother were much taken up with the birth of their own son, Gerald Henry, their only boy.

For her part Caroline realized that all she had done in marrying was augment the stepmother with a pack of interfering in-laws. Her response was to abuse Robert further and become ill again. Robert's was to get out of her way and shoot woodcocks in Boyle. The Henrietta Street house remained a sore point. It was now technically theirs, though Edward and Jane were always aware that the furnishings were not, and Caroline was irritated when she found the family assuming they might use it whenever they wished. When Edward heard of this, he snapped that they seemed to have forgotten "by whose means under God [they] got that house."

Things improved a little when the two families were apart. In autumn 1772 Robert, Caroline, Tickell and the children had a stint at Kingston Hall alone while Edward and Jane, pregnant again and near her time, were in Dublin for the confinement. Little George and Margaret were being inoculated against smallpox by being given a mild version of the disease. The process brought back from Turkey by Lady Mary Wortley Montagu earlier in the century was long, difficult and dangerous; sometimes it miscarried and ended in death, as would happen with the Irish Lord Chancellor's child. In preparation for inoculation a patient had to eat a careful diet for a month; then a wrist was pricked and droplets of the smallpox virus from another sufferer were introduced into the blood. A dressing was applied and the next day removed. Thereafter the spots filled with pus, then formed scabs, lasting three days; after a wait of several more days fever developed together with pimples. These formed "crusts" that in time fell off, leaving the patient for some time immune to the ravages of more virulent smallpox.

Margaret and George had been given the initial treatment under the direction of Dr. Houlton and were ready for the next stage when it was discovered that Margaret had scratched off the scabs prematurely and let out the pus. Treatment had to start again the next day, with new pricking leading to new blisters. Caroline's servant Molly Parker was engaged to

watch over the child and see that she did not scratch again. "They are both taking the disorder very well," said the young father. But this part of the process was slower than anticipated and six days later Robert wrote again to say that neither George nor Margaret had moved to the fever stage but that the doctor expected them to "sicken by Saturday."

By now it was clear to Robert that the two families were better in separate houses. He wanted his parents to remain in Henrietta Street, where Jane was used to having her babies, while he, Caroline and the children stayed at Kingston Hall throughout the winter. They would be no trouble, he assured his father, wanting no "Servant but Tom Cannon." Robert would get a room ready for his little brother Henry, who could join them and play with George, and he would see that all the hay was brought in when the weather was fine; he would also watch over Edward's pet project, the developing of the islands in the lake.

Little Henry duly arrived, together with news that he and Robert had a new sister, Isabella Letitia—soon acclaimed the beauty of the family. Robert wrote the letter of congratulation, also telling his father that George and Margaret had now recovered from their inoculation. Meanwhile Mr. Tickell reported that Robert had thrown himself into rabbit hunting on one of the islands and was supplying the house with five or six pairs each week. Far more than their parents, the tutor interested himself in the children's progress. Little George was beginning to know his alphabet and to count to twenty, he wrote in November; by Christmas he would probably know all his letters. This was tactful. George was a slow child and the family was worried about him. His small uncle Henry called him "Lu Lu." Not much was reported about the girl, Margaret.

Perhaps Jane and Edward did not care to be exiled from Kingston Hall all winter or perhaps Caroline found she did not like being closeted in the country with her husband after all. By mid-December Robert had decided that his best course was to remove his turbulent wife altogether from Ireland by revisiting England. The move at an appropriate time would be perfectly acceptable, for it was customary for Irish aristocrats to

spend some of the winter months in London. But, having determined to do this, Robert was eager to be gone at once. He knew his haste was indecent, especially so near Christmas, but he excused himself by saying they wished to catch the full moon for the crossing.

So in preparation the family returned to Dublin, where Jane "helped Caroline to chuse her house linnen"—coarse for servants and children, fine for themselves and guests. Flush with money from his father-in-law, who was also in town and staying in Merrion Square, Robert was still relieved to find it cost only £63; this was cheap, since only a few years earlier the Duchess of Leinster had spent £150 just to augment her household linen. Jane recommended a cook, whom Robert and Caroline took on, and she told them to raise the wages of one of their other servants. She had not actually come to dinner with them but had accepted an invitation to tea.

The Henrietta Street house was going to be looked after by Caroline's father while they were away; he would see to some repairs and the new furnishings Caroline always wanted. Perhaps this eagerness for the new irritated Jane, who had after all offered her own old-fashioned things, but for the moment everything seemed reasonably peaceful and Robert had hopes of embarking without another domestic storm.

Then on the night before departure a quarrel broke out between Caroline and Jane. It was so violent that Robert told his father, "I am convinc'd it is impossible, after what has passed . . . for my Mother & Wife ever to agree."

He could breathe freely only when Caroline, the children, Tickell, nurses and servants were on board the *Bessborough,* the mail ship he had chosen for their escape. On the afternoon of 15 December they sailed from Ireland for Holyhead in Wales. Robert and Caroline were in charge of themselves and their household for the first time since their marriage.

They arrived next day after a rough crossing, having spent almost a whole night tossing on the sea near the Anglesey coast. All of them had been seasick except baby Margaret and her nurse; George had recovered

quickly, however, and the two children were soon playing happily. An exhausted Caroline, aware of her duty on paper if not in person, scrawled one side of a letter to her father-in-law to tell him of their safe arrival and to send love to little Henry. Robert could write to Jane, she said.

They traveled slowly through Wales and England, achieving not more than thirty miles a day. Their entourage was large and Caroline was a reasonably concerned mother who knew that rushed traveling was bad for small children. Happier out of the social goldfish bowl of Dublin and the tense atmosphere of his family, Robert was interested in all he saw. At Birmingham he noted the burgeoning industries, so different from the backward rural Irish communities with which he was familiar. Already he was thinking acquisitively to the time when he would be master of Mitchelstown, and he bought "two Pair of Candlesticks, very Handsome plated Silver for five Pounds." At Stratford-upon-Avon he and Caroline visited Shakespeare's house, saw his chair, then spent Christmas at Blenheim Palace. "It is very grand and in very good Order," recorded the future landlord.

They reached London at the end of December and took lodgings in St. James's Street. The English aristocracy were known to look down on the Irish sort, but a rich young couple such as Robert and Caroline would always find sponsors and friends. It was essential to live in the correct style and at once they set about assembling the basic materials of a grand life.

Consuming was gendered, although both sexes could trespass on the other's domain and both bought books and novelties. While the lady tended to purchase the clothes, linen, furniture and household goods, the gentleman acquired the house itself and external goods such as carriages and horses. Robert did his part with more concern than might have been anticipated from his performance in Dublin. First he found a suitable place to rent in Hill Street near Berkeley Square, an agreeable and healthy part of town. It was expensive but, as he told his Irish relatives, London *was* expensive. He took it for two years, or rather he had to take it for five but could get out of the lease after two. More in charge than he had been in Ireland, he was keener to take advice.

I am told I have *not* got it very dear considering the high Rent Houses are let at, it has Stabling for Four Horses, and Coach house for one Carriage, besides a Kitchen, Washhouse and Laundry out of the House; I pay three Hundred and Sixty pounds a Year without taxes; it is a very well Furnished & convenient little House.

This was a "little House" only by the standards of Kingston Hall. Then he hired more servants to augment the Irish ones and ordered a fancy coach for himself. Aware of being the Irish rustic, he consulted the fashionable: as a result, he got Caroline an expensive sedan chair from the Queen's chair maker, believing this "genteel" and "more Proper than a Jobb Coach." Only vegetables seemed cheap in London; this neither Robert nor Caroline mentioned but the fact was a source of amazement to another Irish visitor of the time, the lively letter writer Betsy Sheridan, who reported that she had been to Carnaby Market and "bought a very fine sallad Lettice &c. a good dish of Purple Broccola and another of Colly flower for 18d."

Given his misery in Dublin high society, Robert cannot have relished these early sociable weeks, but he did his duty. He attended the King's Levee, then with Caroline went to a "Drawing Room," one of the more or less weekly public audiences at St. James's Palace at which, in a more intimate setting, members of the peerage were presented to the monarch, much as they were to the Lord Lieutenant at Dublin Castle.

Robert and Caroline were again at court for the Queen's Birthday, an important occasion in the London social calendar. The court of the respectable and domestic King George III and Queen Charlotte was stuffy, rather dull and formal, and social events tended to be sober and staid. Like Castle ones, they were also crushed. One guest reported:

the dresses were splendid could they have been seen, but the crowd was so excessive that there was no room to gaze in. I never saw anything so unbecoming the dignity of a Court as the confusion and mobbing of

that assembly. Ladies screaming and fainting from the pressure of the crowd, trains and petticoats torn off, bags and wigs lost, and all for want of the obvious management of opening a door to let out by another road the multitude that continually flowed into the room.

But Caroline was in her element: "Lord Kingsborough and I were at Court [on] the Birthday, it was very full but we got out extremely well, the Queen was not there in the morning, she came in the Evening and I think look'd exceeding well. I believe she will not be at Court any more till after her lying-in," she wrote. Robert reported only that they were at "the Queens Birth Day; it was very full." He was becoming a better correspondent—giving tidbits about baby Margaret already having two teeth in a way Caroline would not bother to do—but he saw no need to elaborate on anything and usually left much of his paper blank. "I do not hear of any news," he customarily wrote.

To his relief peace seemed at last to have broken out between himself and Caroline. The children were thriving, and his wife was more even-tempered away from her mother-in-law. He was proud of himself for arranging things so well: "no people cou'd have lived more regular, than we have done since we left Ireland, & propose to do so."

Given his self-satisfaction, he was unpleasantly surprised when Edward, who was more irritated than delighted by this sudden change in his son's circumstances, reminded him of his past drinking and quarreling. At once he defended himself: "as to Drinking Porter or any other Liquor I never do but when I am dry; my Morning and Evening prayers I neither do nor shall omit, tho' I am sensible of your kindness in mentioning these things." The reference to past upheavals with his wife was more alienating: "really neither Caroline nor I are impatient to return sooner [to Ireland]," he wrote. "I am exceedingly sorry you shou'd express so many doubts of Carolines & my conduct. . . . You very well know how unhappy Caroline & I were when we were with you, I can

assure you, we are now quite otherwise, therefore I hope you cannot blame me for Living seperate with my Wife and Children." The new harmony had an unfortunate result: Robert repeated to Caroline his mother's criticisms—criticisms that he had provoked with his tale-telling. Caroline let it be known that she now was aware of her mother-in-law's opinion of her.

Back in Kingston Hall Edward brooded over his daughter-in-law's rudeness to his wife and Robert's ingratitude to himself: "I am in truth very sensible of the unhappiness you mention between you and Caroline," he wrote, "& was so much shocked at it that I have often wished the match had never taken place, but it was then too late & I kept my mind to myself. I am glad, at any rate, that mutual dislike has ceas'd, & I hope it may continue so."

However, he wished that marital peace had not been built on the "shaking off your Duty to your Mother & me, not to say anything of obligations." Robert had been the cause of the tension by his grumbling about his wife's "brutal behaviour." It was, wrote Edward, "ungenerous in you to betray your Mother & repeat to Caroline what she said in consequence of your complaints & to comfort you, as Her uninfluenced sentiments of Her."

As for Robert's not wishing to return soon, as far as Edward was concerned he could go where he would—England, Mitchelstown, Boyle "or elsewhere"—but, he warned his son, "unless you are Good, you never can be happy." He could begin by asking forgiveness of an offended father.

Robert quickly replied, "You will excuse me if I say I cannot see my conduct in the same light You do . . . [I] know not what to ask forgiveness of."

At this response Edward's fury mounted uncontrollably; he ordered Jane not to correspond with their son and himself wrote a page of incoherent denunciation of Robert, crossed it out, then sent it anyway. Everything was raked up: the fuss over his sister's using the Dublin house, Caroline's unkindness to Jane, "the shocking abuse of your Mother to Me," and Edward's struggle to obtain the fortune Robert now enjoyed

through his marriage to Caroline. "Your Letters are short, cold & void of all affection," he snapped. If little George were eighteen like Robert and acted as Robert had done, could he as a father be satisfied? Edward had thought himself

> the Happiest man in the world in a son and that I once was proud of you and thought you one of the best young men I had ever heard of, foolish partiality of a fond parent, that now I can't make a comparison with any family I know without shame and grief of Heart. I do not know the man of whom I can think so ill of or that I have done for him half of what I have done for you I do not believe he won't make it the study of his life to show his gratitude.

In the face of this ungrammatical onslaught Robert retreated. He did not, he assured his angry father, wish to break with his family but only wanted Edward to stop dwelling "upon every little disagreeable thing, which has passed between us." He desired to live alone with Caroline but also to act properly to his parents.

The letter calmed Edward; despite his sense that "the stile is rather cool and reserv'd," he detected in it some "sense of duty & gratitude." Perhaps he had really been too cavalier with the Henrietta Street house but since the furniture was his, he had thought it acceptable for his other children to use it. In turn Robert felt he had been too hasty: he was saddened to notice that his parents were avoiding the house and that his mother had not been there for her latest lying-in. Clearly his use of his father-in-law as agent in his absence had rankled with Edward and Jane, but Robert assured him that this had been to spare his father expense— the house needed not only repairs but completely new ornamenting.

To all the wrangling there was the subtext of money. Following fashion and keeping the peace with a newly amiable Caroline, Robert was spending lavishly. As a minor, he drew on his father for cash and Edward reimbursed himself from Caroline's father, Richard Fitzgerald, who was responsible for providing his daughter with the £6,000 a year from the

Mitchelstown estates. But Edward was having difficulty keeping up with his part of the bargain, especially since he had laid out so much for Richard at the time of the wedding. On one occasion he complained that he could not easily honour a draft for £258 coming hard on another for over £1,000 but was appalled when Robert proposed to go directly to his father-in-law. To convey his own difficulties he sent his son a copy of the settlement of the family's Boyle estates, which he had expensively disputed with his brother Henry when their extravagant eldest brother had died leaving a will witnessed by a drunken porter, a Swiss servant and a prostitute called Mrs. Jones. The document showed how many claims there were on the rents and how little control Edward had over them. Robert was unimpressed. It was hard for him and Caroline truly to imagine anyone having financial constraints.

Through the correspondence Edward was saddened to observe that Robert set more store by the Mitchelstown lands through marriage than by his paternal Boyle ones. He had asked for a copy of the will of the 4th Baron Kingston, Caroline's grandfather, and Edward replied that his own family property should weigh more with him: "that, and that only, is what you may call your own." Ten or twelve thousand a year from Boyle, together with control of the parliamentary seats in the area, would give Robert more consequence than double the amount in Mitchelstown "in the way you have it." He had struggled to get the Cork estate for his son but, knowing it ultimately remained Caroline's, never thought it overtopped land inherited directly in the male line.

On 12 August 1773 Caroline bore her third child, a second boy, christened Robert Edward after his father and grandfather. The birth made her ill again but not as severely as with Margaret. Typically, the rejoicing was not unmarred by family dispute. Edward had written that he and Jane would be happy to act as godparents, giving as his reason that, since such sponsoring was expensive, they might not want to ask anyone other than a "near and dear relation." Back came the reply that his aunt and Caroline's stepmother were "already engaged."

Despite a new baby and a house with a long lease, Robert and Caroline were soon ready to quit London for the grand tour. Marrying so young, Robert had omitted this essential part of a young lord's education and he was eager to go, even though he must now travel with his wife as well as his tutor. He proposed leaving for Paris in late October, two months after Caroline's confinement. She was not as maternal as manuals were beginning to tell women they should be and she took no notice of the growing opinion in favor of breast-feeding. She craved the excitement of Continental capitals and had no wish to be confined to a nursery. She would take the eldest child, George, with her but leave the baby, Robert Edward, and Margaret, now just two years old, in the care of four nursemaids in a small house they had taken outside town in Kensington Gravel Pits. Young children did better in rural air and infant mortality was lower in the country. Margaret was used to her mother leaving her with servants and she had been given to nurses to feed and care for as soon as she was born, so she cannot have experienced much pain at the parting. Friends assured Caroline that they would look in on the children from time to time and a doctor was engaged to visit and check on their health.

When Robert told his mother of the arrangements she was alarmed and offered to have her grandchildren in Ireland with her. Robert refused: he and Caroline wanted the option of staying abroad a long time and they might wish to send for the children later. Jane was not reassured. Edward had given his son some long-tailed horses, which Robert had found an expensive burden in London; now Edward suggested these might be of some use to give the abandoned children fresh air. No, replied Robert, they would leave no carriage for Margaret and Robert; since Edward did not want the horses back they would be sold. Jane continued to worry. Her daughter had just miscarried with twins and she and Edward were anxious about their remaining grandchildren. As the months rolled by and they heard nothing, they begged Robert and Caroline to get the servants in Kensington to send them reports on Margaret and baby Robert.

The British nobleman, however young, traveled in style and it was essential to assemble maids, men, horses, clothes, books and potions before crossing the Channel. So inevitably there were delays. At the beginning of December Robert and Caroline finally quit London, accompanied by Robert's manservant Peter, a newly engaged French servant, nurse Travis for George, and Mr. Tickell, despite the tutor's having recently married "a Handsome, & very sensible young Lady."

Edward's recent criticisms had awakened Robert to some sense of money—as did his mounting pile of debts. Housekeeping in London had been costly; they had had to set up an establishment and had insisted on acquiring new plate instead of using his mother's. Now there were further expenses, since he must pay the passage for the Irish servants who wanted to return home. Continental traveling was dear if done in aristocratic mode. In only a few weeks in the winter of 1766 the Earl and Countess of Fife had spent over £1,700 living "in the first company in Paris." In 1785 the tutor William Bennet estimated that forty thousand Britons were traveling abroad, draining the kingdom of at least £4 million.

Keen as ever to control his son's affairs, Edward offered letters of introduction for Paris from the previous British ambassador, without which "it wou'd be almost impossible to get into the best Company." Robert replied that he needed no introductions. He was right. His newfound amity with Caroline had given him the social confidence lacking in Dublin and within a few months of arriving in the capital he could report that they had been to Louis XV's lavish court in Versailles four times and been presented to Madame du Barry, the King's lowborn mistress. Du Barry had ousted La Pompadour as reigning favorite some years before and now occupied much of her time in making herself resplendently beautiful with fantastic coiffures and costly materials such as white silk trimmed with shaded silk and colored spangles. In revolutionary times these expensive women would be labeled "cormorants, who wrung the very bowels of industry, to give a new edge to sickly appetites; corrupting the morals whilst breaking the spirit of the nation." But such analyses were twenty years in the future.

Suitably dressed themselves, Robert and Caroline attended masquerades and balls, dined often with the present British ambassador and the French minister of foreign affairs, and were invited to the ambassador of Malta's ball. "[O]n the whole we pass our time very agreeably," Robert pronounced. They were young and rich and the wife was a beauty; everyone at this decadent, novelty-loving court wanted to entertain them.

Although things were better between them, they had no problem separating. After a cold spring in Paris and a fortnight in Lyon, Robert set off with Mr. Tickell down the Rhône to Arles, intending to tour southern France through the summer. Caroline and little George went to Geneva, where Robert would join them later. Though he had expected it to be "insufferably hot," it proved a cool season. It was worse in Ireland, complained Edward, where it was both cold and wet—indeed, he was still having fires lit in his rooms at night. At Toulouse Robert saw the house where he had been born during his parents' grand tour, but he most noticed the seats of the great, mindful of his future role as country magnate. French mansions "have their excellencies, yet upon the whole, they are much inferior to very many seats, I have seen in England," he commented.

In August he met up with Caroline and little George in Geneva and during the next pleasant month the party toured Switzerland. Then they left for Italy through the Mount Cenis Pass, the grandeur and danger of which Robert found much exaggerated. In Turin they paused to send congratulations to Edward and Jane on the birth of yet another expensive child. George was well and they intended a further year on the Continent, he wrote, despite the fact that they had now been away from Ireland two years and from their babies a year. The letter took a month to reach Edward in Ireland; when he wrote back he worried that the young people were not considering their son George enough in their plans—very hot climates did not agree with northern children. He also showed an interest in the abandoned children in England. Robert and Caroline did not mention them in their letters, so he had been glad at last to hear directly from their carers that they were "very well."

Then Caroline was confirmed as pregnant and she and Robert

decided to head home instead of south to Venice. They passed through the Tyrol to Munich. It was winter, much colder than anything they had experienced in wet, mild Ireland, and their carriages had to be fixed to sledges through the snow. Robert was fascinated by the wildlife, especially the Alpine snow birds, which were like grouse but feathered down to the feet. Foxes were everywhere in the forested regions and they came up close to the carriage; Tickell had managed to shoot a huge one.

In February 1775 Robert wrote from Augsburg that Caroline was five months pregnant but they still felt it safe to take another leisurely two months to get to Brussels through Nuremberg, Frankfurt and Holland. Back in Ireland Edward was glad to hear of Caroline's condition. This was her fourth child, but her father-in-law was unimpressed with the fertility and there had been several false alarms. He wanted Robert to "have a handsome family" and he feared that Caroline's health might be the cause of her not breeding "as fast as at first we had reason to expect." By now, after an absence of two and a half years, both father and son had sensibly stopped alluding to past quarrels and were ready to meet again.

. C H A P T E R   3 .

Landlords of Ireland

IN LONDON THE CHILDREN WERE REUNITED WITH THEIR PARENTS.
Margaret was now between three and four; she could have had little recollection of a pretty young mother whom she had not seen for eighteen
months, nearly half her lifetime. On her side Caroline had no special
affection for her daughter. Robert Edward, the second son, was a fine lad;
it was generally thought he was superior to the girlish-looking George.

Caroline bore her fourth child in London, probably another son
named Edward for his grandfather. A few months later she and Robert
took a nine-hour crossing to Ireland. They arrived in Dublin on 25 September 1775 with their entourage and expensive purchases. Presumably
Mr. Tickell remained in England with his handsome wife.

At twenty-one Caroline was now mistress of Mitchelstown and both
she and Robert were thinking of how their fertile estates might be
improved and made lucrative, and the old castle rendered habitable.

They went through money quickly and needed the land to yield them as much as possible. Robert was acquiring a taste for country management not entirely shared by Caroline, but for the time being she was satisfied to be mistress of a great house.

The absentee landlord was a feature of Ireland and a drain on its economy. In the late eighteenth century it was estimated that £2 million was going out of Ireland to absent lords in England. In 1782 Edward alone was said to be removing £7,000 a year from the country. Robert did not intend to follow his father's example: he wanted to become one of the new breed of reforming landlords who were applying English agricultural knowledge to their Irish estates.

England was going through huge rural changes by which old commons were enclosed to make grazing for cattle, while new systems of cropping were improving the yield of arable land. The changes helped form the basis of England's commercial and industrial revolution but took a dreadful toll on the poor. Improvements meant filching the subsistence from cottagers and yeomen, who were transformed into rural and, in time, urban wage-earners or, worse, unemployed paupers. For them the long-term scenario of national power held little attraction.

No more than in England would the concerns of cottiers and peasants have been in the forefront of an Irish landowner's mind, though Robert was aware both of the social dangers of rural unrest and of the glaring miseries of the poorest. A more mature and liberal landowner than the Kingsboroughs, Richard Lovell Edgeworth from the midland counties of Ireland, described improving his "turfbogs" wholly in terms of gain to himself and his ingenuity in draining and watering, with no mention of the people who had used the wetland for their own purposes.

Two parts of the Irish problem that differentiated it from the situation in England were tithes and the agent system. Tithes were the tax paid to the established Anglican clergy by all religious denominations, one-tenth of produce such as milk, pigs and poultry. Indigenous Roman Catholics had also to pay for ceremonies such as marriage, costing 4s and 6d (many circumvented this by finding a friar for 6d and a glass of whiskey), and christening, costing 2s and 6d (to avoid which women tried to hide their infants, leaving tithe collectors to search for cradles and examine breasts for traces of milk). After traveling in Ireland with "a large female family" and being well treated on the road, a sympathetic Englishman, William Bingley, wrote of the sufferings "illegally entailed" upon the Roman Catholic peasantry through the "law, or custom of *Tythes* and *Surplice Fees.*" Matters were made worse when tithes were alienated as a debt from the church to laypeople, and the insolvent poor had to agree to notes and bonds for future payment; these bore interest for years until the debt was too large ever to be paid and the peasant was deprived of all he possessed and thrown into prison. An English agriculturist foretold revolution in colonial Ireland unless the system was changed but young aristocrats were not brought up to consider such matters. They expected the land and the people on it simply to service their needs and the church that served their class.

Many visitors testified to the misery of poor tenants suffering from the disease of agents or middlemen. These stood between the great, often absentee, landowners and smaller tenants, who repeatedly sublet down to the humblest. John Bush, an English visitor in the 1760s, encountered "petty and despicable land lords, third, fourth, and fifth from the first proprietor." In her novel *Castle Rackrent* Maria Edgeworth, Richard Lovell's daughter, defined middlemen as those who took large farms

> on long leases from gentlemen of landed property, and set the land
> again in small portions to the poor, as under-tenants, at exorbitant
> rents . . . The characteristics of a middleman *were,* servility to his superi-
> ors, and tyranny towards his inferiors: the poor detested this race of
> beings. In speaking to them, however, they always used the most abject
> language, and the most humble tone and posture.

For landowners, often regarded as rackrent and fabulously wealthy by the standards of the poor and middle class, the system yet meant that their final rents were less than half what they would have been in England

on similar land. Also it made agricultural reform difficult, since it fell disproportionately hard on the bottom ranks. But, unlike England, Ireland had not yet experienced a population explosion, and if landowners could be made more prosperous, some prosperity might trickle down to the poor and keep them quiescent. If it did not, reform might encourage revolt. The peasants of County Cork were reputedly fierce.

Mitchelstown had a peculiarly inefficient agent and in London Robert complained of this to a friend, who told him of Arthur Young, a sociable Hertfordshire farmer in his mid-thirties. Young was already famous for his books, including *Farmers' Letters to the People of England* in 1767, in which he advocated farming on a large scale. His own agricultural experiments were costly and his habits unthrifty, so he had been pleased when an Irish friend, the politician and parliamentary orator Edmund Burke, pressed him to abandon his farm and study agriculture in Ireland with a view to suggesting reforms. Covering 1,500 miles, Young's Irish tour left him appalled by the improvident and extravagant life of the upper orders, whose estates lacked any "air of neatness, order, dress and *properté*." Mitchelstown was especially ill managed and backward, but he thought something might be done with it. He was therefore delighted to be invited to dinner by the owners, young Lord and Lady Kingsborough, and to be offered a contract as land agent on a salary of £500 a year, with £500 paid at once. He would receive a rent-free house to be designed by himself. He did not hesitate; he packed his books and furniture and sent them off to Cork.

In Ireland the returning Robert and Caroline expected to be treated as equals by their parents. They began by entertaining Caroline's father, Richard, and her stepmother in Henrietta Street, from which the rest of Robert's family were tactfully absent. They then proposed to go to Kingston Hall but without the children. "I long much to shew them to you," Caroline wrote to her mother-in-law, Jane, "and am extremeley sorry that it is not in my power to bring them to wait on you at Kingston." Their own delay was ascribed to the broken wheels of their coach but this did not

explain the nonappearance of the grandchildren, about whom, during the previous years, Jane had shown more concern than their mother.

While his daughter had been abroad Richard Fitzgerald had been angling to become Privy Counsellor, presumably with his kinsman Edward's support, since this was a high and desirable position to which neither his birth nor gifts entitled him. Lord Townshend went so far as to get King George's assent to this promotion but then, considering Richard's unimpressive character and lack of aptitude for politics, withheld the royal letter. A few months later Richard fell ill.

The illness appeared serious, and Caroline was forced to stay in Dublin with her father over Christmas and into the new year. Her apology to Jane was conventional, but she seemed genuinely sad to be missing a sight of Jane's son Henry, of whom she always spoke with more warmth than she did of her own children.

She compensated for her absence from Kingston Hall by doing errands for her mother-in-law in Dublin: buying cloth and sending "a patern of the silk I have chose for your gown." Mulberry grounded silk was, she said, out of fashion and she had picked out something different and "quite new." The silk cost seventeen guineas. She would also dispatch the ornaments for holding candles. Jane must have been pleased by her request that Nelly, always the favorite sister-in-law, come to stay after Christmas. Since Christmas in Boyle was a rather dull affair, Nelly was even more delighted.

Richard's illness proved fatal and he died in Merrion Square late in February 1776. Caroline has left no record of her feelings, but the death seems to have brought her closer to the once resented stepmother Mary, now a widow with four young children. Immediately Edward took note of the parliamentary seat Richard had left vacant; by the end of the year, after expending about £2,000 in bribes and special interest payments, Robert found himself MP for Boyle.

The Kingsboroughs arrived in Mitchelstown to build and reform. According to Dr. Madden, even the great estates in Ireland of several

thousand acres had few houses of lime and stone suitable for gentlemen or substantial farmers. Sir Jonah Barrington, a Dublin lawyer from a gentry family, described his own ancestral mansion as "an uncouth mass, at war with every rule of architecture." The culture of rural hunting made the hall a kind of charnel house, decked with fishing rods, firearms, stags' horns, foxes' brushes, powder flasks, nets, dog collars, heads of deer, extended skins of kites and kingfishers all nailed across the walls. Less extremely, Arthur Young had reported that the nobility and gentlemen of Ireland on salaries of £5,000 lived in a manner a man of £700 in England would disdain.

All this was changing with the generation of young men who returned from the grand tour, for as Young remarked, "a knowledge of the world corrects old manners." The tour fostered a culture of connoisseurship. Owners such as Robert and Caroline brought back physical evidence of their travels in pictures, prints, statues, pottery and copies of Greek and Roman artifacts. The objects would fit the new fashionable style of house, for the rebuilding zeal coincided with the neoclassical movement in art and architecture. Palladian houses, originally designed to combat Gothic taste in Italy, were springing up all over Ireland, inspired by the great mansions of the Irish midlands, Carton in Maynooth, County Kildare, presided over by the Duchess of Leinster, and Castletown in neighboring Celbridge, where her sister Lady Louisa Conolly was chatelaine.

Robert and Caroline wanted a modern stone rather than old brick place, one that avoided the earlier mingling of private and public spaces and kept family apartments away from drawing rooms and halls. Like other rich people of the time, they rejected Gothic taste and the simplicity of earlier domestic architecture and tore down much of the old turreted castle that had been remodeled by Caroline's grandfather. They did, however, keep the round White Knight's Tower, part of the original outworks; it would stand opposite the hall door of the new house and would be turned into a library following the fashion set by Castletown. Initially Robert hired a salaried librarian to catalogue and keep the

books. But the castle inhabitants were not great readers and the White
Knight's Tower was soon used for collecting rents on quarter days.

Meanwhile the old edifice was raised by two stories and recon-
structed in Palladian mode: a large square main house with flanking
colonnades linking it aesthetically to outbuildings. The whole made a
grand and costly impression on arriving visitors. Inside, there was a fres-
coed entrance hall, while the main reception rooms on the first floor, a
riot of portraits, stucco, gilt, marble, Venetian glass, brocade, taffeta and
damask, were approached up an elegant curving staircase. The mansion
cost at least £36,000; another £8,000–9,000 went on the outbuildings:
stables, laundry and offices.

To many, including the Anglo-Irish poet Oliver Goldsmith, the country house seemed a massive indulgence:

> This man of wealth and pride
> Takes up a space that many poor supplied:
> Space for his lake, his park's extended bounds,
> Space for his horses, equipage and hounds: . . .
> His seat, where solitary sports are seen,
> Indignant spurns the cottage from the green.

To others it made a political point. "In a country changing from
licentious barbarity into civilized order, building is an object of perhaps
greater consequence than may at first be apparent," Arthur Young wrote.

> In a wild, or but half cultivated tract, with no better edifice than a mud
> cabin, what are the objects that can impress a love of order on the mind
> of man? . . . when great sums are expended, and numbers employed to
> rear more expressive monuments of industry and order, it is impossible
> but that new ideas must arise, even in the uncultivated mind.

For the Kingsboroughs the house expressed social and political prestige as much as wealth. Neoclassicism was a mode of living as well as build-

ing, the aim being to reproduce in cold, wet Ireland the classical country estate of Pliny or Cicero. To bring this about, the Kingsboroughs had no qualms in simply knocking down the squalid towns and villages on their estate to enhance the position and views of their house. Everything useful and utilitarian was robustly camouflaged; as the old castle had dwindled into an accessory of a modern mansion, so the peasants had to become happy distant rustics in a rural tableau. They were moved from their messy hovels into orderly dwellings farther from the house, while their hopelessly uneconomical strips of fields became lawns of rolling endlessness rather like the lakes introduced to mirror the grassy expanse. There should be no human clutter. The noble family was not to be seen as living on working tenants but as immured in a walled arcadia. The ideal was expressed in a poem on Carton, the Leinster country house:

> Magnificence o'er all the structure shines,
> With lively taste unerring judgment joins,
> Proportion'd beauties every part adorn,
> And bount'ous Plenty opes her teeming horn.

Nature lavished favors in fountains, shades, "shrubby mazes," glistening lakes, and "level lawns," while the peasants became "Arcadian swains": "Like those, here, shepherds tend the care / Of roving flocks, or woo the blushing fair" when not overwhelmed by sultry beams. No mention was made of the Irish potato or the wet Irish climate.

Set on the east side of the demesne nearest the town, Mitchelstown Castle was close to the southern slopes of the Galtees, some of the highest mountains in Ireland; through the grounds flowed the Funcheon River, making red sandstone pools. The grounds were as important as the buildings in expressing wealth and status, and the demesne park of 1,200 acres was laid out in the apparently informal, regulated manner of Capability Brown, who did not himself visit Ireland but whose influence was felt in the new landscapes of lawns, lakes and islands. Clumps of trees, usually hardwoods such as beech, oak and ash, were judiciously planted near the

house to set it off and provide part of the vista from within, while on one side of the building stretched classically designed gardens with statued terraces. Vineyards, conservatories and glasshouses added splendor and provided grapes, melons and pineapples for the occupants and presents for other landowners. There was brisk exchange of seeds and bulbs among the gentry, and letters were filled with details of nurtured native flowers, now combined with the more exotic plants from the new imperial possessions in India. At Mitchelstown there was also a fern house, a boating lake with a gazebo, a fishpond and a circular brick-and-limestone icehouse.

With all this lavish expenditure the demesne was turned into private property and all old roads through it were closed to the public. A traveler now had to approach the castle from King Square in Mitchelstown or through three other suitably ornate gateways. When this style of landscape and private building was attacked in the next generation, which saw the political dangers in such rigorous policing of nature and people, the clean clumps of trees were mocked as army platoons on parade, and the clearance required to make the empty park and private glasshouses was seen as a proud isolationism fed by the severing of aristocracy from the community that served it. For Robert and Caroline, largely untouched by political anxieties in their early years, the style seemed modernity itself.

Although yielding money for its young owners, Mitchelstown had suffered badly from having no resident landlord with political and social responsibility. Before Robert and Caroline came to live there, it had been notoriously disorderly—"a den of vagabonds, thieves, rioters and Whiteboys," according to Young. So called because they wore white cockades and white linen shirts, Whiteboys formed a Catholic movement resisting high rents, tithes and enclosure. Scarce in Robert's childhood home in Roscommon, where tithes were mainly levied on corn and sheep, Whiteboys were violent in Cork, since tithes there fell on the staples of a rural diet: potatoes, milk, eggs and chickens. In their clandestine meetings, their burning of houses and hayricks, and their maiming of cattle, their cutting off of noses and burying of enemies alive, they much alarmed the Protestant gentry, who responded by reasserting the often lapsed penal

laws against Roman Catholics holding firearms. One of Robert's first acts as resident lord of Mitchelstown was to join with fifty-nine other noblemen and gentry in deploring Catholic violation of these laws. They issued a manifesto vowing to bring Whiteboys to justice "at the hazard of our lives and fortunes." One hopes he was not tempted to use his young son George as the Earl of Carrick used his, in hunting Catholics: "I have blooded my young dog," he is reported to have said, "I have fleshed my bloodhound."

In his act against Whiteboys Robert conformed to family tradition— the Kings were violently Protestant, especially James, the 4th Baron, who had endowed Kingston College at Mitchelstown out of his revenues. This was not a school but a refuge for elderly Protestant "Gentlemen & Gentle- women" who had fallen on hard times; they were to lead lives of compul- sory piety, attending the new chapel and being housed in a terraced square in neat, two-story, neoclassical stone houses with ornamental bricks around doors and windows, men on one side, women on the other. James's Protestant enthusiasm was curious, since his father had actually been a converted Catholic and, worse, had married a servant at Boyle. "Few of the nobility of the English extraction have ever contracted mar- riages with Irish papists," remarked his irritated uncle, "but none (up to this case) have married one who was at once an ordinary Servant Maid and an Irish Papist Bitch who had neither Charms of Beauty nor genteel behaviour nor agreeableness of conversation." To retain the inheritance of Mitchelstown, the "papist" had ostensibly reconverted to the Church of England, but few believed him sincere.

With the Whiteboy disturbance largely quelled now, the Kingsbor- oughs meant to "improve" their estates—house, land, and villages— without suffering from troublesome peasants or any worry over the ancient rights which landlords in England had to circumvent. Their aims were the usual mixture of self-interest and altruism, a concern for their own status and wealth combined with a desire to be good landlords as long as the tenantry remained obedient and quiet.

The remodeling of estate towns was as much in fashion as the

rebuilding of mansions. When they had pulled down the old Mitchels-town of hovels and dirty tracks, the Kingsboroughs built a new neat one east and south of Kingston College, reproducing its geometric patterns in streets and trees. The College, completed now by a row of fine town-houses, formed one of two elegant squares of the new town, the other being a large marketplace on an incline. Since the new town was located where the valley plain began to ascend to the Galtees, there were planned views down most of the main parallel streets—each named after one of the King sons. The new houses, inhabited by tenants at low rent and long leases, were two-storied, more like urban dwellings than rustic hovels. Made of stone and slate, they appeared an improvement on the old mud and thatch, although Richard Lovell Edgeworth claimed that "mud-wall houses are far warmer and drier than stone houses. . . . limestone houses unplastered though they have the external appearance of comfort are cold & wretched habitations." In her novel *Ennui,* his daughter Maria described impatient landlords putting people unused to domestic com-forts into modern cottages, which they simply cannibalized to re-create their old thatched life.

Flouting the penal laws, which discouraged Catholic education, a redoubtable gentlewoman, Nano Nagle, had set up a network of Catholic schools in Cork, and the influence needed counteracting. So in time Caroline added a Protestant church, Sunday school and orphanage to her town. As she aged she became more fiercely Protestant, to such an extent that Archbishop Butler of Cashell remonstrated with her over her treatment of Catholic townspeople and her forcible conversion of their children.

On one occasion a child merely sent to Mitchelstown on an errand was grabbed and taken to a house where her hair was cut and her clothes changed. Then she was put in Caroline's new orphanage until her mother's protests released her. When he heard of the incident Robert was furious with his wife, but in fact she was being true to their joint King her-itage: her own Mitchelstown forebears had frequently been in dispute

with the Roman Church. They had blamed local priests for seducing Protestants and marrying runaways, as well as for failing to discourage the more belligerent Catholics from possessing illegal firearms.

The new tenants of the model houses were to be model workers; to this end the Kingsboroughs tried to establish industry for them, such as a cotton mill, but in the early years of their tenure the main occupation of all the tenants was the building and refurbishing of the great house for their masters, together with the hunting lodges and other structures that followed. The ten-foot-high demesne wall alone, stretching for six and a quarter miles, took nineteen years to complete at a cost of £16,000. With all these changes and the constant demand for labor, the once disreputable Mitchelstown was soon reported to be "as orderly and peaceful as any other Irish town."

It took the immense self-confidence of their class for Robert and Caroline in their early twenties to carry out such reforms on people and landscape, a self-confidence born of the unique situation of the Anglo-Irish. England had developed a sophisticated system of financial credit and the Irish aristocracy could benefit from it to invest in magnificence. At the same time they had some political independence, which gave them much local status. Underpinning their luxurious life was the security provided by England's military defense. The life would be threatened only if the defense became fragile.

Prosperity had to be based on revenues from farming as well as credit. In the end the huge house and vast landscaped gardens were simply the decorative face of agricultural coercion. The land had to yield more for its owner; it was well if the tenants profited also.

The main advantage would come from the removal of the middlemen, and Robert set about this as soon as he took charge of the estates. Again he was in fashion—all over Ireland landlords were realizing that some sort of estate bureaucracy controlled by themselves and dealing directly with the hardworking tenant farmer yielded more revenues than the system of middlemen and head tenants. Reaching out to the farmers, Robert tried to encourage them to improve their land by giving longer

leases and offering £80 a year to those who most successfully increased the yield.

In his policies he was confirmed in September 1777, when Arthur Young arrived to take possession of his house and care for his employers' estate.* Young was much impressed with Mitchelstown Castle: it had "a situation worthy of the proudest capital," he wrote. The Kingsboroughs appreciated his comments, since in his tour he had visited numerous elegant mansions—although they may not have welcomed his opinion that the ballroom at Castlemartyr in the south of County Cork, seat of their family rival Lord Shannon, was the best room he had seen in Ireland.

Young began by observing. Like a scientist down a microscope, he stared at the alien population. "The cabins are innumerable," he wrote, "and like most Irish cabins, swarm with children. Wherever there are many people, and little employment, idleness and its attendants must abound." Pigs were everywhere. They basked and rolled about with the children "and often resemble one another so much, that it is necessary to look twice before the *human face divine* is confessed. I believe there are more pigs in Mitchelstown than human beings; and yet propagation is the only trade that flourished here for ages."

Everything needed improvement, beginning with management. The estate had been let out at an average of only half a crown per acre, where rents on land elsewhere varied from 8s to 25s an acre. The small farms and plots were hopelessly uneconomical and Young persuaded Robert to let larger units as well as for longer periods. As a result, the amount held by a single farmer rose from a yearly rent of £5 to one of £20. Young excitedly wrote that he believed Mitchelstown could become one of the finest properties in Europe.

---

* Originally Young stated that Robert initiated these reforms; see Young's *A Tour in Ireland 1776–1779* 1, 459, 462–3: "The size of farms held by occupying tenants is in general very small, Lord Kingsborough having released them from the bondage of the middle men. . . . Many leases being out, he rejected the trading tenant, and let every man's land to him. . . . I never omitted any opportunity of confirming him in this system." But in his *Autobiography*, 78, Young made himself the prime mover: "I was most anxious to persuade Lord K. into the propriety of letting his lands to the occupying cottar as tenant, and dismissing the whole race of middlemen." For the following description of the Mitchelstown estate, see *A Tour in Ireland*, 1:458f., 2:85f.; for Young's ensuing problems with his employers, see *The Autobiography of Arthur Young*, 78f.

Farming practice was harder to attack. The soil had been exhausted by overuse and underfertilizing; it was "a face of desolation." Crops were monothematic: potatoes. Young introduced corn, wheat, turnips and hay. Instead of proper fences and boundaries, so essential to the English agricultural revolution, there were unplanted mounds, with no gates but furze bushes stuck in the gaps or piles of stones. Once there had been trees, but the wood had been sold off by earlier unthrifty landlords. One had, said Young, to "take a breathing gallop to find a stick large enough to beat a dog." He set to planting hedges and enclosing land to allow grazing of cattle, and he urged Robert to give trees to his tenants to help replant the deforested estate. He also encouraged the hiring of a skilled English nurseryman to manage the twelve-acre nursery.

Young's relationship with his employers began well: "that a young man, warm from pleasure, should [improve his estate] has a much superior claim than in the case of an older proprietor." He was impressed that such a nobleman had quit the gaieties of Paris and London for land management. Yet he also understood that all reforms depended on the owner's firmness; here he had doubts. Robert was a mixture of qualities: capable and impressive in many ways, in others still the unsure boy whose staying power was unproven.

Stripped of his childish bashfulness, he struck Young as easy and polite, "having the finish of a perfect gentleman"—though this may have been tact, since Robert still seemed retiring and dour to many—and the power relations between him and his wife had begun to tilt in his direction. At the same time Young noted his employer lacked perseverance even when he knew himself right, and he was easily persuaded out of the proper path by people less intelligent and well-meaning than himself. This weakness, together with the distance still apparent between him and his volatile wife, could be exploited by those disadvantaged by his reforms or who wanted to use these rich young people for their own ends. Chief among these schemers were Caroline's distant relatives, Major and Mrs. James Badham Thornhill of Thornhill Lawn. No doubt they were supported by smaller tenants and peasants who got more through the usual

practice of stealing timber and sponging off the kitchens and gardens of the great house than they expected to achieve under the robust new regime.

The Thornhills held a large farm on the estate and enjoyed profit from the excessive rents charged on reletting the lands in the common rackrenting way of middlemen. The affable Major was a favorite with Caroline, whom he entertained with his boisterous talk. Young was less approving, probably seeing him as one of that "class of little country gentlemen; tenants, who drink their claret by means of profit rents; jobbers in farms; bucks, your fellows with round hats, edged with gold, who hunt in the day, get drunk in the evening, and fight the next morning . . . among whom drinking, wrangling, quarreling, fighting, ravishing, etc., etc., are found as in their native soil." Since, although well related, one of the Thornhills had been among the first batch of poor Protestants admitted to Kingston College, the family cannot all have been as flourishing as the Major. Eager to cement and improve his position, Thornhill wanted to obtain more farms from Robert and Caroline on the same old terms and to become their land agent in place of Young.

Like her husband, Caroline was charmed by the tall, gallant Arthur Young when she saw him at Mitchelstown after her return from giving birth to another daughter (Caroline) in Henrietta Street in September 1777. She found him lively, agreeable and a good conversationalist, although she was perhaps less enamored than Robert by his reforming zeal, which tended to upset the old ranking system. Young knew how to oblige and Caroline took to playing chess alone with him for an hour or so in the early evening when he came to the castle for dinner. Perhaps the affable Major felt socially supplanted. His wife, an "artful designing woman," seized her chance and hinted to Robert that the sessions were not blameless. She also hinted to Caroline that Margaret's Catholic French-speaking governess, Miss Crosby, was Robert's mistress and in league with Young to gain power over their employer. The scheming succeeded, for both Caroline and Robert were ready to believe the worst of each other. Arthur Young and Miss Crosby were dismissed.

Before he left in the autumn of 1779 Young was instructed to draw up a contract granting Miss Crosby an annuity of £50 a year. For himself he negotiated still more favorable terms. He refused to go until he received his arrears of £600. When Major Thornhill—now appointed Robert's land agent, as he had wished—told him that the Kings did not have the ready money, Young proposed a settlement of £72 a year for life. Robert readily agreed.

Were Viscountess Kingsborough and Arthur Young having an affair? Probably not, although gossip made him a libertine who left Mitchelstown not because of his employer's anger but because he had seduced a local girl whose family wanted redress. Heavily pregnant again during Young's last months at Mitchelstown, Caroline was also much concerned with her social status; she loved dressing, show and glamorous company, and she liked being the center of attention and flirting with desirable and desired men. Yet little scandal attached to her name throughout her marriage.

The rumor concerning Robert is more likely to be true, especially in the light of the annuity, which suggests the governess had rendered services outside the classroom. Robert knew that Caroline despised him but he had learned by now that his plain, delicate features were no impediment to sexual conquest elsewhere and that his rank and newly acquired polish made him a very credible lover.

Over the next years Caroline continued to give birth to children to an extent that even her demanding father-in-law must have approved. After Margaret and Caroline came Mary, probably in 1780, and two more girls; after George, Robert and Edward, four more boys, making seven sons and five daughters, twelve children in all. In addition, there seems to have been one infant death and a number of miscarriages.

Despite her fecundity Caroline had little maternal feeling and no knack of endearing herself to her children. Her formal, self-centered and loquacious manner kept them at a distance. With a retinue of nursemaids and governesses they did not cause her undue trouble and she

continued to travel to Dublin and London for the social seasons without worrying about abandoning them in the country. Such parents were "too much occupied by frivolous amusements to pay much attention to their offspring," her daughter Margaret later wrote. The sensuous side of her nature could be filled by lapdogs, on which she lavished caresses and to which she lisped in pretty French.

While aware of her role as chatelaine of Mitchelstown, Caroline did not enjoy long periods in the country. The company was too restricted, and while the setting was lavish, the wind raced too boisterously around the castle terraces for genteel strolling. There is no mention of family theatricals or the children's fancy-dress parties that enlivened the youth of the large Leinster brood in Carton. There was also little evidence of socializing with neighboring nobility, of whom the Kings were wary. The Countess of Moira claimed she had known her rich neighbors in County Down for nearly forty years but, finding them vulgar and illiberal, was "never tempted . . . to exceed the limits of the formal civility of receiving and returning visits once or twice in a year." The aristocracy could feel separate not only from the rural workers on whom they lived but also from their gentry neighbors if they outranked them or if they held different political views.

Yet Caroline was not restricted to her husband and children. The house was commonly filled with relations. Her stepmother and her children stayed for long periods; Mrs. Fitzgerald thought it good for her boy, who had a tendency to think too well of himself in a family of women. She had once irritated her stepdaughter, but her tact had by now won Caroline over and, when necessary, she could restrain her with careful words. She knew her own children had not the Kings' advantages. The dowager Duchess of Leinster married her sons' tutor, to the great dismay of her relatives, and was anxious about the status of daughters from her second family, "not liking to have them run the risk of being looked on as *half* sisters." Mrs. Fitzgerald negotiated this difficult situation with skill and the two families settled down amicably enough, with her girls growing up alongside her stepdaughter's.

Robert did not share his wife's need for Dublin and London society or for constant visitors. He loved Mitchelstown, where his social skills were untaxed, and he enjoyed the bustle of building and planting. There he was not only a landowner but something close to an Irish chieftain. Master in all things, he soon came to hold enormous judicial, political and social power. Young, who admired the Irish nobleman's ability to alter the land and tenantry, had been uneasy at this alien feudal state and had offered some exotic, titillating details to convey it to his English readers:

A landlord in Ireland can scarcely invent an order which a servant, labourer or cottar dares to refuse to execute. Nothing satisfies him but an unlimited submission. Disrespect or anything tending towards sauciness he may punish with his cane or his horsewhip with the most perfect security; a poor man would have his bones broke if he offered to lift his hand in his own defence. Knocking down is spoken of in the country in a manner that makes an English man stare. Landlords of consequence have assured me that many of their cottars would think themselves honoured by having their wives and daughters sent for to the bed of their master; a mark of slavery that proves the oppression under which such people must live . . . It must strike the most careless traveller to see whole strings of carts whipt into a ditch by a gentleman's footman, to make way for his carriage; if they are overturned or broken in pieces, no matter, it is taken in patience.

The humiliating early years of marriage had taken their toll and in time Robert became flamboyantly unfaithful to his dominating wife; no doubt he took advantage of the sexual customs Young described.

The Earl of Kingston had warned his son that he would never be the power in Cork that he could be in his ancestral home in Roscommon, but Robert was clear that the Cork region rather than remoter Roscommon was his political base. While never shining in Dublin, he grew

increasingly interested in local politics. North Cork was a center of large English settlements and the King lands, stretching across twenty miles of the country and controlling the gap in the mountains into Tipperary, made their owners natural leaders. For generations they had been ultra-Protestant and conservative: "there is no family in Ireland more strongly tinctured with religious prejudice," remarked one Catholic observer.

The Anglo-Irish elite, the "Ascendancy," was an exclusive colonialist club headed by such families as the Leinsters, Moiras, Conollys, Shannons, Kings and their neighbors the Mount Cashells. It consisted of landowning members of the Church of England who had benefited from grants to English Protestants made by English monarchs, and it derived power from the Treaty of Limerick following the Glorious Revolution of 1688 and defeat of the Catholic King James II by the Protestant William of Orange. In the early eighteenth century under Queen Anne penal laws prevented Catholics from inheriting estates, entering professions, holding civil office, voting, becoming MPs, serving in the armed forces or bearing arms. At least in theory this was so; in reality the penal laws were only intermittently enforced, many Catholics hid arms in their houses and they managed to control a good deal of land.

As the Whiteboy disturbances suggested, poor Catholics loathed tithes and high rents, but their feeling rarely led them to oppose English rule or the system of landlords. Writing in the early nineteenth century after a period of profound unrest, some landlords looked back to the time when Robert and Caroline were young as a golden age when there was "extraordinary devotion of the lower to the higher orders," when a feudal peasantry was attached to its lords, and when grievances were directed only at tax gatherers and Protestant clergymen. Bishop Berkeley of Cloyne told another story of these years: "it might be better for Ireland if all the fine folk of both sexes were shipped off to foreign countries, instead of . . . spreading moral contagion among the people."

More politically troublesome to the Ascendancy than the poorer Catholics were the equally excluded but more educated Presbyterian Irish, primarily of Scots descent and living mainly in Ulster as small farm-

ers and linen weavers. These saw themselves as the true heirs of the Glorious Revolution, yet they were excluded from its benefits, forced like
Catholics to pay tithes to an alien church and restricted from expanding
their trades, although they had developed the most advanced commercial region in the country. Inevitably they had their equivalents of the
Whiteboy movement, although they rarely made common cause with
Catholics, whom they feared much as the Anglo-Irish did: to both groups
Rome was not only an idolatrous religion but a political threat that
allowed allegiance to a foreign prince. This fear ran deep in all Protestant
classes throughout the three kingdoms. In June 1780 London was con-
vulsed by the Gordon Riots at the mere mention of emancipation for
Catholics, and there were only eighty thousand of them in the whole of
England. Living in the south, Robert and Caroline had little personally to
do with Ulster Presbyterians, but the group would soon have an impact
on all of Ireland and the eldest King children, Margaret and George,
would live and act very much in their shadow.

Although the Anglican aristocracy supported English rule, they usually resented its embodiment in Dublin Castle, outside their immediate
control. As a result, they felt a confusing mixture of colonialist and colo-
nized, holding a hybrid identity, English in Ireland, Irish in England.
Within Ireland they never managed to impose their views and ideals on
the bulk of the population and, despite some liberal traditions and phil-
anthropic activities, they formed an *ancien regime* wedded to their own
power, to patronage and to deference.

In the south the relative numbers of Irish peasants and Anglo-Irish
landowners meant that provincial settlements felt almost like garrison
towns needing defense from within as well as without. During the war for
American independence the French and Spanish exploited England's
predicament by threatening to invade Ireland. Aware that the government had committed most regular troops to America, and faced with an
inept Castle administration, the Protestant landlords organized their
own security. A civilian militia had always provided Ireland with local

peacekeepers; now in the 1780s this body became a new fighting force of Volunteers paid for by landowners, not by Dublin Castle.

Aristocrats were addicted to flamboyant dress and the Volunteer movement fed the habit, as Lord Shannon disapprovingly noted. To sweeten the fact that they were paying, captains were allowed to ornament their troops and lead them out "all bedaubed with lace." The Earl of Mount Cashell, the Kings' nearest aristocratic neighbor in County Cork, dressed his Kilworth Volunteers in scarlet-faced green, gold epaulettes and yellow buttons. Not to be outdone, Robert became colonel of the Mitchelstown troops, who were decked out in scarlet uniform with black facing, silver epaulettes, yellow helmets and white buttons. His officers included his new land agent, Major Thornhill, and the first chaplain of Kingston College, the debt-ridden former landowner Thomas Bushe. So keen was Robert on local soldiering that he became chairman of the convention held in Cork and the Munster representative at the grand National Convention of Volunteers in Dublin.

Not only an excuse for fancy dress, the Volunteer movement allowed the nobility to collaborate with the professional classes. *Exshaw's Magazine* enthused, "What a glorious and pleasing sight to see the laws of a country protected and enforced by her own children, disciplined, armed and clothed by a spirit of loyalty and independence!" Volunteers were, said the liberal Irish politician Henry Grattan, "the armed property of the nation." The Irish parliament had been a sore point since 1688, when England achieved a form of constitutional monarchy, while in Ireland the Lord Lieutenant, appointed in London, still wielded supreme power. Grattan saw the potential of the Volunteers to help steer the country toward a new constitution.

So a meeting of Volunteers at Dungannon in 1782 declared that no one except the King and the Lords and Commons of Ireland could legislate for Ireland. Caught in its war with America, France and Spain, the English government agreed, and "Grattan's Parliament" was established amidst much optimistic excitement: its mover declared "Ireland is now a

nation" free from control by Westminster. Some reforms followed, some
trade restrictions were relaxed, Catholics were allowed to hold property
on the same terms as Protestants, some penal laws against them were
modified, and an interest in Irish antiquities was cultivated, but England
did not much loosen its rule, and ultimate power remained with ministers in London acting through the Castle. The parliamentary vote was
not extended beyond the Anglican elite to Presbyterians or Catholics,
and many believed the parliament from which so much was hoped had
simply increased corrupt Ascendancy power. The later rebel Wolfe Tone
called it "a most bungling imperfect business" and said it was a revolution that "enabled Irishmen to sell at a much higher price their honour,
their integrity, the interests of their country." It had one advantage, however: it kept landowners and their money in Dublin during the winter
parliamentary season and diminished the expensive annual exodus to
London.

Men of the major Ascendancy families, such as the Leinsters, Mount
Cashells, Moiras and Kings, usually involved themselves in politics, fre-
quenting the vice-regal court at Dublin Castle and entering Parliament,
either Lords or Commons depending on status. Edward, as Earl of Kingston, was in the Lords warming the seat for Robert, while Robert had
obeyed his father and become parliamentary member for Boyle. But he
knew his political future lay in the region he now inhabited.

Cork was the most politically powerful county in Ireland, with
twenty-six MPs out of three hundred; as owner of Mitchelstown, he could
expect to influence many of them with money and patronage—indeed,
the Mitchelstown Kings usually commanded 10 percent of the whole
Cork vote. So in 1783 Edward sold his son's old seat in Boyle and Robert
stood for Parliament in his adopted county in one of the traditional seats
controlled by his wife's family. In both places he was classed with the
"independent interest," like so many of his peers, avoiding any close and
stifling contact with Dublin Castle. In Cork, unlike in Boyle, however, he
had to work hard for election, for he had a fierce rival in Lord Shannon,
dubbed the "colossus of Castlemartyr" and "bulwark of the Protestant

religion." A staunch supporter of the Lords Lieutenants in the Castle since the 1750s, the redoubtable Shannon had become used to wielding the greatest political power in County Cork. He did not care to be challenged by young Robert.

Contested elections were expensive—a County Down one in 1790 allegedly cost more than £11,500 to one contender. They were part battle and part festival, with flags, bands, bonfires and gallons of free beer. "Can poverty from Gold withdraw his hand?" asked one losing candidate, the liberal landowner Richard Lovell Edgeworth, about electors' habits of supporting the greatest spender.

Given the tempers aroused and the alcohol flowing, contested elections inevitably became scenes of flamboyant quarrels. In this one, supporters of Lords Kingsborough and Shannon clashed repeatedly. The largest and most respectable Irish newspaper, the *Dublin Evening Post*, reported that nine Shannonites had been horsewhipped and twenty-two duels by sword and pistol threatened—though much was hot air, since only two shots were fired and no hits made.

In the end Robert won. Lord Shannon was irate: "the dignity of the Shannon family is *shorn of its beams* by the loss of a general influence over so great a country," reported one onlooker. Whatever else the election had achieved—and it had certainly made him poorer—it gave Robert a fierce enemy for life in Lord Shannon.

Although Robert did not favor votes for Catholics, he had a sense of their economic grievances, especially over tithes. His "first and highest ambition is to see *this country* [i.e., county] *free*," he declared. Shannon did not follow him so far and in the 1787 election Robert discovered to his disgust that the Anglican clergy this time supported Shannon against himself and his candidate. Lady Louisa Conolly, conservative owner of Castletown, was dubious about Robert's liberalism, so unusual for his family: she wondered whether the fracas in Cork was really about the evil of tithes or simply a matter of personal politics. She thought Robert would by now do anything to distinguish himself from Lord Shannon.

But there is evidence that Robert did for a time lean toward liberalism.

A year after this election, Grattan tried to get Parliament to exempt the food and fuel of the poor from taxation and take dues instead from the grazing grounds of the rich. It was, he said, degrading to the constitution to see "*extortion* assume the *power* of legislation." Robert seconded the motion: "The people who cultivate the poor lands in the county of Cork are utterly unable to pay Tythe of any kind, and yet Tythe of every kind is most rigorously demanded from them." He himself, a great landowner, could oppose the illegal imposition of dues, but the poor had no weapons and suffered disproportionately.

Caroline made no public comment on her husband's opinions. She had written to her mother-in-law that "as for Politics I am too stupid to mind them." Although she was instinctively conservative, she was when young unconcerned with political posturing and, unlike many aristocratic wives, made no effort to campaign for her husband in any of his election contests.

.CHAPTER 4.

Aristocratic Childhood

*Whether for the better or the worse, no matter; but we are
refined; and plain manners, plain dress, and plain
diction, would as little do in life, as acorns, herbage, and
the water of the neighbouring spring, would do at table.*

—*LETTERS OF THE EARL OF CHESTERFIELD TO HIS SON*

THE EARLIEST EXPERIENCE OF MARGARET AND GEORGE WAS OF England, and even the younger daughters were brought up around people more at home in London than Cork or Tipperary. In Ireland the girls traveled between the great family mansions, often left at one while their parents visited the other. They stayed with their grandmother Jane at Boyle before her death in 1784 and spent some time at the seaside, probably near Black Rock in Dublin Bay or Strandhill near Sligo, where Jane used to go for healthy sea bathing with her delicate son Henry, once George's amicable playmate. Margaret remembered how she used "to delight in searching for shells amongst the sand and pebbles."

Life in the castle changed with the seasons. In the parliamentary session Robert and Caroline might be in Dublin in Henrietta Street, but often the whole family, except for the eldest boys, who had followed Robert to Eton, were at Mitchelstown, where men hunted, shot and

gambled and women sewed, played cards, walked or rode around the estate and visited tenants. On Sundays there were afternoon prayers undertaken for political as well as religious reasons. "The rich have all the intolerancy of bigots, without any of their piety," remarked an English visitor.

Domestic life was punctuated by meals taken lengthily at a well-stocked board. Although for much of the day the master and mistress went separate ways, they came together at dinner to sit at either end of their table. In the country some people might dine at one or two but it was not done in upper circles in town to eat before three or four, and Lady Kingsborough cared about fashion. The meal, which was heralded by bells and could last for hours, included fish of several sorts, mutton and some roasted fowl. Young children ate apart in the nursery but were sometimes allowed at the main table; older ones would be expected to join the adults. Girls had to acquire manners and drink enough but not in excess—too much alcohol was indecorous. For men and boys it was different; after the ladies withdrew there were toasts and drinking competitions, and chamber pots were brought into the room.

The girls experienced little social mixing across the sectarian divide, but their society included the nearby Protestant gentry such as the Thornhills, Bushes and Wilmots. Within the castle they were not short of company, since so many relatives and friends stayed for long periods. One frequent visitor, probably a distant cousin of Caroline's, was an impecunious landowner and MP for Wexford, George Ogle of Bellevue. Politically he was a hard-liner, vigorously opposing concessions to Catholics and staunchly supporting Protestant rule despite calling landlords "great extortioners." He popularized the term "Protestant Ascendancy" for his class and regarded any lower-order disturbance as a popish plot.

Inevitably he opposed Catholics bearing arms and insisted they be excluded from his own troops, the Wexford Volunteers. Any concession was an effort "to subvert the Protestant religion of this kingdom, to take the landed property out of the hands of Protestants and put it in the hands of papists." Catholics could not be loyal, for "a papist could swal-

low a false oath as easily as a poached egg," he declared. A whiskey distiller took exception to the remark and the pair fought a duel. Eight shots were fired but nobody was hurt. Ogle claimed he had been misquoted; he had referred only to "rebels," not "papists," he said.

After being, like Robert, "independent" from the Castle for some years, George Ogle had recently thrown in his lot with the Dublin government and, as a result, was receiving a handsome reward, to the disgust of some of his former colleagues: "the patriotic Mr. Ogle . . . has got a government pension and is now the mouthpiece of the court." Usually he and Robert thought much alike except when Robert flirted with liberalism in 1787; presumably they kept off politics while in Mitchelstown during this year.

To Caroline and her daughters George Ogle was less a reactionary politician than a lively, handsome man who enjoyed talking, wearing "pompous apparel" and rather charmingly showing off. He was the author of sentimental love ballads and the encourager of *bouts rimés* competitions, in which he took vigorous part. His most popular work, much anthologized, was "Banna's Banks," which began,

> Shepherds, I have lost my love!
> Have you seen my Anna?
> Pride of ev'ry shady grove,
> Upon the banks of Banna!

It was fashionable for great ladies to have a man of letters in tow and the good-looking, sentimental Ogle was a suitable "flirt," despite the fact that his wife accompanied him. He was not learned but he was entertaining and a good conversationalist, and he spoke with an enthusiasm and energy that were contagious. He was also a good listener, a skill useful to Caroline, who liked best to hear herself talk.

Inhabiting a neoclassical mansion and surrounded by classically inspired artifacts, Margaret and her younger sister Mary entered a bizarre fantasy of the past and present quite at odds with the culture outside their

gates. While Lady Kingsborough was keen for her girls to learn history, it was never the complete history of their country. Margaret commented on the partisan regimen: "to the shame of Ireland I must acknowledge, that it has been too much the custom to neglect instructing our youth in the annals of that country, respecting which they ought to be particularly interested." Parents such as Caroline implanted in their children "a contempt for the land they ought to love" and an exaggerated respect for English customs and culture.

Yet things were changing and the neoclassical isolation of Robert and Caroline was falling out of fashion. Their daughters lived on the cusp of nationalism, and soon the governing classes would develop greater interest in their native land. Then the Greco-Roman would be repudiated in favor of a distinctive Britishness, Germanic and Celtic—an enjoyment of the exotic peripheries at whose expense England was thriving. Buildings would have to change again.

By the time they were adults both Margaret and Mary were aware of being Irish as well as Anglo-Irish in a way their mother never was, and both later revealed some knowledge of native culture. They may occasionally have met the propertied and rich Catholics in the area, some of whom patronized Irish music and literature, although as children they were unlikely to have actually learned Irish, for "the highest sort of people . . . in general, are too genteelly bred to understand anything of the language." They would also have had any Irish accent they acquired drummed out of them. Margaret later criticized the attitude: "No language is considered so unfashionable, no language so discordant, no accent so vulgar, as the Irish." It was a general view among the upper classes and Dublin schools regularly advertised for teachers who spoke "the English Language free from provincial accent."

For centuries Irish songs had been common among the upper orders in England and Ireland. Now in the later eighteenth century Protestant nationalism helped a cultural revival of native music and poetry. Influenced by the vogue for the largely invented Scottish bard Ossian in the 1760s, rapturous and elegiac Irish poetry in translation became popular, and in 1786 the antiquarian Joseph Cooper Walker published his *Histori-cal Memoirs of the Irish Bards,* even providing bardesses of ancient Ireland for an eager modern public. He had collaborated with the Anglo-Irish writer Charlotte Brooke, who, having learned Irish (as well as the harp), translated the poems of the blind poet Turlough O'Carolan. In 1788 she produced her *Reliques of Irish Poetry,* an anthology of verse based on the work of ancient Irish bards. To the English she hoped to teach respect for the older traditions of Ireland; to the Irish she introduced "ancestors so very different from what modern prejudice has been studious to repre-sent them." Through such anthologies girls of Margaret's and Mary's class could see there was more to their native country than its colonial history. For Margaret in particular the volumes of Walker and Charlotte Brooke became treasured possessions.

"It is the misfortune of Ireland that the rich & poor form two such distinct bodies, having different languages, habits, religion & objects, the consequences of the colonising system. . . . there is a strong line drawn between them & they feel that their interests are distinct," wrote one observer. Yet as inhabitants of County Cork, the girls met some poor peo-ple, including beggars and travelers wanting alms, and they attended the annual Mitchelstown fair with its mixture of sellers, entertainers and mountebanks. Although the peasants with their long loose hair, rags or bright flannel petticoats and cloaks were as alien to them as to the aston-ished Arthur Young, they grew up habituated to their presence and they had at least one Catholic governess. Meanwhile, they listened to local tales from the impoverished Protestants of Kingston College. Years later Margaret produced a popular children's book of stories ostensibly told by a character based on an old soldier living on Kingston College green. Irish customs lingered in her memory and she recalled the habit of mak-ing fires on the hills in honor of St. John's Eve.

Some Irish peasant ways also stayed with her. As an adult, she shocked a Polish countess in Paris by eating plain boiled potatoes for lunch in the middle of the day. The timing and fare had been picked up in childhood in Mitchelstown, where cottiers sold their meat and poultry to pay their

rent and lived on milk and potatoes, that "root of poverty," as the radical English journalist William Cobbett called it. Potatoes were "eaten by way of bread, even the ladies indelicately placing them on the tablecloth, on the side of their plate, after peeling them." In the early 1800s, when her potato eating was commented on, national awareness had increased and Margaret, now a firm patriot, was making a point about her ethnic identity. When the upper orders appropriated aspects of lower-class life, these aspects tended to grow sophisticated: her aristocratic friend tried to please her by preparing a breakfast of potatoes dressed in fifty different ways.

While sorties into the wider culture punctuated their lives, most of the girls' experience was within the great house. In Margaret's words, she and her sisters were "placed under the care of hirelings from the first moment of [their] birth." All the King children were breast-fed and cared for by other women. Although they recognized their mother as a source of authority, they experienced the nurturing aspects of mother-hood through paid women and occasionally minor relatives. It was nor-mal for their rank.

At all times of the day the children were surrounded by retainers, many in the family livery. A great house such as Mitchelstown probably employed eighty or so grooms, maids, nursery maids and workmen— more than most Irish factories. The castle was largely self-supporting: baking, brewing, spinning, weaving, tanning and the raising of horses and hounds all took place there. Only luxury goods and services had to be imported.

Just one group of hirelings, their governesses, were set over the girls, who had to put up with the moods and rages of young women often resentful of their role within the family. This, Margaret claimed, spoiled the children's temper and made them difficult. The governess Miss Crosby, who presided over Margaret's early time at Mitchelstown, could have taken what liberties she wished, since she was almost certainly Robert's mistress. After her came a succession of women, all instructed by Caroline to make her girls accomplished ladies. None lasted long.

Some were ill-natured and rude; Lady Kingsborough treated them with contempt and they took this out on the girls with sarcasm and arbitrary punishments.

Other servants were simply hired to do the children's bidding and teach them to act with the authority of their rank. Such ubiquitous service led to self-centeredness. As the Earl of Clonmell remarked of the large country house, "It is a prison, unless you have society; and that society are the instruments of the landlord's ruin." Servants, he wrote, could become a power in themselves, corrupting the owners by their flattery and bad habits. They taught aristocratic children to be both fearful and arrogant. Even as a freethinking adult, Margaret saw servants solely from the employers' point of view: an ugly or deformed servant should not be hired to tend sensitive children, she wrote, oblivious of the needs or value of an imperfect retainer.

Caroline emerges as a harsh, self-centered and distant parent to many of her sons and daughters. By the mid-1780s George, her eldest, was showing a character that neither she nor Robert approved—so much so that they did not even want his portrait. Like his father before him, George was at Eton College in England, where it was customary for the pupils to have their pictures painted. To do George his parents had commissioned the artist Romney, a celebrated painter, but not as expensive as Reynolds or Gainsborough. Whether or not the Kingsboroughs had considered cost in the choice of artist, when the portrait was completed they failed to pay for it and so it was never delivered. Presumably they were not eager to have a likeness of their eldest son on their wall to remind them of his failings.

George was not given to recording himself in words but he may have sat for a sketch by the adult Margaret, his closest sibling. She wrote about the effect of parental tyranny on children, insisting that it made them timid even if they grew up knowing they had fortune and a noble name. The temperament of childhood was never eradicated and the child made nervous by harshness and never treated as a rational creature would emerge either wicked or obstinate. Something like this seemed to

be happening to George. In early childhood he had been slow and delicate, the kind of boy who, if wrongly treated, would become sullen and violent. Now he was big, rowdy and so boorish that both Robert and Caroline preferred their second son, Robert Edward. Caroline no doubt blamed her husband's dissoluteness, while he might have retorted that his cold wife was at fault.

Books told parents how to bring children through the newly labeled stages of growing up. The Irish-Scots philosopher Francis Hutcheson stressed that children should obtain "their liberty as soon as they can safely enjoy it, since without it they cannot be happy." Everyone knew they had a duty to parents—it was much stressed—but he pointed out that the reverse was also true. "Generation no more makes them the property of their parents, than Sucking makes them the property of their nurses. . . . the child is a rational agent, with rights valid against their parents." Lady Kingsborough would not have agreed; textbooks on child rearing were aimed mainly at the middle classes, not the aristocracy, where children were still swapped as counters in dynastic games. Yet many in the upper orders testified to a growing respect for children and an emotional closeness between them and their parents. Surviving series of letters such as those between the Irish bishop Edward Synge and his daughter and between the Duchess of Leinster and her large brood indicate much expressed affection and openness.

Her sons George and Robert Edward at Eton were now beyond Lady Kingsborough's concern but, since aristocratic daughters had no formal schooling, the girls were hers to mold, and although she lacked warmth, she was dutiful. She had often been bored in the country and she assumed that her eldest girls would feel much the same. She let them have the amusements of their class: they could walk, string beads, draw, embroider, look at prints of dresses and ride out with their brothers or grooms. At the same time they must learn the duties of their station, how to act benevolently to those below them. Charity was less the fashion in Ireland than in England, but even there well-brought-up ladies were encouraged to visit the poor and soften the lot of those who supported

their cushioned lifestyle. Caroline was a great patron in Mitchelstown with her churches and schools, and she encouraged her daughters in proper patronage.

She decreed that her girls should read only improving books—or, as was most usual, read books to each other while they took it in turns to do their needlework or practice drawing and copying. She disapproved of novels, believing they promoted imagination over common sense and romance over dynastic interest. The aristocratic anxiety about novels for growing girls was general, and history was regarded as a proper antidote; yet few guardians were as strict as Lady Kingsborough. Bishop Edward Synge divided his daughter's reading into the grave and idle and allowed both, although the grave had to predominate. Frivolous reading hurt and enfeebled the mind, he believed, and he prescribed a good dose of history to neutralize fiction.

The King daughters were taught by traditional methods.

They learned historical and geographical facts by rote and their factual education sounds like that of Maria and Julia Bertram in Jane Austen's *Mansfield Park:* these girls could put the map of Europe together, tell the principal rivers of Russia and recite the chronological order of the kings of England and the Roman emperors as low as Severus, "besides a great deal of the Heathen Mythology, and all the Metals, Semi-Metals, Planets, and distinguished philosophers." The King girls "learnt a little of many things & nothing well," Margaret later remarked.

Yet despite her daughter's adult hostility, Caroline's system was not fruitless. Although Margaret might mock, she and her sisters grew up knowing well foreign languages such as French and Italian, useful for the grand tour they would make with their parents or future husbands. Margaret also became fluent in German, Latin and Greek: later in life she translated from German, referred knowledgeably to Tacitus, Sallust, Livy and Cicero, and read Greek drama. Presumably her sister Mary was similarly skilled. Caroline saw some learning as part of feminine display, rather like music and painting, but it is to her credit that, as her girls exceeded the usual requirements, she did not immediately worry that

they would become Bluestockings, too masculine to make suitable marriages. In many cases, if a girl liked her skipping rope more than her doll, or Latin more than sewing, it alerted a watchful mother to the looming danger of spinsterhood.

Despite the strictures on novels, it is unlikely that the girls avoided the very popular works of Frances Burney, whose heroines like their author moved in aristocratic circles, although they also showed the miseries of the poor and the struggles for significance of middle-class girls without status. Their plots often revolved around the engrafting of middle-class morality onto the nobility—Lady Sarah Napier, one of the more liberal sisters of the Duchess of Leinster, especially recommended *Cecilia,* in which a rich heiress gave up everything for love—rather as she herself had done earlier in life. Possibly the girls also came across the few novels produced locally, such as Sophia Briscoe's *A Fine Lady* (1772), which displays an exemplary wife and a wicked aristocrat. Such novels followed the sentimental form of the time, usually written by vicars' daughters or gentry girls imagining what it would be like to live in a castle in Ireland or Wales—as the King girls actually did. The sensation of the year 1785 was *The Recess* by Sophia Lee, a novel in which Mary Queen of Scots is given middle-class virtues and aristocratic sovereignty, a delicious combination with which to identify.

Frequently Caroline's quick temper set the house in an uproar and she was used to getting her way with it. She did not stay angry for long but was not accustomed to be crossed for long either. As an important only child, she had been spoiled and it was too late for her to learn complete self-control, although her stepmother, Mrs. Fitzgerald, had been a calming influence in recent years.

Caroline believed that girls should be properly punished for bad behavior and insubordination, although she followed contemporary opinion in avoiding beatings. When her daughters displeased or disappointed her she deprived them of treats and favorite foods or gave them especially boring chores. The adult Margaret remarked that this was wholly the wrong method: children had irregular appetites and should

not be denied what they liked best or they would start to crave luxurious foods. Chores could not cure a dreamy child; they simply made her resentful. As an adult, Margaret was much concerned with regimens for well-being and she tried out various combinations of rest, entertainment and proper eating.

A hint of the treatment she and the other girls received when ailing comes from a book Margaret later wrote for young mothers. It advised them to prevent rather than cure disease, insisting that many illnesses were due to the imprudence of parents and the neglect of children. Presumably she had Caroline in mind. Margaret was always worried about her "capricious" health, and some, including her mother and later her eldest brother George, believed her a hypochondriac, manipulating others through feigning illness. Margaret did not look delicate, but as an adult she was prone to colds and lung infections and was often sick, as she had probably been as a child. Confined in the castle with so many children, she would have needed a strong constitution to avoid a succession of common and contagious fevers. The girls lived through some severe national outbreaks—for example, the general influenza of 1782; the only remedies were sweating, taking physic and drinking brandy or wine. Mary was a small child at this time and the family must have feared for her life.

Irish letters constantly advise treatments. The sequence of purges, laxatives, bleedings and spa waters suggests a general belief in the old humoral physiology of the ancients, still current in the eighteenth century: blood, phlegm, yellow and black bile interacted with the four elements of air, fire, earth and water, and health was the keeping of all in balance. If lost, balance could be restored by ridding the body of the particular excess through blistering, bloodletting and vomiting. Partly at war with this theory was the newer fashionable one of nerves, which, stressing the interactive powers of the body and mind, gave some value to physical delicacy in women.

The doctor in whom Caroline trusted most was aware of such theories but, true to his profession, he also believed in intervention and

immediate cures through heavy use of drugs and potions, something of a luxury commodity in this era. Indeed, Lady Louisa calculated that in one year she spent £42 on physicians and drugs, more than Caroline was paying her governesses. Having suffered under this doctor's treatment, Margaret came to disagree profoundly with him, believing that children should not have medicines such as mercury sulfide thrust down their throats.

> The very idea of being the patient of a medical practitioner, and liable to take remedies continually, is, sometimes, enough to create disease in a person whose nerves are already agitated by the vicinity of an important revolution in the frame: and, therefore, it should be one of the first objects of those, who are about a girl in this situation, to prevent her from supposing herself in bad health, and keep her mind as cheerful as possible.
>
> Treatment should be natural: warm water for stomach ache, castor oil for colic, rinsing the mouth with tepid water for toothache and camomile flower infusion for sore bowels.

Mary and her sister Caroline were not yet pubescent but Margaret probably already had irregular periods since in later life she devoted much attention to the subject. The "periodical evacuation" of females can be entirely erratic, even stop for a year or more, but this should not be treated as a disease, she warned, suggesting that something like this might have happened to her. It was a difficult subject to discuss, since the modesty demanded of a young girl prevented her asking questions. A few years earlier Bishop Synge resorted to embarrassed French when he mentioned "*ses Ordinaires*" to his daughter, admitting he could "scarce write it in English. Such is the force of Custom."

By her mid-teens, when pretty Mary was still in the nursery, Margaret had grown into a difficult, awkward and too tall girl. The only area in which she pleased was her skill at music. She had a good ear and hand and played with taste. As a result, she was often hauled into the drawing

room to exhibit before company. Despite the praises showered on her, she loathed such exhibitions and her resentment of her mother grew.

She had a serious, needy temperament to which Caroline could never respond, while she lacked the art to charm her mother into the affection she wanted. The harshness and regular punishments were ineffective, and the contempt Margaret soon felt for her unloving parent became corrosive, decaying her own self-respect. Both had violent tempers and both succumbed to them. Margaret was not the only daughter to be alienated in these years. A younger sister, perhaps Mary, a "poor little girl . . . was so much afraid of being alone with her mother, she wept herself sick" when Lady Kingsborough proposed to take her on one of her many visits.

Margaret's response was to retreat into mimicry, mocking the affected, lisping way Caroline talked (when the wilier Mary grew up, she took the opposite course and copied it). Lady Kingsborough was unamused, never glancing at the vulnerability the mockery masked. "No person . . . can be more thoroughly [sure] of the injurious consequences of unkindness and tyranny to young minds," Margaret later wrote, "for few (I believe) more severely experienced the baneful effects." She warned adults against being deceived by appearance and not understanding the insecurity of a clever child, noting how much the imagination and agitation of nerves could destroy health. She knew herself to be an open, expressive girl who wanted to be liked. She responded effusively to kindness and was stung to the quick by rebuffs from the mother she only intermittently saw. For the rest of her life the vacancy Lady Kingsborough had left at her core would be filled by other women, the relationships made the more intense when the central male ones also failed her. Neither as child nor as adult did Margaret ever make common cause with her brother George, whose later hatred of their mother quite equaled hers; their temperaments were too distinct and they disliked each other quite as much as they did their mother.

As girls of rank, Margaret and Mary had to dress accordingly, and here there was much opportunity for friction. Aristocratic ladies spent much of

the day adorning the body and head with the help of maids and expensive preparations. It was important to look decorative at all times, since the great house was a public space. Margaret's features were delicate and regular, her eyes blue, her complexion pale and her thick hair a deep chestnut brown, but by her teens these advantages were offset by an angular shape. In time she could make herself striking if she took the trouble but when young she was aware of her mother's dislike of her gawky appearance and found it hard to compromise—she even suspected that Caroline drew attention to her ugliness by trying to load her with ornaments.

The 1780s were an unfortunate time to be young and big. Dress was still quite complicated and the simpler, soft outfits such as the polonaise, using an overskirt held around the hips in three soft puffs, and the French court muslin dress, with its broad sash and billowing neckerchief, required a form very different from hers. They suited the prettier Mary, although not her liking for energetic outdoor playing. In contrast, Margaret believed that flannel, not silks, satins and muslin, was right for winter, however unfine, and that girls ought not to have their arms and breasts fashionably exposed so they could look pretty and catch cold. Clothes should be plain to allow movement; instead, all dolled up, spirited girls were reproached for spoiling finery and timid ones avoided exercise for fear of ruining their frocks. So, from her earliest years Margaret waged war on Caroline's addiction to "flounces and trimmings, and lace and trumpery of all sorts." This was unusual for an upper-class girl and here her mother was far more conventional. The common interest can be observed in the letters of Jane Austen or the Irish Betsy Sheridan from England. In 1785, for example, Betsy wrote:

> Washing gowns of all kinds are the ton. Dark dutch Chintzes are very much worn, and now I think of it I must tell you I never had a gown so admired as my Irish Lawn. It has been wash'd three times and appears now if any thing better than when new. . . . It is always taken for a dutch Chintz but I take care to publish its country. . . . The undress Hats are straw, chip or Celbridge or Cane, of the dimensions pretty nearly of

your round tea table, two rows of narrow ribbon or one of broad round
the crown and three or four yards pinn'd loosely at the back. I have got
a Celbridge for the Honour of Ireland, these are for walks or Church,
as a more dressy one I brought from London a white persian Hat—
Tiffany quilt'd on it and bound with pale pink ribbon.

Nothing in Margaret's copious writings compares with this.

Indeed, by her mid-teens she hated the whole cult of feminine prettiness, insisting that a healthy, good-humored child could not be "ugly."
Unhappily, most mothers disagreed. Like other daughters Margaret suffered from the tyranny of stays and tight lacing, both meant to give girls
the exaggerated feminine shape of minute waist, high plumped breasts
and upright figure. The squeezing damaged internal organs and sometimes even led to death. In Margaret's and Mary's case nothing so drastic
occurred, but Margaret's big-boned figure pushed against the restraints:
"I have very good reason for believing that this mode of acquiring a slen-
der shape does not always succeed," she later wrote. Some girls' mothers
did not demand stays and lacing, yet their daughters grew up with fine
figures, she noted. "Beauty is by no means to be neglected; but it cannot
exist without proportion; and if a girl be so formed as to have broad
shoulders and broad hips, (as many handsome women are,) surely nothing is so calculated to destroy the symmetry of her form as to pinch in
her body until it is as small as her arms." Beauty, she would later say
firmly, was a matter of physical and moral culture, which depended on
education, not haphazard attributes.

In compensation for all this female constraint Margaret took to
dressing as a boy when she could. Years later, when she was nearly fifty,
the habit persisted, and the poet Shelley, a close friend in Italy, even suggested that she disguise herself as a male suitor to rescue his latest
amorous enthusiasm from her convent.

Possibly it was the conspicuous failure with her son George and his inabil-
ity to nurture any moral restraints that prompted Caroline to look again at

the education of her daughters, especially the eldest, whose childish rebel-liousness reminded her of George's insubordination, only it was worse in a girl. She feared that her daughters lacked something essential, some sound principles to guide them in marriage or spinsterhood. The rude-ness of Margaret indicated a failure in morality, which demanded respect for parents. She wondered perhaps if their ethical and religious education had been insufficiently attended to in her concern for their learning French, Italian and music. She feared that, in the educationist Hannah More's stern words, she had sacrificed "principle as a victim to sounds and accents." A clergyman called Barry had been brought in to tutor the younger children in religion but had little effect on the elder daughters.

The latest governess had just left and the choice of a new one was cru-cial. The girls, now growing up and learning to assert themselves against their paid tutors, had already broken several and a woman of strong char-acter and principle more than skill in French was needed if they were not to turn out wild. Having seen the Catholic French-speaking governess off the premises for seducing her husband and having watched other unsat-isfactory women pack their bags, Caroline decided she had had enough of frivolous and feeble governesses. Instead, she required a woman of good morals and firm principles who would not sleep with her husband and who could control and refine the girls, teaching them standards as well as facts. Despite the school's failure with her son George, she had come to trust one of the undermasters at Eton College, John Prior, whose wife too was a sensible woman. Prior associated with men of intellectual stature while having an understanding of the proprieties of rank. He was the man to advise her, so she sought him out while she was on one of her periodic visits to England.

She was offering £40 a year, not princely—£10 less than the pension given to the disgraced Miss Crosby—but adequate, and perhaps she and the Priors thought more would attract the wrong sort of person. The usual demand in governesses for the higher ranks was spoken French and fancy needlework, but Caroline had had sufficient of these expen-

sive skills; rather, she left it to Mr. and Mrs. Prior to find her someone of suitable character and morality.

The Priors were friends of the leading nonconformist thinker of the day, Richard Price of Newington Green, a serious, kindhearted man, who often befriended earnest, intellectual women. Among his friends was his neighbor, a schoolmaster's widow, Mrs. Burgh. Both these elderly people had recently encountered a young woman who had moved into the Green to set up a school with her friend and sisters. The circumstance had been rather irregular, since one of the women was a runaway wife, but both Dr. Price and Mrs. Burgh had been won by the seriousness of the prime mover in the scheme. Her name was Mary Wollstonecraft.

Recently the school had collapsed and the young woman was in need of a position. Dr. Price and Mrs. Burgh believed her to be just the right-minded spinster for Lady Kingsborough, while Mrs. Burgh, to whom she owed a great deal of money, also hoped she might make her fortune away from her dependent sisters. They passed on her name and description through the Priors. Lady Kingsborough responded with an "advantageous" offer.

. C H A P T E R 5 .

The Governess

*Children will necessarily delight in the company of those,
who make them happy.*

—MARIA EDGEWORTH,
"THE GOOD FRENCH GOVERNESS"

AT TWENTY-SEVEN MARY WOLLSTONECRAFT HAD HAD A LIFE different from anything Margaret, Mary, or their pampered mother could imagine. The eldest girl of seven children, she had been dragged back and forth across England and Wales in the wake of a downwardly mobile and increasingly drunken father, who had mistakenly exchanged his trade of weaving for life as a gentleman farmer. Angry that the diminishing family fortune was being lavished on the eldest son and inspired by her love for Fanny Blood, a delicate, clever Anglo-Irish girl, Mary herself had grown into a remarkable and determined young woman. The contrast could not be greater with Lady Kingsborough: Caroline had retained her power at the expense of father and eldest son, while Mary Wollstonecraft saw herself sacrificed to both.

Sustained by a dream of life with Fanny, at nineteen Mary left home to support herself as a companion in Bath. She was brought back to help

care for her dying mother; after her mother died Mary moved in with the poor but welcoming Bloods, her sojourn interrupted by another family demand when her married sister, Eliza, sank into depression after childbirth. Fearing a complete mental breakdown, Mary did not wait to investigate the circumstances but whisked her away from husband and baby. It was to provide for Eliza, a younger sister, Everina, and Fanny Blood that she established her school at Newington Green. It was interrupted when the ailing Fanny left for Portugal to marry. On hearing that Fanny was pregnant, Mary abandoned her school to be by her side. Fanny died soon after she arrived and Mary returned to England to find her school in ruins.

Desperate for money, she now used some of her teaching experience to write her first book, an advice manual called *Thoughts on the Education of Daughters.* In it she lamented the need for superior females to work for unsatisfactory mothers and described the social horror of being a governess, above the servants yet patronized by the family. Her advice to other serving young women was to cultivate patience and faith in a better life hereafter while being on guard against any enjoyment in this and any indulgence in seductive games with men who would not marry them or even in condescending female friendship. In a private letter she wrote, "I by no means like the proposal of being a governess. I should be shut out from society—and be debarred the *imperfect* pleasures of friendship—as I should on every side be surrounded by *unequals.*" Mary could never be the kind of governess whose happiness was complete with a private parlor and gracious mistress or even the affection of her charges.

The book was not yet published when Lady Kingsborough hired its author. So she had no means of knowing the "disagreeable" expectations her offer had raised. Also she was unaware that the young woman suffered from periods of melancholy and that one such mood had descended since the death of her friend. Her austerity she probably approved. Wollstonecraft had trained herself in restraint and self-denial. She never read for pleasure, not even poetry, concentrating entirely on serious, improving works. In diet she had become almost vegetarian and

she avoided all the luxuries of life. She dressed plainly, even carelessly, and was unconcerned with what people thought of her appearance. It was a good regime for the soul and allowed her to save money to help her family. Such a person was the sort Caroline declared she wanted as example for her children, but it was not a character that would easily fit with her own.

Mary Wollstonecraft knew little of Ireland. Although her mother and closest friend had been Protestant Irish, her family was culturally English. Her sortie to Portugal had confirmed her Protestantism and she regarded Catholicism with the common English contempt, even revulsion. After contemplating Portuguese nuns, she concluded that Catholics degraded women. Expecting to be alien in Ireland, she made no effort ahead of time to acquaint herself with the culture and politics of either the indigenous Catholics or their Protestant overlords.

Hoping that Mrs. Burgh had not exaggerated her skills, she primarily prepared by brushing up her inadequate French and smartening herself, though she had little money and depended primarily on presents from well-wishers. Among such presents was a stylish blue hat, the only part of her wardrobe that would be admired in her new home: "[it] is the first phenomenon of the kind, that has made its appearance in this hemisphere," she wrote.

Then she stored her books at Mrs. Burgh's and set out for Eton to meet and travel to Ireland with the King sons and their tutor. But the boys did not arrive and as she waited she learned to despise the upper orders from experience as well as theory. "I could not live the life they lead at Eton," she wrote, "nothing but dress and ridicule going forward." Everywhere she saw tyranny and slavery to convention. It was discouraging that her future employer had been educated in this trivial place and that he was training his heir there also. "Vanity in one shape or other reigns triumphant," she declared. Both censorious and depressed, she raised some anxiety in the Priors, who had recommended her; prudently Mrs. Prior did not pass on any fears to Caroline, perhaps hoping that her young guest would learn the necessary social hypocrisy when actually employed.

Meanwhile, Wollstonecraft tried to find out something about the Kingsboroughs. Mr. Prior was of humble origins and had acquired caution in his rise, but from Mrs. Prior she gathered that Lady Kingsborough was serious and unhappy, mainly because her husband was "very extravagant." She had no grasp of the huge incomes of aristocrats or of their habit of living on credit, and she imagined an anxious wife. That it might have been *sexual* extravagance she did not consider. She also learned that Caroline believed the children had been "neglected and left to the management of servants." Surprisingly, Wollstonecraft did not blame their mother for this: "These sentiments prejudice me in her favor—more than any thing I have heard of her." Other favorable opinions about Lady Kingsborough's character were irrelevant, she thought, for they were probably influenced by her exalted status. Wollstonecraft was determined to be impervious to rank.

After waiting some tedious weeks, she set out for Ireland alone. She enjoyed the calm boat trip from Holyhead to Dublin, enlivened by conversation with a handsome Englishman from Oxford, who discussed theology and individual suffering with her, just the sort of serious talk she relished. From Dublin she was escorted south to the Mitchelstown estate by a man about whose status she was unsure. He turned out to be the butler of the castle and she was relieved she had not been too familiar. She was aware that she must keep herself apart from the servants to retain her own and the family's respect.

The plainly dressed young woman who came up to the newly fashioned mansion intended to be unimpressed; to her it was simply a magnificent shell. She was not a reader of Gothic romances, so the remaining sections of medieval castle failed to interest her. "There was such a solemn kind of stupidity about this place as froze my very blood," she wrote, "I entered the great gates with the same kind of feeling as I should have if I was going into the Bastille."

She was displeased when she learned she would not immediately be greeted by Viscountess Kingsborough, who was in bed with a cold and sore throat. When she was later summoned to the bedchamber she found her employer surrounded by pet dogs on whom she was lavishing "infantile expressions." Caroline quickly dashed her hopes of companionship, but Wollstonecraft did find her fairly polite, and she wrote of her first meetings, "Lady K. is a shrewd clever woman a great talker." Soon the talking, along with the lisping and baby-speak, grew irritating; Wollstonecraft had been used to dominating other women and a garrulous, commanding, affected aristocrat was difficult to tolerate. Her irritation masked some fascination, however, for, self-absorbed herself, she had never seen anyone take the habit to these lengths, and she found herself thinking and writing a great deal about her new employer. "Lady K. is a *clever* woman—and a well-meaning one; but not of the order of being, that I could love," she concluded.

It is unlikely that Viscountess Kingsborough expected to be "loved" by her governess. She left no record of her first impressions, but if she was repelled by a gauche manner, depressed looks and dire dress sense, she determined to overlook them; a woman chosen for her mind and morals might be pardoned for woodenness of manner. She wanted a serious mentor for her girls and for herself a companion on demand. This last requirement had not been made clear to Mary Wollstonecraft. So she was rather surprised to find herself sought out for talk.

Lord Kingsborough did not make a good impression. "His Lordship, I have had little conversation with—but his countenance does not promise much more than good humour, and a little *fun* not refined." She noted that husband and wife were not much in each other's company.

The other ladies of the castle were mostly dismissed as "*Mrsus* and *Misses* without number," although one stood out above the rest: Mary Fitzgerald, Caroline's stepmother. Wollstonecraft noticed how she restrained her stepdaughter's bad behavior and made her more tactful. To this friendly lady she opened up, telling of her luckless sisters. Mrs. Fitzgerald agreed to look out for posts among her friends—although she soon discovered the difficulty of placing genteel, inexperienced, largely uneducated young women.

Despite her good qualities Mrs. Fitzgerald had not brought her children up well. Her three daughters were trivial, "such nothings," their
heads stuffed with dresses and balls, while her only son, Gerald Henry,
fatherless from a young age, was spoiled and selfish. When she heard
that Wollstonecraft had written a book on education, she asked her
advice about this beloved but trying young man. Unlike George and
Robert Edward at Eton, he had been kept at home so long that not much
could be done with him, Wollstonecraft feared, but, eager to help, she
wrote to her old friends in London asking if they could find a place for
him in a respectable family where he might learn religion and restraint.

The interchange with Mrs. Fitzgerald heartened her and led her to
write of the "civility," even "kindness" of the castle inmates: "I am . . .
treated like a gentlewoman by every part of the family." At the same time
she knew she must be on guard: "I cannot easily forget my inferior station." She was the moral equal of any woman in the kingdom and the
intellectual superior of most, but she was saturated with the British class
system and feared being snubbed.

The person who made most impression was another constant castle
visitor, Caroline's "flirt," a successor to the charming Arthur Young. In
George Ogle, Wollstonecraft, like her employer, saw not the reactionary
Protestant politician but a sensitive poet. She enjoyed engrossing his
attention, especially once she realized that Caroline was her rival. Melancholy was much in fashion and Wollstonecraft's very real depression
mimicked it; she was delighted to be complimented on her sensitivity.
She liked Ogle's "gentle pleasing" wife too and his beautiful sister-in-law,
Mary Moore, yet she could still most admire Ogle as "a *genius,* and
unhappy," and she received his sentimental poems with rapture. To her
he seemed good, clever and handsome, a combination she had rarely
encountered. He became for her the model of a perfect gentleman.

As for the girls who were to be her special care, they were not initially
prepossessing. The youngest children of both sexes still in the castle
were rather sweet, but the three eldest daughters struck her as uncon-
trollable and "not very pleasing." Margaret had not inherited Caroline's

looks and she seemed an overemotional, highly strung girl whose violent temper and hostility to her mother rather shocked the new governess. She reminded her a bit of her own spirited but unfocused sister Everina, who always found it hard to restrain her moodiness. The youngest promised to look well and she had some of her mother's pretty ways, while still being tomboyish.

Collectively the girls struck her as wild young animals with little refinement of manner. When she later wrote a book based on her experiences, she created two girls of fourteen and twelve called Mary and Caroline who, despite the names moving down the sisters, seem a pretty good stand-in for Margaret and Mary. At the outset they were described as "shamefully ignorant" but with "tolerable capacities." The eldest had "a turn for ridicule," the younger was "vain of her person. She was, indeed, very handsome, and the inconsiderate encomiums that had, in her presence, been lavished on her beauty made her, even at that early age, affected."

The girls did not expect the new governess to last long. They had despised the previous one, taking their cue from their mother, who gave the governess little respect and then expected her to dominate the girls. But, despite her depression and complaints, there was a purpose and self-confidence about Mary Wollstonecraft, and not much time passed before Margaret grew intrigued, then moved, then overwhelmed by this powerful personality. Finally she had found a woman to respond to her adolescent yearnings for significance and love.

She and Mary Wollstonecraft were alike in being eldest daughters of mothers who did not care for them. When Wollstonecraft came to fictionalize some of the characters she met at the castle, she used Margaret's experiences to reinforce her own, accepting her pupil's version of her early life and its resemblance to hers. Of the heroine's mother she wrote, "In due time she brought forth a son, a feeble babe; and the following year a daughter. After the mother's throes she felt very few sentiments of maternal tenderness; the children were given to nurses, and she played with her dogs." The "feeble babe" does not sound much

like Wollstonecraft's assertive brother and may have been Margaret's response to the uncongenial George.

Herself lacking much formal education and seriously deficient in French, Wollstonecraft could still be scathing about the girls' upbringing. As a serious middle-class woman believing in proper development of skills and specialization, she despised such upper-class training. The girls had had "a multiplicity of employments," she wrote, all aimed at "a heap of rubbish miscalled accomplishments." The clergyman tutor Barry, dismissed as a "*good sort* of a man," had made little impression on their principles. Caroline had hired Wollstonecraft because she wanted her girls more self-disciplined but she did not give the governess free rein to abandon their initial studies: "I am grieved at being obliged to continue so wrong a system," Wollstonecraft commented. She was opposed to it on social as well as intellectual grounds. She believed that the day school she herself had attended was preferable to hothouse family education: girls needed to tumble up with children from different backgrounds and classes. Young Mary was only seven, and her governess concluded that she would be better mixing with the poor in a national day school. After that age talents emerged and different routes could be followed but until then coeducation of gender and class should occur.

Yet if their mother did not interfere too much, perhaps something might be done with the girls. Caroline had always insisted on her daughters acting as patronizing noblewomen. Not yet the vindicator of the *rights* of the poor, Wollstonecraft accepted this as their duty and she agreed to go with Margaret to visit "the poor cabbins" as part of her education. She also meant to find out tales "of the humbler creatures," although she never did; Margaret took up the idea when she grew up and published her stories of Irish humble life. Meanwhile, such activity helped the girls understand what Wollstonecraft described as "the luxury of doing good"—not quite the attitude Caroline intended.

Quickly she saw the tension between Margaret and Caroline. Lady Kingsborough was not used to being thwarted and she had met her

daughter's increasing sullenness with hard words and coldness. Margaret responded with more emotional outbursts and now Caroline's only hope was that the new woman might do something with the child's temper before she became unmarriageable or, in the current phrase for spinsterhood, "remained upon hands." For this reason she gave orders that Margaret should always be with her governess.

Soon after Wollstonecraft arrived a fever struck down the children, including Margaret and Mary. Caroline put herself into mothering mode, since she felt most comfortable when thinking about physical ailments and most caring when she could bustle around a physician. Later Margaret remarked, "The moral feelings are, often, too little considered, and the physical too much; for mothers who make no scruple of wounding a daughter's sensibility, or mortifying her pride, will yet be very ready to cram her with pills and draughts, if she happens to look pale, or complain of a head-ache." With much experience caring for the sick, Wollstonecraft became a soothing presence, but Caroline's state visits terrified the children; they were relieved when she turned her attention again to her lapdogs, addressing them in her lisping baby talk.

By the time the children recovered Mary Wollstonecraft knew herself a firm favorite in the nursery. When she appeared, the little ones clustered around her, trying out her outlandish long name and begging a kiss. In contrast, when their mother swept in they trembled and ran to hold the governess's skirts. One little boy whom she especially liked pretended he was her son. The affection shown during their illness tied Wollstonecraft to the "wild" girls. The tall, plain Margaret became a "sweet girl" with "a wonderful capacity." She knew she was making a strong impression on this young mind and was not above feeling pride in rivaling the mother; she did not believe it part of her business to instill respect for inadequate parents and she had no fear of bonding with her charges. When she saw the fear Caroline provoked in Margaret, she exclaimed, "[T]hat such a creature should be ruled with a rod of iron, when tenderness would lead her any where."

Wollstonecraft began her work by partly breaking with the past. She followed Lady Kingsborough's initial instructions but was soon conscious that she was teaching her pupils to disregard much that their mother valued. Since Mary liked boisterous games and Margaret saw no purpose in making useless items, the girls were relieved to find their governess had no skill in fancy needlework and they were probably amused to hear her rather basic French. All the cramming had caused "very little cultivation," in Wollstonecraft's view: the French, Italian and Spanish remained so many words. Instead of teaching words, *she* would cultivate reason through encouraging the girls to enjoy thinking and to learn morality from vicarious experience. They could do this while improving their French with the fictionalized ethics of Stéphanie de Genlis and other edifying writers. She was not worried about going against Caroline's prohibition of novels, since those she chose were quite different from the trivial fantasy romances she herself despised—although she noted that they would not necessarily have harmed her pupils: "I almost wish the girls were novel readers and romantic, I declare false refinement is better than none at all."

Herself so comforted by her strenuous piety, she tried to impart to the girls her brand of Anglican religion, her reliance on afterworldly comfort to compensate for misery here and her sense that unhappiness betokened superior sensibility and trial. At odds with her mother and too old to find companionship in the younger girls, Margaret was fertile ground for such teaching.

Nearer Christmas, Margaret became violently ill again, so much so that her life was feared for and even Caroline grew anxious. Wollstonecraft was energized by nursing "my poor little favourite."

As ever, the medical treatment was interventionist. Probably the doctor used a sinapism made by wetting coarse mustard with vinegar to make a paste, then applying it to gauze and putting it on the chest until it caused a sharp pain and redness on the skin; the raw spot would then be covered with soft linen and flannel. This kind of treatment and her

mother's fussing increased the problem, in Wollstonecraft's view; she believed bed rest, plenty of liquids and avoidance of strong medicines were the remedy for most ailments. "Nothing should be done to disturb or to vex a child attacked by a fever; as a fatigue of body or uneasiness of mind may change a slight into a dangerous malady," Margaret later wrote; "the child should be treated with the greatest gentleness, kept as silent as possible, and, if the eyes are affected, in a dark room." Nature, not the doctor, should be the healer.

Margaret recovered, but Wollstonecraft feared that under the system of drugs Caroline and her physician favored, she would relapse—especially since, after treatment, she was pushed out of bed and onto her feet too soon. In Wollstonecraft's view strong medicines "prematurely stopped" the illness, allowing a "remnant" to lurk in the blood, and the sudden activity gave it rein. She had watched her friend Fanny die of consumption; she knew the disease was in Margaret's family—perhaps Caroline's young mother had died of it—and she feared for her favorite under the robust regime.

Despite all her wariness, Mary Wollstonecraft could be duped by manner. Margaret's illness had brought her and Caroline together, and, seeing what appeared to be some maternal care, Wollstonecraft had softened to her employer and even begun to think that her polite inquiries about her sisters were genuine. She imagined she might bring them to Ireland with Caroline's help and have them stay at the castle for holidays. With her usual peremptoriness, she told them to get ready for the move by improving their French and needle skills. "I am a GREAT favourite in this family," she wrote, "and am certain you would please them."

But she had misjudged aristocratic manners. The intimacy could not develop and the charm declined with the fever. When Margaret was out of bed, her mother returned to her dogs, withdrawing from both her daughter and the governess. Wollstonecraft was mortified, and her comments on Lady Kingsborough became harsher: "I think now I hear her infantine lisp—She rouges—and in short is a fine Lady without fancy or sensibility. I am almost tormented to death by dogs." Forgetting that she

had once judged her sympathetically, she now declared she had always disliked the haughty Caroline.

She never forgave her and in her most famous book, *A Vindication of the Rights of Woman,* Wollstonecraft took revenge by telling the world of a very "handsome" woman who "takes her dogs to bed, and nurses them with a parade of sensibility, when sick," while suffering "her babes to grow up crooked in a nursery," a woman who "lisped out a pretty mixture of French and English nonsense, to please the men who flocked round her." In this female, "the wife, mother, and human creature, were all swallowed up by the factitious character which an improper education and the selfish vanity of beauty had produced." Toward the end of her life her mind still ran on Caroline and when she described the French queen Marie Antoinette, whom she had never seen, the Irish aristocrat sat for the portrait: "besides the advantages of birth and station, [she] possessed a very fine person; and her lovely face, sparkling with vivacity, hid the want of intelligence."

The incident with Caroline made Wollstonecraft more censorious than ever about upper-class life, and she expressed her disgust more openly to her pupils. The triviality of words and habits appalled her. The Kings and their guests did not really converse in the way the people of Newington Green had done, nor were they silent as her parents were when locked in their miserable marriage. Instead they simply chattered affectedly in prepackaged phrases. Most of their time was taken up in adorning their pampered bodies. With the austerity of her class and temperament she was amazed to watch the rituals of the dressing table. The ladies rouged and used cosmetics lavishly and without shame. Dressing took at least five hours a day, while much of the rest was used in getting ready for the night and bathing the body in the expensive preparations that supposedly kept it young, such as "Milk of roses."

Increasingly alienated and homesick, she now realized that she could never feel comfortable in Ireland despite her growing fondness for Margaret. The Irish were not her people. "The family pride which reigns here produces the worst effects—They are ingeneral proud and

mean. . . . As a nation I do not *admire* the Irish, I never before felt what it was to love my country; but now I have a value for it built on rational grounds," she wrote.

In early February 1787, Lord and Lady Kingsborough removed to Dublin. Some families in their station went to town for the winter season in November, staying around until March or remaining for a kind of miniseason in the spring before returning to their country estates for the quieter summer months. The February-March season the Kings were keeping was the most fashionable. Despite her initial fears that they would as usual leave their governess and the children in the country, Wollstonecraft found she and the elder girls were to be of the party. Perhaps Caroline thought they should learn how to comport themselves in wider society; perhaps she wanted the company of her odd governess for solitary moments. Wollstonecraft would form an interesting exhibit at supper parties.

So she was sent on ahead to Henrietta Street with the children. Following Mrs. Fitzgerald's advice to woo the governess who was proving so useful with the difficult Margaret, Caroline put at her disposal the kind of accommodation most employees craved: a good big room to teach the girls in and the use of a drawing room complete with elegant harpsichord—which Wollstonecraft could not play. She also had her own parlor, where she could properly receive even male callers. "Here is no medium!" she exclaimed. "The last poor Governess—was treated like a servant." An old London friend called at once to see the new arrangements; Wollstonecraft was eager to show Margaret how intelligent women might talk together rationally without the gushing, artificial compliments and faked warmth of high life. Margaret was charmed.

It was a good time to be in Dublin, now at its most elegant after half a century of building, improving and municipal investing. Parliament's money had been spent on roads and canals, since any surplus supposedly went to England. With about 180,000 inhabitants, about a quarter the size of London, Dublin was a small, compact city with everything and

everyone close by. It had very much an Anglo-Irish and English center, set out by neoclassical architects and landscapists in wide boulevard-like streets opening into squares and greens. Along the streets and squares the townhouses of the nobility formed austere but grand terraces, while the center included the newly built Houses of Parliament—far more elegantly fine than their Westminster equivalent—the Royal Exchange and the library of Trinity College. The Church of Ireland was modeled on the Church of England, and the institutions of the state followed London lines; bookshops stocked English books and magazines as much as Irish and Scottish, and in Trinity College the conforming youth read Newton and Locke together with an English Oxbridge curriculum of the classics.

Of the Dublin poor the King girls cannot have known much. They saw them from their carriages or noticed them sitting raggedly on the steps of the grand houses of Henrietta Street or Merrion Square, where Mrs. Fitzgerald still lived with her son and daughters. In response to the enclosure of so much once common land, dispossessed peasants were now pouring into Dublin and the city was growing fast. The landowners who benefited from the new wealth brought it to spend and they were served by an army of merchants, importers, artisans and tradesmen. Although Wollstonecraft was teaching the girls to value poverty and thrift so that they could be benevolent, they could not have expected ever to be poor themselves.

Entertainments for the wealthy were lavish. There were two good theaters, one at Smock Alley and another at Crow Street, both appreciating the patronage of the Lord Lieutenant. Major actors from London came for the season: famous comedians such as Andrew Cherry and budding tragedians such as Sarah Siddons. Audiences liked innovation: new scenery, new costumes, even gimmicks such as performing dogs. The theaters had recently been refurbished in gilt and real gold, and elegant Smock Alley had exchanged the usual green stage curtain for a painted drop scene showing a view of the Parliament House and the façade of Trinity College, together with allegorical figures of wisdom and the arts. Plays followed London fashions and no distinctively Irish drama was per-

formed, although a national inflection was given by the playing of Irish airs at intermission.

The theater was a place of social display where a lady should wear fashionable clothes well and exhibit those charming natural gestures practiced in private. For the upper ranks it was formal, even requiring court dress when the Lord Lieutenant arrived with his entourage. In the past only aristocratic ladies sat in boxes, but by the 1780s it was alleged that women of any rank and sufficient money or influence could obtain a box seat. It was not entirely luxury and decorum, however, and the violence endemic in Dublin in all ranks ensured drama off as well as on the theater stage. One dramatic moment touched William, Duke of Leinster, Caroline's failed suitor. There had been a fracas between actors; the wife of one shouted to the Duke, whom she knew, to save her husband. A dutiful man, William responded by leaping over the stage box, then falling on the spikes. With four wounds in the thigh, he hung there until lifted off. It might have been purely comic had he not been so seriously wounded. In general young bucks in the pit confined themselves to shouting comic remarks and disturbing the performance by throwing orange peels or apple cores. In London such rowdiness was still common but growing unfashionable.

Outside the theater there was Italian opera in the Great Musick Hall, Fishamble Street—although it never quite caught on, associated as it was with scandalous doings: the parliamentarian Henry Grattan was said to be having an affair with one of the Italian singers. There were also the pleasure gardens of the Rotunda, the first maternity hospital in Britain or Ireland. Elaborately built on the lines of Leinster House, it had been established by Dr. Bartholomew Mosse and financed by himself, public subscription, lotteries and grants from Parliament. The gardens behind it were laid out in imitation of London's Vauxhall and to the east was a round assembly hall; both were intended to bring in revenue for the hospital. They were a great success and in 1784 to augment the income two more assembly rooms were added. In winter fashionable people listened to concerts and attended masquerades, card parties and balls in the

assembly rooms, while in summer in the Rotunda gardens they displayed their fine clothes as they paraded along the paths, through the shrubberies, beside the bowling green, and along the grand terrace, on which an orchestra played. They bought tea, ices and other light refreshments in between strolls and stared and bantered with each other as they met and parted. People such as the Kings visited the Rotunda on Sunday evenings when the gardens were illuminated, suffering the congestion to appear in the mode.

George and Elizabeth Ogle, as well as Mary Fitzgerald, lived in Merrion Square, and they called on Wollstonecraft and the girls before their mother arrived. Mary and young Caroline were not of an age to notice such things, but Margaret might well have observed how the compliments George Ogle formerly paid to her mother were now going to the governess; he was a sensual man who enjoyed pleasing ladies of all ranks and types. However, he seems to have made no effort to engage Margaret and it is possible that his robust political views, unnoticed by the governess, were already alienating the pupil, who was growing alert to the inequities of her native country.

Then the rest of the family arrived in a "*hurly burly*" of dogs and tutors. The girls were no longer center stage and the self-expression that their governess had encouraged was not tolerated. Since Caroline preferred the town to the country, they all hoped she would be caught up in balls, plays and visits and leave them alone. "The hours I have spent with L[ady] K[ingsborough] could not have been very pleasant—now she must visit— and my spirits are spared this weight," Wollstonecraft remarked. Caroline certainly threw herself into high society. She was mentioned in reports on lavish occasions and listed as keeping modish carriages and sedan chairs; she belonged to clubs and assemblies, and patronized fashionable charities. For instance, she was vice patroness of the Magdalen asylum for unfortunate seduced females who "preferred a Life of Penitence and Virtue to Guilt, Infamy and Prostitution." The patroness was the Lord Lieutenant's wife and visiting ladies included, beyond herself, the Countess of Moira, Lady Louisa Conolly and Mrs. Ogle.

From Wollstonecraft's point of view the disadvantage was that Mrs. Fitzgerald was no longer staying with the family, so Caroline's behavior would not be tempered by her influence. In any case, Wollstonecraft was discouraged to find Mrs. Fitzgerald also preoccupied with trivia now that she was near the vice-regal court, choosing materials and fitting clothes in preparation for grand events.

Drawing Rooms, Levees, state balls, dinners and investitures made up the social round of formal magnificence in Dublin as in London. The emphasis was on fashion and novelty as well as show and expense. Local hairdressers and dressmakers traveled to foreign capitals specifically to bring back impressions of court gala nights to Dublin for copying. On the royal birthday in London in January 1786, for example, at least two Dublin observers were in the crowd: one noted court dresses and head ornaments, the other patterns of dresses, which were then made up and displayed at home.

Ladies had to be elaborately adorned. Real and false ornamental hair of rare colors and fine quality was shaped into height with rolls, cushions and wire, then worked into various ethnic styles: Italian, French or Turkish. The whole was powdered in shades of pearl, brown, gray or white, an expensive business, since a powder tax had been introduced in 1786. The top of the edifice was fitted with a small cap and ostrich feathers, or perhaps artificial flowers, fruit or vegetables. When a grand event was about to occur, ladies were urged to make early hair appointments.

Exploration and new imperial possessions encouraged the imitating of foreign clothes, the use of pompoms, tassels, ruffs, feathers, and plumes. Ethnic styles came in and out of vogue: Circassian or Levantine outfits at one moment, polonaise or creole at another. There was endless debate about the cut and placing of ribbons and tassels, about the newest embroidery and lace, about whether a jacket should be loose or fitted and whether the petticoat should be shown or not and what should adorn it.

For the "hurly-burly" of Castle functions a lady had to dress in an old-fashioned way and colors were often dictated. Lady Clare at a Drawing

Room in the Castle in 1795 wore "a white crape petticoat, trimmed with embossed satin beads etc., white satin gown trimmed also with embossed satin in a new style; her head, arms and sleeves, looped up with diamonds in a most superb style; on the whole, her dress displayed the woman of fashion, the most refined elegance of taste, and a novelty of effect," glowed the newspaper account. On the same occasion the Misses Tighe had white crêpe petticoats with silver fringe and white satin ribbon, pink tabinet gowns trimmed with silver, white satin caps and fancy feathers; Miss Crokshank had a white gauze petticoat ornamented with flowers, white satin gown and cap with feathers and flowers. The pale theme was broken only by the poor Viscountess Ranelagh, who, being in mourning, had to wear a black gauze petticoat, black satin gown, black velvet cap and black flowers.

Wollstonecraft discouraged her pupils from caring about fashion. She taught that plainness was superior to ornament. Although it was poor training for the adult aristocratic life, the contempt for dress comforted Margaret, who came to add her governess's middle-class dislike of indiscriminate consumption to her own distaste for unflattering finery. Soon she had "a premature disgust to the follies of dress, equipage & the other usual objects of female vanity." The austerity helped Margaret see foreign luxuries as improper and this in time would urge her toward nationalist concerns. It also taught her that women, barred from conventional politics, could make moral stands in all areas of life including the domestic.

Despite the governess's contempt, the younger children, including pretty Mary, probably enjoyed the social commotion of a great event and were glad to be included in preparations when a party was being thrown in Henrietta Street. On these occasions no one could entirely escape: "the whole house from the kitchen maid to the GOVERNESS are obliged to assist," Wollstonecraft declared, "and the children forced to neglect their employments."

The expectation that in Dublin Caroline would be busier and less demanding of her time was at first partially fulfilled and Wollstonecraft

had some "quietness" in her fine apartments. But after the initial flurry of visits Caroline seemed to want her company even more than in Mitchelstown. Difficulties with Robert that she could not easily discuss with relatives and friends might have made her seek a confidante in her melancholy governess. If so, she was disappointed; the gap between them was too great and for once her condescension was not met with gratitude. Instead, Wollstonecraft wrapped herself up in misery. "Here I feel myself *alone,*" she wrote, "dead to most pleasures."

So Caroline set about wooing her. She invited her to sit in the drawing room, not just to enter it with the children, as was the usual custom. Wollstonecraft was on guard. She knew that sometimes ladies used their governesses to make themselves shine by contrast or to play off their wit against them. She had no intention of allowing this to happen. After one disagreeable episode she resolved never to enter the drawing room again; she would not be used as a prop for wit or treated publicly with condescension. She wished, she said, to avoid going in at all. Her excuse was that she did not want to spend the kind of money necessary to fit her for the society of brocaded and coiffed ladies and gentlemen. It would cost her half her income to dress her hair appropriately and acquire the right millinery.

George William Tighe, a modest landowner and lawyer from a gentry family in County Wicklow, a little below the rank of the Kings, caught what Wollstonecraft experienced but which neither Caroline nor her daughters would ever quite understand: the uneasiness of being in the train of a woman of society and rank. These hangers-on are "generally speaking, the despised part of the community," he wrote. "They are either a sort of fiddlers & singers who are expected to entertain the company by their talents; or they are Mutes in the train of some of the principal personages; or they are a species of *Figuranti* who fill up empty spaces & serve as food for scandal & contempt."

The girls must have been aware of the tussle between their mother and governess and sided with the latter, especially since Margaret loathed being a spectacle in the drawing room quite as much as Woll-

stonecraft. Beside the frills and flounces of Caroline, the governess's coarse cloth dress, black worsted stockings, lank hair and beaver hats seemed insolent and attractive, and she underlined her choice with arguments that Margaret lapped up. She saw no need for girls to "disfigure" themselves in hooped skirts, tight lacing and enormous hairdressing for the sole purpose of attracting the opposite sex, she said: "[They] only dress to gratify men of gallantry; for the lover is always best pleased with the simple garb that fits close to the shape. There is an impertinence in ornaments that rebuffs affection."

Failing to understand puritan pride, Caroline attacked Wollstonecraft with presents. She followed the practice of great ladies by offering a cast-off poplin gown and petticoat. This was appropriate for a lady's maid, in Wollstonecraft's view, and she refused the gift. Caroline was furious and said so. She consulted Mrs. Fitzgerald, who urged care and caution. Swallowing her pride, Caroline asked pardon and let the matter drop. She then offered Wollstonecraft two tickets for a masquerade, thinking that the glamour and glitter of fashionable people in decorated mansions would cheer her, but again Wollstonecraft found objections. Costumes would need to be fine and they were too expensive for her; her money was already bespoken for repaying debts and for her sisters' upkeep. So Caroline offered to lend her own black domino, a large cape that enveloped the whole body and allowed much erotic bantering in a false voice—lend, not give, since she had already found Wollstonecraft prickly on that score.

Wollstonecraft was "out of spirit—and thought of another excuse." She was unused to going to grand entertainments and would not know how to act. Caroline controlled her temper and offered to go herself with Wollstonecraft and her friend, and also bring along Mary Moore, George Ogle's sister-in-law, as a South Sea Islander in a rather risqué costume of thin wraps, shells and wreaths of dried flowers. Thus garbed, the four ladies would visit "the houses of several people of fashion who saw masques." At last the governess agreed—and in the event enjoyed her-

99

DAUGHTERS OF IRELAND

self: "the lights the novelty of the scene, and every things together con-
tributed to make me *more* than half mad—I gave full scope to a satirical
vein." Frightened of their commanding mother, the children must have
looked on with awe at this display of power in an inferior.

When Caroline left for a fortnight's visiting, the governess and girls
were alone again. They were relieved. But, curiously, Wollstonecraft grew
more depressed than ever. She shut herself up with her friend to mourn
her beloved Fanny Blood. "I am, at present, rather melancholy than
unhappy—the things of this world appear *flat, stale* and *unprofitable* to
me, and, sometimes, I am perhaps, too impatient to leave the *unweeded*
garden. I do not now complain, a listless kind of dispair has taken possession of me, which I cannot shake off," she wrote miserably. Her only
comfort was the contemplation of her superior sensitivity.

In this state, even the girls were little compensation and she cher-
ished the times alone when they had gone to bed: "I sit up very late. 'Tis
the only time I *live*." She read the works of the French philosopher Jean-
Jacques Rousseau, with whom she thoroughly identified: both were
lonely idealists among boors. (Despite Wollstonecraft's admiration, the
adult Margaret came to distrust the self-absorbed character of Rousseau:
"I think him an eloquent madman with his heart in the wrong place &
his mind distorted by morbid sensibility & extraordinary selfishness," she
wrote.)

But Rousseau was more than an egotist and his views on education
also struck a chord with Wollstonecraft. The child, he thought, ought not
to be oppressed into good behavior but led to adult rational morality
and goodness through his senses and needs: "there must be no submission to authority if you would have no submission to convention [later]."
Wollstonecraft agreed and taught that "[t]he absurd duty . . . of obeying
a parent only on account of his being a parent, shackles the mind, and
prepares it for . . . slavish submission." The teaching reinforced Margaret's attitude to her mother's "faults" and justified her habit of mimicry. Meanwhile, Rousseau's placing of authority in a tutor as much as the

parent suggested that the young might find substitutes for failed mater-
nal authority. Rousseau was no anarchist, but a disdain for the primary
parental figure could develop into political disdain for parental monarchy or hereditary government of any sort, though as yet neither governess nor pupils had a sense of this.

When she returned home, Caroline continued to feel challenged by
the moody Wollstonecraft. She would try once more. She had noted her
liveliness at the masquerade and concluded that the poor woman was
starved for elegant entertainment. So, along with Margaret, she carried
her to fashionable plays and introduced her in the Rotunda and Green
Room. They also went to the Handel commemoration concerts at fashionable St. Werburgh's Church, possibly even taking the younger girls,
since Handel was regarded as the next best thing to going to a church
service. Listening to Handel had also become a patriotic act, for he had
first performed *The Messiah* in the New Musick-Hall in Fishamble Street
in 1742, where it had been far more rapturously received than in London; consequently the Irish regarded themselves as his true supporters.
He was *the* Protestant musician and his music and oratorios seemed to
confirm the special status of British Protestants as the equivalent to the
chosen Israelites. On this occasion the huge event, numbering hundreds
of performers, was graced by the Lord Lieutenant, who arrived with his
entourage just before the performance and sat on an elaborate throne.
As the *Daily Universal Register* reported: "A more elegant or brilliant auditory never appeared to honour the memory of that great musical genius.
The church could with difficulty accommodate the numbers."

Margaret, whose musical skill Caroline had wished to exploit for her
visitors, must have relished the performance and probably felt like a
near Irish contemporary, Betsy Sheridan, who attended a Handel commemoration in Westminster Abbey:

> [N]ever was I more truly delighted. The beginning of the Te Deum was
> so truly great that my whole frame thrill'd and the tears ran down my
> cheeks in spite of me. I would have given any thing to have been behind

a Pillar to have cried in comfort—but I was forced to struggle and almost choak to behave decently. . . . I thought it the only homage worthy of the Devine being which I had ever heard offer'd up.

While not rising to these emotive heights, even Wollstonecraft admitted herself "obliged"; the music haunted her and under its influence she softened a little to Caroline. "Lady K. and I are on much better terms than ever we were," she wrote; she "really labors to be civil." Yet she was not won over. When the enthusiasm of the moment wore off she reverted to her opinion that Caroline was vain, foolish, dull and demanding. Her voice grated and her opinions were trivial, couched in fashionable sentimental style but with no real sentiment behind them. She did not hide her scorn. "Why she wishes to keep me I cannot guess," she wrote. Perhaps Caroline sensed the difficulty she would have with her eldest daughter if there were no buffer between them.

The tension in the relationship between governess and employer is well caught in an awkward social moment with Edward, Earl of Kingston, who had been dining privately in Henrietta Street with his daughter-in-law, together with Mrs. Ogle and Mary Moore. The conversation turned to the governess writing a letter upstairs. The Earl was curious and Mary Moore and Mrs. Ogle, followed by Caroline, went up to bring her down. She refused despite repeated requests. Finally cajoled by Mary Moore, she agreed. She capped this display by outstaying her welcome and, when male guests arrived, flirting with George Ogle.

Surrounded by gossiping servants and relatives, Margaret and Mary understood more of the fashionable world than their governess and probably always knew what came to shock her: that modish sentiment could mask sensuality. They cannot have been entirely unaware of their father's peccadilloes. Wollstonecraft was fascinated by the indolence and self-indulgence of the castle ladies, the gluttony and luxury of their lives, and she had watched with distaste the effete flirting of effeminate men with coquettish women while both pretended to play at cards. But she did not at first imagine real sexual impropriety. She never accused Caro-

line of adultery, among her many failings. Now she heard gossip about the admired George Ogle. "I am sorry to hear a man of sensibility and cleverness talking of sentiment sink into sensuality," she wrote; "such will ever I fear be the case with the inconsistent human heart when there are no principles to restrain and direct the wayward impulses of it."

The hint of new knowledge was combined with an admission of sentimental lovesickness. To her sister she coyly described herself as "a *lilly* drooping" and she asked, "Is it not a sad pity that so sweet a flower should waste its sweetness on the *Desart* air, or that the Grave should receive its *untouched* charmes." She wrote of her "broken heart" and declared, "Certainly I must be in love—for I am grown 'thin and lean, pale and wan.' " Such curious admissions suggest that someone was worrying her. There are several possibilities.

The first is George Ogle, although, given her comments, this seems unlikely. Another is an earlier friend now perhaps in Dublin, but that does not quite fit the case either. A closer possibility is Robert, Lord Kingsborough, who surprisingly makes hardly an appearance in her copious letters except for the remark "Lords are not the sort of beings who afford me amusement—nor in the nature of things can they." Later in life she could be very tart with privileged men, but Robert is absent from her tirades against aristocracy and privilege. The closest she came to discussing this sort of man was in her novel *Mary*, where Lord Kingsborough may have sat for the husband who spurns his dog-loving, lisping wife and looks for more robust fun below his rank.

Given his reputation by now, it seems likely that he made some sort of overture; later there would be gossip linking the pair. To her sisters Wollstonecraft was open about her miseries and physical ailments but always secretive about directly revealing matters of the heart: some years later her infatuation with the married Swiss painter Henry Fuseli made no clear entry into her copious correspondence. With Robert there are a few hints. Once when he appeared in the drawing room where she was sitting she blushed redder even than Caroline rouged. Later she told her sisters that a "friend" had offered her a large sum of money with which

to educate and settle them but that she could tell no one who it was. The usual suggestion is that this was her publisher, Joseph Johnson, but why in this case would it be a secret? Mrs. Fitzgerald was touched for small sums but there is no sense that she would lend the amount Wollstonecraft was supposing. Lord Kingsborough is the most likely candidate for the "friend." In the end the money was not forthcoming, which fits with Wollstonecraft's sudden acrimonious departure from the family. While in Ireland she showed no understanding of specifically Irish politics, so she was probably unaware of Robert's specific views, but she was already radical enough in her sense of general social issues to see the danger of severe inequality. It may be significant that it was during her year with him that Robert uncharacteristically supported Henry Grattan in his desire to alleviate the miseries of the poorest.

After some months Caroline grew as tired of Dublin as Wollstonecraft. It was time for a tour of the Continent. It might give her daughters some polish. In London, too, she might see and influence her difficult son George, who, about to go to Exeter College, Oxford, was disgracing himself with the Prince of Wales's disreputable set. Neither she nor Robert relished the fact that the Mitchelstown estates would in time proceed to this intractable youth, who, although he had his own property at Glandon Harbor in West Cork, already cast an envious eye on their larger acres. The trip might even shore up the always shaky relationship between Caroline and Robert.

Wollstonecraft knew nothing of Lady Kingsborough's problems as wife and mother. She had dreaded returning to rural Mitchelstown and was pleased to be told she would accompany the girls with their parents on the tour. It was worth putting up with Caroline to get to France, which she had always longed to see. The party would cross the Irish Sea at the beginning of June and on the way visit Bristol Hot Wells, famous for its "balsamic air & charming Scenery." Richard Lovell Edgeworth mocked the annual outing of the Anglo-Irish to English spas as refuge from their luxurious living at home: they flocked to such places "like regular birds

of passage," he wrote. Maria was more caustic: noblemen left "their delightful country-seats, to pay, by the inch, for being squeezed up in lodging houses, with all imagined inconvenience, during the hottest months in summer."

When the party arrived at the Hot Wells, they were all out of sorts. Caroline felt the sad associations of the place, for two years earlier Robert's youngest brother, Henry, so much her favorite when a small child playing with her own baby son George, had died there before he was twenty. For her part Wollstonecraft wrapped herself up in her usual nervous complaints, at one moment feeling immensely sorry for herself, at another self-important with her new intellectual status of author—*Thoughts on the Education of Daughters* had just been published. Caroline was irritated at her airs. She was equally annoyed by Margaret, who had grown more insolent and mocking under her governess's teaching. She had added rudeness to gaucheness.

At Bristol Hot Wells Wollstonecraft completed her first novel, *Mary*, in the process providing a vicious portrait of Caroline as the virtuous heroine's feeble, despised and unfeeling mother. The good Mary, whose virtue, like her author's own, sprang from neglect and unhappiness, was a woman of "sensibility," the classless quality that separated Wollstone-craft from Caroline and had attracted the discerning George Ogle.

Writing the novel renewed her irritation with her employer, who was now behaving with less restraint than ever since her stepmother was not even in the same country. Unhappy in marriage and increasingly upset by the attitudes of her eldest children, Caroline found it hard to control her temper. She was sick of having her overtures spurned and being despised by a social inferior. Also the affair with Ogle rankled and per-haps the attention shown by Robert to the governess did as well.

An uneasy peace prevailed as they all traveled from the Hot Wells to London, from where Wollstonecraft was to visit her sisters for a short vacation before the family left for France. Margaret felt the approaching separation with all the dread of a neglected child who had at last found a surrogate mother. Having seen the discord between Caroline and her

governess, she probably feared that Wollstonecraft would not return. She had not learned her mother's intermittent control and displayed the feelings of real grief that Wollstonecraft's teaching had encouraged her to think natural. Caroline found the unseemly emotion distasteful. She blamed Wollstonecraft for alienating her daughter's affections and for encouraging insubordinate behavior. She had had enough. She gave the governess her wages and told her to go.

Although the relationship had lasted only a year, the adult Margaret throughout her life "glorie[d] in having had so clever an Instructress, who had freed her mind from all superstitions." Without Wollstonecraft, she would, she declared, have become "a most ferocious animal." As it was, it had been her "peculiar good fortune to meet with the extraordinary woman to whose superior penetration & affectionate mildness of manner I trace the development of whatever virtues I possess." When she came to assess her life for her own children, she was similarly enthusiastic: "almost the only person of superior merit with whom I had been intimate in my early days was an enthusiastic female who was my governess . . . for whom I felt an unbounded admiration because her mind appeared more noble & her understanding more cultivated than any others I had known." Mary, though younger, may well have thought the same. She was growing up a child of her time, valuing expressed emotions far more than her parents had done.

As for Wollstonecraft, she felt like a new woman away from the Kingsboroughs. Unemployed, she presented herself to her publisher, Joseph Johnson, who in the most remarkable act of her life took her on as an author and editorial helper. No wonder she exclaimed that she would be the "first of a new genus."

At once she set about using her experiences with the King girls in a storybook for children. She had painted herself and Caroline in her novel; now she would paint the daughters and herself. Her alter ego was Mrs. Mason, an independent, strong-minded mentor charged with rectifying the corrupt upbringing of two noble children. In this fantasy the

children mature from privileged aristocrats into the sensible, benevolent middle-class sort of young women who learn that aristocratic magnificence is "state," not "dignity." Margaret was moved by the book and years later, when she abandoned her role of aristocrat, called herself Mrs. Mason in honor of her old governess. She also wrote about the relationship in her own works. In an unpublished utopian novel named "Selene" a rich boy has a worthy, austere and benevolent tutor of whom he says, "To this excellent man I am indebted for most of those moral principles which have so much conduced to my welfare in latter years. . . . [He] soon attached himself to me with parental affection."

Once Wollstonecraft had left them, the Kingsboroughs changed their travel plans. Perhaps Caroline could not face touring the Continent with an unfaithful and despised husband and a resentful, sullen daughter who did not want her company. The family returned to Ireland, and Margaret and Mary never saw Mary Wollstonecraft again. Yet it is possible that, without this catalyst, neither would have strayed from the path mapped out for aristocratic girls. Wollstonecraft had not made them anarchists or democrats nor indeed dented their belief in the ideals of nobility to which they were heirs. She did not criticize the institutions of family or marriage, but she had taught them of a life outside the charmed Ascendancy, and she encouraged them to question received family wisdom and follow their own bent. Compromise, they had learned, was not essential.

.CHAPTER 6.

Marriage and Separation

*When I married him, I knew not to what I had
condemned myself. As his character gradually
discovered itself, my reason also encreased;
and now, when I had an opportunity of comparing
him . . . I felt all the horrors of my destiny!*

—CHARLOTTE SMITH, *EMMELINE*

THE YEAR MARY WOLLSTONECRAFT LEFT THE EMPLOY OF THE
Kingsboroughs, Irish politics began to impinge on the family. Soon after
their return from England in 1788, George III stepped out of his carriage and addressed an oak tree as the King of Prussia, then declared the
loyal prime minister William Pitt a rascal and the Duchess of Leinster's
hostile nephew, Charles James Fox, his friend. As a result, Pitt's control
of the government faltered and many anticipated the regency of the
Prince of Wales. This would bring to power his progressive allies—Fox in
London and the liberal Irish Ascendancy of the Leinsters, Moiras and
Grattan in Dublin.

Gambling that the King would recover, Pitt and the Lord Lieutenant
prevaricated. Following George Ogle earlier, Robert now swung over to
the Castle, his flirtation with liberal politics over, his political Protes-

tantism reinvigorated. He acted opportunely, for George III did rally and the opposition in both countries was confounded. Robert's foe Lord Shannon, insufficiently partisan at the right moment, was dismissed as governor of Cork, a position he had held for nearly a quarter of a century. Robert was appointed in his place.

Fearing further troubles in Ireland, Pitt was persuaded that its semi-independent Parliament had simply given power to an irresponsible Anglo-Irish oligarchy; a merging of Dublin and Westminster assemblies might best defang opposition and lead to more peaceful relations between the two kingdoms. Heading toward this goal, he formed an alliance with John Fitzgibbon, a difficult, vitriolic but politically canny man. Fitzgibbon's schemes and ambition would make him Earl of Clare and Lord Chancellor, or chief law officer, of Ireland, the first Irishman in the eighteenth century to rise to the highest legal post. Over the next years many realized that Clare had become the true ruler of the country whoever was Lord Lieutenant. Pitt found him useful: a colleague commented, "[Clare] has no god but English government."

The dreaded "Black Jack" of later nationalist tales, vicious hound of defenseless Erin, the Earl of Clare was a complex man. He came from the small Catholic professional class and his opponents taunted him on his lowly sectarian background as the son of a Catholic lawyer descended from doctors and farmers. Far back, his line of Fitzgibbon derived from the same source as the more elevated one of Caroline's maternal ancestors; indeed, the latter-day Fitzgibbons regarded themselves as the true heirs of the White Knight, with the Kings but a lesser line.

Clare thoroughly rejected his Catholic forebears, identifying closely with the Protestant interest. Like George Ogle and Robert King, he knew that concessions to Catholics would dispossess himself and his allies. He also understood that, whatever the rhetoric, Ireland was a colony whose land was largely owned by descendants of successive sets of English adventurers: "Confiscation is their common title." He knew too the miserable position of the Catholics: "I am very well acquainted with the province of Munster," he wrote.

I know that the unhappy tenantry are ground to powder by relentless landlords. . . . When we speak of the people of Ireland, it is a melancholy truth that we do not speak of the great body of the people. This is a subject on which it is extremely painful to me to be obliged to speak—but it is necessary to speak out. . . . the Act by which most of us hold our estates was an act of violence.

Clare understood *realpolitik*: "So long as the nature of men continues as it is, it is impossible that a zealous Catholic can exercise the efficient power of government in support of a Protestant establishment in Ireland, or in support of the connections with the Protestant Empire of Great Britain." If the Catholics were ever aroused, they would menace the power to which he had so firmly aligned himself. So he constantly warned his English and Anglo-Irish friends that danger lurked below the surface. England had just lost its American colonies and Ireland might follow. Himself an *arriviste* and convert, he was irritated by liberal hereditary aristocrats such as the Leinsters and Moiras, who did not take their Protestant cause seriously, held themselves aloof from the Castle, and failed to understand how dependent they all were on London. He opposed the romantic, unthinking enthusiasm for Catholic political participation, believing adherents failed to realize how much it would diminish their power.

While mocking the great families, he forced them to socialize with him, accepting his house in Ely Place as second only to the Lord Lieutenant's Castle as the place of preferment and patronage. The Kingsboroughs, Mount Cashells, Moiras and Leinsters were among the frequent guests entertained in style there. With his ostentation, his love of finery and display and his fashionable carriage imported from England, Clare almost dared the old families to despise him.

So things stood in Dublin when London newspapers for July 1789 reported, "Advice is received from Paris, of a great revolution in France." The English were excited and Mary Wollstonecraft and her friends reiterated old liberal views in a new revolutionary context: "Civil governors are

properly the servants of the public; and a King is no more than the first servant of the public, created by it, maintained by it and responsible to it." This went for his viceroy in Dublin Castle. Reform had once seemed the only answer to the status quo; now rebellion and revolution were possibilities. The administration sensed the change. The period of slow reform initiated by the Volunteers and Henry Grattan was over.

Despite the volcanic events over the water, in Cork local issues dominated. Lord Shannon had been incensed by Robert's strategic support of the government in the Regency crisis. He had felt his own commanding position at risk and in 1789 he complained to the Castle of

> the want of sufficient power and patronage. He declared that he thought well of Mr. Pitt but that he did not care who was Lord Lieutenant unless the principles were admitted upon which alone he could support government, namely that he should always have the nomination of one bishop, one judge, and one commissioner of the Revenue, besides office for himself, inferior office for his dependents, and the whole patronage of the county and city of Cork.

With such grand expectations it was inevitable he should find Lord Kingsborough a continuing thorn in his side and at the next parliamentary election in 1790 he put up a candidate to oppose his rival. The quarrel that ensued, fueled by riots and brawls, upset Robert, who was soon "distressed and distracted"; "his looks and conduct shew it and he has lost his temper," remarked a gleeful Shannon. As well he might. A contested election now cost on average £5,000 in alcohol, bribes and entertaining and Robert too had grown used to political obedience.

Before the vote was taken, Shannon accused his rival of "desperate corruption and perjury" and inciting his followers to lies and violence. As opposed to his own supporters, "gentlemen of property & character," Robert's were an infamous set of villains, covered in "rags & lice." At one point Shannon managed to get a committee set up to look into the irreg-

ularities, but to little effect. The sheriff was Robert's man and saw to it that the courthouse was almost filled with his followers, who, according to Shannon, functioned as banditti by night. They were allegedly locked up till the committee sat, so that Shannon's men could not get in, while in the chair was one of Caroline's relatives, who simply passed resolutions approving Robert and all he did. Shannon was furious: "[Robert] supports himself by the most infamous, perjured, tutored set of villains that can be conceived," he raged. Some of the King men did go to jail for perjury, but Lord Shannon could not stop the progress of corruption. With revenue from his great estates, Robert was spending profusely: Shannon reckoned at least £500 a day.

In his dilemma Robert fought a duel with his opponent, though neither was wounded. He also called on his rowdy son George to help him, and George rode into Cork at two in the morning, bringing with him a "coach stuffed with bucks for the next day." "What an education for an eldest son!" exclaimed Shannon. "A witness and accomplice in every scene of infamy, and bosom companion to every fellow who can be hired to corrupt and suborn others. The whole country cries shame, and every moderate man is enraged."

Over in Kilworth Stephen, the new young Earl of Mount Cashell, was in a dilemma. He was a vacillating man. He had promised Lord Shannon his support but he was a neighbor of Robert's, and Robert was the richer and closer. In the end, much to Shannon's disgust, he came out "violently" for Robert.

Robert lost the election but managed to get his way through a by-election the following year. It was all bribery and perjury in Shannon's view. The whole had not been an edifying episode. Appeals followed, but both sides grew sick of the expense and were happy to let grander voices such as Lord Clare's intervene. They had been part of a national struggle, and over in Wexford the Castle-leaning George Ogle had also had trouble holding a seat in these difficult times. Shrilly he warned that if men like himself and Robert did not prevail, there would be massacres of Protestants all over Ireland.

In 1793, Robert moved even nearer to the government by raising both the Antrim militia, of which he became colonel, and the North Cork in Mitchelstown. Replacing the old Volunteers, these new militias were urged on landowners as a duty by the Castle, which also wanted to make a political point by insisting the men be drawn from Anglican, Presbyterian and Catholic communities, although the Catholics were decidedly lukewarm about joining. Aimed at the protection of the "realm and its constitution," these militias were also clearly intended to curb potential domestic unrest and negotiate between new Catholic assertiveness and Protestant anxiety. The qualification for the higher ranks was simply various amounts of property.

By October 1794 Robert's Mitchelstown unit was embodied; it had 26 officers, 24 sergeants, 16 drummers, 12 fifers and 540 men. He had a novel way of getting recruits: he put a notice in the Cork newspapers and elsewhere offering each of the first 244 volunteers a small farm in Munster at a low rent provided he remained living there when his military service ended. Contrary to the Castle's inclusive aims, Robert's notice was for the "encouragement to protestant volunteers" only and he became the sole militia commander to insist openly on sectarian allegiance; some thought it a betrayal of "the benign intention of the sovereign which had for its object a generous fraternity of his people." If Robert's soldiers were all Protestants, many yet spoke Irish and bore old Gaelic names. Such seemingly turncoat men would be especially offensive to Catholics when they came into conflict with them later in the decade.

Despite her earlier lack of interest in politics, Caroline too was growing clearer in her views: she never would give her "interest to any but a good Protestant," she later wrote. Both she and Robert were now associated with the Castle interest against many of their rank. When a new Lord Lieutenant, the youthful and untried Lord Westmorland, and his wife progressed together, then separately, in state from Dublin to Cork, there was so much hostility toward them among the Anglo-Irish that Castle supporters had some ado to find people willing to meet and be civil to them. In Cork the mayor laid out the considerable sum of £231 2s 3½d

to prepare his house for the Lord Lieutenant's arrival and entertain his important guests, while Robert was arranging for the corporation to put on a dinner and card party for him. But he found himself in a quandary: although many invitations had been sent out, in the end only two country gentlemen supported him in entertaining Lord Westmorland. "Cork is a very popish and gossipy place, and a whisper becomes the tittle-tattle of the town," remarked Lord Shannon.

Lady Westmorland was similarly unpopular and at a breakfast in Waterford with the Bishop's wife she actually had to drink her tea alone. She expected a better welcome at Mitchelstown, knowing the firm support of the Kingsboroughs, and Caroline was indeed most happy to receive her. But she too had trouble rustling up company. Then both she and Margaret came down with measles and were too ill to be hostesses. In the circumstances Lady Westmorland felt obliged to return north. (Clearly the Westmorlands were not skilled politicians, but it was often hard to find governors of caliber for Ireland. Betsy Sheridan had reported the gossip that, among the more suitable noblemen, the Duke of Norfolk was "afraid of drinking himself out of the world, and Ld: Derby . . . won't leave Miss Farren.")

Given the volatile politics of the region, Robert needed to cement alliances where he could. His near neighbor Lord Mount Cashell would be a useful ally if he could be prevented from wavering again. The Kings were enthusiastic Freemasons: the 4th Baron, James, had become Grand Master and set up the first Irish lodge, and his rakish relative Lord Kingsborough had followed his example. Robert was true to family tradition and he liked the fact that young Stephen was also a Mason. So with such factors in common he may already have gained his neighbor's support for the future by hinting at what further he might do. Lord Mount Cashell was twenty-one and a bachelor.

After Mary Wollstonecraft left, Caroline hoped the connection between her and Margaret would be severed, but the pair managed to write clandestinely through Fanny Blood's brother George in Dublin. They were

careful with their secret. Wollstonecraft told George never to send a letter directly to Henrietta Street but always to wait until someone came to collect it from his home.

Both needed this underhand correspondence. Margaret hated being deprived of the one person who approved her serious, affectionate character, while Wollstonecraft was saddened without her love. Margaret told her what she wanted to hear: "She says, every day her affection to me, and dependence on heaven increase," Wollstonecraft reported. "I miss her innocent caresses—and sometimes indulge a pleasing hope, that she may be allowed to cheer my childless age—if I am to live to be old.—At any rate, I may hear of the virtues I may not contemplate—and my reason may permit me to love a female." Margaret shared the dream and years later, when she wrote "Selene," she described her damaged hero spending his later life near his worthy old tutor.

In present real life, however, there were difficulties. Encouraged by her governess's approval of her loving adolescent sentiment, Margaret wrote again too often in the same vein. Wollstonecraft grew bored: "her childish complaints vex me—indeed they do," she declared immediately following her enthusiasm. Yet, nearly a year after she had left, Wollstonecraft was still hearing from Margaret, her "dear girl," and musing, "I scarcely knew how much I loved her till I was torn from her."

Then the letters stopped. Perhaps Caroline heard of the correspondence and objected; perhaps Margaret was simply growing up and away. After not hearing for a year, Wollstonecraft asked George Blood to inquire about Margaret's welfare. She was still missing her pupil and her affectionate heart. She wished she had set up a correspondence with Mrs. Fitzgerald, from whom she would at least have heard news of the girls, but she hesitated to initiate one.

Meanwhile, her governess's teaching continued to dominate Margaret's life, often to the detriment of relations with her mother and family. Later she looked back a little ruefully: "from the time [Wollstonecraft] left me my chief objects were to correct those faults she had

pointed out & to cultivate my understanding as much as possible: my intentions were good but I wanted advice, perhaps more than those who had less exalted views." She continued at odds with Caroline. Indeed, the pair got on so badly that Margaret was sometimes sent off to stay with relatives. Robert approved the separation, remembering the old tension between Caroline and his mother, which had soured the early years of his marriage.

Given their touchy home life, both Caroline and Margaret probably agreed that early marriage would be a good idea. From Caroline's point of view it could not be soon enough. Mary Wollstonecraft had written of her fictional heroine's mother that "she did not wish to have a fine tall girl brought forward into notice as her daughter." Also girls should be disposed of chronologically and the eldest needed to be chosen before Caroline could attend to her younger daughters. Margaret's failings in temperament could only become more glaring with age.

So it was time for her eldest girl properly to "come out." Wollstonecraft described the ritual: "Without having any seeds sown in their understanding, or the affections of the heart set to work, [daughters] were brought out of their nursery, or the place they were secluded in, to prevent their faces being common; like blazing stars, to captivate Lords." Through Wollstonecraft's training the King girls were rather different but they could not avoid the process. Caroline would be no help: "The mother, if we except her being near twenty years older, was just the same creature."

Once accepted as a "marriageable miss," Margaret had to be properly initiated into aristocratic adult life. She had some advantages in the marriage market. She was accomplished, spoke languages well, and, if rather opinionated, also had a refreshing eagerness of manner. She remained serious and concerned with duty and in the last year she had learned some politeness, while the excessive piety Wollstonecraft had encouraged had lessened, along with the cultivated melancholy she had shared with her governess. She now had the sophistication of her

aristocratic upbringing; she was a citizen of her world, of London and Dublin.

On the other side, she was still oversensitive and too apt to lose control of herself. Her appearance did not please everyone. An onlooker described her as "brawny" and as "stiff as a grenadier." Although she had a handsome face, she had bad teeth. But something might be made of her through careful dressing. She too was eager to leave her family home and the only route was marriage. Dress, which she might rebel against in childhood, had therefore to be accepted.

Fashion was not as demanding as it had been. By the early 1790s the immense headdresses had shrunk, although the hair was still frizzed, curled and forced into ringlets. As the decade progressed gowns became simpler, more revealing of the body's curves, more high-waisted and flowing; stays fell out of fashion. Neither the simpler fashion nor the more elaborate one much suited Margaret; nonetheless, she had to overcome her hatred of "frippery" and face the pageant of aristocratic city existence. She needed to be seen to good advantage, enter a room and move through it gracefully without disturbing the powdered curls and feathers on her head and fine lace on her body. It was difficult, but for the moment she had to appear genteel whatever the provocation or discomfort.

Caroline and Robert subscribed to the public assembly rooms at Rutland Square, where events were held in weeks when there were no balls at the Castle. No doubt Margaret was dragged along. These were occasions for immense displays of wealth and, since girls were attractive for portions as well as appearance, jewels glowed finely and seductively on young arms and bosoms. One St. Patrick's Day masquerade, when Lord Delvin went as Bajazet and Lady Catherine Freke as the wife of Vandyke, their diamonds were estimated to cost £40,000.

To show girls to best advantage it was necessary to entertain lavishly and in April 1790 newspapers reported that Viscountess Kingsborough put on a large evening party or "rout ball," which included supper, card

playing, negus (a kind of wine punch) and a sumptuous ball. Though it gave no figures—simply declaring that "the entertainment was perfectly magnificent, taste being in it united with expence"—such events elsewhere were of staggering cost and size. Experts were brought in from Paris to manage the decorations and special chefs hired. A few years earlier the Leinsters had given out a thousand double tickets for a masquerade at Leinster House.

To Caroline's rout ball everyone of importance was invited, including the Lord Lieutenant, now more comfortable in Dublin than he had been on his frosty progress through the south. To honor her friend Caroline, his extravagant wife, Lady Westmorland, arrived wearing a dress whose ordering had been reported in the paper as "reviving the real magnificence . . . which should be adapted to the splendour of a Court, and to the dignity of station." It consisted of Brussels lace laid over pink Irish satin, all worth the amazing sum of £500. Margaret was presumably one purpose for the ball; she would be launched in style. She may, however, have been enough of Mary Wollstonecraft's pupil to realize that her governess would need to have worked for twelve years to earn the cost of their guest's new frock.

In addition to balls and assemblies Margaret had to endure ritual visits to country houses outside Dublin such as the Leinsters' Carton and the Conollys' Castletown. Such outings cannot have appealed: "The ladies sit and work and gentlemen lollop about and go to sleep—at least the Duke does, for he snored so loud," one visitor reported of Carton. There was little to do except eat; breakfast was "an immense table—chocolate, honey, hot bread, cold bread, brown bread, white bread, green bread and all coloured breads and cakes," chewed to the sound of French horns. The boredom was interrupted by drunken romps and boisterous horseplay.

The most interesting of the Leinsters, young Edward Fitzgerald, was hardly ever in Dublin. Caroline could only have welcomed the absence, since a younger son was unsuitable for an eldest daughter. Had he returned and had designs on Margaret he would certainly have been

shown the door, as he was by his uncle Lord George Lennox when he made overtures for his fair cousin Georgiana in England. In any case he had a liking for conventional beauty and was having an affair with the beautiful and dying Elizabeth Sheridan, Betsy's sister-in-law.

The Dublin elite was small. Gradations of rank were as great as in England, but the smaller numbers meant more mingling and more acceptance of merchants and clever lawyers into fashionable society once they were sumptuously dressed—although such people rarely attended Castle functions. The Tighes, English-educated, literary and clever, often socialized with people with noble titles; they were good friends with their kinsman Lord Shannon, which perhaps prevented intimacy with his enemies, the Kings. Further down the social scale, wealthy upstarts could gain partial entrée into high society, men such as Francis Higgins, who had been in prison for inveigling a lady into marriage by presenting himself as a man of breeding and fortune when he was actually a tavern waiter. Now out of prison, he had grown wealthy as a newspaper editor of the government-supported *Freeman's Journal* and owner of illegal gambling tables. With his new wealth he had moved to St. Stephen's Green, next door to the mansion of the Kings' aristocratic neighbors from Cork, the Earl of Mount Cashell and his family. The "Sham Squire" could be seen parading along Beaux Walk with gold tassels on his Hessian boots and violet gloves on his hands. This was not the sort of man Caroline wished her daughters to meet, but many accepted that fine clothes and riches obscured low birth.

Caroline had been sold before she knew her own mind, but the experience did not persuade her or Robert to give more liberty of choice to their daughter or take less effort to see her suitably married. Many years later Margaret quarreled with the father of her second family, who wanted to continue in his retired life despite the fact that his daughters were arriving at marriageable age: she knew that girls did not make "good" matches without maternal effort and she desired to give her eldest child "an opportunity of being married by letting her be seen and known." To this end she was prepared to surrender her own income

and valued privacy for two or three years. Something of her despised mother's efforts had rubbed off on her.

Despite her acceptance of aristocratic marriage Margaret yet had some romantic feelings beyond her family's dynastic aims. These had settled on a young man she had known from her childhood in Mitchelstown: Charles Kendal Bushe.

A few years her senior, Bushe was the brilliant son of the chaplain of Kingston College, who had given his boy a good education but no funds. Indeed, on his majority the young man, who had just started practicing as a lawyer in Dublin, had been greeted with papers to sign, making him responsible for the family debts. Margaret was charmed by young Charles, who had grown into a clever, bookish, humorous man with a soft melodious voice. He was a distinguished classical scholar and good orator, and in time would become Lord Chief Justice of the King's Bench in Ireland. Even had the Kings known his future, he would not have matched the social advantages and wealth they would expect for their daughter. There is no record of Margaret's internal or external struggle over her affection for such a man.

It is perhaps a measure of the fading of Mary Wollstonecraft's teaching that she resigned herself to it. Her governess would have told her either to stay a spinster or to follow her heart. Margaret did neither. She must by now have read the novel *Mary,* in which the heroine, daughter of parents based on Caroline and Robert, is married off to unite two adjacent estates. She is never happy. But this was a middle-class fable and Margaret was enough of her parents' daughter to expect to marry a nobleman.

Now a suitable peer had presented himself: the handsome, neighboring Lord Mount Cashell, approved by her parents. In return for her agreement to the match Margaret wanted a life dictated by her position but allowing some freedom of thought. Her mother had been a formidable woman whatever her failings and Margaret had inherited some of her qualities. A malleable man would suit her best. Wollstonecraft did not agree with young marriages, having seen her sister a victim of one—as

well as her Irish employers—but nineteen was not unduly young in this circle and Margaret was ready to escape her family with minimum fuss.

Stephen Moore was already the Earl of Mount Cashell and sitting in the House of Lords, from which her own father was excluded while her grandfather lived. His father had only recently died and he had been recalled from his grand tour. He was looking for a wife to help him cope with his new life as landowner and head of the family. It was unusual in Ireland to marry a neighbor, but in Munster for some reason it had become common. A conventional, affable man "with gentle manners & the appearance of an easy temper," he sought above all a woman of his rank, a woman of substance and breeding, not too much of a Bluestocking, since he himself had little education, one who came from a family with which it would be an honor to be allied and one who brought a good portion, since he liked money. Although awkward, Margaret was young and interesting-looking, had an average portion of £6,000 from the family estates—she would have had more if there had not been quite so many girls—and could expect further cash when her parents died. Since a sum of £360 was later mentioned as coming to her from Mitchelstown, it is likely that the portion was intended to remain invested in family property to provide money for the younger children she might bear, as was the custom.

The Moores were not equal in lineage to the Kings. They had been glovers and merchants until, having grown wealthy, they gave a loan to King William III. It remained unpaid, but honors followed, including the earldom of Mount Cashell. Now they owned more than twelve thousand acres in Cork and Tipperary and nearly fifty thousand in County Antrim; they had their seat at Moore Park in Kilworth. The closest great house to Mitchelstown and sharing the Funcheon River, it was a few miles south within the Blackwater Valley, surrounded by a thousand acres of parkland and bounded by a twelve-foot wall stretching for seven miles.

Moore Park was a solid, rather graceless Palladian structure of three stories and symmetrical wings, noted for its fine drawing room adorned

with classical frescoes, its grand pedimented doorway set off with Corinthian columns, and its magnificent stables. It had been built to accommodate the usual army of servants and dependents and to provide elegant public rooms for hospitality, while its windows commanded organized views over the demesne, one including a ready-made folly: a fifteenth-century tower house, remnant of the seat of earlier owners of Moore Park. In Dublin the Moores also owned Mount Cashell House, a dilapidated but enormous town house in fashionable St. Stephen's Green, a square of tall trees surrounded by handsome gravel and grass walks, which Mrs. Delany said might "be preferred justly to any in London." Number 80 had been purchased by Stephen's extravagant father from the queenly widow of the Bishop of Clogher. He enlarged and embellished it, putting in a fine ornamental plaster frieze in the dining room that was much admired. In the process he nearly made himself bankrupt. (Mount Cashell House continued something of a trial to the family, since the lead from its large, jutting portico was irresistible to thieves. A few years after he inherited, Stephen gave up the unequal struggle and tore it down to save the cost of repairs.)

If not especially solvent, Stephen was, like most Irish lords, rich in land and buildings and he was a splendid catch for any young woman. The Kings might have done better with Margaret had she been more tractable and prettier, but Robert was above all keen to buy political power in south Ireland and this he was doing with the Moores. Stephen's father had been a Privy Counsellor, Stephen was in the House of Lords, and his brother William was MP for the Moore borough of Clonmel; the family also controlled the seat of Cashell. Such an alliance must help Robert's general position in Cork. There would be no question in the future of the Earl of Mount Cashell siding with Lord Shannon's party.

Caroline's refusal to provide romantic fiction to her difficult daughter seemed to have paid off. No one insisted that Margaret be in love—but she had not been sold in quite the way her mother had been. She had been "out" for several seasons and was old enough properly to assent to a family choice. The marriage settlements do not survive but a younger sis-

ter making a suitably aristocratic marriage and bringing in a similar sum as portion received £200 pin money a year and would, should she be widowed, have all the use of her own property.

For Margaret the advantages of being mistress of Moore Park outweighed the possible disadvantages of marriage to a man she did not admire. With Jane Austen's Elizabeth Bennet contemplating Darcy's Pemberley, she may have thought that to be mistress of a large Georgian house would be "something." Also her pride in ownership answered a need for significance nurtured by her mother's contempt. Years later her son said his mother married for position. Despite her fascination for the middle class, rank was important to Margaret and she understood that a high social status allowed a woman to do much in society. She had been bred to see patronizing the poor as part of her duty; as her own mistress, she would have time and money to give to good causes and people. Less planned and elegant than Mitchelstown and consisting of just one long street, the small town of Kilworth could yet be a proper scene for her benevolence, although she pulled away from the example of her mother and other ladies of establishing Protestant Sunday schools there to teach the next generation patience and respect for superiors. In fact, the reading skills intended for Hannah More's exemplary *Tracts for the Times* were used on Tom Paine's inflammatory *Rights of Man,* and to Margaret's amusement the benevolent ladies at once changed their minds about the instruction: "the rage for Sunday Schools" was "principally promoted by the very people who now exclaim so violently against their natural effects," she remarked.

No more than her mother was Margaret naturally a country person but she thought partial residence on an estate her duty and she was not as averse to rural living as many people of her rank, who regarded themselves as exiles when out of London or Dublin.* The farms of Moore Park had undergone enclosure, as at Mitchelstown, but like most noble-

---

* Lady Moira described herself as "exiled" when she had to spend much time in the country: "I hate the North. I detest Ballynahinch [the Moira Estate]."

women, Margaret would be insulated from the damage inflicted on the poorer classes through the reforms. Besides, in Ireland it was always easier first to blame England, the Westminster government, or its puppets in the Castle than to look to native causes for any harm done by landowners.

Before she married him Margaret knew Stephen's limitations—his friendship with her brother George was proof of them—but he seemed well-meaning and she believed she could influence and make him more what she wanted. She later regretted the notion: "Guilty of numerous errors & none greater than that of marrying at nineteen a man whose character was perfectly opposite to mine . . . To my shame I confess that I married him with the idea of governing him, the silliest project that ever entered a woman's mind."

On Saturday, 12 September 1791 Margaret King, eldest daughter of Viscount and Viscountess Kingsborough, married Stephen Moore, Earl of Mount Cashell, amidst all the splendor and lavish consumption usual in such events. The wedding took place in Mitchelstown, where the tenants and town were festively decked out for the occasion; probably her father's militiamen were brought in to make a ceremonial guard and there would be balls, plays and concerts, as well as a great feast.

Just as Margaret was preparing for her wedding and being forced to think of her trousseau—gloves, stockings, trimmings, gowns, dresses, riding habits, hats, feathers, cloaks and shawls—Mary Wollstonecraft in London was writing her most famous book, *A Vindication of the Rights of Woman,* in which the aristocratic woman is a materialist child, kept in a gilded cage by pretended respect and expensive toys, and her friend Tom Paine was publishing *The Rights of Man,* which suggested a completely new social order of men born equal with equal rights. "It is an age of Revolutions, in which everything may be looked for," he declared.

Wollstonecraft had known Charles Kendal Bushe in Mitchelstown and may have heard of Margaret's liking for him. She would have been shocked to hear of the wedding to the Earl of Mount Cashell. Secure now in her own revolutionary ideas, she may have written to Margaret,

presuming on their old relationship. Certainly something untoward happened and in her letters Wollstonecraft referred bitterly to the "thoughtless ungrateful Lady Mount C" just after mentioning Bushe. It was easy for such a rift to occur: Margaret had become an adult and would not wish to be treated as a child; Mary Wollstonecraft had always been quick to see arrogance in a noblewoman.

Whatever the case, Charles Kendal Bushe did not break his heart at losing Margaret and two years later married someone else. He produced a large family.

During her time in Mitchelstown and Dublin, Mary Wollstonecraft made no mention of the fissures in her employers' marriage or the tensions their obvious incompatibility caused within the household. But for some years Caroline had taken every opportunity to be away from her lord and Mitchelstown, and those close to the couple were aware that they were virtually separated. Divorce was unseemly and difficult, requiring a private act of Parliament; Robert's string of mistresses was insufficient grounds and he was neither insane, impotent nor excessively violent, the only causes allowed to a woman. As the judge Sir William Scott remarked in a case about this time, "What merely wounds the mental feeling is in few cases to be admitted where they are not accompanied with bodily injury, either actual or menaced. Mere austerity of temper, petulance of manners, rudeness of language, a want of civil attention and accommodation, even occasional sallies of passion, if they do not threaten bodily harm, do not amount to legal cruelty." In any case Caroline, little concerned with sex and much concerned with social surface, seems to have had no desire to try for divorce.

It was remarkable that any aristocrats, raised by servants to consider their own desires paramount and their own persons effortlessly significant, ever managed to live together. Big houses and separate bedrooms took some of the strain off cohabitation but married life in isolated castles, however splendidly furnished and stuffed with grateful relatives, must have taxed the insufficiently regulated tempers of many. The mar-

riage of Caroline and Robert had never been happy. Repeated infidelity was not uncommon in the aristocracy—the Duchess of Leinster had had no difficulty coping with the errant Duke and in due course herself fell in love with her sons' tutor—but Caroline had never been fond of her husband and, as the source of the largest portion of the estate, found it difficult to put up with his promiscuity and boorish treatment. Robert had always been socially unsatisfactory and he remained as reserved and sullen as ever when not on his best behavior.

By now he had a permanent and public mistress called Eliner Hallenan, who was often with him in Mitchelstown, Dublin and London; with her he had two acknowledged children. He made no effort at discretion and rumor even had him exercising his *droit de seigneur,* the taking of maidenheads from the virgins of the estate, the "mark of slavery" that had so struck Arthur Young. It was later said of Robert that he "was famed for the beauty of his mistresses, one of whom inhabited each of his seats." Perhaps he compensated for the ridicule he had suffered at Eton owing to his childish appearance and the contempt of his wife in their early years together. Margaret said that the report of mistresses was "much exaggerated," not that it was entirely false.*

Caroline had never really enjoyed being at Mitchelstown with her family for long periods. She remembered her happiness as a young woman at court in England and determined to recapture this time. She was still a beauty and a vivacious talker; if there was no scandal, her rank and appearance would make her popular wherever she went. Her family was growing up and although Margaret was out of her control, the younger girls could only be advantaged by separation from their dissolute father.

In the past she had used ill health to get away; now she planned a more permanent move. The Kings used a London town house in George

---

* Another quarrel concerned an old graveyard on the Mitchelstown estate. Perhaps resenting his wife's family pretensions, Robert had buried some records of the White Knights nine feet under the surface of the graveyard, then leveled the surface. The place would thenceforward be called the New Orchard. See *Unpublished Geraldine Documents,* ed. James Graves (Dublin, 1881), 4, "The White Knight," 53f.

Street, Hanover Square; she would leave this for Robert and his mistress while she herself would take a "small cottage" out in Windsor. Liking a regular, methodical life, George III and Queen Charlotte now spent most of their time nearby at what the Queen called "our sweet retreat"; the King even had a special uniform for his residence there, dark blue with red facings. On Sunday evenings at seven, accompanied by the princesses, the royal couple descended to the Windsor Terrace to walk arm in arm through waiting crowds while regimental bands played. They talked to anyone they knew: the local nobility and gentry who were sure to be there, sometimes along with farmers, tradespeople and servants, who more usually gathered in the Long Walk where another band was playing. The walkabout had some of the informal appearance of the squirearchy mingling with tenants but it remained regal, and people were kept on their best behavior by the royal condescension. The Queen's own private rustic retreat of Frogmore, purchased just before Caroline took up residence at Windsor, as well as the royal "cottage" nearby at Kew, gave a certain cachet to other people with "cottages" in the area. Ladies amused themselves with country fêtes and pastoral games, including raking hay in white kid gloves. The French queen Marie Antoinette, who so enjoyed playing the shepherdess before the Revolution guillotined her, seemed far removed from Windsor.

Lady Kingsborough relished being at a court, especially one that had taken a serious Protestant turn. The war with anti-Christian France made piety a peculiarly British possession in the 1790s. With her political Protestantism Caroline fitted well into the circle of a queen who was criticized for coldness to her children and who wrote, "Lack of principle, forgetting all duties to God and Man, and lack of Religion, is seen as the main reason for the distresses amongst our neighbours"—a statement Lady Kingsborough found relevant to Ireland. In Windsor Caroline became acquainted with society ladies, many Anglo-Irish or with Irish connections, and some who were family friends such as Lady Harcourt, daughter-in-law of the Lord Lieutenant of Ireland succeeding Lord Townshend. This lady much suited her, for Lady Harcourt liked busying herself

with her tenants' occupations and moral lives, as Lady Kingsborough did at Mitchelstown, and she was praised for her activities by the leading evangelical writer Hannah More. In More's words, Lady Harcourt's spinning feasts and other morally improving events "contribute[d] to reconcile the lower class to that state in which it has pleased God to place them."

Margaret had little enthusiasm for Hanoverian royalty or politically useful religion, and she never understood her mother's love affair with the monarchy; no doubt she had her in mind when she mocked Irish nobles who "seek for refuge in the splendour of a Court and the smiles of Majesty."

Although gossip columnists had noticed that Lady Kingsborough spent much time in England without her husband, she did not appear a publicly forsaken wife. No scandal had besmirched her name, if one discounts Mrs. Thornhill's accusations against Arthur Young so many years before; even the gossiping Horace Walpole could find none to repeat, and Mary Wollstonecraft in her fictional portrait had to declare she was "chaste, according to the vulgar acceptation of the word, that is, she did not make any actual *faux pas.*" For all her childbearing—or perhaps because of it—Caroline seems not to have been a very highly sexed woman. There would be no impropriety in the separation, and appearances would be kept up; the couple would be together on great state and family occasions.

Probably it saddened Robert to accept that the tomboyish and beautiful Mary would now be in Caroline's sole charge and away from him. From his wife's point of view, Windsor, near the court, was a sensible location for a woman with unmarried daughters. It was common practice for Irish aristocrats to troop to England to fashionable spas and towns hoping to get their girls off their hands. The Duchess of Leinster was spending time in Tunbridge Wells on just such an errand. Caroline had high hopes for Mary, who was her favorite among her girls. Indeed, her affection for the child suggests that her failure to inspire any love in Margaret hurt more than Mary Wollstonecraft had understood.

Meanwhile, Robert, always keener to be in the country, chose to live

almost entirely at Mitchelstown Castle or at nearby Mountain Lodge. Although his father had asserted he would never quite feel they were his, he had thrown himself into improving both house and land, and he went on tinkering with both after the split from Caroline, busily enclosing, planting trees and hedges, copsing, draining and renewing old bridges. Margaret, who shared her father's dislike of the vice-regal court, place of "Lords-Lieutenants, their *pets,* and their parasites and their partizans," as she put it, admired her father's decision to remain a resident landowner: the nobility should use their income on their estates rather than living abroad and pressing their agents to squeeze more income from the tenants.

Education of a Rebel

I cannot submit to be controled in my Way of thinking.

— COUNTESS OF MOIRA

THE ARMY AND POLITICS WERE THE ONLY PROFESSIONS OPEN TO A young peer. At the age of twelve Stephen had been enrolled as an ensign by his father in the Kilworth Volunteers, but he showed no real military inclination. So by many, probably including Margaret, it was assumed that he would make a mark in Parliament. In this again his friends and relatives were disappointed. Stephen did not seek to use his family power for his own or anyone else's good. When he later managed to say something sensible in the House of Lords, some assumed it was through Margaret's influence and she was complimented as if he had been her son rather than her husband. The liberal Presbyterian pamphleteer William Drennan called Stephen "a patriotic if not democratic nobleman," much like the majority of the Anglo-Irish establishment.

Whatever his limitations, he did not cramp his new wife's style. Earlier in the century the celebrated Lady Mary Wortley Montagu famously

remarked that a woman should hide her knowledge as she would a deformity. But now aristocratic girls and married women were often allowed to immerse themselves in science and the arts as a leisure activity. They could be escorted to talks by philosophers, itinerant scholars and inventors, and it seems likely that during these early married years Margaret attended public lectures on the theories of the body and its nervous sensitivities. Mary Wollstonecraft thought girls should be taught the elements of anatomy and medicine so that they could care for themselves and their families—and, indeed, in a more ideal world become physicians—but she did not have the learning Margaret acquired, the basis of which was probably gained in Dublin. Later in life Margaret translated German medical books into English and doctored those around her, as well as giving advice on childhood ailments. Abroad she attended medical lectures dressed as a man—an easy business with her tall, angular figure—and she may have used the ruse in Dublin for more advanced courses. The famed cross-dressing actress Sarah Siddons perhaps inspired her here, since Siddons complemented her risqué male roles with a much-vaunted maternity and virtue in private life.

Margaret was maturing in character as well as intellect. At the age of fifteen she seemed whining and clinging; by her early twenties she struck people as sympathetic, cheerful and resolute, if rather too concerned about her health and oversensitive to slights. Much must have been due to the separation from Caroline and her new status as her own mistress. She never became interested in dress like her mother but she could when she tried achieve an alternative style that was neither Caroline's elaborate one nor her governess's careless one. (Unknown to Margaret, over in London even Mary Wollstonecraft was smartening herself up under the influence of her passion for Fuseli.) While some continued to think Margaret ugly and gauche, her striking androgynous features and height meant that she could occasionally look stunning in dramatic attire. As she aged some people found her face had a haunting quality derived from her kindliness and mental energy.

A few years after her marriage she was the subject of a fulsome poetic

tribute that caught her appeal, including the emotionality that so attracted other women. The admirer, signing herself A. Maria, was probably female:

> Mount Cashell! dear,—revered,—exalted, name!
> Oh! had I power half equal to the theme.
> But vain's the wish!—no mortal e'er expressed
> Such Heavenly virtues as adorn her breast.

Even this "artless" flattering poet could not ascribe beauty to Margaret but she allowed her to compensate for her lack of "heart-insnaring eyes":

> Vain are their charms! gay sparklers of an hour;
> They droop neglected like some fading flower.
> Such charms could ne'er my artless muse inspire,
> For sordid flattery ne'er profaned my lyre.
> The charms I sing are pity streaming tears,
> A generous soul and ever open ears.
> A hand that never closes at distress,
> A noble heart that only beats to bless.
> Virtues that make no ostentatious shew,
> But from benevolence still sweetly flow.
> Those inward virtues that adorn the mind,
> All in Mount Cashell sweetly are combined.

Probably the young couple visited London, as Robert and Caroline had done when they were first married, and were introduced at court, but the war with France prevented a more extended wedding trip to the Continent. Wherever they stayed they found it impossible to get on and they quarreled continually. Margaret followed her governess's advice and refused to use feminine arts of persuasion to control her husband, wanting to be neither a dominating wife nor a humble flatterer. Instead she was straightforwardly judgmental. Quickly she came to regard Stephen's understanding as "uncultivated & his mind contracted"; she deplored his

aversion to literature and found him "incapable of comprehending the feelings of a noble spirit." For his part Stephen was bemused by his highly strung, censorious wife and the stimulation she required.

Margaret was not used to suffering in silence. She was often sickly and tended to see her illnesses as psychosomatic, with a particular person as cause. It had once been her mother; now it was Stephen. In addition she was hurt when unappreciated. Her childhood insecurity made her want to be liked, by everyone from servants and tenants to children, where he, the prized eldest son, was concerned with status rather than popularity; she found it difficult to adjust to putting a husband's interests before her desire for promiscuous approval, however dearly bought. Yet, despite such differences in temperament and expectations, in time the couple did find a *modus vivendi* and life, often led apart, became tolerably tranquil—although Margaret later implied that she and Stephen were always ill-matched.

Especially in Kilworth she did not have the company she craved. Beyond herself and her new husband the most permanent resident was Stephen's unmarried sister, Helena, whose timid character differed greatly from her own. Given the difficulties Caroline had experienced with her mother-in-law, Jane, following her marriage, perhaps it was as well for Margaret that Stephen's mother died soon after her husband and within a year of her son's wedding; on the other hand, a new wife might have welcomed an older woman's help and company in her early housekeeping years. Until she could provide her own circle of friends, Margaret must often have yawned at the daily routine of country house living, as described by another young aristocratic wife:

> As soon as I am up and have breakfasted I ride. I then come in and write or do anything of employment, I then walk, dress for Dinner and after Dinner I take a short walk if it is fine and I have time 'till the Gentlemen come out, and then spend the remainder of the evening in Playing at Whist, or writing if I have an opportunity and reading.

The main stimulus in Margaret's life at Moore Park was reading. She probably received the new Dublin magazine *Anthologia Hibernica,* since it suited her serious and curious temperament. Responding to the improved civility and knowledge of the kingdom, it aimed at a readership wanting "intellectual enjoyment" and bored by insipid novels. It even mentioned Mary Wollstonecraft, though criticizing her for her opposition to hereditary titles and wealth. Like other journals, it declared it avoided politics, but its antiquarian interest in the Irish past and language and its "general hints" for improving the state suggested a broadly liberal agenda. It implied that revolution was not required but that reform would be a good idea. It ensured its Ascendancy credentials by dedicating the collected edition to the Lord Chancellor, Lord Clare.

Like her mother, Margaret began breeding quickly and she arranged to have her babies in Dublin at St. Stephen's Green. No doubt she followed aristocratic habit and used a male doctor or accoucheur rather than the midwife her governess favored for *all* women, not only the lower classes. The first baby, Stephen, appeared nine months after the wedding, in August 1792. Then followed another son, Robert, the next year, and another the year after. Then there was a gap of nearly two years, suggesting lack of cohabitation in so fertile a lady. Her new relatives speculated on the state of the marriage bed, as her mother's had done when Caroline seemed momentarily to falter in the almost annual ritual. Childbearing resumed with the birth of Helena in March 1795. Margaret was fulfilling the first duty of a woman in her position.

With her children she intended to act differently than her mother. She would start by breast-feeding them in the way Mary Wollstonecraft urged and she would be cheerful while doing so for the sake of the baby. Caroline had been a forbidding parent and Margaret had turned to surrogates; she would bring up her own children more closely, although it never occurred to her not to delegate most maternal duties. While they were young she had total control of them and took pains to plan their raising. She read widely in books on education and became attuned to

the stages of childhood and adolescence. She studied Wollstonecraft's works and laughed with her at Rousseau's notions of girls' education as contingent on boys', but she followed her governess in accepting some of his general principles: encouraging systematic development through experience and allowing much open air and exercise. Her regime stressed the physical side of life, especially in the first five years; with the care she had given she was proud that her children had better "constitutions" than she herself possessed.

She wanted to treat both sons and daughters with "mildness, kindness and respect." They were to learn to think for themselves as soon as possible, as Mary Wollstonecraft had taught. "My greatest object is to make my children happy and virtuous," she wrote. But she herself was scarcely out of childhood when she began her mothering and she had missed exploring her own desires fully. So, for all her goodwill and intentions, she emerged as an unsympathetic educator of some of her young brood, a cross between her mother and the mother Wollstonecraft wanted to be to her. Her eldest son found her as uncongenial in her careful child rearing as she had found her more trivial mother.

In the end she was Caroline's daughter and did not have the enthusiastic affection the Duchess of Leinster showed her children. She did, however, make a bond with her daughter Helena and second son Robert that was strong enough to withstand the vicissitudes of their later lives. For those who suffered from her principled rearing, the less dedicated father, Stephen, seemed a kinder presence. He had had a fairly lax education in Ireland and did not believe knowledge of literature and science necessary for a proper nobleman—or indeed political theory and practice. If his sons and daughters were good landed ladies and gentlemen, it was enough. Naturally he and Margaret quarreled. She accused him of being mean and of not wanting to spend money on his children by hiring tutors and sending them to costly schools: "Lord M. never considered education as a matter of any importance and my children have never had the most trifling advantage of this sort," she later lamented. For all their faults, the Kings had spared no expense in the raising of their family.

The running of the households of Moore Park and Mount Cashell House was definitely the lady's preserve: she dealt with the superfluity of servants Irish aristocrats seemed to require. Although much business would be delegated to the housekeeper, the clerk of the kitchen and the butler, as at Mitchelstown, a sensible wife aspired to control and take care of as much as she could. But good servants were hard to find and keep. Letters between ladies were full of problems, particularly the hiring of cooks who could cope with the new menus from France and England as well as the old-fashioned Irish ones. Ladies groaned at the difficulty of keeping up the new grand houses: the cleaning of stucco, the polishing of silver and the varnishing of pictures. As with the educating of children, despite much goodwill Margaret found she had no easy way with servants, whom she could neither persuade nor coerce.

Perhaps she felt between worlds, caught both by the patrician noblesse of her mother and Wollstonecraft's mingled concern and anxiety of influence. Her governess cared for the poorer classes while deploring their vulgar effect on the higher; at the same time she oscillated between seeing them as an equal citizenry and viewing them as a service class designed to give her own some intellectual leisure by shouldering the material burden of life: housekeeping and child care.

Margaret also had to negotiate the new sentimentalizing of class relations. At the time when servants were moving from being family retainers and dependents into forming contract labor, the service tie was being sentimentalized in literature. As a result, while social differences remained firm, some employers liked to think they kept their employees through their own benevolence and their servants' loyalty. A few egalitarian nobles in the 1790s became more radical, inviting the lower orders to their table and mixing them with the gentry—to the horror of Bishop Percy, who thought the practice savored "rather of French *Equality and Fraternity*, than of the old English Baronical System of Manners. Our ancient Barons nobly protected their Vassals, but made them keep their proper subordinate Distance."

A friend later remembered how badly Margaret dealt with inferiors.

"Often her frank & generous disposition misleads her & she suspects no one, as I have perceived in her being a dupe to servants who have practised towards her the most glaring duplicity." She herself agreed with this verdict and later admitted she had "no talents" for being a "good severe mistress."

Undisturbed by literature or social anxieties, Stephen was yet no better with his employees and he often found himself dominated by his grooms. For some time both he and his wife were in thrall to a moody retainer who grumbled about them around Dublin and whom they could not shake off. Each tried to make the other speak to him.

For all her difficulties, there were worse predicaments than Margaret's as young wife and worse husbands than the ineffectual Stephen. In the year of her marriage, her father's old enemy Lord Shannon went to stay with his beautiful daughter near Cork and was appalled at her treatment—"an immured State Prisoner," he called her. He described her plight to his son:

> [S]he . . . looks wretchedly & has a constant Pain in her Head occasioned I am sure by the Life she is sentenced to lead & goes through more Drudgery than all the Servants in the House, for she has not only the Family to regulate, accounts to keep, all things out of doors to attend to, but the personal Slavery of doing the duty of Maid to all the Children, to attend their rising, & going to Bed, their Drinking, Meals, airings, & watching every thing that goes into them or comes out of them.

The poor mother was made to sleep near the heir; he kicked off his nightclothes and she had to wake every half hour to cover him and to listen to him if he chattered when he woke. Meanwhile, her husband—dismissed by his father-in-law as "a composition of Bile, Melancholy, & bad temper"—lay in a separate bed so as not to be disturbed.

Wollstonecraft had prepared the ground for Margaret's interest in politics, as had her father in his reactionary way. Now through Stephen she was related to a family far more politically and socially to her taste than the Kings, the Moiras—Stephen was grandson to the first Earl of Moira by his first wife. The Moiras were liberal-minded grandees, associated with years of opposition to the Castle of a more decided character than Robert's when he had been in his independent phase. They were not radical and did not seek complete separation from England but they wanted more autonomy in ruling their own country and balked at legislation from London. Without having sympathy for Catholicism as a creed or accepting its nationalist potential, they favored Catholic participation in Parliament as right and politically expedient.

Political labels do not easily stick on the liberal Anglo-Irish nobility. Most accepted Britain's limited monarchy and Grattan's Parliament and thought them worth preserving, although many believed Ireland ill served by the present rulers. Much was less ideological than personal and familial. The great families were aggrieved when Castle patronage did not reach them, even as they criticized Castle policies. In England, the terms *Whig* and *Tory* signified temporary alliances of families and interests; in Ireland the Ascendancy was vaguely Whig, loosely divided into Protestant conservatives and liberal progressives. Whigs tended to use *Tory* as a term of abuse to indicate enthrallment to royal power, but in reality Whigs could also be defined according to their adherence to various royal personages. The unruly Prince of Wales allied himself with liberal Whigs primarily because they drank and gambled and because his father, George III, hated them and him, and the difference between the Westminster government of William Pitt and the opposition of the liberal Whigs under Charles James Fox sometimes seemed a matter of style. Fox, cousin of the Leinsters, was short, squat, untidy, unbuttoned, exuberant, uncontrolled and generous; William Pitt was thin, priggish, buttoned up, careful, secretive and suspicious.

Like other thinking Anglo-Irish lords, the Moiras picked their way through English politics, now siding with Pitt, now with Charles James Fox. Francis, who became the 2nd Earl of Moira on his father's death in 1793, was about the age of Margaret's father; he was an impressive and

earnest man, tall, stately and athletic, a brave and skilled soldier of inflexible and undiplomatic principle. He was also extravagant, spending wildly to promote his career, and he was soon indebted to Stephen, whom he had to reimburse by selling some of his estates. Only Lord Moira's huge political ambition explains his friendship with the self-indulgent Prince of Wales, whom he supported with unflagging loyalty. Much concerned with Ireland, he yet found his natural home in London; so it was in Westminster that he most often spoke of the outrages against the Irish poor, whose fierce supporter he became. Back in Ireland he was guest at a banquet given by grateful Catholics and he acted as godfather to the child of Wolfe Tone, an increasingly radical ally of Grattan and, inevitably, opponent of the Earl of Clare.

Although the Moiras and Leinsters both resented Castle power and often achieved an uneasy alliance, the tightly knit group around the Richmond sisters—the Leinsters, Conollys and Napiers—was also viewed as a faction opposed to the Moiras. Certainly Lord Moira's mother was no fan of these ladies, whom she dismissed as "a bastard race of an adulterous king" on account of their descent from Charles II and his French mistress. On the other side Lady Sarah Napier thought Lord Moira a "toad-eater" in his desire to advance himself. The distaste did not, of course, prevent the two families from socializing together.

The Moiras were a political force in Dublin—although the dowager Lady Moira hoped that no Irish quixotism would spoil her son's promising political career on the wider London stage. They were leaders in politics, entertained Grattan and Fox and loathed Lord Clare, who loathed them in return. When in Dublin Margaret and Stephen were often guests at the splendid Moira town house on Usher's Quay overlooking the River Liffey. It was famous for its elegant high-ceilinged octagonal room, the sides of whose window were inlaid with mother-of-pearl—it had been much admired by the evangelical John Wesley when he toured Ireland.

For Margaret the crucial tie was a surprising one, with the dowager Countess of Moira, the Earl's third wife, a woman now nearing sixty. A close friendship developed and after some formal visits the pair began dining with each other "in a family way" and Lady Moira became familiar enough to urge Margaret to stay with her when unwanted company arrived. Despite the great age difference of over thirty years, the two ladies had much in common. Both had unfulfilling marriages, both were intellectually curious and both were seriously interested in social issues and Irish politics. Both suffered from "nerves," were often ill and were much concerned with their health. They swapped advice on regimes of living and eating and discussed plants, potions and their favorite remedies: herbal teas, clarified honey, antimony, elixirs and spirit of hartshorn. Both enjoyed the Moira library: "Recesses where you may sit and read books of all kinds, to amuse the fancy as well as improve the mind—telescopes, microscopes, and all the scientific apparatus. Everyone chooses their employment; it is the land of liberty, yet of regularity." In Lady Moira Margaret, who had so painfully missed her strong-minded governess, had found another congenial mother figure.

Like Mary Wollstonecraft, although with more humor, Lady Moira encouraged her friend's satirical turn as well as her mental independence. Once when planning to dispute with a bigoted bishop, Lady Moira wrote, "[H]e is not willing that I sh[oul]d even have a little scrap of a Mind of my Own, & when he disputes that, then I grow resolute & will have a greater Share of Opinion & free Will." Lady Moira wrote warmly of Margaret: "Her attachment to me is from the liking of me, notwithstanding the difference of age, and her tribute of the mind is most flattering, and is not to be confounded with . . . chilly propriety." Despite being Stephen's stepgrandmother, she was clear which of the pair she most admired. Margaret was "sensible, rational & good natured to the utmost degree" and she wrote of her and Stephen, "I love her sincerely, & think most highly of her Understanding & Ability of Mind—Ornamental Merits that certainly Providence did not endow *him* with."

In many ways the curious, cultivated and snobbish Countess of Moira was a more useful role model for an aristocratic young Anglo-Irish woman developing a liberal conscience than an opinionated middle-class governess. She had much of Wollstonecraft's firmness of mind and added to

it a grasp of the contemporary Irish political scene. She herself was an English woman with her own hereditary titles, daughter of the 9th Earl of Huntingdon and his formidable wife, the Calvinist Methodist patron and religious leader Selina—a lady as unconcerned with her appearance as Margaret and Wollstonecraft; Horace Walpole said she looked like "an old basket-woman." At eighteen Lady Moira had been at court as a Lady of the Bedchamber to the young sisters of George III, then in 1752 she married Lord Rawdon, later Earl of Moira; she was his third and most fertile wife, producing eleven children, of whom five died young.

Mrs. Delany judged Lady Moira "modest & civil in her manner, neither handsome nor genteel" but having "good sense & delicate sentiments." Others, more fulsome, said she combined

> the bounty and beneficence suitable to her noble birth and elevated rank in society, with all the tender traits of humanity, and the amiable graces of her sex. To strong natural powers of understanding, she added a refined taste, formed upon the best principles, and cultivated in an eminent degree.

With such gifts she easily became a leader in Irish society, and Moira House was a "favourite spot where every person of genius or talents in Dublin, or who visited Dublin, loved most to resort to." She reflected "grace upon every beneficial fashion."

Lady Moira warmly embraced Ireland as her husband's country and his elegy applied to her: he "strove to plant the Arts on Eirin's [*sic*] strand." She commissioned translations from Gaelic and patronized the Irish poet Thomas Dermody, whose habitual drunkenness she forgave. She subscribed to a book of poems by the young poet Henrietta Battier, who, even as she hymned George III, the Lord Lieutenant and his wife, declared herself above all the singer of Erin, "nurse of Beauty—Isle of Saints."

Lady Moira aimed to be a practical reformer. She wanted, for example, to make cheap coarse cloth for "some alleviation to the miseries of the unhappy beings that surround me, the excess of poverty that reigns

here being such, that in my native land, I am persuaded, it would not be imagined to exist." She gave details of how the work was to be done, using fired or mildewed flax divested of oil through fermented urine and boiling; she had tested the method and in addition had experimented with herbs and boiled fish as common dyes. Despite her enthusiasm, she was frustrated by professional weavers who saw a threat to their trade in foreign cotton—absurd, she snapped, for the poor would never have bought their expensive stuff.*

Lady Moira moved in a circle of politically interested and active women. She was Protestant but not pious or even very religious, and she detested "fanaticism." She had strong likes and dislikes, having, for example, no time for her eldest son's wife but idolizing her own youngest daughter, her "angel" Selina, married to the Earl of Granard, another opponent of the Castle regime. Lady Moira's marriage was punctuated by domestic quarrels and sharp words. "Mend your temper for the convenience of others and the good of yourself," her husband told her on one occasion, while she complained that he covered his pictures with foul-smelling turpentine varnish with no thought for her health: it "kills me with the head-ache," she protested. Selina was her compensation; she clung to it even though it made her husband jealous. Margaret became a good friend of Selina but saw little of her, since she was often away with her numerous children in her fortified home, Castle Forbes, near the Edgeworths.

Many aristocratic women both in Ireland and England interested themselves in their men's politics but remained independent in some of their views. When her son was fighting for the British cause in the American war, Lady Moira called it a "humiliating contest" and openly supported the enemy. She was not alone in independent-mindedness; her friend Lady Londonderry actually opposed her husband's politics and, even more strikingly, Lady Clare sometimes disagreed with Lord

* The letters containing the proposal were written in 1775, but the *Anthologia Hibernica* printed them in 1794 to bolster its point that Ireland should be economically independent.

JANET TODD

Clare's strident views. Lady Moira encouraged Margaret to read widely in Irish history and come to conclusions not necessarily endorsed by her husband.

As they had begun to do when she was Mary Wollstonecraft's pupil, Margaret's opinions were diverging widely from those of her family and family friends such as George Ogle. With Lady Moira and her allies she came to understand a political philosophy that would in her mind rival her governess's belief in natural rights. This was a genteel sort of republicanism much in keeping with the new classical houses. Without much threatening the status quo, the republican philosophy provided a moral challenge to the corruption of venal and nepotistic rulers. Noble republicans were rarely separatists or democrats, regarding it as an aristocrat's duty to govern, but they wanted substantial reform.

In England, Scotland and Ireland republicanism had a long history and meant different things to different groups. Based on the Roman and Greek traditions of military and civic male virtue, it implied that the state should promote the good of the whole people—though it was unclear who defined this. To espouse republicanism in Margaret's rank was more a mode and way of thinking than a specific political program, and many versions coexisted easily with hierarchies of class and established religion. Even Charles James Fox, the king-hating republican, was no democrat and was greatly alarmed by the egalitarian notions of Wollstonecraft's friend Tom Paine. Later in life, when Margaret imagined a political utopia in her novel "Selene," she gave it a classical republican government: a prince chosen by the nobility over the age of twenty-five and the plebeians over fifty.

With the Moiras and their friends Margaret came to define herself more clearly as Irish. Unlike her brother George she had spent most of her childhood in Ireland and knew it as her country. She disagreed profoundly with Lord Clare, who saw the Anglo-Irish as colonialists living in defended enclaves. In her view the distinctions of the past should be effaced in the present. Protestant settlers, from whom most of her family were descended, had been so long in Ireland—rather longer than most "Americans" in North America—that they were as rightfully there as any

other group and could not be called usurpers. The good among the Anglo-Irish opposed corruption and oppression just as forcefully as the descendants of old "Irish chieftains." Indeed, she was beginning to find the term *Anglo-Irish* as irritating as George Ogle's favored word, *Ascendancy;* all the Irish were mongrels and "the man who has now the best title to the appellation of *Irishman,* is the inhabitant who loves his countrymen, who promotes the prosperity and who respects *the independence of Ireland,*" she wrote. Like Lady Moira, she came to believe that the country's divisions were primarily due to the divide-and-rule policy of London and its lackeys in the Castle.

Also like Lady Moira, she retained a belief in the ideal of nobility. With all her goodwill toward the poor and suffering, Lady Moira scorned "the Mobility" and had a horror of an armed "rabble": "As to making a democrat of me, that, you must be persuaded, is a fruitless hope," she wrote to a radical friend. She was appalled at the "vulgar Freedom" and "jocular impertinence" of the multitude, and she summed up her position:

> An Aristocrat of the genuine Brand . . . I loved *the People* & thought my duty to protect & serve them, I shou'd not, nor do I chuse to be tyrannized by the mob having never had the least inclination to practice tyranny over those who were subject to my influence, I am loyal & National—but I sigh when I behold those who never had a Great Grandfather, to whom the Noble Feudal Feelings of grateful attachment to a faithful Follower, & the Indulgence of the power to protect & serve are unknown.

Margaret followed this line in deploring the venal lawyers and placemen around the Lord Lieutenant. When in "Selene" she imagined a baseborn boy ruined by flatterers of his wealth, she called them "professed Democrats." "[T]heir *cant* was particularly agreeable" to him and he joined in "their ridicule of high birth and noble ancestry." His rich uncle had failed to get a peerage, so he agreed with "the sentiments of these liberal youths" and was as proud as "the haughtiest descendant of a Norman

Prince," although he had no ancestors whose deeds of valor had transmitted to posterity "the splendour of a noble name"—like that of her own family's White Knight. In her fantasy Margaret could imagine unicorns with grass-green eyes, eight legs and two tails of purple, green and gold, all covered in small feathers, with striped zebra-style panniers, but not a world without rank or where people whom one spoke to did not have attendants. There had been a time of equality, she wrote of her utopia, but as numbers increased "an aristocratic race naturally sprung up."

Yet despite her tenderness for the ideal of nobility, Margaret valued ability and enthusiasm where she found it and she thought Stephen's crude pride in lineage misplaced—the kind of pride that made him pay extra rates when traveling in Europe rather than take the coronet off his carriage. And she later claimed that she agreed with her governess that the middle class was the best situation for developing personal virtue. She even wrote that she "sighed" for the "middle rank of life" though born noble. Also she was scathing about her own class when it failed to live up to its noble ideal: "excepting very few individuals, our men of high rank and large fortune, are creatures whose hearts are contracted, whose minds are vulgarized, and whose morals are depraved." She probably had her brother George in mind when she castigated the education of a young lord as a training in idleness, ignorance and debauchery. Inevitably such men became easy instruments of corrupt power.

Margaret was in her element with Lady Moira and her circle. Some became her friends and were entertained at Mount Cashell House and Moore Park. The cause of reform, propelled in 1782 by the landed class, had passed to a lower order of lawyers, merchants and teachers and with these she could now mix. There is no record of old acquaintances such as the Ogles visiting but instead she welcomed the kind of people unthinkable at Mitchelstown Castle: Denys Scully, a Catholic lawyer from Tipperary who was a friend, sometimes almost a factotum, for Lady Moira; the Reverend John Murphy, another friend of Lady Moira, who often lodged him in her house; Robert Orr, a snobbish barrister delighted to be entertained by a countess—he boasted of being familiar with Moore Park; his

friend the radical pamphleteer William Drennan; and the gentlemanly
Protestant liberal MP Arthur O'Connor, a clever, attractive, egotistic man
who may have met the King girls earlier, since he was born at Mitchelstown and was only a little older than Margaret.

Among the women she met the most radical was Mary Anne Emmet,
sister of Thomas Addis and Robert Emmet, all living near the Mount
Cashells in St. Stephen's Green West. Like Wollstonecraft, Mary Anne
became a pamphleteer and journalist, and her example declared that
women could be politically active and write in Ireland. But not necessarily on women's issues. The Presbyterian Mary Anne McCracken eagerly
read *A Vindication of the Rights of Woman* and declared it was "almost" time
"for the clouds of error and prejudice to disperse" so that "the female
part of the Creation as well as the male" might throw off its mental fet-
ters, but there is little evidence of such thinking in Lady Moira's circle.
Margaret's utopia did not envisage votes for women and she did not follow Wollstonecraft into any specifically feminist agitation.

Margaret also probably came to know Henrietta Battier, the poet
whom Lady Moira had patronized and who in turn praised the Moiras as
virtuous Irish patriots. Battier had begun as a conventional writer of
eulogies and songs, helped on her way by encouragement from the old
English Tory Samuel Johnson. Now in "these degenerate days" she had
found her "patriot heart, that throbs with honest pride" and was writing
political and satirical verses, lashing out at Castle hacks and declaring
that "absent Honour leaves the rein to power." Freedom bled through all
of Ireland's arteries and its treasures were drained "for an assassin tribe."
She especially loathed Lord Clare, whom she called "that proud plebeian," a "glitt'ring snake" and "evil counsellor." Poetry did not bring her
affluence and she lived with two daughters in a single Dublin room, into
which she unashamedly invited like-minded radical friends to tea.

For future events Margaret's most important acquaintance was
another man from County Cork, the Protestant lawyer John Philpot Curran, a short, ugly, depressive man with very black hair and a protruding
lip. His mother had wanted him to be a bishop and was disappointed to

find him consorting with local peasants; as a result, he understood Irish Gaelic, felt much sympathy for the poor and became the enemy of tithes and high rents. He had once been so slovenly a student that he despised Trinity College for putting up with him, but in later life he realized that, despite the physical disadvantages of a shrill voice and stutter, he could speak eloquently—and attract women. Little Henrietta Battier wrote of him, "For though his monkey face might fail to woo her, / Yet, ah! his monkey tricks would quite undo her." After a spell in London Curran began a brilliant career as a lawyer in Dublin, specializing in unpopular causes. One of his first cases was the prosecution of the Kings' neighbor, an ally of Lord Shannon, the Protestant Lord Doneraile, for horsewhipping a priest. When Curran won, Lord Doneraile ordered every mass-house (Catholic church) in his estate nailed up.

Curran did well from the law and moved into a grand house at 12 Ely Place, near the Earl of Clare, who was for a time a close friend. He then became MP for Rathcormac in Cork and joined Grattan's party. He attacked the extravagance of the ruling regime, mocked the Castle's control of power through selling honors and advocated parliamentary reform and Catholic participation. "He animated every debate with all his powers; he was copious, splendid, full of wit and life and ardour," wrote an admirer. When George III went mad, Curran joined the formal opposition, but the King's recovery took away his hopes. Rupture with Lord Clare followed. Clare called Curran a "puny babbler" and the insults led to a duel. Neither hit the other but spectators said Clare intended to hit. When Clare became Lord Chancellor of Ireland, Curran lost much of his Dublin practice. In return he attacked Clare viciously and often.

For a time it seemed that the early French Revolution was following the modest American one and held little threat for Britain. England and Ireland were not as oppressive as France under the *ancien regime* and, for the ruling class, there was much freedom of opinion. As long as they paid lip service to the Church of England, the upper orders could be as deist in religion and as liberal in politics as they wished. The social structure

seemed secure, and God, the King and the squirearchy were more or less aligned. People might grumble about government in Westminster and Dublin Castle but they rarely proposed to destroy it. This orderly stratification was threatened by France, which suddenly veered off into quite uncharted waters. Now it had a profound effect on Ireland and England.

In August 1792 Louis XVI was dragged from his palace, deposed and imprisoned with his wife and children. Early in September 1400 French prisoners including priests were murdered by the mob. A few months later, the King was tried, found guilty, guillotined and buried in quicklime to prevent any fetishizing of his royal body. His death threatened every crowned head in Europe. George III and the British court went into mourning, as did Dublin Castle.

Then the radical Jacobins under Robespierre seized power and the Terror began. Like most moderates, Charles James Fox was uneasy; yet he saw French atrocities as no worse than those of the absolutist regime it destroyed. Mary Wollstonecraft came to agree. It was not a popular view.

Ireland always made the notion of English nationhood insecure. At times of crisis the island fortress that Shakespeare had extolled as being built by nature—rather ignoring the Scottish dimension—became more of a porous group of islands. The French disease of leveling and anarchy might come into England through any opening but the most likely ones were in Ireland.

In February 1792 Pitt had surveyed Europe and announced to Parliament that he expected "fifteen years of peace." By early 1793 war with revolutionary France was inevitable and inevitably Ireland was involved. Fearing internal and external threats, Pitt's government was eager to control the home as well as the war front. Books and views that had simply irritated a year ago now became threatening; spies were recruited to watch suspected republicans in the three kingdoms. Meanwhile, new journals fanned patriotic enthusiasm and loyal societies supporting King and Country were founded in England and Ireland to counter sedition. Paine's effigy was burned in town squares without interference from the government. Some even proposed the same fate for Mary Wollstonecraft.

Fox had no problem with the demonizing of Paine and Wollstonecraft but, like other liberal Whigs, he opposed the French war. He saw it as supporting kingly power and threatening both the traditional liberties he revered and the order on which the landed power of Whig grandees depended.

Through these changes Mary Wollstonecraft remained firm in her democratic views, and had she still been communicating with Margaret she would have given her the advice she gave a Liverpool friend: "do not mix with the shallow herd who throw an odium on imutable principles, because some of the mere instruments of the revolution were too sharp." To some extent Margaret agreed. At the same time she probably joined Lady Moira in stopping short of welcoming a French invasion of Ireland to oppose England.

In 1794 Margaret and Stephen's life at Moore Park was interrupted by a surprising wedding: that of her boisterous brother George to Stephen's sister Helena. George had had a poor preparation for marriage. After Eton and Oxford and the riotous sojourn in London in company with the Prince of Wales, he had returned to Dublin, where he had allegedly walked through St. Stephen's Green near his sister Margaret's house with a Miss Johnstone. "What a fine night to run away with another man's Wife in," he remarked. She replied, "And why not with another man's daughter?" "Will you?" he asked; "Yes," she replied. "Done then," said George. "Done," said she, and they sailed away to the West Indies, where she bore him three children. It was claimed that he married her.

In due course the irate Robert brought him back. Miss Johnstone (or Mrs. George King) was "disposed of in England"—presumably the marriage, if it existed, was annulled and the children boarded out (it was relatively easy for marriages to be "broken" if they had occurred out of Britain or in rural Ireland). George was found suitable roles as page to the Lord Lieutenant and captain in his father's North Cork militia. He was also provided with a suitable wife from the family.

So in early May, at Margaret's home of Moore Park, Captain George

King married the Lady Helena Moore, described as "a pretty, pleasing little woman" and in another, more tactful account as "amiable & accomplished." There were rumors that George had married a large fortune,
but this was not the case; his own revenues proved insufficient for his
increasingly expansive personality, and he and his father were soon at
loggerheads over rents from Mitchelstown. Marriage did not interrupt
his rollicking sexual career, and he spent much time in London while
Helena remained with Stephen and Margaret at Moore Park. Nonetheless, they managed in time to breed three sons and two daughters.

Both Margaret and Helena shuttled between Kilworth and Dublin,
presumably enjoying the season in their different ways. Despite signs of
discontent, the Dublin world seemed fairly secure. At the state opening of
Parliament in January 1794 Lord Westmorland declared, "His majesty has
the fullest reliance upon the loyalty and attachment of his people in Ireland." That he spoke only to the Anglican Anglo-Irish subjects was implied
when he appealed to their desire "for the preservation of every privilege
which upholds the social order" and their need to resist "the desperate
designs of men, who are endeavouring to erect their own power and
dominion on the ruins of law and order." The world he defended was at its
most brilliant. Mrs. Siddons, now at the height of her fame, was playing in
the theater and Castle entertainments under the jovial Lord Lieutenant
were lavish: at least he spent his salary in Ireland, some commented. Sarah
Tighe wrote to her nephew George: "These are terrible times for balls and
gaiety and yet things of that kind go on amazingly. . . . I am sure that those
who are in the midst of danger in the county must think us mad or at least
very unfeeling."

With nurses and governesses to care for children, motherhood did
not weigh heavily on the aristocracy. So, despite her young family, Margaret now made a trip to London. Unhappily, there was no chance of a
remeeting with Mary Wollstonecraft, who was away in France. After her
unfulfilled relationship with Fuseli she had gone to Paris and fallen in
love with an American speculator, Gilbert Imlay, and, impetuous as ever,
entered a union outside marriage and borne his child. Probably Mar-

garet heard the gossip in London about this strange affair. She also observed the fame of her governess's great tract, *A Vindication of the Rights of Woman,* and was proud of their old association. Her own increasingly liberated stance could be justified through the older woman's accepted achievements.

While in London she probably learned a good deal of another revolutionary conversion: that of the Leinster son, Lord Edward Fitzgerald. He had been radicalized in 1792, when he became a disciple of Tom Paine in Paris. Both had attended a famous dinner in White's Hotel, where he called himself a "Friend of the Rights of Man," discarded his title and proposed that everyone else do the same. More interestingly for the British government—which received details of the event—he drank to the armies of France: "may the example of its citizen soldiers be followed by all enslaved countries, till tyrants and tyranny be extinct." Full of enthusiasm for the Ireland he had rarely inhabited, he convinced Paine that it was a place worth liberating. Together they should try to persuade the French authorities to undertake it.

Once war broke out with Britain such intention was, of course, treasonable. It might also be ill-advised. As a more thoughtful Irishman remarked, "Seek French co-operation but take care what you are about." The French were quite capable of using the Irish cynically, then betraying them: "You will be swopped for some sugar island," he warned.

When she arrived in London Margaret found it in a political ferment over the French war, the Revolution and its relevance to England. Eighteenth-century conduct books strongly advised women in the middle ranks to live privately, but, as in Ireland, here many aristocratic ladies were loud in their opinions: they electioneered, heckled in Parliament and spoke robustly in public. An Irish agent commented that "the women, even in the highest ranks, were absolutely democratic. Out of party spirit: they all have their hair cut *à la Jacobine*"—a short "Grecian" style. Lord Edward's youngest sister, Lady Lucy Fitzgerald, embraced this radical chic, and she and her friends went to the London opera with their hair tucked up. They were mobbed, as they presumably expected to be.

Margaret too was beginning to play at revolution. By 1794 the increasingly worried British government was turning against radical political societies, which were felt to be weakening the country from within. Men once seen as misguided fools were now labeled traitors. Even though many wanted reform and made no threats against royal heads, Pitt had arrested twelve of them for high treason, including the veteran political agitator John Horne Tooke, the dramatist Thomas Holcroft, and the radical shoemaker Thomas Hardy. Amidst much publicity and comment, they were acquitted by a jury and the case was dropped. It was all rather foolish, but frightening for those involved.

Margaret had openly supported the accused and was so elated when she heard of their acquittal that she dashed around to Hardy's shoe shop to congratulate him. She found him a "good, strait forward man with great firmness & some understanding." She asked him whether he had been committed to the Tower and he replied that he had had "that honor." Like the Duchess of Devonshire electioneering with her open purse some years before, Margaret expressed her appreciation by ordering a pair of shoes from Hardy—indeed, the activity became so fashionable among the upper orders that poor Hardy was kept busy during his first weeks of freedom making trophy shoes for liberal ladies. Unhappily, Margaret's were "shockingly made" and her enthusiasm for lower-order insubordination did not extend to shoddy workmanship. She took a hackney coach back to his house to return them for altering, remarking, "Mr Hardy I am very sorry for it but my feet are democratical and your shoes are aristocratical and they don't agree at all—Pray have the kindness to put them on the last for me." Instead Hardy made a new pair, not much better but not as painful to wear, and he refused payment. She did not press him and the transaction of condescension and gratitude pleased both. It was harder to escape the class structure than either the countess or the shoemaker imagined.

In London Margaret saw the imperial Parliament at close quarters. Ladies could enter the ventilator room above the ceiling of the Westminster Commons to see and hear debates or they might sit behind the

red curtain on either side of the throne in the Lords. Margaret was unimpressed with what she heard. With her father in Cork she had been aware of corrupt electioneering and in Dublin had listened to quarrelling parliamentarians. London was worse. In her utopian novel she imagined a moon man expecting much from the extolled English legislature but on examination finding it no different from any of the foreign absolutist regimes that so appalled the British, except that

> there is more corruption & more expence in the support of it. And as to the liberty they boast of, one of its chief privileges seems to consist in the power of scolding each other within the walls of a large building where some hundreds of them assemble at certain periods under pretence of legislating for the nation at large.

In the same novel she also criticized an aspect of English political life Mary Wollstonecraft approved: the lowliest in England think themselves entitled to share in government and "fancy their opinions, of consequence to their rulers, and thousands write and read newspapers." Other visitors had been impressed that ordinary Englishmen were reading about current events, and men such as Thomas Hardy were a product of this culture. As usual Margaret's opinions were hybrid.

Mostly she encountered people of her own class, some of whom shared her liberal enthusiasms. One may have been another Irish visitor, Valentine Lawless, with whom her husband, Stephen, had been in school in Black Rock. He was from a liberal Catholic family, the eldest son and heir of Lord Cloncurry and, like Margaret, he supported the accused in the Treason Trials. While she visited Hardy, he went off to dine with Horne Tooke in his cottage on Wimbledon Common. Margaret and Lawless would meet again in Dublin.

Of her mother and sisters out at Windsor she probably saw little, although they were within easy reach. The rift between her and Caroline had not been bridged by Margaret's obedient marriage. When a mother severely treated a child, she could not, in Margaret's view, expect that

child to grow up to become a friend, however much the parent might have wished it. Also their political views continued to diverge. Caroline was now closely connected to Queen Charlotte and playing a role in her household. She was even closer to Lady Harcourt, one of the Queen's most intimate ladies-in-waiting. In this milieu Caroline was struggling to fit Mary for court appearances and would not wish to be deflected from her purpose by an opinionated older daughter. Margaret shunned such society and such events and, during her stay in England, was not listed in the court assemblies and Drawing Rooms the Irish aristocracy would be expected to attend.

Her avoidance was intentional. She had by now seen enough of high life to notice that English aristocrats looked down on their Irish cousins. She came even more to despise people such as Caroline, who chose to spend so much time in a foreign country, where they had nothing of the status and significance they enjoyed on their family estates:

> Sorry am I to say, that a contempt for their native land is a sentiment, which will without difficulty be acquired by the majority of our nobility, amongst whom it has long been a fashion to despise, and to ridicule the country and the people which support them. But we should console ourselves with the recollection that they compose but a small part of the inhabitants of the Island, and that the share of talents and virtue which they possess is *not* considerable.

Her sojourn in England made her realize the necessity of the Parliament in Dublin, however corrupt and inadequate.

Stephen failed to follow his wife in her developing opinions. Like Caroline, he enjoyed hobnobbing with noblemen, where Margaret actively sought out freethinkers and radicals. He thought her odd and eccentric; she said he respected "nothing but wealth and titles."

.CHAPTER 8.

United Irishmen and the Orange Order

What have you got in your hand?
A green bough.
Where did it first grow?
In America.
Where did it bud?
In France.
Where are you going to plant it?
In the crown of Great Britain.

—FROM THE UNITED IRISH CATECHISM

MARGARET RETURNED FROM LONDON WITH POLITICAL VIEWS closer to Wollstonecraft's, a contempt for the British government in Westminster and an increased desire to help the struggle for Irish independence, whether or not this meant complete separation from England. Back in Dublin her revolutionary play became more earnest and she joined the political group that would dominate Irish politics through the next four years: the United Irishmen. It was a momentous step. Lady Moira did not openly identify herself with the society, some of whose egalitarian aims she could never have approved, but she often acted as a fellow traveler and useful ally, and she probably knew of Margaret's loyalties. Like most thinking Anglo-Irish women, such as the novelist Maria Edgeworth, Lady Moira held to a sense of the political "feminine" role, preferring personalities and manners to abstract issues. Margaret, pupil of Mary Wollstonecraft, was quite different.

The United Irishmen had developed only slowly into a great force, built by middle-class people who first supported reform, then became radicalized. In 1791, the year when the Honorable Margaret King married the Earl of Mount Cashell, the first society had been founded in Belfast. Believing that sectarian divisions and the Castle's exploitation of them had kept Ireland weak, the Presbyterian William Drennan submitted a plan to the Belfast Volunteers for an Irish brotherhood that would seek Catholic relief and diminish Castle influence. Then in October, with his fellow Protestant Wolfe Tone, he founded the first society of United Irishmen in Belfast: the initial article of the constitution was the "forwarding a brotherhood of affection, a communion of rights, and an union of power among Irishmen of every religious persuasion." Three weeks after Belfast, an equivalent society began in Dublin.

For both the object was to "make all Irishmen citizens and all citizens Irishmen." Henry Grattan's reforms were no longer enough and the United Irishmen wanted speedy and structural change. They saw this change as inevitable, almost ordained. As their newspaper, the judiciously radical *Northern Star,* declared: "The present is an age of revolution. Everything is changing, every system is improving and mankind appear to become more wise and virtuous, as they become more informed. This is the consequence of knowledge, the effect of intelligence, the result of truth and reason."

Initially the society posed little threat to Dublin Castle. In 1792 Wolfe Tone took part in the Bastille Day demonstrations in Belfast, consisting of a parade and dinner. The parade was led by dragoons; then came a portrait of Benjamin Franklin and the flags of "the Five Free Nations," namely, Ireland, the United States, France, Poland—and Great Britain. There followed the Irish Volunteers and the artillery of the Belfast Blues, all props of the Ascendancy. At the center of the procession was a great standard on a cart drawn by four horses, on one side of which the "Releasement of the Prisoners from the Bastille" was represented while on the other was the image of Hibernia in chains being offered the statue of liberty by an Irish Volunteer. The standard was

escorted by the second brigade of the Volunteers and the procession was closed with a portrait of the French patriot Mirabeau with the inscription "Our Gallic brother was born in 1789. We are still in embryo." At the subsequent banquet Tone thumped his glass on the table so hard after each toast that he finally broke it. The first toast was to the "King of Ireland," George III, called "the best of kings."

In his speech at his court-martial six years later Wolfe Tone declared, "From my earliest youth I have regarded the connexion between Ireland and Great Britain as the curse of the Irish nation; and felt convinced that whilst it lasted, this country could never be free nor happy." But clearly this had not always been his view. The notion of Irish independence had surfaced intermittently as an idea but only in the 1790s did it seem possible that the nation could exist entirely alone, unconnected not only with England but also with Spain or France, the usual alternatives. Lord Clare early denounced all United Irishmen and all reform as separatist, but most believed Castle policy as much as United Irishmen ideology responsible for making independence the main issue. In this view Clare, not Wolfe Tone, was the catalyst.

Initially the idea of independence was perplexing. Many Protestants realized that unless sects melted away, an independent Ireland would be Catholic and not republican. Also *English* ideals of liberty, on which much of the thinking was based, had precisely been defined against the despotic regimes of Continental Roman Catholicism. Yet now *Catholic* France had managed a secular revolution. Could it be a model for Ireland?

Another difficult area was equality—financial and social. The natural rights preached by Wollstonecraft and Paine emphasized considerable redistribution of wealth. But although United Irishmen praised Tom Paine and sang French revolutionary ballads, there was not much in the published program about social reform and economic equality— intentionally so, since they wanted "to attend to those things in which we agree, to exclude from our thoughts those in which we differ." Some aimed to split great estates into small farms, as Mary Wollstonecraft proposed, and reform the agrarian laws. Others were unsure, desiring merely

"a more equal distribution of the benefits and blessings of life." Most hated the Ascendancy but not the entire system of rank: the middle-class lawyers at the head of the movement were not of the people and did not speak in brogue. "By liberty we never understood unlimited freedom, nor by equality the levelling of property, or the destruction of subordination." All in all it was easier and more immediately necessary to concentrate on remedying sectarian inequalities than class (and gender) ones. Catholics should sit in a new state Parliament; few thought women, or men without property should be there.

Since revolutions were supposed to end history—as the French one had done in France—the United Irishmen tended to believe there was little need for concentrating on the confusing and bloody past that pitted Catholic against Protestant, Irish against Anglo-Irish, settler against native. Now this unjust past would be swallowed up in a clear present. Wolfe Tone was especially keen to make the new society, born of northern Protestant Dissent, appeal to Catholics, so ceremonies were invented to cut across the sectarian divide. There were parades, meetings, festivals and songs using popular Irish tunes. The harp, a symbol both of old Ireland and of Ireland's relationship with Britain—Henry VIII had associated the two when proclaimed King of Ireland—was adopted as emblem. It was given a modern motto: "I am new strung and shall be heard." Green was the chosen color and it became fashionable to wear it, if only in a handkerchief, ribbon or garter. Members adopted the cropped hair of French republicans and were nicknamed "croppies" by their enemies.

In 1793 the United Irishmen changed. War had been declared between Britain and France, and as Pitt's government grew hostile to reformist organizations in England and Scotland, so it came to see the United Irishmen as a terrorist society in league "to deliver the kingdom to a FOREIGN INVADER." They were banned and went underground. From then onward, separation from England became a common goal. France had led the way to a new future, and England and Ireland would follow once they had broken their suffocating connection. The privileging of an alien elite in Ireland supported by England had led to corrup-

tion; when the link between the countries was gone, the Ascendancy would collapse.

Forbidden open meetings, the movement chose other means to gain and support members. They enrolled recruits through clubs, fairs, horse races, lottery groups, social gatherings, funeral processions and Masonic meetings—no doubt to the horror of loyalist Masons such as the Kings and Ogles. Ominously for the government, they infiltrated the militias and used their musters to bring in new members. To get their message across they employed newspapers and pamphlets, and they stuck anonymous broadsheets in coffeehouses and on public walls. The Lord Chancellor, Lord Clare, acknowledged the power of the media campaign, admitting the press was "used with signal success as an engine of rebellion. Sedition and treason have been circulated with increasing industry, in newspapers and pamphlets, handbills and speeches, republican songs and political manifestos."

Secret signs and words welded the disparate outlawed groups together. William Drennan proposed a test for members that would "strike the soul through the senses." Masonic-type rituals had a purpose. For example, two members would recognize each other by a series of actions. The first lifted his right hand and drew it down the right side of his face; the second lifted the left and took it down the left side of the face. Both shook left hands, then one asked, "What do you know?" to which the other replied, "I know U—. What do you know more?" To which the reply was "I know T," or any other letter of the word *unity* or *united*.

Oaths frightened as well as bound, and rumors circulated about their content. Some groups made members vow to "assist the French in case of invasion," while others distrusted foreigners. Some oaths were said to urge the killing of their enemies, but the official United Irish oath in 1795 simply made a member swear to persevere in obtaining "an equal, full, and adequate representation of *all* the people of Ireland." Even here there was a new radicalism. The formula dropped a phrase in Drennan's initial oath: "in Parliament." Over the years the agenda had become more republican and populist.

The activity appalled Lord Clare. He saw the United Irishmen as corrupt, cynical men preying on gullible people, a conspiracy of "a deluded peasantry aided by more intelligent treason." In the London Parliament, in which he sat by virtue of his mother's English family, Lord Moira tried to counter this view and to alert Pitt's government to the danger of responding with unthinking repression. The "desperate body of men denominated *United Irishmen* were a product of government terror," he asserted. Persecuting them could only inflame matters in Ireland and this in turn would impact on England, already in turmoil: following an attack on George III's coach, the government rushed through Sedition and Treason Bills giving themselves powers to suppress political meetings and unwelcome pamphlets.

Within Ireland the United Irishmen were flanked by more sectarian movements. One was the predominantly Catholic Defenders. These invoked history, looking more to an idyllic Celtic past before the Ascendancy gripped the land than to the enlightened future of the United Irishmen. They concentrated on the traditional Whiteboy goal of reducing tithes and rents—although they were less antiproperty and raided Protestant houses more to grab arms than to destroy. Their genesis was obscure. In the American rebellion the Catholics had made use of English troubles to gain economic and political concessions at the expense of Protestants, especially Presbyterian weavers in the north, who saw their wages undercut. Some of the more militant became Peep O'Day Boys, making dawn raids on Catholics to steal their weapons and smash their looms. It was claimed that Defenderism, the most secretive of the opposition movements, was a response.

By the early 1790s Defenders had spread throughout the north down to Dublin, and their demands were becoming revolutionary. In Ulster they might fight Presbyterians, but there were few of these in the midlands and the south, and there they turned their force on landlords. Soon they went further, swearing to "quell all nations, to dethrone all kings and plant the Tree of Liberty in our Irish land whilst the French Defenders will protect our cause, and the Irish Defenders pull down

British laws." Like the United Irishmen, they learned from Masons and called their cells "lodges." They made joining exciting and staying out terrifying, and they frightened landowners by meeting at night and blackening their faces for raids.

Opposing the United Irishmen and Defenders, a third group now started up: the Protestant Orange Order. Its members feared that concessions to Catholics would make Protestants a beleaguered minority in Ireland and diminish their influence and power. There was immediate friction between the groups. Some United Irishmen allegedly made members vow to "kill the Orangemen," while they spread the rumor that Orangemen had sworn an oath to exterminate all Catholics. Both used belligerent songs, such as this Orange one:

> We'll fight to the last in the honest old cause,
> And guard our religion, our freedom and laws,
> We'll fight for our country, our King and his crown,
> And make all the traitors and croppies lie down.
> Down, down, croppies lie down.

Like other societies, the Orange Order thrived especially in Ulster among the lower and middle classes, but as battle lines hardened, gentry and men of property joined. By the end of the '90s the Dublin Orange lodge included lords and prominent men, and the movement was estimated to have about eighty thousand members professing king and country. Inevitably such a group could be harnessed by the Castle administration, while all three organizations had potential for violence.

The radical poet Henrietta Battier saw the Defenders as entirely patriotic and defensive, while the Orange Order, the "boys of the ascendancy," expressed "malice, virulence and spleen" and existed to support the "bondage of our hundred years." To Margaret, however, there was little to choose between the two: one was a Protestant rabble, the other a Catholic one, but she was appalled to see the Orangemen being used by the Castle: "Government . . . considering the Orange party . . . the most

dangerous, adopted the method which has since been pursued, of protecting and countenancing them in opposition to the [Defenders]; by which means they have been rendered the dupes of designing men, who regard their welfare as little as the welfare of the Papist mob."

Before the land was given over to what appeared inevitable violence, there was a last chance for peaceful reform. In the early months of the French war Pitt in London had ordered the passive Lord Lieutenant Westmorland in Dublin Castle to allow a measure of change in Ireland. To the horror of Robert King, his son George and their ally George Ogle, the Catholics could now vote for MPs on the same basis as Protestants, sit on juries and hold junior commissions in the army, though they could not be in Parliament. Liberal politicians in Ireland and England such as Lord Moira and Charles James Fox believed it sensible to continue and complete the process of emancipation. Otherwise there would never be lasting peace in Ireland.

In both London and Dublin the opposition of such men had been weak and disorganized ever since the French war began. They had disapproved the belligerent government policy but found themselves wrongfooted when the war assumed the form of a patriotic crusade against anarchy and atheism. So Lord Moira's warnings about the oppression in Ireland went unheeded. By 1794, however, the war was going badly and Pitt needed the support of the opposition. He made overtures and in July the most conservative of the group, the Duke of Portland, joined his cabinet. To Fox and Moira it was a sellout but Portland made one useful condition: that his friend, a rich Yorkshire magnate and absentee Irish landowner, Earl Fitzwilliam, be sent to Ireland in place of Westmorland, that "dull cipher of a Lord Lieutenant," as Lady Sarah Napier called him.

Fitzwilliam made no secret of his dislike of Clare and his allies—the men whom Lady Sarah called the "toad-eaters of the Castle"—or of his admiration for Henry Grattan and the reformist agenda. A social conservative, close friend of Edmund Burke and neutral on the emotive

topic of the slave trade, he realized that Ireland under the Ascendancy had fewer necessary constraints on power than England:

> Its being so completely aristocratical leaves the lower orders *without protection;* and in that example we may learn what tyrants we aristocrats can be when there is no check whatever on the selfish bent of the human mind—Happy the country where there is such an alloy of democracy as brings the overbearing inclinations of the great to a fellow feeling for the low.

On 4 January 1795 Fitzwilliam was sworn in at Dublin Castle. He had strict orders from Pitt to dismiss no crown officers, to continue old policies and to move slowly. This seemed to contradict his remit from Portland, so he disregarded Pitt. Margaret, Lady Moira and their circle were hopeful. In early February he started on his "new system" by allowing Grattan to introduce measures for complete Catholic equality—in Grattan's view the only way to head off a threat of outright rebellion from the United Irishmen.

The policy might have worked, but with so many enemies in the Castle it had no chance. "To reform all these flagrant abuses, which so immediately prevent the securing peace in Ireland . . . must raise the hornets' nest," Lady Sarah remarked.

Indeed it did, and for once Robert and Lord Shannon found themselves on the same side, along with the irate Lord Clare. They formed a committee to oppose Fitzwilliam's policies and alert the Westminster government. Soon messengers reached George III and Pitt telling them of the Lord Lieutenant's disobedience. The King was especially appalled at the notion of Catholics in Parliament—he had sworn a coronation oath specifically to defend the Church of England against them. When he heard of Fitzwilliam's activity, even Portland observed that his protégé was moving too quickly. It was put about that the new Lord Lieutenant was covertly supporting the French.

So Pitt recalled Fitzwilliam at the end of February. He had been in Dublin only a couple of months. In his place came Earl Camden, appointed to defend the Ascendancy at any cost. While shops were shut in mourning and Fitzwilliam's carriage was drawn to the water's edge by cheering crowds, his successor was sworn in to the sound of riots stirred by the oratory of Grattan, who said of Clare and the Castle junta, "They will extinguish Ireland, or Ireland must remove them." Clare's windows were broken and his forehead hit as he rode home from the ceremony in his stylish carriage. Fitzwilliam's recall left Ireland "on the brink of civil war."

Camden, who declared that the "English Interest" required firm resistance to reform, began his reign by appointing Protestant hardliners, including Robert Stewart, later Lord Castlereagh, as acting chief secretary for Ireland. This aristocratic young man, fresh from his grand tour and a stint in the militia, was his nephew by marriage as well as being nephew to Lady Louisa Conolly, who valued him highly. Her sister Lady Sarah disagreed and called Castlereagh "ignorant, vain, shallow," but politically he and Lord Clare made a formidable pair.* From now on few expected peaceful change. Clare boasted he would "make the seditious as tame as domestic cats," a quip that would return to plague him even in his coffin. Soldiers were licensed to seek out illegal arms and use torture to find them. They could use whatever measures they needed to prevent dangerous assemblies without consulting the civil authorities.

While Robert, his son George, Ogle and their allies felt relief at this turn of events, elsewhere there was a sense of betrayal and many rushed to join the United Irishmen: "Great classes who were as yet very slightly disaffected, now passed rapidly into republicanism, and Catholic opinion, which had been raised to the highest point of excited hope, experienced a complete, a sudden, and a most dangerous revulsion." The United Irishmen decided the country was becoming ripe for revolution

---

* For my story the chief politicians are Lords Clare and Castlereagh, but I am aware that in the wider history of the 1790s Edward Cooke, undersecretary of state and controller of the secret service, was of equal importance.

and they resolved to appeal directly to France for military aid. Wolfe Tone was dispatched as agent to negotiate. Despite his broken French, he found Paris responsive. When she later contemplated this crucial time, Margaret echoed Thomas Addis Emmet's view that rebellion had been provoked not by democratic ideas and French principles but by Castle policies. Lady Moira and her daughter Selina agreed. Both were alarmed at the government's handling of dissidents around the Moira estate, many of whom on flimsy evidence were flogged and sent to the fleet without proper trials. They were no keener on democracy than they had been before, but Castle policies were radicalizing even them. Both believed the government was fomenting sectarian differences to thwart change.

A new development now alarmed the Castle. To hurry on the revolution the United Irishmen merged with the Defenders; in the patronizing words of the Irish poet Thomas Moore, the one brought intelligence and republican spirit, and the other deep-rooted discontent and numerical force. Despite different aims, the two organizations were allies in struggle and the merger allowed the United Irishmen to use the Defenders' network of cells. Violence accelerated and government accusations of terrorism became apt.

Horrifying to men such as Clare, the combination of United Irishmen and Defenders troubled moderate landowners such as Richard Lovell Edgeworth, who began calling the disaffected peasants by the emotive French revolutionary term "sans culottes"—though he noted this was a literal description, since they had no breeches:

> [N]ow the sans culottes of Ireland are inured to blood and murder. . . .
> an insurrection of such people who have been much oppressed must be
> infinitely more horrid than any thing that has happened in France—for
> no hired executioners need be sought from the Prisons or the gallies
> every man is ready to be his own executioner.

The spectacle was frightening: "the lowest order of the people has been long oppressed—they are ignorant from habit cruel & vindictive— they are crass sans culottes & without prevention the most horrid

calamities may ensue." The Arms and Gunpowder Act of 1793 had
restricted firearms and made it illegal to import or move them across the
country, hence the need to manufacture weapons at home. As a result,
trees, so aesthetically planted by landowners, were cut down at night to
make the eight-to-twelve-foot staffs for pikes, while rebellious black-
smiths forged metal heads. Although crude weapons, pikes were effective at close quarters against cavalry and ferocious in the dark. The
United Irishmen openly celebrated French victories against the British
with bonfires. Dublin became "combustible."

The other side was no less forceful, and its force destroyed many traditional public rights. As Edgeworth also remarked, "The monied &
landed Interest are Whipped in with the old Cry of Church & State, and
ten to one but in the bustle a leg or arm of the Liberty of the Press may be
pulled off as if by accident." Well informed by spies, the Castle government
responded to the threat of rebellion with draconian measures. The Insurrection Act was passed in March 1796, condemning to death any who
administered unlawful oaths and imposing curfews on disturbed areas; in
October Habeas Corpus was suspended.

Now to strengthen British regiments and local militias the Castle
established the Yeomanry; it was put under strict Castle control and Grattan at once labeled it an "Ascendancy Army." It pleased few: the United
Irishmen found it provocative, the Yeomen saw themselves as overcon-
trolled, and civilians still felt unprotected. Lady Sarah Napier, wife of a
disciplined regular army man, was afraid of all kinds of "*rabble*," including this one: "I am not the least afraid of the Catholicks, but very much
of the mob in all places," she remarked.

Most householders dreaded soldiers being billeted on them, but some
ladies in provincial towns foreshadowed Jane Austen's younger Bennet
girls in welcoming the increased masculine presence. The Bishop of Limerick wrote to his unmarried niece,

If you have a mind to make your choice out of all these valiant Hero's
make Haste before they get themselves otherwise engaged . . . I walk'd

out this evening to Parade, and every House in that Quarter, had all the
Windows fill'd with Three Dress'd Caps in each, Like the Hot Roasted
Pigs in Lubberland, with Knives and forks in their Backs, crying come
eat me.

With its troops and new powers the Castle now went on a military
offensive; Clare and Castlereagh ordered no concessions to dissidents or
their supporters. The often undisciplined militiamen and yeomenry
burned cabins and tortured those suspected of concealing arms; they
even flogged a schoolteacher because he knew French. The United Irishmen were similarly brutal and there were stories of scalping and hacking
of limbs from captured soldiers and recalcitrant landowners. Anger
against the rebels ran so high that Clare even agreed with a supporter
that summary executions would be appropriate, since civil and military
trials were too slow; all those suspected of being United Irishmen should
be executed at once: "We should put to death ten for every one."

A picture of Margaret in these troubled years comes from Hugh
MacDermot, a Catholic doctor with whom she became friendly while
staying in Roscommon. He described her as a "second Lady Bountiful . . .
the cleverest of the family . . . She is above the little frivolous vanities and
amusements of her sex; she is young, handsome, rich, high in rank and
happy in situation."

If she struck an onlooker so, it was perhaps because she now had an
identity and knew what she stood for. Despite her Ascendancy position
and ties of blood and marriage, she was committed to the United Irish
cause. As society became polarized "it becomes the duty of an individual
to declare his opinions, and to throw his mite of disapprobation into the
national fund," she wrote. There was a difference between the "peer who
dwells in the decorated palace" and "the peasant who exists in the moul-
dering hovel" but each was oppressed as an Irishman; they must combine
to resist, accepting that the connection with England was "unnatural."

Margaret now saw herself as ineradicably Irish, not *Anglo*-Irish. Many

of her society felt "in-between," both different from and similar to their English relatives, but Margaret was sure she was simply Irish, connected with everyone living on the island. Her "Countrymen" were those "who first drew breath in this persecuted land . . . who inhale the native air of Ireland." A maneuver of the Castle and London was to rewrite the non-sectarian dream of the United Irishmen as "*a Catholic republic.*" Her own Protestant background ensured that she disliked Catholicism as a religion as much as Mary Wollstonecraft had always done, but she was firm in desiring 'universal toleration.' On property she still remained ambivalent. Patriotism required some ownership, for why should a man fight to defend what he did not possess? Yet redistribution of property was not at the top of her list of wishes.

Without the nationalist agitation of these years, Wollstonecraft's teachings might have born other fruit and Margaret have developed a feminist consciousness that could have moved her governess's enlightened middle-class feminism into something more sensitive to difference. But national problems were too great, and national identity overrode sexual identity, as it did in the movement as a whole. Without any particular feminist agenda, many vigorous women such as the poet Henrietta Battier also joined the United Irish and took the "oath of secrecy." In Dublin and Belfast they formed groups much mocked by Castle supporters as "teapot societies." The libertarian *Press* urged women on, however: "In political changes you have been frequently the actuating principle," it noted. "Determine to act for the melioration of your country in the *mighty crisis which awaits her.*"

Women became useful as spies and couriers but inevitably not much of their activity was public; as Lady Moira noted, "*All that Matter . . . is matter* to talk over, not to write upon." They could take secret messages and carry into prisons weapons and ropes hidden on their bodies. The lively sisters of Valentine Lawless, well known to Margaret, had joined the society and helped United Irish prisoners by enabling their friends secretly to enter their jail each evening after dark, with the connivance of a sympathetic jailer. Highly placed women could work to control news

and useful rumor through their network of letters and drawing-room gossip. As a rich aristocrat, Margaret had some freedom of movement denied more sheltered middle-class women, and with her six-foot height and bearing, she could dress as a man and probably did so when need arose. She could liaise between leaders and keep her ears open for information in public rooms and assemblies, then pay for private couriers to take her messages; everyone knew "the power of Post-Office tricks," as Lady Moira put it.

The Castle, which had a developed intelligence system using the post office, paid spies and coast guard and Revenue services, also employed women to do their business. Some were aristocrats, acquaintances of Margaret; others came from the lower orders, such as the prostitute Bella Martin, who kept busy identifying spies, double agents and active dissidents for her masters. Then the republican *Union Star*—dubbed the "assassination sheet" because it ran lists of "detestable Traitors, as Spies and Perjured Informers"—identified her. She was a

> middle size woman, about thirty years of age, dresses in black, appears like a servant, speaks a northern dialect remarkably broad, she is very yellow, goes about at night as a woman of the town, in which character she has made several captures, by the assistance of two soldiers, who are always within reach of her signals; she was brought from Belfast by Government, lived some time in the Castle, at present lives in Pembroke-court, Castle-street.

There was not a lot she could do after this.

Without Stephen's knowing, Margaret could also provide safe lodgings in the family's capacious houses to those arriving with the correct tokens or passwords; there is some evidence she employed the cellars of Moore Park for the purpose. But her main use was probably with her pen. She was certainly involved in the intellectual debate of the United Irishmen—whether to rely on themselves or foreign powers; whether to have single or collective leadership; whether to stress democratic or

nationalist, social or economic aims; how much violence was justified to attain the desired ends—and she seems to have written pamphlets for the cause, though with their repeated rhetoric the anonymous documents are hard to attribute with any security. Even Henrietta Battier wrote her radical poems anonymously, although she made it clear that hers was a "female pen."

Margaret understood the power of patriotic history and in these years she also set about writing a large novel. It would transpose the present Irish rebellion into the reign of Queen Elizabeth I, when the English were menaced by the Spanish as they were now by the French. In the three volumes of her fiction "The Chieftains of Erin," stalwart and noble Irish chieftains, spurred by the "unjust acts and unwarrantable tyranny of the English," come together in romantic locations to plot the expulsion of their oppressors in Dublin Castle—so allowing Margaret to rhapsodize about native Irish customs while displaying her sense of aristocratic blood honor. In the novel the English and Irish are completely distinguished by language, dress, habits, food and weapons, details of which Margaret took less from childhood observation in County Cork than from the antiquarian books of Joseph Cooper Walker and Charlotte Brooke. Lady Moira probably encouraged the project since she herself was fascinated by ancient Irish customs and had earlier supplied much information to Walker for his descriptions of historic costumes. It may have been at this time that Margaret began to study the Irish language in earnest.

But not everyone among her United Irish friends approved this mythicizing project or found it helpful in the present circumstances, when the overwhelming need was to unite Irish and Anglo-Irish, Ulster Presbyterians and Catholics. So Margaret abandoned her book. Years later, looking back on the stalled novel, she declared that "the spirit of party . . . ran too high and the prejudices of those days were too bitter, to allow such a composition to be viewed with impartial eyes." Also fiction had a way of escaping its declared political aim and in the tense moment of political discussion it might have been "mistaken or misconstrued"

even by the well-meaning. She put her manuscript by until more peaceful times.

If Margaret was not unique as a woman in joining and writing for the movement, she was rarer in being rich and noble—although again not unique. Others among the well-born included Valentine Lawless, now an influential member of the Leinster executive, his sisters, and the lawyer and landowner Archibald Hamilton Rowan, secretary of the Dublin branch.

Despite Curran's defense of him, Rowan had been imprisoned for distributing revolutionary leaflets, but he quickly escaped to France, where he encountered Mary Wollstonecraft—in whom he was shocked to find an unmarried mother. In the end he managed to tolerate her "republican marriage" and, while always disapproving, was happy to have "spirited conversation" and tea with her. It was ironic that a few years later her name would be blackened by an accusation of an affair with this handsome, chunky man who could countenance political but not sexual revolution.

First among the few noblemen of the United Irishmen was the flamboyant son of the Duchess of Leinster, brother of the present Duke, Lord Edward Fitzgerald, now back from France. Margaret had always known him or of him, but now they were brought together by politics. She left no direct description of him but in "The Chieftains of Erin" she portrayed a noble son of an Irish chieftain as "young, bold, impetuous and enthusiastic," a man "to be dreaded as a leader of the rebels," and it is likely that Lord Edward sat for the portrait. Edward spoke openly to Margaret of his changed views, telling her how much he regretted serving with the British army in America and wishing he had fought on the rebel side. Now he had abandoned the cause of parliamentary reform in his cousin Charles James Fox's manner and was seeking revolutionary change. Only an armed struggle against Castle rule could make an Irish republic. The young man in "The Chieftains of Erin" thought the same.

Despite their similarities of status, Margaret and Edward had contrasting family backgrounds. Although having little sympathy with Catholic

natives, the Leinsters had long felt irritated with English rule and often with Castle dictates. However, the Kings had by now thrown in their lot very thoroughly with the Castle and were staunch upholders of the British monarchy. Emotionally too the families were distinct. Beside the coldly conservative and mannered Caroline, the Duchess of Leinster, Lord Edward's mother, was in sentimental mode, gushing and family-oriented and as demonstrative as demanding with her affections. Letters between her and Edward read like love letters and were pored over with similar intensity by both.

Edward had chosen a wife in the same emotional style as his mother, the exotic Pamela. She was termed "Mademoiselle Egalité" by the press, who, along with most of the Leinsters and probably Pamela herself, suspected she was the natural daughter of the revolutionary Duke of Orleans, Philippe, nicknamed "Egalité." Her supposed mother was the Duke's mistress, the educational writer and woman of letters Madame de Genlis, whose books Wollstonecraft had taught Margaret and Mary during her stint in Ireland. Though probably the daughter of an English couple, as Madame de Genlis always maintained, Pamela had been raised in the hothouse atmosphere of the Orleans court, where her foster mother encouraged her theatrical quality. "Act Héloïse," Madame de Genlis commanded one day for the benefit of her friends, and the seven-year-old Pamela immediately let down her hair, fell on her knees and assumed the ecstatic posture of Rousseau's heroine. On the day of the Bastille's fall she dressed in red and rode out on horseback with a plumed hat. No wonder Lord Edward at once fell in love with her. His emotion was helped by her white skin, dark eyes and curls, resembling those of his dead mistress, Elizabeth Sheridan.

On 27 December 1792 they were married. On hearing the news his aunt Lady Sarah Napier commented, "Edward Fitzgerald has acted a romance throughout all his life, and it is finished by his marriage to Pamela." Their existence together continued theatrical: "Pamela has frenzies of fondness for Edward, and he takes her off, throwing her arms round his neck." The pair were effortlessly celebrities. Even the *Anthologia*

*C*aroline King, Lady
Kingsborough (later
Countess of Kingston),
as a young woman

*R*obert King, Lord
Kingsborough (later
2nd Earl of Kingston),
as a young man

George King when a pupil at Eton, painted by George Romney

Mary Wollstonecraft, Margaret and Mary King's governess, painted in 1791

Early miniature of Margaret King, Wollstonecraft's favorite pupil, from a miniature attributed to Charles Robertson

"*Economy* and denial are necessary in every station
to enable us to be generous." William Blake's illustration to
Mary Wollstonecraft's *Original Stories* (1788)

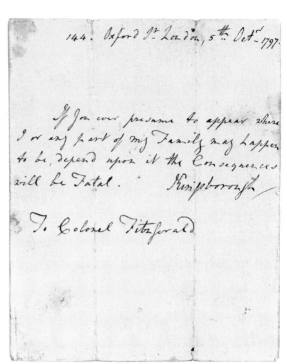

Letter from Robert King, Lord Kingsborough, threatening his daughter's lover, Colonel Henry Gerald Fitzgerald

Robert Stewart, Lord Castlereagh, Chief Secretary for Ireland, after a portrait by Sir Thomas Lawrence

John Fitzgibbon, 1st Earl of Clare, Lord Chancellor of Ireland, from a painting by Gilbert Stuart

Pamela Fitzgerald
(née Sims) painted in
theatrical attitude by
George Romney

Lord Edward Fitzgerald
after a portrait by Hugh
Douglas Hamilton

Elizabeth Rawdon-
Hastings, Countess of
Moira, Margaret's friend
in the 1790s

A militiaman pitchcapping a suspected rebel in 1798

ℛebels piking Irish loyalists during the massacre on
Wexford Bridge, by George Cruickshank

George King, Lord Kingsborough (later 3rd Earl of Kingston)

Margaret Moore (née King), Countess of Mount Cashell, now calling herself Mrs. Mason, ca. 1810

Hibernica, which recorded few social events, noted the arrival and departure in Dublin of Lord Edward and Mademoiselle Egalité. When Drennan
spied them, he remarked, "[Edward] and his elegant wife will lead the
fashion of politics in a short time." Their combined appearance and her
background fascinated everyone. Light, quick, talkative and not especially
intelligent, Pamela enchanted with her "candour and sensibility."

Both had the aristocratic obsession with symbolic clothes. Even
before it became the uniform of the United Irishmen Edward had taken
to wearing a short jacket, pantaloons, a round hat, a loose handkerchief
at his neck with its ends hanging down and unpowdered hair cut in
"croppie" manner. Shoes were tied by string. It was an upper-class version
of lower-class gear and a French revolutionary statement. Often the
neckerchief was green or red silk, openly declaring Irish nationalism or
revolution. On one occasion when he was leaving a race in Kildare the
obnoxious green cravat was spied by crown officers. They demanded he
remove it. He stood firm and dared any man to step forward and take it
off. He heard no more of the matter. He was even more impulsive where
Pamela was concerned. At the theater in Smock Alley an actor added the
line "Damn the French" to his text; seeing offense to the Revolution and
Pamela, Lord Edward jumped up and hissed. Many in the pit loudly
applauded him, but one bystander remarked of the young man, "I think
he will come to some untimely end."

Pamela too assumed aspects of peasant style, sometimes appearing
in black stockings with a red cloak, her head bound with a red handkerchief. She wore short petticoats and either black gowns or skimpy white
dresses, and she tied black and scarlet ribbons round her stockings.
Ladies adopted her style, although to avoid too heavy a tinge of democracy they embroidered their gowns heavily in white.

The pair also adopted "low" habits. To the relief of his stuffy brother,
William, Duke of Leinster, they moved out of Leinster House into a small
lodge in Kildare. There they lived a domestic idyll with Lord Edward's
black servant and several helpers from the nearby town. It was based
more on fashionable English rusticity than rural Irish reality but Edward

was enthusiastic about his "dear wife's" performance "in her little American jacket, planting sweet peas and mignonette." "When I am with Pam and the child, of a blustering evening, with a good turf fire and a pleasant book, coming in after seeing my poultry shut up, my garden settled, flower beds and plants covered for fear of frost, the place looking comfortable and taken care of, I shall be as happy as possible," he enthused. Adding the spice of treason, they put a picture of Tom Paine over the mantelpiece and drank rebellious toasts by their turf fire in Irish whiskey punch to "Mother Erin, dress'd in green ribbons by a French milliner, if she can't be dress'd without her!" To make theater more real they dined with apothecaries and danced with servants.

Lord Edward was so entranced with his wife he thought all felt the same. "Everyone seems to like [Pamela], and behave civilly and kindly to her," he wrote. But there were many scoffers. One lady mocked the red cloak and ribbons, "which we have an idea here is the Jacobin Uniform in France and when her head is bound up with a dirty handkerchief people suspect it is soiled with the Blood of Louis the 16th."—an allusion to the fact that her supposed father, the Duke of Orleans, had voted for the death of his royal cousin. At a Rotunda ball in her strange dress Pamela danced so enthusiastically that she kept revealing her stockings. "The Company (some of the genteelest in Dublin) star'd at her with so much curiosity that she went away crying." Happily, Lord Edward's family approved of her, especially his aunt Lady Sarah, who called her "a sweet little, engaging, bewitching creature"—she might have been talking of a child.

Margaret became a close friend of Pamela and Edward, and both came to stay with her at Moore Park. On such occasions George, the antithesis of everything his sister stood for, presumably whisked his wife, Helena, away. They also met often in Dublin. Pamela spoke poor English and the friendship was much enhanced by Margaret's excellent French. Although they came to their position from different routes, both women were unconventional in dress and both stood out from the crowd. Both negotiated different worlds. Margaret remained with her socially conser-

vative husband, continued close friends with the haughty Lady Moira, and associated with United Irishmen. Like Lady Moira, she was not pious—the religious influence of Wollstonecraft had long worn off—and therefore had little problem with Pamela's Catholicism. She did not record whether she believed her new friend the daughter of the Duke of Orleans; if she did, she would have been less impressed had she seen her old governess's views of "Egalité": the "grossest libertine . . . the grand sultan" of a "den of iniquity," his heart as "tainted as the foul atmosphere he breathed.—Incapable of affection, his amours were the jaundiced caprices of satiety."

The United Irishmen welcomed the arrival of the high-profile Edward into their ranks, although there was some uneasiness at his assumption of natural leadership. As middle-class lawyers found it difficult to associate with "fellows with their elbows out," so Wolfe Tone could say that some were "too much connected with the aristocracy, to be really the friends of the people." He was thinking of Lord Moira rather than Edward but the point applied. All of them, including Margaret and Lady Moira, could be accused of wanting to retain some of the privileges of the nobility while claiming to speak for and understand all classes.

In the great debate about military tactics—of how Ireland was to be wrested by force from the English and their puppets in the Castle—many supported the idea that the uprising should be decentered and depend on the loyalty of peasants to their regional landlords. Edward, who had experience in the regular British army, insisted on forces being organized on a national scale, then augmented by disaffected militiamen once the rebellion started. He expected himself to be the leader; others were not sure. The rancorous discussions lasted nine months; then Edward became generalissimo. It was an opportune moment for action: oppression against Ulster, the usual site of disaffection, was now so intense that the initiative for rebellion had passed to Dublin.

The liberal landowner Richard Lovell Edgeworth remarked: "This Kingdom is at present hushed to grim repose—5000 men landed from

France in this country would make a strange disturbance." But he did not expect such a landing. Lady Sarah Napier had a similar impression. She noted how peaceably the regiments divided on Sunday mornings on the Parade to go to their several churches. Thus both watchers were taken unawares—as the Castle also was—by what happened next.

Ever since Wolfe Tone had formally invited them to Ireland, the French had been waiting for an opportunity to act. Now they learned that the Castle administration had dispersed its troops around the country while the rebels had managed to infiltrate most areas. So they appointed General Lazare Hoche, rival of the up-and-coming Napoleon Bonaparte, to take an invading force to Ireland with the object of discomfiting England. He would have fifteen thousand men and a fleet of forty-six ships; they would land at Christmas 1796 in the south of the island, seize Cork, then march to Dublin. They had been told the local Defenders and United Irishmen were well organized and that fifteen thousand men and five thousand horses would be ready to join them, but Tone stressed that the strength of the support would depend on French success.

Nothing went according to plan. Storms scattered the fleet and only seventeen ships arrived in Bantry Bay. No one was ready for them—the United Irishmen had expected an invasion in the spring and, when they had reports of the French in the south at Christmas, simply disbelieved them and imagined a Castle plot to disperse their forces. To the soldiers who had set off in high spirits from France the outlook was bleak: "Nothing in the world could have looked more sorry or desolate than the country which appeared before our eyes," wrote one. "It seemed uninhabited and we could see neither church towers, nor villages, nor any trace whatsoever of cultivation or population."

Although some Catholics did join the French, others saw them as atheists rather than fellow religionists and declared loyalty to George III. The winter was cold, the poor hungry and reluctant to let their animals fall into the hands of invaders, so some drove them from the coast. With so many setbacks the French became "a crippled fleet . . . uncertain of

their purpose"; they had nothing to do but straggle back to France in January. They had come to the wrong place at the wrong time. Above all they had not successfully liaised with the United Irishmen.

Although a failure, the invasion frightened the Castle. Despite their thick network of spies, they had had little warning and they knew they had won mainly through the Irish weather: as Castlereagh remarked, "the wind has saved us the trouble of driving the French away." But "those ancient and unsubsidised allies of England," as Sydney Smith called them, "allies upon which English ministers depend as much for saving kingdoms as washerwomen do for drying clothes," could not always be relied on and France was an increasingly powerful force. Pitt grew anxious and responded by covering the Irish coast with troops.

The invasion also sobered liberal aristocrats such as Lady Moira, who, for all her dislike of the Castle, did not approve "Gallic Ruffians" or "the Chimera of the Rights of Man." She was glad that, despite bribery, the peasants had not rallied to the cause of "Hoche and his Banditti."

The situation was delicate for her and her son. Both had some residual distrust of the United Irishmen, as their scorn for egalitarian rights suggests, yet both helped the movement, sometimes inadvertently. One United Irishman claimed he was "engaging & humbugging Ld Moira to advocate their cause." The nobleman was preparing a speech for the British House of Lords on the sorry condition of Ireland; to this end he employed a dozen clerks in his house noting down atrocities committed against Catholics. Unbeknownst to him, all were United Irishmen. Poor Lord Moira found it difficult to please anyone now. He was distrusted by the English and Anglo-Irish rulers, but also mocked by the United Irishmen, who at one meeting discussed his character "at full length, to know whether he was a man to be depended on, or not, by the people? It was agreed, that he was as great a tyrant as the Lord Lieutenant, and a deeper designing one."

The divisions in the Leinster family had clarified: although he later resigned, William, the duke, was at this point a colonel in the Kildare regiment of militia, his younger brother Edward the military leader of

the opposing United Irishmen. Indeed, they were so at odds that Edward avoided meeting his older brother and sometimes disguised himself when in the region of his old home, Leinster House. Their sister Lucy sided with Edward and when she visited Ireland spent many of her days in his rustic retreat. Meanwhile, the government's chief secretary, Lord Castlereagh, passed his time with their aunt Lady Louisa and went out riding with Lucy, who chattered to him about her enthusiastic views, which so completely opposed his own.

On one occasion when she was with Edward and Pamela, republican friends came to talk politics (and, it was said, atheism). Louisa got wind of it and sent Castlereagh to rescue her niece. She herself was staunchly against the French and their Revolution and feared the arrival of both in Ireland and specifically in her house at Castletown. In this she was prompted by her timid husband; as her sister Sarah commented, "he terrifies dearest Louisa with his croakings. And when she wakes she expects Robespierre or Danton to guillotine her before night." Deeply fond of Edward and Pamela, Sarah distanced herself from their politics, believing that "becoming an Independent people is not practicable without horrors worse a million times than the English Government, nor can it be done without the French whose *alliance* is sure to be usurpation, despotism and complete poverty if they succeeded."

Despite their disagreements, however, all the family members continued visiting and being visited. Lucy, Edward and Pamela were seen at a ball given by Lady Carhampton, wife of the courageous but intemperate military commander who, asked to suppress Defenders and United Irishmen, responded by cruelly impressing a thousand suspects into the Royal Navy. Lucy also attended a ball given by Lady Clare, wife of the Lord Chancellor: she compromised by wearing her "hair turned close up," so "was reckoned democratic and was not danced with."

The division in the Kings was more raucous. In contrast to Margaret's involvement with the United Irishmen, her eldest brother, George, joined the Orange Lodge and became a zealous supporter of the Ascendancy.

With the family friend George Ogle he took the oath that he would never forget William of Orange and Oliver Cromwell, "who assisted in redeeming us from popery, slavery, arbitrary power." Despite the lapsed Catholic background of many, the North Cork militia now under George's command openly wore signs of their Orange allegiance.

In sexual matters George was royally abusing his position as colonel; in this he followed family tradition. His father, Robert, was openly promiscuous and his great-uncle, Edward's elder brother, was so notorious a rake that his seductions had been memorialized in novels and ballads. George had become famous for having his will with women who needed his help for their menfolk. One officer reported his boasting that "a number of pretty women had come to him in behalf of their husbands, fathers or brothers; that he always said to them, 'If you'll grant me one favour, I'll grant you another.' " Apparently few refused these terms. When a soldier asked him for a pass, he denied it unless the man sent his sister to him; then he even promised to make him a corporal. He forced prisoners to bring women for his use and he was known to push his way into their rooms at night demanding services. Yet George was disgruntled: "I have been very unfortunate, since out of all of these I have hitherto only had two maidenheads," he complained.

He bullied men as well as women. There were stories of his entering houses to look for United Irishmen, declaring he would simply hang them "on the nearest tree" if found. His North Cork soldiers became notorious for their "pitch-cap" torture, instituted in mockery of the short republican hairstyle of the "croppies." In this the victims' hands were tied behind their backs and a cap of heavy paper or linen filled with tar or pitch and gunpowder placed on their heads, then set alight. They ran screaming as the burning tar ran down their faces, frequently blinding them; when the cap was pulled off it took the skin with it. Victims of such torture usually found something to tell.

One such incident was described by a horrified spectator near the Customs House in Dublin. He saw two men covered with pitch and blood

running blindly through the street followed by George and his friends, who were laughing immoderately and pointing at the "tortured fugitives." They were a ferry man and a coachman flogged to extract confessions but "having none to make, melted pitch was poured over their heads and then feathered." The right ear of one was cut off and both were stripped naked. George "superintended the flogging and almost at every lash asked them how they liked it." It is difficult to remember that this is the George about whose infant good temper his mother had boasted years ago.

Other King family members were less ferocious but equally loyal to the Castle. In Boyle, George's aging grandfather Edward joined neighboring landowners whose fear made them forget basic rights. He intercepted letters at the local post office and found one from a refugee in America to a prisoner in Castlebar jail for high treason. As obtuse as ever about what would please the government, he forwarded the letter to the Castle. It was promptly returned "and misapprobation expressed that the Post Master should give up any letters even to his Lordship." It was a comic reminder of Edward's earlier impolitic zeal for his earldom. With hindsight, however, his sort of officiousness was justified—the appointed government interceptor of mail in Dublin was later discovered to be a United Irishman.*

Ireland was by now "*really*" in a bad way, according to Lady Sarah Napier. The government was behaving so disastrously that she regarded it as actually fomenting civil war: "they *force* insurrection." The anxiety on all sides led to rumors and false accusations. People were turned into rebels by suspicion. Servants of great houses such as Mitchelstown, Moore Park and Castletown were arrested as thieves and United Irishmen, then punished; then their families took revenge. The violence sometimes brought together owners and servants, sometimes polarized them. Certainly some

---

* According to a London informer, William St. John was "a person in the letter department of the post office in Dublin. He used to have the care of searching suspicious letters. He joined the rebel camp at Wicklow and was a chief. . . . St John is a very desperate man for whom it is imagined the Irish govt. are in search." Information given by H.M. [November?] 1798, NLI MS 33, 043.

retainers were persuaded to plunder their employers' houses for arms; others, when urged, simply got drunk or frightened and took the oath of the United Irishmen without much thought of consequences. Some moved deviously, as a lady from County Wexford illustrates:

> Yesterday, rather a genteel looking man came up the lawn to me, and said he wished much to have the pleasure of instructing a few young ladies in geography, and begged I would allow him to teach my family. I told him my daughters were too young, and that I did not think he was likely to get any pupils in the neighbourhood. This day, as I was walking in the shrubbery near the road, I looked out, on hearing a number of horses, and saw the same young man under an escort going to jail, from information sent to Mr. Boyd by government. There was found upon him a plan of all our houses, the names and numbers of the inhabitants, and a copy of "Paine's Age of Reason."

In the midlands Richard Lovell Edgeworth and his daughter Maria saw cruelty on both sides. The soldiers dragged men from their beds, then shot them without trial. In one nearby village Maria heard of thirty-six houses burned down, leaving only two standing. Her father had just married the last of his four wives; on her way from Dublin to her new home the bride noticed the empty villages and was surprised until a woman at an inn whispered, "The boys [the rebels] are hid in the potato furrows beyond." Later she saw "something very odd on the side of the road." Her new husband told her to look away: "it was a car turned up, between the shafts of which a man was hung, murdered by the rebels."

They arrived home to find everyone safe and resigned. "We laugh and talk, and enjoy the good of every day, which is more than sufficient," wrote Maria. "How long this may last we cannot tell. I am going on in the old way, writing stories. I cannot be a captain of dragoons, and sitting with my hands before me would not make any of us one degree safer." Other Ascendancy families were quitting the country; good riddance, exclaimed the *Press*: the "corrupted and enslaved" Irish aristocracy had

long indulged in "senseless revelry and ruinous expence"; they were political prostitutes.

After the Bantry Bay fiasco the debate among the United Irishmen over whether or not to rely on the French intensified. Some in Dublin doubted that any foreigners could be of much help; surely it would be better if they relied more on themselves. Others felt the uprising could never succeed without outside assistance, however disastrous this first French essay had been. The debate was so acrimonious it slowed down proper preparations for rebellion with or without foreign help and Valentine Lawless, who wished to please both sides, was glad to be sent to London away from it all. There he would act as a center for Irish patriots and relay messages from the United Irish agent in Paris, though very little communication now came.

Meanwhile, those remaining in Dublin and supporting self-reliance noted that, following the failed French invasion and the dispatch of troops around the coast, the capital was left relatively undefended. It might be possible to take the city at once by themselves through seizing certain key spots—if allies outside Dublin could then prevent government reinforcements coming in from provincial garrisons. After that, armed with captured weapons and strengthened by new recruits, they would surely find all Ireland open to revolution.

Lord Edward liked the plan. He grew excited and ordered a new uniform ready for his combat role and military triumph. A fusion of Gallic and Celtic symbolism, it was based on the costumes designed by the artist David for the revolutionary French; it would have a green cape and jacket, with scarlet braiding, and a matching green and scarlet silk-tasseled cap of liberty.

At this point Margaret's Windsor family surfaced embarrassingly into public view. They provided a respite of entertaining scandal from grim news of house burning, pitch-capping and vengeful servants.

. C H A P T E R 9 .

Romance

Love is . . . an arbitrary passion, and will reign,
like some other stalking mischiefs, by its own authority,
without deigning to reason.

—MARY WOLLSTONECRAFT,
A VINDICATION OF THE RIGHTS OF WOMAN

THE SECOND HALF OF 1797 DID NOT BEGIN AUSPICIOUSLY. THE
nation was on edge and at the end of June an eclipse of the sun seemed
ominous. The Sedition Acts had largely quelled the rebellious in London but the outlying kingdoms and provinces remained insecure. A
resentful Prime Minister Pitt indulged in his vice of secret drinking.

Despite the precautions taken in the three kingdoms and despite
the unattractive imperial politics in Paris that had superseded the
French Revolution, British conservatives still sensed that radical infec-
tion was spreading. They were uneasy and made more so by the death,
just at this moment, of Edmund Burke. He was the great Irish theorist of
traditional England whom Mary Wollstonecraft had combated in her
first polemical work in 1790, the man who had so strenuously opposed
all violent revolution as prelude to tyranny. After what had happened in

France during the Terror, he now seemed more correct than many moderate people had supposed.

In Ireland both sides were ready for extreme measures. Attracted rather than deterred by the bloodletting that had followed the Revolution in France, a large meeting of rebels in the northern mountains considered massacring all aristocrats in the French manner, beginning at the top and working down through dukes and earls. The *Press* believed that, with Castle policy, "fathomless abysses yawn with destruction beneath our feet."

At first the Kings were out of step with this national misery. In early June a rich relative, Mrs. Walcot, died, leaving a rumored fortune of £60,000. Dublin speculated about the heirs; Lord Shannon remarked that there was more gossip about the matter than about the troubled times. To his dismay one candidate for the great legacy was the hated King family.

When the will was read, his fears were realized. The Kings had received the prize. Edward, the old Earl of Kingston, "arrive[d] to take possession of his immense acquisition, in a very heavy chaise heavily loaded, his valet by his side, and a pair of miserable rips that could hardly stand, and the driver discontented at his fare," wrote the irritated Lord Shannon. Edward and his son Robert each pocketed more than £20,000.

Politically too Robert was flourishing. Having given up his initial independent stance, he now found no difficulty holding his parliamentary seats. In 1797 he took the expensive course of getting himself elected for both Cork and Boyle, intending to use Boyle as a safety net should Cork fail him. Lord Shannon was predictably contemptuous at this display of power and wealth, although, given the desperate times, the feuding pair had occasionally now to collaborate for the sake of the "Protestant establishment." It was not easy for either.

Still deeply involved with his militia, Robert held positions in both Antrim and Cork. Margaret had approved his work with the Volunteers, whose "*Western* energy" she admired, but she did not relish this later military involvement, especially with the North Cork; the insistence on only

Protestant soldiers hardly helped heal the country's sectarian wounds. She cared even less for the violent militia activities of her brother George, who was increasingly making his mark on the country.

Given reports of troubles in Ireland and disagreements in her family, Caroline was pleased she had removed her younger daughter Mary to England, out of harm's way. In London and Windsor she continued her round of socializing with the well-connected, attended court and went to the opera and select parties. She was still a good-looking woman, but increasing years had accentuated the loquacity and arrogance that had so tormented Mary Wollstonecraft and appalled her young husband. "How [she] does talk!" remarked the Honorable Mrs. Calvert, an Irish beauty and one of her "friends." "And poor woman, how excellent does she think her own understanding and judgment. She really does not want for good sense, but by overvaluing it so much, one does not give her credit even for what she possesses." A few years later Mrs. Calvert was still being bored by the garrulous Caroline, who managed to silence even the overbearing French woman of letters, Madame de Staël.

Her daughter Mary was now fifteen. She had grown into a spirited, energetic and whimsical girl, less intellectual and more confident than her eldest sister at the same age. Like Margaret, she was not actually robust in health, despite her glowing appearance, but she avoided Margaret's interest in her own symptoms and was more of a tomboy. She was attractive but, again like Margaret, careless of her appearance. She could be strong-willed, although she appeared conciliatory and, like other pretty upper-class girls, expected life to please her, assuming, usually rightly, that her wishes would be attended to. This would be fine as long as they coincided with her mother's.

Mary had a good friend in a slightly older girl called Adèle, the pretty daughter of French émigré parents, who shared her enthusiastic temperament and passion for self-dramatizing. Adèle's mother had been lady-in-waiting to Mme. Adelaide, daughter of Louis XV, and Adèle had grown up at court, petted and spoiled by the royal family, rather like Pamela in the household of the Duke of Orleans. Mme. Adelaide would take the pretty

child for walks followed by a flock of servants, who carried Adèle's pet spaniel in a linen bag to prevent his paws becoming muddy. After the Revolution, the family fled the Terror and arrived in Naples, where Adèle appeared with Nelson's Lady Hamilton as one of Niobe's children in the kind of living tableau that had become the rage among the gentry.

Then they came to Brighton, where Adèle first met up with her mother's cousin Mrs. Fitzherbert, the Prince of Wales's morganatic wife, before moving on to London. The family had salvaged little money from revolutionary France and Adèle was now living with her parents in a small house in Brompton Square. Despite her romantic, courtly past, she was grateful to be friends with a girl like Mary, from such a rich family, and to receive frequent visits in her modest lodgings. Adèle regaled her new friend with her history and it was easy for both girls to see their future as a long, adventurous romance. When Mary shifted her own life into exciting romantic mode Adèle was on hand to record it.

Mary got on far better than Margaret with her mother, from whom she had learned to hide her feelings. Consequently Caroline, who did not often look below the surface, enjoyed her company. Mary did not disguise the fact that she was unattracted by the artificial society in which Caroline chose to move and, to her mother's annoyance, she refused to "come out" and be properly presented at court. In her dislike of formal society she seemed to repeat Margaret, and her mother must have cursed the year her daughters had spent with Mary Wollstonecraft, who made such parade of liberty and self-assertion for girls.

In the end Margaret had married satisfactorily; there was no reason to suppose Mary would not do the same. She had the kind of skill that always brought her mother around and would surely be attractive to suitable young men. Her appearance was far more conventionally pleasing than her elder sister's. She was shorter and prettier, with striking features and a graceful figure. Her glory was her very long, luxuriant hair, not unlike her mother's when she had been for sale among the Irish aristocracy a few decades before. Despite her enjoyment of the outdoors, she had cultivated a soft manner and she copied Caroline in speaking with

an affected little lisp. Prince Pückler-Muskau summed her up as "one of the most attractive girls in Ireland." Caroline was proud of her.

In Windsor and London a pretty girl from a noble family could come to the attention of the British as well as absentee Irish aristocracy and could anticipate marrying an elder son. Caroline hoped Mary would learn more manners and civility than she had mastered in Mitchelstown before serious suitors presented themselves. As people had remarked, despite her prettiness and charming ways, she was in need of some refinement. Years ago even Mary Wollstonecraft had thought her and her sisters rather wild and uncultured.

Mary and her mother saw their various relatives in England. Gerald Henry, Caroline's spoiled half brother, whose education Mary Wollstonecraft had tried to influence, had grown up without mishap and was now living in the fashionable resort town of Bath, though retaining the family estate of Kilminchy and the Dublin town house in Merrion Square. In July 1794 in Dublin he had married the gentle, pretty Isabella Staples, daughter of the baronet Sir Robert Staples and niece, as every account pointed out, to Viscount Vesci; they had produced two children.

Nearer to home there was another young man from their past, Colonel Henry Gerald Fitzgerald, with whom Gerald Henry was frequently confused. He was about to affect all their lives. There are many suggestions as to who he was.

Newspapers and contemporary accounts consistently conflate the two young men, yet Gerald Henry continued to live peaceably with his family in Bath long after Colonel Henry Gerald disappeared from the scene, and when Isabella died in 1803, he waited ten years and married again. He was, as far as one can see, never in the regular army, as his near namesake certainly was.

To bring together these two disparate men many interesting fictions were invented. One created an illegitimate son for Gerald Henry; indeed, the twentieth-century King descendants retain this spectral young man who, it was declared, was brought up within Caroline's fam-

ily with the greatest kindness. It is an attractive invention, for a pampered young man might well have sired a child and left it to his rich older sister to raise. But the dates do not work: they require the lad to reach a colonelcy by the age of ten or so.

Another story is more extreme and provides a full elder brother for Caroline, son of her father, Richard, and mother, Margaret. The romantic version authored by Mary's friend Adèle subscribes to this story. Her Henry then becomes the legitimate son of Caroline's dead brother; in the story the brother married but Richard would not recognize his marriage or the infant he sired, and the child was cared for by Caroline, who, to humor her father, had to "hide her interest in the young orphan." She had him carefully educated and, when she took possession of her Mitchelstown property at twenty-one, provided for the boy.

There may be some truth here, for, although an incorrigible romantic, Adèle did, after all, know Caroline, Henry and Mary. Yet the central point of the story is surely made to render the Colonel's birth exciting—indeed, perhaps he himself was the source, since he too was a romancer in his way. Apart from the frisson of incest, the genealogy gives Henry every reason to feel bitter toward the Kings, who would have come into the fortune that should have been his. It also explains what many noticed in the events that followed: the almost intentional degradation of Caroline and Robert.

But there are insuperable problems with the account. First of all, it denies one obvious fact: Caroline's significance to her father and grandfather even when a small child. There is no evidence of a son to Richard and Margaret, and the will of James, 4th Baron Kingston, mentions only his daughter and granddaughter. Also there does not seem much time or opportunity for the nurturing of a "young orphan" during Richard's lifetime, since Caroline, after her youthful marriage, lived with her in-laws, then embarked with Robert on the grand tour. When she returned, her father died almost at once.

There is more plausibility, if less sensation, a little farther distant. An appropriate Henry Gerald Fitzgerald was the son of the late George

Fitzgerald, elder brother to Caroline's father, Richard. George became a colonel in a regiment of Volunteers and died in 1781, leaving a boy, Henry Gerald. The nearest rich relative for this boy was Caroline; he would have been her cousin as well as Gerald Henry's. In his description of the Kings, Prince Pückler-Muskau declared that Colonel Henry Fitzgerald was "a cousin on the mother's side, a married man." When she contemplated his often fanciful account Margaret, who knew the truth, did not refute this part of it.

Adèle declared that the King girls "were brought up almost at [Henry's] knee," perhaps an exaggeration, but all accounts do agree that he was raised in part by Caroline with the King children. When he came to maturity, presumably his cousin bought him a commission in a good British regiment: the first battalion of the First Foot Guards, commanded by the Duke of Gloucester, part of the army headed by the Duke of York.

Of all the professions open to an upper-class youth the army was by far the most expensive; the price of the lowest commission in an old regiment was £500 and that of a higher rank could be over £4,000. Henry was entering a smart regiment, made famous earlier in the century in the Duke of Marlborough's campaigns. By 1793 he was listed as either lieutenant or captain. In October 1797 a handwritten entry crossed the name out and in the army lists of 1798 he is not mentioned. This sounds like the right Henry.

Boys who grew up in a milieu of money and status not theirs might develop odd attitudes. They might have expectations that could not be met and irritations that their fortune was not equal to their supposed merits. They would probably be arrogant and haughty through mingled pride and uncertainty about their status. They might also be resentfully dependent on the families that patronized them. All the accounts assert that, whatever his lineage, the tall, distinguished-looking Henry Fitzgerald was arrogant and assertive in the way of young men with good connections. Prince Pückler-Muskau claimed he "enjoyed the greatest celebrity as a resistless seducer"—but, like Adèle, the German prince wished to heighten a tale. It is more certain that, with his advantages of

appearance and aristocratic patrons, Henry married an heiress—"a very beautiful Lady," according to newspapers. They set up home in a handsome house at Bishopsgate on the Thames, possibly belonging to the Kings. Two children were born, a boy and girl. The girl was called Caroline in honor of his cousin and patron.

Officers at home had many pleasures. A young man such as Henry had to inspect his men's arms and equipment at roll call and do his duty in parades and drills, and he needed to study some maneuvers and the use of weapons like muskets and bayonets, but for the rest of his time he was free to drink, gamble and visit, in much the same way as other young men about town. Onlookers noted that Britain was not much of a military nation, appointing as officers mere boys whose families happened to have interest and allowing these gentlemanly officers to choose the uniforms of their men—hence the absurd frills of the Irish militia. Such young men were in no position to enforce discipline among their men or indeed to pay much attention to their welfare, and the brightly clad soldiers were more or less jettisoned when they were wounded or fell sick.

Then the war with France impinged. It had been declared at the beginning of February 1793 and by the end of the month Gerard Lake embarked for the Continent in command of a brigade composed of the first battalions of the three regiments of Foot Guards. They included the Duke of Gloucester's regiment under Charles Asgill, a harsh man whose experience of being under an American death threat in the War of Independence had not increased his sensitivity to fear in others. Among his men was Henry Fitzgerald.

The regiments were the first British troops actually engaged in the war. They had to face a grueling time of skirmishes and small, costly battles. By April the brigade had with difficulty joined the Duke of York's army of thirty-five thousand British, Hessians and Hanoverians. Their brief was to take Dunkirk and help the Dutch get the invading French out of their country.

While their titular head the Duke of Gloucester enjoyed a civilian life of parties and bathing visits to Weymouth, his Foot Guards waded through the Flanders mud. However, a few events enlivened their dreary and dangerous time. In Holland the officers were guests of local magnates and they in turn gave a ball, at which they made the social mistake of inviting nobles and bourgeois together. The nobles were horrified and the bourgeois were disinvited. The latter's disgruntled feelings led several into the arms of the French enemy.

One military success stood out. In August 1793 some English troops under Lake were sent to rescue the Dutch forces under the Prince of Orange. Unable to rally the Dutch, Lake's troops fought alone and routed the more numerous French with very few losses. Yet the campaign as a whole was a disaster—indeed, these months formed one of the lowest points for the British in their twenty-year war with France. Dunkirk was not taken, and the lower and middling classes among the Dutch population they had come to help were uncooperative; like the disinvited bourgeois, they were often inclined to side with the French republican invaders.

Then Lake fell ill and went back to England. He sold his commission in the Guards, became a colonel of an infantry regiment in Ireland, and was appointed to the command of Ulster under Lord Carhampton's authority. Meanwhile, Lord Moira and seven thousand more men were sent out from Britain to reinforce the failing army of the Duke of York, an inveterate womanizer with little ability. Lord Moira was keen to make his mark, having the previous year taken part in an abortive attempt to help French royalists in Brittany rise against the new republic. He wished to compensate for this disaster, which rather stained his reputation for military skill.

After a lengthy and fraught march, Lord Moira and his men caught up with the main troops under the Duke of York. But then he was appalled to learn he would receive only a low command in the combined army. He resigned in a huff and returned to England. His loyal sister Selina blamed the government for her brother's chagrin; later she remarked, "I build

little on any of Pitt's expeditions, he may be a lucky Minister, but he certainly is a bad General, for sketching out Military Manoeuvres."

No such escape was possible for Henry Fitzgerald, still struggling against the odds in Holland. The winter of 1794 was unusually harsh and the flat land of the Netherlands became one sheet of ice. In early December the Duke of York was recalled to England and Lord Harcourt, brother-in-law of Caroline's friend at the Windsor court, took over as army commander. The French captured the icebound Dutch fleet and the Prince of Orange gave up the struggle. He ordered the Dutch to offer no more resistance and left the British army to fight on alone in the dreadful winter conditions. Lord Harcourt was having no more success than the Duke of York and had no choice but to retreat from the Continent. The rearguard of this operation was managed with some redeeming skill by the Scottish soldier Ralph Abercromby.

By now the cold and sickness had decimated Henry's regiment. Half the British army was sick and the other half weary from the vile weather and the hostility of the people they had originally come to help. Supplies had not been delivered and there was insufficient food for marching men—some days they had none and drank only water, yet they had to trudge through drifting snow, sand and wind. Many were tempted to lie down and end it all. Wagons were sent to locate the absent, but often they found them simply dead on the route.

Finally, weakened by frostbite and hunger, the regiment limped into the camp they had been aiming for, only to find it filled with unwelcoming Hessian soldiers. By now most territory had been lost to the French. The future Duke of Wellington noted the inefficiency of the army and its administration in this forlorn campaign; he would try not to make the same mistakes when he came into command some years later against Napoleon in Spain.

But at least Henry was alive and he had acquitted himself so well in the arduous time that he had taken over from Charles Asgill as lieutenant colonel of the King's Company. It was a significant promotion.

In early May 1795 the unvictorious First Foot Guards set sail for

England from Bremen with the rest of the army. They had remained gallant and disciplined, according to the official record, and had put up good resistance against a numerically superior enemy.

They landed in Greenwich, where, to inspirit his demoralized troops, King George III himself was on the pier to welcome them. They were billeted in Southwark.

Through 1796 and 1797 the First Foot Guards remained in London. Henry returned to his wife and ordinary life—his family was now living in Bury Street, St. James's. From there he visited his cousin Caroline in Windsor and she again enjoyed his company. He had added the stature of an experienced military man to his charm as a handsome gentleman.

He remained useful. Her social calendar was as full as ever and Henry could be left to entertain young Mary when, as so often, she refused to accompany her mother. The pair had played tomboy games from an early age. Now they enjoyed walking and riding together and, even more, driving fast in the dogcart. They made a strange but striking couple—the battle-hardened commander nearing thirty and the young, spirited girl of sixteen who had known nothing but ease.

Although fond of Mary, Caroline had never been consumed by child raising and did not spend a lot of time giving her daughter her own sophistication. As a result, Mary was "more uninformed of the vicious habits of the world than happens to most young people, even at that early age." She was therefore fitting company for the young Adèle, who, despite a past of French royalty and Lady Hamilton, claimed that she too was naive and innocent when she met Mary and her family. She later made a point of this since she did not want to appear a failed chaperone—or, indeed, a pander.

For some time Adèle watched the virginal Mary and the married Henry gambol and horseplay together, noticing nothing untoward in their relationship. But by now their feelings were changing: they were falling in love. Mary was no longer a child and the age difference of more than a decade seemed less than it had been a few years earlier. When she

was at home in Windsor with her mother, Mary became moody and dif-
ficult. Caroline tried to question her, but she was not forceful enough
and did not interrupt her social routine to deal with her increasingly
secretive daughter.

During these months Adèle remembered long morning and evening
visits from Mary and Henry to her little house in Brompton Square.
Whenever he was absent, Mary spent the time praising his virtues to
Adèle: she thought this natural, for Henry was indeed a fine man. When
he was present the pair beguiled the time with music. Henry had a good
voice, though he was not a musician, and when he sang he made mistakes in Italian. Mary Wollstonecraft had noticed the linguistic skills of
the King girls and Mary presumably knew the language well, as did Margaret. In revenge for mockery of his errors, he said he would force Mary
and Adèle to sing in Irish, implying that the native language had not
been part of Mary's education, though it had been of his. So he and Mary
"used to sing Irish melodies together with the utmost perfection." It was
quite respectable: they were not alone, nor had they an improper public
audience, since only Adèle, her father and mother were present.

The songs reminded them of Ireland, about which they all spoke.
Despite her royalist background, Adèle's opinions were liberal, even radical, and her guests probably shared some of her sentiments. There are
no existing letters between Margaret and Mary, but many may have been
exchanged and it is hard to imagine Mary knowing nothing of her eldest
sister's political activities.

Adèle is probably right in saying that Mary was the first to be aware
of love, for in all accounts she emerges as a quick, impetuous and head-
strong girl. She is less likely to be accurate in declaring that Henry did
not suspect the infatuation or his danger. Neither had yet admitted their
feelings to the other, however.

At this crucial time Caroline was recalled to Ireland by the illness of
one of her sons. Mary could not be left alone at Windsor and so she and
her mother were both to set out for Ireland. But, perhaps because of her
recent moodiness, Mary's health appeared especially delicate; it could be

worsened by speedy traveling. So Caroline, who did not wish to endanger her favorite daughter for the sake of a son, set off at a fast pace alone. She asked Henry to bring Mary over more sedately.

It was "during this fatal journey" that both young people admitted their passion. Adèle insisted on mutuality in their disclosure. Henry was not the seducer, and neither was Mary; the pair were simply overwhelmed and had to succumb. Other observers were not so sure. Some had long noted Henry's particular attentions to Mary and regarded him as the instigator of an open passion, the older manipulator of the emotions of a young girl little more than a child. They were surprised at Caroline's blindness. For some time the pair had been spied being too intimate at parties and even the servants were gossiping.

After a stay in Ireland all three were ready to return to England; Caroline was not keen to be near her husband for long periods. Henry presumably had to rejoin his regiment. So they traveled back together. Both Henry and Mary were actors and controlled themselves so carefully that Caroline suspected nothing. Perhaps she was simply relieved to find her daughter cheerful again.

During her friend's absence from England Adèle had married a distinguished French mercenary, Benoît de Boigne, who had grown wealthy through soldiering in Ireland and the British colonies. He was thirty years older than she but her family was in financial trouble and when this rich man proposed she felt it her duty to accept. As a result of her marriage and her moving away, she saw less of Henry and the Kings on their return and her account trails off just at the momentous time. By the following year she and the Comte de Boigne had separated and she was back in Brompton Square with her parents, accusing him of jealousy, intolerant conservatism and a temper made irritable by withdrawal from opium. Because of her brief marriage she missed the most sensational episode in her friend's life.

By now Mary and her mother were on bad terms again. Mary seemed as willful as Margaret at her age. Her refusal to go into society, attend the

proper parties and take part in the necessary social round of the marriageable young girl was thoroughly irritating. A change of scenery and company might help; Caroline therefore sent her to the country to stay with Lady Harcourt in her elegant Oxfordshire house at Nuneham Courtenay. Perhaps she thought her friend's combination of sensibility and piety would gently help the girl to see her duty: Lady Harcourt was famous for her gardens of sensibility, in which wreaths crowned busts of Rousseau and other philosophers of sentiment; the leading evangelical writer Hannah More praised her as the cynosure of womanhood in her combination of religion, sensitivity and taste.

Considering her own age at marriage Caroline ought not to have been unduly surprised at the romantic proclivity of her daughter. Mary was about the age her mother had been when she bedded Robert King. Yet since there were no young men very present in her life beyond their cousin Henry, she may have seen no danger, believing, like Mrs. Norris in Jane Austen's *Mansfield Park,* that two people who had grown up almost as brother and sister would be unlikely to fall passionately in love. Also, from her own experience (and indeed Margaret's), she did not believe passion a family failing. She and her daughters all knew that an aristocratic girl had to marry well to further the interests of her brothers and maintain her own social position. They also knew that, while adultery was aristocratic and common, romance was less so.

Perhaps Henry, with his tangential relationship to the great family, had some conscious or unconscious desire to disgrace his benefactors, in which case Mary would have been as much a pawn of her kinsman's intricate desires as she was of her mercenary and ambitious family. Yet Mary, although naive, does not emerge from any accounts as docile. Rather, she seems to have been eager for sensation. It remains as likely that Henry was coerced by a willful girl into wounding a family he had learned to respect. He himself emerges as a complex character, antagonistic to and in awe of the high-ranking family of which he was only just a member. Flexible, needing to play the courtier to his cousin while pursuing his own military

status, he seems also to have been at moments unruly in emotions. He obviously enjoyed role-playing and reveled in his power to dupe others, but he could be dominated by stronger personalities. In some ways in character he resembles Lord Edward Fitzgerald. He had just had the excitement of war; peace must have been a difficult adjustment.

Henry had been raised with Mary as a sort of brother but they had had long periods apart. Both could have been actuated straightforwardly by lust, which turned into an obsession, blinding the man to claims of self-preservation and family gratitude. Yet a young woman of Mary's temper was likely to have gratified him clandestinely to his heart's content, and there seems no need to have taken matters further than a secret affair. Wollstonecraft had suggested that sex before marriage was not morally wrong, only socially unwise. If this had become her pupil's view, then Henry could have enjoyed his relative without destroying his social position, marriage and promising military career. Such indulgence, even if known and resulting in pregnancy, could be covered up or, if not entirely so, a quick, inferior marriage could be arranged for the girl. Henry was married and apparently fond of his wife—and she of him.

By early summer 1797 the affair had been consummated. It continued through the next months despite Mary's stay at Lady Harcourt's sentimental retreat. Caroline remained unaware. Then Mary realized she was pregnant. She grew more difficult and secretive; Caroline became annoyed and anxious.

And here the story deviates from the usual aristocratic peccadillo, since the pregnant Mary and the married Henry now decided to elope. For the young girl it was an exciting romantic adventure with a dashing older man; for him it seems an extraordinary jettisoning of everything he had worked for. If the elopement became known, he could not keep the patronage of the powerful Kings or, presumably, his family. Mary was a minor with a good fortune and, since he himself was married, he was dishonoring one of Ireland's first families. Whoever took the initiative, he would be most condemned, she most sullied.

For all these reasons it is difficult to know what his intentions were. Perhaps at first he hardly knew himself; perhaps he merely thought to help Mary get away from her relatives and hide her state in a secret place until her time came, then return her slim again, himself quite uninvolved.

Probably it seemed best to both if they or she alone left the country and went to France. The war between the two nations continued but, under the Directory, France was a more hospitable place for the British than it had been when Mary Wollstonecraft was exiled from Paris during the Terror. It was not as free or libertarian as some had expected in the early 1790s, but there was some freedom not available in England and a new frivolity was conducive to irregular lovers. Mary may well have read her old governess's latest book, *Letters from Sweden,* where she described her desire to be out of censorious England—Wollstonecraft failed to make it clear that she herself was an unmarried mother who wanted to hide her status, but several people in London knew the truth.

They decided that it would be best to explain Mary's absence by suicide; the moodiness of the last months would give some credibility to this. Again Mary Wollstonecraft might have been a guide. Her lover Imlay had believed that variety alone conquered satiety and he felt overwhelmed by her affection. So he extricated himself from their relationship and in despair she twice tried to kill herself. The fact was not generally known in England, but Margaret probably heard of it from her radical friends, and she could have told Mary when she was over in Ireland.

Suicide through love or passion was not regarded as unusual for women. English melancholia had recently been enhanced by such introspective works as Charlotte Smith's sonnets, which had been reading matter in Mitchelstown Castle when Mary was a child. These suggested an inconsolable anguish that could be ended only in death. In fact, some cynical observers believed that suicide had become fashionable. Contemporary manuals reported that ladies preferred drowning to shooting because it disfigured the body less.

There was therefore no reason to suppose the ruse would not suc-

ceed. When Mary was believed dead, Henry could go on playing his usual role of courtier with Caroline. To aid their plan he hired a maid; she would help Mary escape, stage a suicide by the River Thames, then accompany her mistress to secret lodgings in London.

So one morning in early September Mary did not come down to breakfast. Her apartments were searched and a suicide note found. It declared that she was about to throw herself into the river.

Caroline acted swiftly. Servants combed the house and garden, then dragged the Thames near the house. They found no corpse but did discover a convincing bonnet and shawl on the bank, supposedly placed there before Mary took her final plunge. According to Adèle, a workman said he had seen young Mary getting into a post chaise at five in the morning, but his report was initially discounted.

For a while things went according to plan. Mary realized her mother had accepted her cover story and believed her dead. Then she had qualms. She knew Caroline loved her and she pitied her grief. After three days of indecision she wrote a note to her mother declaring she was still alive. She did not say where she was, nor indicate that she would return. It was posted from Windsor itself, so no secret location was given away by a peculiar postmark.

Lady Kingsborough had indeed been distraught at the notion of her daughter's suicide, but distraction mingled with anger when she received this letter. It suggested that the girl had some regard for her mother, since, to reassure her, she had prejudiced her chance of going undetected, but an elopement implying scandal was one of the worst things that could happen to a respectable family. Much cultural opinion believed it worse for a mother to bear than death itself.

Despite the estrangement Lady Kingsborough now considered a husband essential, so she alerted her lord in Ireland. Robert was aghast at the news and immediately blamed his wife's guardianship. He set out for London at once, summoning to his aid his second son, Robert Edward, now a professional soldier. By the age of twenty-five, Robert Edward had

achieved the rank of lieutenant colonel in the army and served in the West Indies. He too would be concerned for the family's reputation. George as champion of female honor was out of the question.

When Lord Kingsborough and his son arrived in London, they took up residence away from Caroline in the house in Great George Street, Hanover Square. Although the times were troubled in Ireland, both had taken leave from their military duties for such an important affair. Immediately they resorted to advertising—with no clues, there seemed absolutely nothing else to do, although newspaper notices were more common for missing servants and horses than for noble daughters. Robert also contacted the family lawyer, Mr. Lowten, who would handle the details and let his inconspicuous name be printed in the newspapers.

So on 23 September 1797, the London *True Briton* and *The Times* ran the following:

Young Lady Eloped

Whereas a young lady went from her Mother's House near Windsor, on Sunday Evening the 3d inst. and has not since been heard of, except by a letter of Wednesday the 6th inst. having the post mark Windsor upon it.

The Lady is about 17 years old, clear brown complexion, with very dark brown hair, light blue eyes, Grecian nose, long oval face, is about 5 feet 5 inches height, rather slim made, and a pretty elegant figure; speaks with a little lisp, and rather quick.

Whoever will give information of the place of abode of the Young Lady, so that she may be restored to her Family and Friends, shall receive a Reward of ONE HUNDRED GUINEAS, by applying to Mr Lowten, in the Temple.

The picture was attractively girlish and the money substantial.

Over the next five days the notice reappeared in newspapers, delighted to have an aristocratic scandal to watch unfolding. It also appeared on printed bills pasted on outside walls and in coffee houses. Few people in London could have avoided it. On the twenty-seventh an

added announcement promised, "The Name of any Person giving information, shall, if required be concealed. It is thought that the lady went to a new Place of Residence on Saturday or Sunday last."

The name of the "lady" was hidden but would not be so for long; it was a measure of the family's concern that they had resorted to such methods and risked regaling the public with their domestic problems.

Then the identity was revealed. Gossip spread that the missing girl was Mary King, third daughter of Caroline and Robert King, Lord and Lady Kingsborough of Mitchelstown Castle in County Cork. According to Adèle, it was Caroline's friend Lady Harcourt who made it known. Adèle's mother thought the publicity improper but the increasingly religious and conservative Lady Harcourt was intent not so much on finding as on punishing the girl: "she has sinned, morality demands that she should pay the penalty," she is supposed to have said. She would have been more ferocious had she realized that the other sinner was an officer under her brother-in-law's command in the recent British retreat through Holland.

Back in her cottage in Windsor Caroline turned more and more to her cousin Henry, who had shown such fondness for Mary. At first he was not to be found, but it was reasonable for him to be away on regimental business. Presumably he had told his wife something like this. Then he returned to answer Lady Kingsborough's appeal. One or two people suspected something and challenged him, but he flatly denied any involvement. Indeed, he was so indignant that he threatened to fight any accuser. Caroline was convinced. Henry appeared deeply distressed at her loss and called daily to console her.

A few days after the advertisement had first appeared, a postboy reported he had spied just such a young lady walking by herself along the roadside. A gentleman came up in a post chaise, stopped by her and helped her inside. The couple traveled into central London together. Then a maid came forward to Caroline declaring she had seen a gentleman and young lady arriving to take lodgings at a rooming house in Clayton Street, near the Kennington Turnpike. Caroline dreaded her

next words: the pair had spent the night together and the man had not left the room until six-thirty in the morning. There was no question of Mary's being returned intact. Indeed, the mother now learned through the scandal sheets that the affair had been going on a great deal longer than she had supposed.

The maidservant—who curiously, appears to have been the maid in Henry's pay—continued with devastating detail: left alone, the young lady had sent her out for a newspaper. When she received it, she read the advertisement her parents had placed. Coolly she remarked that the description of the missing girl seemed something like herself. The maid claimed that she failed to see the significance at once but later, when she entered the lodger's room and found her cutting off the long dark brown hair mentioned in the notice, her suspicions were aroused. At this stage Caroline had no reason to disbelieve the story. The gentleman who had delivered the young lady had called constantly to visit her.

As the maid was speaking—lengthily, in hope of receiving the full reward of the hundred guineas—the door opened on Colonel Henry Fitzgerald. He had come to pay his daily call of condolence to his cousin. The maid saw him and exclaimed, "There's the very gentleman who visits the young lady." Henry dashed from the room and away from the house at full speed.

Mr. Lowten was now summoned and dispatched to the place near the Kennington Turnpike; there he learned that Mary, possibly alerted to the exposure of her hiding place, was out searching for new lodgings. On her return she was greeted by Mr. Lowten. At first she refused to accompany him but, underage and with no Henry near for support, soon saw resistance as useless. She agreed to get into the waiting carriage but insisted on taking the maidservant along—an odd act, considering she had just been betrayed by her.

Perhaps it was in all their interests or part of a complicated plan of Mary's that the maid receive the Kingsborough reward; or perhaps Mary was supposed to have decamped from Kennington by the time her captors arrived. One account suggests that the maid was herself in love

with Henry, so perhaps she exposed him when he failed to respond to her, then repented of her betrayal. Most likely she was simply being employed by both sides, like so many political agents in Ireland. Unlike a good number of these, she was actually paid for her services.

Mr. Lowten drove Mary to her father's London mansion in Great George Street. On 28 September *The Times* announced under the heading "A Young Lady Who Eloped": "The Mother and Friends of the Lady desire to return their Thanks to the numerous Persons who have offered their Services on the occasion, and beg leave to inform them and the Public (to prevent further trouble) that she has been recovered." Lord Kingsborough did not add his name to those of the grateful.

He continued to berate Caroline for her care of their daughter, while she herself realized she had been too indulgent with the girl. When the Queen, who knew what it was to have rebellious children, visited to give some regal consolation, she found Caroline uncharacteristically subdued, "reproaching Herself with having Idolized Her Mary too much." She now accepted that she had failed as a mother and that her daughter would have to be returned to Ireland without her.

For some time Mary was interned in the Great George Street house, where, to prevent further gossip about the estranged Kingsboroughs, her mother joined her. According to the Dublin *Press,* Mary was much affected by what had happened. Then Mary was whisked off by coach and boat to Mitchelstown Castle. There her scandalously short hair could grow again without daily comment from the press. Perhaps the story would die down. When she left, Mary took with her the Kennington maid; presumably both she and her parents thought they might make an ally of her.

The romancing Adèle's version of events was more colorful. In this Henry and Mary were discovered by her father about to embark on a boat on the Thames for America. Mary was dressed as a boy and the pair were traveling as father and son. Seeing Robert, they covered their faces with their hands. They did not justify themselves; Mary remained calm, even cold, but she exclaimed, "I am very guilty." She was led away from Henry without resistance.

An interview was then arranged between Mary and Henry's still-loving wife. Mary had advised Mrs. Fitzgerald to go to her husband's aid through the device of bearing a message from Mary. She had agreed and had met him. He was affectionate and shed tears of blood for his abandoned family but was definite that he could no longer live with them. He must devote his remaining years "to the unfortunate victim whom he had brought to destruction." He resigned from his regiment and retired to a small village near London. All this seems a little unlikely; by now Adèle was the Comtesse de Boigne and no longer in close contact with the Kings.

If Robert and Caroline really believed the scandal would die down, they were mistaken, although the *Hibernian Chronicle* had declared, "Delicacy towards the parties concerned . . . prevented us from entering into a detail of the unfortunate affair." The *Times* continued its interest and provided new information; it was they who reported the previously suppressed fact that Mary was pregnant. There were various suggestions of what might become of her when her lying-in was over. The newspaper declared she would be dispatched to a convent in Portugal—a strange location for a Protestant girl but at least far from scandalmongers. In Prince Pückler-Muskau's account she was to be placed in safe custody in the north of England. In more plausible versions elegant Kingston College for decayed Protestants became a prison: "The family have an asylum for reduced gentlewomen at their country seat in Ireland, where they propose fixing this wretched girl. I ventured to foretell such a place would prove her ruin," wrote Lady Harriet Skeffington, sister-in-law of Caroline's half sister, Margaret Jocelyn.

In her alternative story Adèle entered Gothic mode. She related that Mary was incarcerated in an empty house in Connaught on the shores of the Atlantic in the wildest and most desolate area. Two guards in her father's pay ensured that she could not escape.

The scandalous affair continued to be the talk of Dublin and London and the subject of excited letters to the provinces. With her close rela-

tionship to the Kings, Margaret Jocelyn was the source of much-wanted information. She gave news to Lady Harriet Skeffington and Lady Harriet relayed it to Martha McTier, who told her brother William Drennan. They all listened to the "tragedy" and found it very "shocking."

There was now general comment on Mary. Much could be explained by youth and the failure of a social mother to supervise and curb her daughter. In such cases blame was usually thrown on the novels young girls were addicted to and which frequently made claims for romantic love over duty and rank. But Lady Kingsborough had discouraged novels as corrupting and middle-class, the kind of reading suitable for daughters of curates and tradesmen. Perhaps she had gone too far and the girls had not had the moral benefit of the better sort of fiction; forbidden proper outlets, perhaps they had read the servants' trash.

Looking elsewhere for explanation, the public found it in the year she and Margaret had spent with the notorious Mary Wollstonecraft, scourge of aristocratic privilege and manners. Her middle-class sense of individualism, hatred of the legal prostitution of dynastic marriage and political views on the equality of the sexes had, it was supposed, sunk deep into her pupils' minds. She had recently married the radical philosopher William Godwin and a few months later died in childbirth, leaving a grieving husband and baby daughter Mary, so her death was uppermost in people's thoughts. She had been the most famous radical woman in the country, used as a symbol of enlightenment by liberals and as an unsexed monstrosity by conservatives. She must have had an influence on fallen Mary King.

As well as her teachings, Wollstonecraft's character had also supposedly had an ill effect on her pupils. They say, wrote the gossiping Irish Bishop Percy to his wife, that the governess wanted "to discharge the Marriage Duties, with [Lady Kingsborough's] husband." Others connected her known extramarital passion for Imlay to Mary King's action. Wollstonecraft had, it was asserted, led young girls to "the vestibule of the Corinthian temple of Seduction and Adultery." Her "*suicide* and *lib-*

ertinism" had inspired Mary's faked suicide and "intrigue." A lady correspondent to *Gentleman's Magazine* summed up the public interest by
writing:

> I shall be obliged to any of your numerous correspondents who can
> inform me, whether *Miss K.* whose unhappy story so lately engaged
> the public attention, be one of the daughters of Lord Viscount Kings-
> borough, in whose family the late Mrs. Mary Woolstonecraft [*sic*] God-
> win was a governess. Whether this may have been the fact or not, is not
> every degree of indiscretion, and profligacy, the natural consequence
> of such principles as Mrs. G. maintained in speculation, and exhibited
> in her own conduct?

The magazine editor replied that indeed Mary had been "an unfortunate pupil of the renowned Mrs. Mary Woolstonecraft; and the sooner
they are both consigned to a long oblivion the better."

The Kingsboroughs wished the same. For the moment Robert and
Caroline tried to limit damage by prompting notices in the English and
Irish press presenting themselves as conventional loving parents. They
were not really estranged, these notices reported, and their living apart
"has not proceeded from any domestic differences" but simply from
Lady Kingsborough's "strong predilection in favour of [England],"
where she is "often visited by his Lordship": "We are also well authorised
to say, there is no family in Ireland more universally esteemed and
beloved, and consequently, that their late domestic misfortunes must
excite general and sincere concern." The Kingsboroughs also answered
the conservative newspapers that linked Mary and Wollstonecraft by
downplaying the tie and stressing their daughter's exceptional innocence and naiveté.

Robert had to do more than limit damage. He and his son Robert
Edward must seek out Henry for proper satisfaction and assert family
honor by violence. To this end he immediately summoned a nephew to

town, Major Robert Wood of Ashford. After some difficulty the trio managed to discover Henry's hiding place, and on 29 September Colonel Robert Edward King sent Major Robert Wood as his second to challenge Colonel Henry Fitzgerald to a duel.

Henry agreed to meet Robert Edward but without a second—he simply could not find one, he said. He had had an acquaintance with him at this first meeting but declared that no one in London would formally act on his behalf, since his name had been so blackened. Wood, whom he knew well, would have to be friend for both. Absolutely not, replied Wood; if his cousin Robert Edward had not fought, he himself would have been Henry's opponent. He advised Henry to find a replacement friend quickly. They decided that the duel would take place on the next day.

So on Sunday morning, 1 October, the men met in Hyde Park. "Where is your friend, Sir!" asked Colonel Wood. Henry replied, "I have not been able to procure one—I wish the matter to go on, I rest assured that you will do all fairly" (or so Colonel Wood later reported). He did have a surgeon, however, and Wood suggested he ask this man to be his second. The surgeon, a paid professional, was not eager to become involved in this aristocratic affair and declined, but said he would at least be in view. Since both men wanted to proceed, nothing stood in the way. As Wood remarked, "It was no common business."

Dueling was strictly regulated, especially among the Irish, for whom it was a "national taste." Although it was illegal, juries rarely convicted duelists, since few jurors would have avoided the practice themselves and in Ireland even Lord Chancellor Clare, head of the legal system, had fought several duels, including the one with John Philpot Curran. As was customary, Henry, the challenged, chose the weapons—pistols—and the ground; the challenger, Mary's brother, chose the distance, ten paces. As the only second, Major Wood placed the duelists at the chosen ten paces, though he himself thought the distance, which allowed for fatal mistakes, too great. He consented, however, believing that Henry, "sensible of the vileness of his conduct," would ask pardon of Robert Edward after the first shot. Wood loaded the pistols for both; firing would begin at his signal.

The duelists took up positions and exchanged shots. Initially Wood thought Robert Edward the most determined, but as the shots rang out, he realized appearances were deceptive: Henry was "obstinately bent on blood." Having expected him to fire athwart his opponent, as the guilty party often did, he was appalled to see that Henry was shooting directly at him; he even wounded Robert Edward slightly. It suggested some deep antagonism to the benefactors he had injured.

According to Irish rules, seconds should attempt a reconciliation before the meeting or, as now, after the fourth shot, when an explanation and full apology might end the matter. This apology must include precise formulas of abasement, since a lady's honor was involved. Major Wood remained silent. Henry paused to ask his advice "as a friend." The major declared he was no friend of such a scoundrel but if Henry would acknowledge himself the vilest of all human beings and accept with no right of reply any insult and affront the aggrieved brother might wish to bestow on him, then the duel could be declared over. Henry agreed he had acted wrongly but would go no further; he refused to abase himself.

This was insufficient. Henry tried to address Robert Edward directly but the latter was now too enraged; Henry was, he said, "a damned villain, and . . . he would not listen to any thing he had to offer." The duel resumed.

After two further shots, aimed directly at the wounded man, Henry's powder and bullets ran out. This was wrong; since the quarrel concerned a "gross" affront, had he had a proper second, Henry would have had two pistols, with his friend holding another ready charged in reserve. He asked to take one of Robert Edward's weapons, but this was strictly forbidden by rule. The duel had to be stopped—interrupted, not terminated. It would be resumed on Monday. "It shall not end here," Robert Edward declared.

Major Wood went home and wrote a detailed account of events from his—and the Kings'—point of view. Ostensibly to a friend, it was soon published in the newspapers and formed part of the family's efforts to control public opinion and blacken Henry's character. On the other

side, some reported that Henry had purposely had insufficient bullets so that he would not be tempted to kill his relative and might the more surely be killed himself. Ever the supporter of Henry, Adèle explained that he had extracted bullets from his pistol because he did not wish to add to the wrong he had already done to Caroline and her family. He hoped he would die in the duel. If so, and if Major Wood's impression of his ferocity is correct, then the duel changed his mind.

The duelists were to meet at Tyburn Turnpike. But by the next day the news had got out and they were intercepted. The Duke of York, now commander of the troops in England, heard of the affair and sent an officer of the Guards to arrest Henry; another order went to Robert Edward. The Duke himself had no problem with dueling and had indulged in it himself—a decade earlier he had fought the Duchess of Leinster's nephew Charles Lennox on Wimbledon Common using Lord Moira as his second. The Duke, who declared he had no animosity against Lennox and had merely come out to give satisfaction, had fired in the air while Lennox's bullet had grazed the Duke of York's curl—to the horror of George III, who later, out of sight of his disapproving queen, embraced his son and "with tears congratulated him on his safety." Despite his own performance on this occasion, the Duke, as commander of the army, could not allow such activity in others. The men had to discontinue their business.

Aggrieved not only at the ruin of his daughter but also now at the insult and injury to his son, Lord Kingsborough suggested the two young men disobey the injunction and take the consequences; to compensate Henry for the inevitable loss of his commission and his military career should he do so, he ordered Wood to offer him the large sum of 5,000 guineas.

But overnight some of Henry's bloodthirstiness had evaporated. He refused to go on with the duel or take the money; if they wanted his life, he would simply stand in front of Robert Edward and let him fire. Naturally Major Wood replied that his cousin would not be an "assassin." Henry would not budge and he declared he would not fight again, what-

ever insults they threw at him. So the duel had to be abandoned. Lord Kingsborough wrote furiously to Henry on 5 October 1797: "If you ever presume to appear where I or any part of my Family may happen to be, depend upon it the Consequences will be Fatal." It was a written threat of murder.

Over in Windsor Caroline was dismayed by events, for she had now lost two favorites, her beautiful daughter Mary and her entertaining cousin Henry. She had been berated by a dominating spouse she disliked and humiliated publicly as an inadequate mother. Queen Charlotte tried to comfort her by continuing to visit but she found her friend "a most melancholy sight." The overbearing, talkative Caroline had become "very resigned, & queit, and Mild about every body."

It was further embarrassing that Colonel Henry Fitzgerald should be confused with her half brother and the whole affair made a matter of incest. Possibly Gerald Henry himself was tired of being questioned about the scandal and contacted the press. Most likely the beleaguered Kings resorted again to the newspapers, for on 10 October *The Times* ran the following notice:

> We are desired to correct a mistake which has appeared in some of the Morning Papers, relative to the relationship between Lady Kingsborough and the Seducer of her daughter. It states, that Colonel Fitzgerald is half-brother to her Ladyship. This is not the case. Colonel Fitzgerald is son to the late George Fitzgerald, elder brother to Lady Kingsborough's father. Gerald Fitzgerald, Lady Kingsborough's brother, is a young man of unsullied character, and possesses a large fortune in Ireland.

Murder and Unrest

What uproar and what strife may now be stirring
This way or that way o'er these silent hills—
Invasion, and the thunder and the shout,
And all the crash of onset; fear and rage,
And undetermined conflict.

—SAMUEL TAYLER COLERIDGE,
"FEARS IN SOLITUDE WRITTEN IN APRIL 1798"

THE IRELAND TO WHICH MARY WAS DELIVERED WAS FAR LESS peaceful than the one she had left. Around Mitchelstown there were major disturbances: men assembled at night intent on burning farms, destroying orchards and laming the cattle of those who failed to support them. They threatened to kill any soldiers they encountered.

The lawlessness fitted Mary's condition. She was unrepentant, seeing herself as both victim and liberated heroine, just the sort of woman Wollstonecraft had been writing about: romantic but determined, justified by radical theory that valued fulfilment and desire over obligation and rank. Knowing her self-willed and theatrical, Robert had her carefully guarded. He suspected she was plotting with the Kennington maid, who, he now discovered, had helped her removal from Windsor despite later betraying her for money.

So he dismissed the girl. But he did not watch her carefully: she left

for England with a letter addressed to Henry hidden in her clothes. The letter begged Henry to come and rescue his mistress.

Adèle's more colorful account here takes note of Mary's pregnancy, which in other versions drops from the tale. A prisoner in Ireland, Mary feared both for her own life and for her unborn child's. Her maid and jailer seemed sympathetic and offered if necessary to take the baby, when born, out of the castle and care for it. She also agreed to deliver a letter to Henry asking him to send someone reliable to Ireland to rescue their child. The maid proved feckless or treacherous and the letter fell into Lord Kingsborough's hands. He read it, sealed it and sent it on to Henry. In this version Robert knew that Henry had been invited and would come, and he both welcomed and prepared for his coming.

Whatever the truth—and it seems unlikely that Robert, though he had grown despotic and in some accounts more gloomy over the years, would have turned into the kind of man who would plan to murder his daughter, grandchild and cousin—Henry was certainly summoned to Ireland by Mary.

One newspaper reported that since the duel he had become sensible of the enormity of his crimes and had even tried suicide. He had shot himself but not mortally. Another claimed he had been reconciled with his wife. This appears to have been true. Nonetheless, when he received the summons from Mary, he proposed to obey and risk losing his family and infuriating the Kings. He had little else to lose. His reputation had already been destroyed and he had become one of the most despised men in London. Also, time had not moderated his amorous feelings—or histrionic tendencies.

He told his wife he was going to Dorsetshire. This was plausible since, although a section of his regiment was preparing again to leave for the Continent, another part had been sent to Winchester in March for deployment along the coast. Since he had no money, he needed to borrow from his wife for the journey, or so the English newspapers later reported, now for the first time allowing some blame to fall on a girl who summoned a man so abruptly from his forgiving family. The Irish papers

remained firmly on the side of the Kings and kept Henry's villainy uppermost in their readers' minds.

Perhaps Henry was waiting for such a call or perhaps he was used to obeying the King ladies, for he set out at once. Whatever he had purposed after the duel, he was not now going on a suicide mission. He disguised himself heavily and carried with him the letter in which Robert had threatened to kill him; if he was attacked, he would implicate Lord Kingsborough.

Soon after the two Roberts had returned to Ireland they were summoned to Kingston Hall, where Edward, the old Earl of Kingston, was dying. Many members of the family were gathering for the death, including Margaret and Stephen. Caroline, who had once shown some affection for her father-in-law, remained in England; presumably she did not want further dealings with her censorious husband and eldest daughter. Despite the famous prejudice of the Kings, a Catholic doctor, Hugh MacDermot, was treating the dying man. Edward lingered, growing steadily weaker, giving his heirs time to savor the implications of his going.

Given their family scandals as well as the political gravity of the times, they kept very much to themselves. No doubt there was talk of the Henry Fitzgerald affair, but on this occasion nothing leaked out; they had had their fill of publicity. The usual gay nights of the aristocracy were curtailed, and Dr. MacDermot was amazed to report that they retired every evening at eleven, then breakfasted at ten, hardly the hours kept by fashionable society. They consoled themselves each night by eating Lissadel oysters of the finest kind for supper.

It was as well to avoid much conversation even among themselves, since there were so few innocuous topics, especially between a follower of the United Irishmen and her hard-line relatives or between a father and his undutiful children. Margaret compensated for the limited society by spending more time with Dr. MacDermot, who was involved in agitating for Catholic rights. He was impressed with her medical knowledge and courtesy: "Lady Mountcashel and I are very great," he wrote to his cousin.

Perhaps in private they spoke of a common enthusiasm. Unknown to the dying Earl and his son, MacDermot was one of the leaders of the United Irishmen in his area. There is no mention of Mary in the family letters from Kingston Hall, but it is likely that, while the family attended the deathbed, she was moved for safekeeping to Dublin.

Stephen dutifully remained with his in-laws, but his mind was on his estate of Moore Park. Indeed, he was so anxious that he wrote to Lord Castlereagh for special help. He had heard of disturbances in County Cork and of rebel meetings and lootings near his home. Insurgents had tried to kill a tithe collector by throwing him from the bridge at Kilworth. The law-abiding citizens of the area were defending themselves but they were desperate to have soldiers posted in the town to help their yeomanry. Stephen endorsed their plea: "I believe it to be absolutely necessary," he concluded.

Castlereagh, who had requests from panic-stricken landowners all over the country, including Lord Shannon at Castlemartyr, answered wearily and offered no special help; Stephen should apply to a general stationed at Fermoy, a developing garrison town nearby. Castlereagh well knew the views of the lady of Moore Park and perhaps was disinclined to help her family. Others openly blamed the Mount Cashells' liberal sentiments for the disturbances around Kilworth, where rebellious attitudes had been allowed to develop—much as the Moiras were blamed for unrest near their northern estates and the Leinsters for that in Kildare. Presumably in Kilworth this was primarily Margaret's fault, although it was also noted that Stephen had not been as staunch a Castle supporter as he should have been. As one neighboring officer remarked, "It is generally thought, that Lord Mountcashell's conduct in Parliament, has had the same ill effect in the country of Cork, as the Duke of Leinster's in the country of Kildare." It was now easy to criticize the Leinsters, for, torn between factions he could not wholeheartedly support, William had prudently left the country along with his wife and children. His heart had never been in politics and as a young man he had declared he was "not calculated for it"—any more than Stephen had been.

At midday on 8 November 1797 the Earl of Kingston died; he was seventy-one. The *Hibernian Magazine* with some exaggeration called him "a nobleman whose worth will be remembered, when all who knew him have long ceased to exist." He was buried at Boyle Abbey, near his old unfashionable home, King House. His death made Robert the 2nd Earl of Kingston, with a seat in the Irish House of Lords and lands in Roscommon and throughout the midlands to add to his wife's substantial holdings in the south. He was at the pinnacle of ownership: if he wished, he could move into a position of great political power in Ireland.

Financially he was not hugely advantaged. Edward had never managed to disentangle himself from the debts to which he had referred in the negotiations over Caroline. With his building and improving of houses he had recently contracted more and, despite his recent large legacy, he died owing £71,981.

George too was affected. He became Viscount Kingsborough, and after a fight—which to Lord Shannon's disgust he won—took one of the County Roscommon seats his family expected to control. Like the rest of his male relatives, he wanted the seat to increase or underpin his power and showed no interest in the needs and hopes of the common people in the region he represented.

Stephen and Margaret returned from Kingston Hall to Moore Park to find both Kilworth and Mitchelstown in disarray. An irascible magistrate in the area near Fermoy had written to Dublin Castle that "the revolution has commenced." During the next months this magistrate used a loyal soldier called Jasper Uniacke to infiltrate the rebels. Uniacke was informed against and unmasked; then, while the magistrate was visiting him and his wife, rebels hacked both men to death and hurled Uniacke's wife over the banisters. Stephen was appalled and summoned dragoons from Fermoy to ride with him to capture the assassins and burn the village that harbored them. But a priest dissuaded them, pointing out that if they burned the village houses, their enemies would certainly burn Moore Park in return. These particular rebels were in the end captured, tried, found guilty and hanged, but the incident frightened the land-

owners, who could not be sure that law would always—or even usually—prevail. Margaret's views on the incident are unknown, but she later said that she and Stephen had often spoken of separating; perhaps this was one of those moments.

Terror was employed on both sides. By mid-April one United Irishman claimed that Castle repression had become "so atrocious that humanity could no longer endure it . . . men were taken at random without process or accusation." The rebels were not behind. Everywhere "dreadful outrages" were being committed and a "ferocious spirit" was abroad. Houses continued to be plundered for arms, trees cut down for pike handles and the rich relieved of their "redundancy of victualling." Those unsympathetic to the cause received threatening letters, and landlords were warned to expect reprisals if they evicted tenants for suspicion of rebellion or refusing to pay rent. Government spies and informers scoured the country, smelling out disloyalty, intimidating, blackmailing and paying off old scores with rumors and false information, while United Irishmen frightened property owners with midnight raids, house burnings and murders of collaborators or those suspected of betraying their society to informers. The area around Kilworth was so disturbed that an officer from Waterford offered to go restore order there; if he did not, gentlewomen would have to quit their houses and leave the "country to be ravaged by a popish banditti."

With so many different groups now united against Ascendancy rule, the provincial militia was ordered to be in readiness for national and regional uprisings anywhere. The Castle government feared infiltration of troops by United Irishmen and urged landowners responsible for the militia to be especially vigilant. Rebels had also penetrated great houses as servants, the better to keep a watchful eye on the enemy and their own sworn members. Landowners should be on their guard and note anything suspicious. In particular, the hunt was on for a fierce United Irishman said to be prowling around the countryside near Mitchelstown and forcibly taking oaths of membership from country people, stirring them

to rebellion. It was important to catch the man and Robert had given orders that anything unusual was to be reported directly to him.

It was in this troubled time that Henry Fitzgerald decided to travel to Ireland to find Mary King. The crossing from South Wales to Waterford would bring him nearer to Mitchelstown, but there were good links between the latter and Dublin since the Royal Mail coach went every day from Dawson Street, while post coaches set out three times a week to Cork, traveling through Mitchelstown.

Henry chose the more anonymous Dublin route, then took the mail coach south. He had heavily disguised himself and was assuming a strange voice, pretending that he was not a native speaker of English. Either this was not one of his better roles or he was enjoying the part he was playing and hammed it up. Presumably he trusted to his disguise to save his skin, but there was also something exhibitionist in the overacting. A Mr. Phillpott who traveled down from Dublin in the same mail coach found his companion quite "extraordinary . . . of a very suspicious appearance" and did not know what to make of him. Throughout the journey Henry had examined a map of County Cork with rapt and conspicuous attention.

Arriving in Mitchelstown, he did not try to enter his old home but instead went to stay at the King's Arms, a new hostelry in King Square across the road from Kingston College and the gates of Mitchelstown Castle. He knew it was kept by an old family retainer called Richard Barry, one of whose relatives was at present serving in Robert's militia. He expected to avoid recognition by his disguise and by the precaution of staying in by day and being seen only by candlelight. At night he left the inn to try to find Mary and get word to her.

Henry was consciously living a Gothic plot: a wandering lover seeking his beloved, immured in a castle. He was also conforming to the later romanticized image of the United Irishman. In the early nineteenth century, when she revisited these years in her patriotic novel *The Wild Irish Girl,* Sydney Owenson described a "stranger of noble stature, muffled in

a long dark cloke" who appears mysteriously in an ancient Irish hall during a time when "every man regarded his neighbour with suspicion or considered him with fear." Like Henry, the stranger always departed and returned "under the veil of night."

Outside fiction Henry's unusual nocturnal habits and bizarre speech patterns struck a curious note—as he must have known they would. United Irishmen were notorious for assuming odd, rather flamboyant disguises, so much so that Lord Chancellor Clare on his travels, when he spied a man dressed up as a Turk and speaking in a funny accent, had him arrested. It turned out that the suspected United Irishman was neither Turk nor rebel but a simple costumed crook busy defrauding the locals. In Henry's case the bizarre show alerted Barry, the innkeeper, who did not recognize him as the young man who used to live at the castle. It also roused suspicion in John Hartney, the manager of the inn and a former private in the Roscommon militia, of whom he asked many questions about who was in the area. His questioning and strange shifting accent led Hartney to conclude that he was the notorious United Irishman for whom they had been told to look out. He informed Barry of what he suspected; Barry decided to tell Robert, his landlord. When abroad Henry again proceeded with such theatricality that he was bound to be noticed. He lurked around Mitchelstown Castle and the surrounding estate, as several testified. Presumably he had not made contact with Mary, who might still have been kept in Dublin.

It was now the evening of Friday, 8 December. Robert had followed government orders about inspiriting his men and had gone to inspect them at Fermoy, about three miles south down the road from Mitchelstown. As he had turned out of the estate gates with his retinue, he had passed by the King's Arms and had probably been watched by Henry, who may have concluded that his going suggested Mary was not in Mitchelstown after all. Perhaps she was being kept at Kilworth with her sister Margaret. He decided he would take the Mitchelstown chaise to Kilworth. He could even have believed that the freethinking Margaret would help him and Mary.

Meanwhile Barry arrived in Fermoy, where he informed the Earl of Kingston about the suspicious stranger. Given the hunt for the United Irishman, Robert may in part have expected to find such a man but, hearing the description, probably he suspected the truth. He ordered a chaise to be got ready, took up a case of pistols and collected his son Robert Edward, who, as well as being a regular army officer, was acting as a colonel in the local militia. They set off through the night for Mitchelstown to interrogate or capture the stranger.

At Mitchelstown they questioned the servants and postboys, learning that their quarry had moved to Kilworth. There again informers reported they had seen a man "lurking in disguise." Robert asked Barry if he could come with them to identify the suspect when they found him. Barry doubted he could recognize him, having seen him only in the dark, but he believed that John Hartney, with whom the stranger had long conversed, could help. A horse was obtained for Hartney, and the three men set off for Kilworth.

Having come the ten miles at full speed, they arrived in the early hours of the morning at the Kilworth Inn, opposite the road to Fermoy. There the innkeeper, Simmons, confirmed that his guest had come from Mitchelstown and was now sleeping upstairs. Obviously he had not found what he wanted at Kilworth or he was beginning to doubt the efficacy of his disguise, for Simmons reported that he intended to take the mail coach out next morning; it should arrive about eight and he had asked to be roused when it came. It was now six o'clock.

The three men were told which room the stranger occupied. Robert sent up a message saying they wished to speak with him. Since the Earl of Kingston was a personage in the region, it is unlikely the message was delivered without the sender's name attached. The guest refused to come down, so Robert, his son and John Hartney went up. They knocked loudly and repeatedly at the door, but it remained closed.

Many versions relate the next events. In some Henry simply opened the door; in others he declared he was locked in and would receive any communication in writing through the gap under his door. In most ver-

sions the three men broke down the door and forced entry into the room. Then again accounts diverge. The official report from the King camp has them expecting to find a United Irishman and being "amazed" to discover Henry, whom the Earl had forbidden to enter the country. Most accounts assumed Robert saw what by now he anticipated.

The pro-King *Times* at first reported that a duel ensued in which the Earl shot Henry dead. The similarly pro-King *Gentleman's Magazine* was more circumstantial. It recorded an unarmed Robert Edward going up alone before his father. He gained entry to the room; then, seeing a case of pistols on the side, he took one up and told Henry to grab another and defend himself. The young men both seized weapons but were grappling together when the Earl arrived, furious to find Robert Edward in danger from a scoundrel. With Henry suddenly about to fire and his son unwilling or unable to defend himself quickly enough, the Earl took his own pistol and "fired upon the colonel, not we believe with an intent to kill him, though his aggravation was great; but the shot however took effect, and the colonel lost his life, but not lamented by any one who has heard of his very dishonourable conduct in this affair."

However glossed, it was clear that the Earl of Kingston "with one bullet from a five-shilling pistol" shot his wife's cousin Henry. He made a wound three inches deep and half an inch wide; it was mortal and Henry died instantly—although in *The Times* report Robert at first tried to get medical help for his victim. It was also clear that this was not the usual duel but something akin to murder. The lowly John Hartney, brought to identify the stranger, was by all accounts unarmed.

What must have happened next, although no account delivers the detail, was that, before leaving the inn, Robert rifled through his dead cousin's pockets and belongings and retrieved the letter in which he had threatened him with murder if he came near Mary. The three men then left the corpse and rode to Moore Park to rouse Margaret. Stephen, it appears, was absent, probably on military business himself.

Margaret may have sympathized with Henry's love for Mary, impressed that one of her family at least was following her heart in the

manner Mary Wollstonecraft approved. Or she may have recognized an impetuous, confused man torn by conflicting emotions. In her patriotic novel "The Chieftains of Erin" she described with more psychological realism than she could usually muster in her fiction an Irishman who is disloyal to his clan. While pursuing his treachery near his original home, he disguises himself and assumes a strange accent; he lurks in dark corners and trembles whenever he sees people whom he knows. In the end he tries to make amends for his always confused and troubled actions. Whatever her attitude had been to the living Henry, he was now dead and she saw a chance to serve her father instead. He had not repulsed her, as Caroline had done, and she had been on good terms with him in her adult life; when A. Maria had made the flattering poem to Margaret, she had thought to please her by declaring, "Those virtues that adorn bright Kingsborough's breast / With equal lustre are by her possessed." No mention was made of her mother.

Margaret was in no doubt about events. When he arrived at her house, Robert exclaimed at once to her, "God! I don't know how I did it; but I most sincerely wish it had been by some other hand than mine." It was an impolitic exclamation but it fitted with his daughter's opinion, "that things which cannot be concealed, are better told at once." She could have advised her father to escape—there were routes out of Ireland for an earl with money—but it was a high-risk strategy: if he failed, he would be killed; if he succeeded, he would lose reputation and property. It would be better for him, his son and Hartney to let themselves be arrested without a struggle.

That Margaret had some pity for her father becomes clear from another fiction she wrote. In "Selene" she portrayed a man in a similar predicament to Robert's. This man has been betrayed by those he trusted, his wife and his best friend, who then refuses his challenge. He becomes frenzied and sets off in pursuit with loaded pistols. "In truth I was not perfectly in my senses," he confesses. "I felt as if some strange revolution had taken place in my feelings and mode of existence, but had not a perfect consciousness of what it was." His anger increases as he

travels. "The instant the carriage stopped, I opened the door, sprung out before any one could reach it, and rushing into the house demanded in furious tones to be shown the room." He is taken upstairs to a door "which I burst open in a paroxysm of rage, which was only checked by the appearance of two old ladies as pale as ashes. . . . This recalled me to my senses, and after making some incoherent apology for my strange conduct, I retired." Margaret was rewriting paternal events to give them a happier ending.

For Lord Shannon, Robert's fierce rival in Cork, a man whom he had ousted for the governorship of the county, events had already yielded much joy. They yielded even more when he realized that his son Viscount Boyle would be foreman of the grand jury appointed to investigate the Kings' crime. In her novel *Ennui* Maria Edgeworth wrote that in Ireland "A great man talks of *making* a justice of the peace with perfect confidence; a very great man talks with as much certainty of *making* a sheriff; and a sheriff makes the jury; and the jury makes the law."

The Shannon party was enthusiastic to see all connected with the murder punished, to such an extent that they even wanted to include John Hartney in the charge. This they succeeded in doing. The coroner's inquest, packed with Lord Shannon's supporters, gave their speedy verdict: Henry Fitzgerald had been killed by Lord Kingston but he had been aided by Colonel Robert Edward King and John Hartney, quaintly described in the indictment as "being moved and seduced by the Instigation of the Devil." It was a shrewd move to implicate all three since, had Hartney not been charged with murder, he could have given testimony on behalf of the two Roberts, that the one was not guilty and the other had acted to defend his son and should not be accused of the worst sort of cold-blooded crime.

The King family understood the point well and at the beginning of February Robert's uncle Henry wrote to the Lord Lieutenant asking for a pardon for Hartney, so that he could give evidence in the trial of the Earl and his son. The poor man was a victim of the feuds between the Kings and Shannons, he said.

But the Shannon party prevailed and in early April 1798 Colonel Robert Edward King and John Hartney were arraigned by the Cork Assizes. Robert Edward, a haughty man, was noticeably nervous in court, deeply embarrassed at the indignity brought on his family, especially in front of so many ill-wishers. Yet even the Kings' enemies could not find the two men guilty of murder. More irritating was the fact that the new-made Earl of Kingston, who must surely be found guilty, could avoid justice in Cork altogether; as a nobleman, he could demand trial by his peers—his father had died in the nick of time. Robert would therefore now be tried by the House of Lords in Dublin. Friday, 18 May was assigned for the event. In the meantime he remained in jail in Cork.

Colonel Henry Fitzgerald was buried where he had been murdered: in Kilworth at the church. Margaret, though living so close by, did not attend the funeral, nor did any of the Kings or indeed Henry's wife. The only mourners were the Kilworth innkeeper, a corporal and five privates.

As for Mary, accounts differ. In Adèle's version, Mary's letter of invitation and her portrait were found on Henry's body; the letter was brought to his beloved covered in blood, while her heartless brother Robert Edward boasted of the stratagem that had delivered Henry so neatly to him—in this account the Kings knew of the invitation and had welcomed it. Thereafter Mary produced a stillborn baby and "went raving mad." Fits alternated with apathetic imbecility and the sight of any of her family led to violent outbursts. Just as eager for scandal but usually more accurate, Bishop Percy wrote of the rumor that Mary "lives concealed in this Town [Dublin], where she has been brought to bed of a daughter." If not stillborn, the baby probably died soon after birth since there is no further mention of her.

While the Kings were preoccupied with family matters, the Moiras were pursuing national politics. In July 1797 their tenants at Ballynahinch had been accused of being United Irishmen and both Lord Moira's groom and gardener were found guilty of taking the oath. Worse, they were accused of recruiting government soldiers into rebel ranks and of making and con-

cealing pikes on his estate. "My tenants and my servants must be as open to seduction as those of other people," remarked Lord Moira. He believed the government, especially Lords Clare and Castlereagh, were targeting him through arresting "underling trangressors." "The tranquillity of my town was an effusive proof of the advantages that might arise from kind treatment of the people."

Castle policy was alienating many, he believed: "there exists a general detestation of Government in this part; the universality of which sentiments will produce all the effect of concerted plan as soon as circumstances give any invitation for attempting revenge." Yet whatever the provocation, landowners—including himself—could not be in favor of outright rebellion since "all of us who have property would be sacrificed to private cupidity in the confusion of public vengeance."

Undeterred by the hostility from his own class, in November Lord Moira brought a motion in the British House of Lords asking the crown to interfere directly in Ireland, now in thrall to "the most absurd, as well as the most disgusting, tyranny that any nation groaned under." Ireland could be no help to England in the war with France, since it had been reduced "to such a state of wretchedness that men actually died for want." The Castle forces were out of control, burning and scourging the country and menacing anyone they chose. Indeed, it seemed as though Ireland were ruled by the Inquisition, he said. It was an emotive image for Protestants.

Such open attacks on the government of a country which, as his enemies pointed out, Lord Moira rarely chose to inhabit, angered Lord Clare. Why did he speak in the Westminster Parliament, not the Irish one? he asked. "[T]he noble lord, secure in another kingdom, conceives that we are all safe—that the Lords and Commons know nothing of the situation of the country, because they do not wait until their throats are cut by the rebels, without making any preparations for defence." Moira was a dupe, the "High-priest of sedition," an ally of the United Irishmen; his speech was treason, an open invitation to the rebels to rise and the French to invade. He had insisted that the unrest was due to lack of par-

liamentary reform. Clare responded that most peasants had not the slightest idea of such a thing; they were simply incited and intimidated by a frightening secret society, the United Irishmen. There was a massive gap between liberal aristocrats and the peasants they purported to represent. Lord Moira "might as well read to them the quotations from Cicero, with which he had favoured the house."

In Dublin Lady Moira responded to attacks on her son with fury. She shrank her social circle and banished from her home lords and bishops, even former close friends, who had opposed him. Anyone in good odor with the administration was ostracized. "[T]hey are all off," wrote Bishop Percy to his wife, and "no body from the Castle is allowed to enter [the] old Lady's Doors, &c. &c. &c.—Green here is the disaffected colour & Lady M. carries it so far, that she wears Green Stockings & takes care to lift up her petticoats to show them, as she gets in and out of her Carriage." It was as well that she had Margaret and Pamela to visit and invite.

Mary Wollstonecraft also became a factor in these polemical wars. She had been blamed for the fall of Mary King and the old scandal that she had wanted to get Robert into bed was resurrected. In this heated atmosphere the Bishop of Ossory preached a sermon in Dublin in which he condemned "atheistical writers," apparently including Mary Wollstonecraft. He also mocked freethinking ladies of the "higher ranks" who had been influenced by "conspirators" to work toward the undermining of religion: "in no work of their's did they so much glory, as in that monster of Christian days a female Libertine, a female Atheist." Everyone knew "atheism" was a political term, and the St. George against this particular dragon was Lord Clare, whose name the bishop followed with a prayer: "May the work he has performed be permanent! be eternal! May no infamous seducer ever cross that hallowed threshold, to pollute that virgin hope of the state!"

His remarks made Margaret as furious as the attacks on her son had made Lady Moira. The allusion to Wollstonecraft was an obvious reference to the fracas in the King family and the comments on high-ranking libertines and subversives were aimed directly at herself and Lady Moira.

Faced with her fury, the bishop retreated: he had never intended to insult the noble family of Kings, he pleaded. But, recorded Bishop Percy, "this was so far from appeasing her, that she made a Caricature of him" and Lady Moira robustly backed her up: "his Lp is banished Moira House for that, as much as for voting agst. her Son. The Old Lady openly professes the most violent Enmity to all Religion & has banished all Bishops from her house." Margaret and Lady Moira made a formidable pair.

For some time Margaret had probably been supporting her opinion by concealing fugitives in her large town house and country estate. Now in her fury Lady Moira followed her example. Lord Clare certainly suspected that the many rooms of Moira House assisted his enemies in evading justice. Not only were rebels hidden in Usher's Quay but they were then helped to escape from Ireland through boats moored on the river Liffey nearby. As one informant testified, "The late Mr Thomas Geoghegan, solicitor, informed me that two uncles of his named Clements, who were United Irishmen, obtained refuge at Moira House while warrants were out for their arrest, and finally succeeded in escaping all pains and penalties owing to the precautions taken by Lady Moira."

Pamela and Edward were, of course, open and constant visitors to Moira House; Edward also called on the Moiras' near neighbor, the United Irishman Francis Magan, living at no. 20 Usher's Island. He was a Catholic barrister who had inherited the large house from his rich grandfather. Magan had been a longtime member of the United Irishmen, so his home could be used for asylum and illegal meetings. The unlikely pair of Protestant patrician Lady Moira and middle-class Catholic Francis Magan made the whole area something of a safe haven for refugees.

Despite the extra powers of the army, the pacification of Ireland was not going as well as the administration claimed to its masters in London. So in November 1797 Pitt appointed Ralph Abercromby to take charge of the Irish army in place of the punishing Lord Carhampton, whom even the Lord Lieutenant, Lord Camden, had admitted "did not confine himself to the strict rules of law." Abercromby had recently learned in Flan-

ders how disastrous, demoralized and undisciplined troops could be and how dangerous they were to the population they supposedly defended. He at once criticized the license of the troops under General Lake, commander of the north, and, after surveying the Irish situation in general, blamed Dublin Castle for the mess in the country—the unrest was due not to revolutionary principles but to "the oppression of centuries," he said, echoing liberals such as Lord Moira, his mother and Margaret. As for the army, it was "in a state of licentiousness which must render it formidable to everyone but the enemy."

When they heard these opinions, Lords Clare, Camden and Castlereagh were appalled, as was George King, whose militiamen were probably also on the new commander's mind; they all called Abercromby a "Scotch beast." The combined outrage was transmitted to London, where it had its effect; Abercromby in March 1798 was forced to resign effective 25 April. In his place came his second in command from Ulster, General Lake, who had done gallant service with a small brigade on the Continent and was famed for calm courage in the field, but as an overall commander was mediocre and blustering. He reversed Abercromby's cautious policies. Confrontation was again the order of the day and Ireland became "the prey of the Orange and Castle bloodhounds." Since the country was said to be in rebellion, General Lake was to have a free hand in quelling it.

The United Irishmen had not, so far, been infiltrated by informers to the extent the Castle wished, but now they had a setback, not from a Castle agent but from one of their own followers. After agonizing over his decision, Thomas Reynolds, whom Lord Edward had recruited into the society, decided to change sides and betray his fellow members. He told the Castle where the United Irish leaders were next meeting and, unusually for informers, said he was prepared to testify against them in court after they were taken into custody. To Edward he hinted that the government was about to seize him; as a result, he did not attend on the crucial day.

On 12 March 1798 Lord Camden's constables arrived at the United

Irish meeting and arrested the committee. Apart from Lord Edward, one who evaded capture was the member from Wexford: he had been flirting with a barmaid at a local inn and had thus missed the crucial beginning of the session. From his absence the authorities mistakenly assumed that Wexford had few United Irishmen and no important cell of activists.

After the multiple arrests Lord Edward went into hiding in safe houses in Dublin, probably including Moira House, which had a useful subterranean passage joining its two pleasure gardens on either side of Island Street. From here he could easily visit his men in disguise. Like Henry Fitzgerald, Lord Edward had a theatrical streak and zestfully assumed various roles: now a doctor, now a woman and now a poor drover complete with sheep. He remained the single free leader of the United Irishmen.

When necessary he also left Dublin to hide in outlying counties. Here Margaret was invaluable. The authorities suspected he was sometimes traveling the country and they ordered householders in suspicious districts to supply lists of all people sleeping under their roofs on any particular night. For Edward the safest house was undoubtedly Moore Park when Margaret was in residence. So on one occasion when fleeing Dublin he arrived there unexpectedly, presumably using one of his colorful disguises. Margaret at once hid him within the cellars. Soon Castle troops followed, having been tipped off by agents who claimed they had spied the fugitive in the area. Presumably they were apprised of Lady Mount Cashell's views if not her allegiances. Margaret invited the troops into the house and persuaded them of the absurdity of expecting to find Lord Edward in residence. Then she entertained them all, commanders and ordinary soldiers, with some lavishness. They ate and drank their fill in rooms on top of the cellars where Lord Edward was hiding.

Back in London Margaret was also on hand to help Lord Edward's wife. In April Pamela went into labor prematurely, with Lady Moira intermittently in attendance. She and Margaret saw to it that their poor friend had good treatment despite the frantic times and the absence of her husband, and Lady Moira was especially impressed by the attentive doctor. After a long labor Pamela bore her third child, whom she named Lucy

after her enthusiastic sister-in-law; she was tired and did not recover her energy for some time.

However they helped ease her labor, Lady Moira and Margaret could not ensure Pamela's peace, and one day when she was still bedridden at her brother-in-law's Leinster House, she was disturbed by soldiers sent from the Castle to find evidence in her chamber of Lord Edward's hiding place and schemes. Hurriedly she tried to burn bundles of incriminating letters between herself and Edward, but there was little time and many were discovered. She was terrified and tearful, especially as she assumed from the raid that Edward had been captured or killed. Softened by beauty in distress, their commander whispered, "Your husband has not been taken."

Pamela also had a visit from her stepfather-in-law. Hearing the news of the capture of so many high-profile United Irishmen and knowing the involvement of his stepson, Mr. Ogilvie had arrived posthaste from England. He called on Lord Clare, who, wishing to rid Ireland of Edward rather than make him an aristocratic martyr, told Ogilvie to get the young man out of the country quickly; he would leave the ports open for this purpose. Ogilvie relayed this to Pamela, but she distrusted the offer. When he caught up with Edward, he learned that his stepson was in too far to "withdraw with honour." Ogilvie left in tears. Shortly afterward printed sheets went up all over Dublin offering a reward of £1,000 for the capture of Lord Edward Fitzgerald.

Margaret, meanwhile, had her own family to worry about. Her father's trial was now drawing near. The attitude of the Lord Lieutenant to the Kings was uncertain. He had been a friend of Robert, who had been a government supporter in recent years. At the same time he might have wanted to show impartiality to the nation by sacrificing one of his own class. Lord Clare, with the addition of his hereditary dislike of the Kings, may have felt the same. Or, since Margaret and Stephen had both been blamed for failing to aid the Castle, Clare and the Lord Lieutenant might have wished to teach some members of a treacherous family a lesson. George King, the

heir, was a committed Orangeman and loyalist; with his father executed for murder he would be Earl of Kingston and a member of the House of Lords.

The first thing Margaret needed to do was provide a good defense advocate for her father. Undoubtedly it was she who asked her friend, the radical John Philpot Curran, to become one of the lawyers representing him; otherwise it is hard to explain such an appointment by an ultraloyalist family. Even her earlier friend, the liberal Charles Kendal Bushe, would have been a more appropriate person. The choice of Curran suggests both that Margaret had come closer to her father during his troubles and that he himself had moved further from his opinionated Orangist heir, George. In Curran Robert was retaining a man frequently accused of being a United Irishman—there are even hints that he was negotiating for a position in the new government to be set up once the rebellion succeeded.

This was a man who had recently thundered, "I warn ministers of the present example in a neighbouring country, where 24,000,000 people, galled by their oppressions, have risen up to vengeance at the great call of Nature, and rend their chains upon,—upon the heads of their oppressors." Curran had appeared in all the recent state trials to defend terrorists and traitors; as the *Anti-Jacobin,* a conservative magazine, observed of his methods and stance, if his sort of arguments were admitted, no such thing as high treason could subsist in the kingdoms.

The most eminent lawyer in Ireland, Curran was a good person to defend a man clearly guilty. He was famous for bullying witnesses unhelpful to liberal causes, for shredding the evidence of the perjured and for dominating the jury with commands and oaths. If he lost, he attacked the members as drunken and unfit, noting exactly how many bottles of whiskey had been passed to them through the window while they deliberated and who had vomited before the verdict.

Margaret probably had other things in mind for her father's trial as well. She herself was heavily pregnant now and could help her fellow United

Irishmen best by planning and subterfuge. Surely this unhappy family event might be turned to good advantage, while any political use made of it must also save her father, a state prisoner.

Whoever first proposed the plan, the Dublin United Irishmen were soon seriously considering the Kingston trial as a possible beginning of the long-awaited rebellion. Since Reynolds's betrayal, the organization had foundered and the leading Dublin group had been censured for delay by the provincial branches, which felt support ebbing from the movement. The previous year had seen hardships and the people were known to be in a volatile mood and desperate for decisive action and leadership. Some blamed the Dublin members for being slow to revolt, for dithering when they should be decisive, and for hanging back from open assault. Others accused them of putting too much faith in French help, which, given France's aggressive policy in Europe, might in any case turn out a double-edged sword (the counterargument put forward by a minority was that a French-led insurrection would be more disciplined and fierce than a wholly native one).

After much debate in secret houses and inns, Lord Edward and his colleagues decided that they would cooperate with the French if they landed but that they would be better relying primarily on themselves for their revolution. There could scarcely be a more favorable event to begin military action than the Kingston trial before the House of Lords. The whole aristocracy of Ireland, the whole corrupt administration, would be assembled, dressed up and vulnerable.

The plan demanded little initial force. The approaches to Dublin were unfortified and, owing to the decision to disperse troops around the country in case of a French invasion, there were relatively few regular soldiers within the city. Although there were various yeomanry corps, some of these were less than menacing. For example, lawyers, doctors, and even elderly gentlemen living in Merrion Square had formed their own corps. The last of these paraded in the square on fine evenings before playing whist and drinking tea; on wet and damp nights they patrolled sedately in a file of sedan chairs. Although the Castle rulers despised the Dublin

crowd as drunkards and potential looters, the United Irishmen were more sanguine about their abilities when roused, and they believed they could easily mobilize and control their followers once an open uprising began.

So, with one single well-planned rebellious act using minimum force, it ought to be possible to topple the government in Dublin and capture most of its important members, including the Lord Lieutenant and Lord Clare. Once this was achieved, supporting crescents of United Irishmen outside Dublin but close by would rise in their tens of thousands and prevent government troops coming from garrisons elsewhere to reinforce the city's soldiers. After the capital was secured, the rest of Ireland would be easy to take.

The Kingston plan was to be finalized at a secret executive committee meeting the night before Robert's trial. Meanwhile, it was much discussed in preparatory sessions. Many members were for it, most importantly the charismatic Lord Edward; he urged it on his wavering fellow members. The trial was, he pointed out, an unprecedented moment to neutralize the aristocratic landowning class and free the country from political and economic oppression. With such a move the rebels would bring the French Terror to Dublin. The United Irishmen had numerous caches of hidden weapons about the city that could arm their city followers, and there was no reason to fear failure, he argued. The only question was the aftermath: when they achieved power, should they simply confiscate property and banish the aristocrats or should they massacre them in the French manner? Happily Edward's brother, the Duke of Leinster, remained out of the country.

Hiding out in Thomas Street, a thoroughfare parallel to Usher's Island, Lord Edward was not especially fearful of capture, since friends were all around, including Lady Moira at Moira House and his fellow conspirator Francis Magan, living a few doors away. Magan had just been elected to the executive and was now a respected and trusted member of the inner circle. So the meeting of the final committee on the evening of 17 May was held in his house on Usher's Island. The committee had to decide on final tactics and give the signal for action to their followers.

In a meeting of three Irish conspirators there are, it is said, always two informers. The committee that met that evening had forgotten this saying; indeed, they were so bent on treachery against the government that they failed to worry about it in their midst or suspect that any one of them could act as traitor. Thus they had no inkling that all their words and plans were reported directly to the Castle. The source was their host, Francis Magan, who was now in government pay.

Although financially independent thanks to his rich grandfather's legacy, Magan perhaps wanted more money. Spying and informing were not often well paid but in these troubled times those who pleased the government could expect to be handsomely rewarded, and there was on offer the £1,000 for the capture of Lord Edward—which Magan confidently declared he could accomplish. Perhaps, though, since he was unmarried and did not live luxuriously, he simply gained a thrill in an otherwise unremarkable life by his double dealing. At the same time he may have believed he was heading off a secular rebellion that would in the end be injurious to his fellow Catholics and their faith.

Whatever his motives, Magan had already contacted an old friend of his father's, the "Sham Squire" Francis Higgins, the journal proprietor who secretly doubled as spymaster for the Castle—the radical, spy-busting *Union Star* had already targeted him as an agent. Magan offered to inform against the United Irishmen and Lord Edward in particular. The *Union Star* had been suppressed or else he might not have had so easy a time of his treachery.

The Castle administration had been delighted at Magan's offer, knowing he had an unrivaled position within the inner sanctum of the United Irishmen. Furthermore, from his stable doors at the end of his untidy garden on Island Street behind Usher's Island he could actually see what was happening at Moira House on Usher's Quay and other houses where intrigue was suspected. Both his house and stables commanded a fine view of who was lurking in the area at any given time. He had left his stable doors open a good deal over the last weeks and kept in the shadows. His Castle paymasters would not speak directly to Magan

for fear of compromising him, but both sides could liaise with Higgins, who, as a neighbor of Margaret's, could himself keep an eye on any comings and goings at Mount Cashell House.

Through Magan and Higgins the Kingston trial plan was relayed in full to the Castle: "on the day of Earl Kingston's trial . . . a shocking scene of blood and havoc in the city" was intended. Higgins added that the aim was to involve "the nobility and Government as well as the city of Dublin" in a "scene of blood." As a result of such information, Lord Clare saw to it that Lord Kingsborough, now a keen part of the Castle's military force, was ordered speedily to move his North Cork troops to Dublin. George's appearance together with his notorious reputation would itself strike terror in many: he had hurt his eye and now wore a large green eye patch; it made him look as ferocious as he acted.

Quartered in George's Street Barracks, George's men were ordered for the moment to keep the peace in Dublin. It was small-scale work. For instance, he took his soldiers to the defense of a man who was being attacked as an Orangeman and whose house was being pulled down. The relieving soldiers were pelted with brickbats but managed to take five prisoners. After the incident George was irritated to find blood on his glove and his dress discomposed. Fortified with Magan's information, Lord Clare was expecting that the North Cork militia would soon have more strenuous work to do.

. C H A P T E R   1 1 .

Trial and Conspiracy

Those nicknames, Marquis, Lord and Earl,
That set the crowd a-gazing,
We prize as hogs esteem a pearl,
Their patents set a-blazing.

— *PADDY'S RESOURCE*

LORDS WERE DUELING EVERY DAY AND THE DEATHS WERE A FORM of murder, yet few paid the penalty. The Kingston killing was not a duel, however, and most of Kilworth was aware of the details. Times were tense and to be lenient to a lord was perhaps unwise. It was rare to execute landowners for murder but it was occasionally done. A distant Fitzgerald relative, George Fitzgerald of Turlough, after a rollicking career of heiress snatching, dueling and mayhem, which included imprisoning his father in a cave with a muzzled Russian bear, was to his great surprise hanged for murder and incitement. A good number hoped that Robert would be similarly served, Lord Shannon among them.

The presiding judge at the trial was Lord Clare as Lord Chancellor. He relished ceremony and a chance to dominate an old family such as the Kings. The trial would become a great social event, himself at its center. Involving the cream of Irish society and drawing an immense num-

ber of ordinary spectators, it would be a welcome diversion in grim times. So huge was the expected crowd that the House of Lords, the proper location for the trial, was judged too small; instead the event would be held in the larger neoclassical rotunda of the House of Commons on College Green. This could accommodate a mass of participants as well as seven hundred spectators, all with a good view of the chamber.

Preparations were elaborate: the trial was intended as "the most impressive and majestic spectacle ever exhibited within these walls," as one awed watcher put it. Scarlet fittings and rich Turkey carpets increased the pomp, and the Speaker's chair was gorgeously adorned to receive Lord Clare. The ritual would be carefully choreographed; lacking much precedent, a Lords Committee had been set up to inspect descriptions of old trials in parliamentary journals to find out how things should be done. This trial would outdo the past. Tickets were sold, as for an opera or play; they turned into such hot items that officials were soon being bribed to release them. Participating nobles—two marquesses, twenty-seven earls, fourteen viscounts, three archbishops, thirteen bishops and fourteen barons—were assigned three each for their families, one for the body of the House, and two for the galleries. The defendant was treated no differently from his judges, though he had a wife, a mistress and twelve legitimate and several illegitimate children. Seats were color-coded for rank: peers' wives sat on crimson cushions. It was all theater, "one of the finest Shows wch. can be exhibited in this Kingdom."

There was enough glamour, luxury and potential sensation in the trial to attract spectators outside the Parliament house as well as within, and these interested crowds needed policing. Since Dublin was experiencing an unusual spell of sunshine, it was expected that more onlookers than usual would be tempted out. So streets nearby were closed off and sheriffs placed officers conspicuously in squares and main streets around town.

It appeared a civil precaution but it would do duty for a military one as well. Knowing before the trial about the violent intentions of the

United Irishmen, the Castle had decided to close off the city and use the pretext of policing the crowd to restrict access to the Parliament buildings. Yet Clare and Castlereagh must have feared that, despite all the panoply of ticketing and guarding doors, there might be some among the rank-and-file spectators within the chamber who had taken the secret oath to the United Irishmen and who were not just double agents but triple agents, some who knew of the trial plan and might have pistols and knives hidden under their clothes.

By eight o'clock in the morning of 18 May ticket holders assembled outside the building. At ten they were let into the Commons galleries. An hour later the peers who would do the judging—including the Earl's son-in-law Stephen—assembled in their own House of Lords in rich robes of state, even the notorious drunkards and slovens looking splendid in their regalia. There were some absentees, while some of those present were coming to Parliament for the first time in their lives. The peers walked two by two from the Lords to the Commons in self-conscious pomp, led by the court judges and followed by their eldest sons, George of course among them. The star of this part was Lord Clare, who carried a white wand. He then sat in the Speaker's chair with the lords on his left and the bishops on his right. The robed judges went to a table in the center. The names and titles of the peers were elaborately intoned by heralds and ritual salutations made. King George III's commission was delivered appointing Clare Lord High Steward for the trial. Then the grand jury's indictment was read.

Just at noon Robert was brought into the chamber and led to the Bar by the Constable of the Castle. The shouts that often greeted murderers were absent, for although the Kings were not a popular family, there was some sympathy for a father provoked beyond endurance by unruly children. One MP watching from the gallery shuddered with suspense: he was, he recorded, seeing history.

The Earl too had a sense of theater: alone in all the gaudy crowd he

was an austere figure, dressed in black, his eyes fixed on the ground. He was in mourning for the dead man, who was, after all, his wife's cousin, and appropriate dress was required. To sensitive spectators he appeared to move with a slow and melancholy step.

Sir Charles Fortiscue, Ulster King-at-Arms, carried before Robert the armorial bearings of the Earls of Kingston emblazoned on a shield. Beside him the constable bore the symbol of his potential fate, an axe with a broad blade, painted black except within two inches of the edge, which was of brightly polished steel. The axe was held level with Robert's neck, the shining edge turned away; if the trial condemned him and judgment of death was pronounced, the blade would be turned toward the neck.

The tension was great. All reports confirmed that spectators had no inkling of what would happen. The Kings were unpopular and many inside and outside the House expected to enjoy the thrill of a peer's beheading. At the same time acquittal after a contest of lawyers could be equally satisfying.

The trial proceeded ritually. Lord Clare warned Robert that he had been "brought here to answer one of the most serious Charges which can be made against any Man—a Charge of the Murder of a Fellow Subject"; he feared that the solemnity of the occasion must "materially discompose and embarrass" the accused but stressed that he was being tried by the laws of a free country, laws framed to protect innocence and punish guilt and which had separated out accidental homicide from malicious murder. He would be heard by the lords, Clare went on, "the supreme judicature of this nation . . . upon whose unbiased judgment and Candour" the Earl could have "the firmest Reliance"; this must be "a great consolation" to the accused. It was good propaganda: the English tradition of justice that was treating Robert fairly contrasted with the rebellious aims and terrorist methods haunting Ireland outside the law and even now threatening Dublin and good order.

Clare continued, "Culprit, how will your lordship be tried?" Robert

replied, "by God and my peers" and pleaded "Not guilty." The clerk of the court responded with his formula, "GOD send you a good Deliverance." All, including the accused, were now poised for the climax, when witnesses were brought in. On these people the outcome of the trial rested: the victim's wife, for example, who would have known of the death threat to her husband, as well as the people who had almost witnessed the murder at Kilworth and seen incontrovertible evidence in the smoking pistol and blood-bespattered clothes. What the prosecution did not have and could not see was the incriminating letter written by Robert to Henry Fitzgerald; this remained in the hands of the Kings.

"It is not easy to describe the anxiety and suspense as each name was called over," wrote one observer, Sir Jonah Barrington. "The eyes of every body were directed to the bar where the witnesses must enter, and every little movement of the persons who thronged it was held to be intended to make room for some accuser." The silence that followed the calling was therefore tense.

And prolonged, for no one entered. A second proclamation also resulted in silence. Who was surprised? Lord Clare, the lawyer John Philpot Curran, the Earl of Kingston or all of them? Certainly most of the men and women watching from the gallery were amazed.

A third and last proclamation was made; each name was called again. The same silence followed. Nothing remained but to order the Earl of Kingston's removal from the chamber and give a verdict. The peers adjourned in their hierarchical rank and Lord Clare told them they must unanimously acquit the Earl; yet, in view of the solemnity of the proceedings, each lord must give his opinion individually. Perhaps Clare felt that the ceremony was truncated and that the audience, like so many at the theater, would riot at too brief a piece.

So it began; each peer's name was read out and each stood hatless to pronounce "Not Guilty, upon my Honour!" with his right hand clamped to his breast. The performance took an hour. The Earl was brought back:

he knelt and was then told he had been acquitted "without a dissenting voice." Clare broke his white staff of office and the lords processed out in order, rustling again their gorgeous robes of state.

"It is pity but you and your Daur. cd. have seen the Show," wrote Bishop Percy to his absent wife after it was over. Less easily impressed, the Bishop of Limerick had been bored even by the preparations for the trial:

> I am in Dublin for a few days, brought here by a call of the *Whole* House
> of Lords, to regulate matters for Lord Kingston's trial; But had I known
> how Trifling and uninteresting the Business was for which I was call'd;
> They might have call'd often enough before I should have answer'd. I
> am going Home again on Saturday.

There were two other notable absences: the Earl's estranged wife and his most prominent enemy, Lord Shannon. Presumably the resignation that Queen Charlotte had noted kept Caroline quietly in Windsor away from the "Show" her family was providing for Dublin. Lord Shannon was, of course, an invited peer and should have been present as a judge, but he feared that Robert would be acquitted by some loophole. "Amen" would have stuck in his throat, he wrote.

Always ready to support the powerful Kings, the *Hibernian Journal* declared that "every virtuous and feeling heart" was contented by the verdict of acquittal. According to Mary's friend Adèle, however, Henry's wife cried for vengeance but failed to get it because of the despotic power of the Earl of Kingston in Ireland. "Lord Kingston and his sons . . . were the objects of general opprobrium in their own country," she insisted. Prince Pückler-Muskau made a similar hostile point. "The sequel proves how lightly the laws sit on great men in England," he wrote with some confusion of the two kingdoms. Yet Curran testified that Henry's wife and children had been summoned for the trial and this was supported by the officer who had served the summons in Bury Street, London. Perhaps they had indeed been warned off—or heavily bribed—by the Kings or perhaps the wife's love for her husband had not triumphed as much as

Adèle assumed. The other possible witnesses from Mitchelstown and Kilworth must have shared in the bounty of the Kings and Mount Cashells—Robert had had the large sum of 5,000 guineas available to buy off Henry Fitzgerald and it had not been used.

Why had the nobility been allowed to process in such pointless show without disturbance from the United Irishmen? What had happened to the planned uprising? The answer must be found with Francis Magan.

On the previous evening at the meeting of the United Irishmen he had been in a delicate position. It was his business to stir rebellion, since the more he had to tell the more he would be paid. But a plot to wipe out the nobility and his main Castle paymasters was not in his interests, and it was imperative to dissuade Lord Edward, a rash young man in his view, from following this risky plan. There was also the matter of the £1,000 he had been promised for his capture—either dead or successful, Edward would have escaped his intended betrayer. Never again would Magan be likely to have the amazing good fortune of having in his grasp a man with such a sum on his head.

He knew he must not move precipitately. By now he was terrified that his fellow conspirators would discover his treachery and deal with him. He needed above all to stop the rebellion beginning. After that he would see to the capturing of Lord Edward.

With these aims Magan had earlier argued to the United Irish executive that failure of the Kingston plan could result in disaster for them all and cause heavy casualties. The Castle just might be more prepared than they anticipated. The argument convinced some committee members but not Lord Edward. This was troubling; Magan feared to press his view in case he aroused suspicion.

Before the final meeting at his house he had told his fears to his control, Higgins, who urged him on; too much was at stake for faltering. Magan remained worried about his safety and Higgins had to advance his own money to keep him "steady"—or so he later claimed. Perhaps when he reported this episode to the Castle Higgins magnified his own part: he

declared that the bloody attack would certainly have occurred, "if I had not prevailed upon [Magan] to come forward and act in the manner he did when the first attack was intended at the H. of C."

Higgins's persuasion, political or financial, worked and Magan did indeed become "steady" and resolve to act in the Castle's interest. The plan he knew was finally to go to the executive for a decision at this meeting and the members were then bound to abide by the majority vote. Lord Edward continued to support the plan, as did many of his followers, but when heads were counted it was found that it had been defeated by one vote—Magan's. The revolt was called off.

The meeting over, Magan's account of it was sent to the Castle through Higgins, but it is not absolutely clear when the report was received and read by Lord Clare: before or after Robert's trial.

Both Magan and Higgins deserved their pay in the affair. As Lord Castlereagh reported, "Had this infernal plot not been so fortunately discovered, the Capital of Ireland would now have been flowing with the blood of its inhabitants." Good people as well as deluded wretches would have died. But "the discovery was so timely as to defeat their designs before they had arrived to more decisive execution."

In other words, had the United Irishmen attacked that night, they could possibly have taken Dublin for, only just forewarned, the Castle was not really prepared for a major assault. If the rebels had risen and been successful or partially so, Irish history would have taken another course and Mary's affair with Henry Fitzgerald and Margaret's involvement with her family and the United Irishmen would have been crucial within it.

Like the other United Irishmen Margaret heard of the postponement but had no inkling of Magan's treachery, no notion that the Castle knew of the intended rebellion. So she, like her fellow members, was unprepared for what happened next.

After abandoning their plan, the executive of the United Irishmen had decided on a new scheme: a rising a few days later, on 23 May, using the combined rebel forces of the surrounding counties: Dublin, Kildare,

Meath and Wicklow. The date would give them time the better to prepare their troops. Magan duly relayed the plan to the Castle: "the banditti of traitors had by no means relinquished their plan of attack on the metropolis." They would, he reported, be helped by a band of seventy thousand men from the country along with the "armed circuitous horde" already in the city. All were inspired by United Irish propaganda that insisted the Castle meant to exterminate the Catholics. Higgins, who relayed the information, pointed out that among the detailed plans for Dublin was an attack on the houses of the great, the head of the list being those of Clare and Castlereagh. It was time for the Castle to strike hard at the United Irishmen by capturing their impetuous military leader.

Among his many tactics Castlereagh had tried to neutralize society women such as Ladies Moira and Mount Cashell, who thought it amusing to support Lord Edward and play at revolution. He needed to counter like with like, so he turned to the more pliable and timid Lady Louisa Conolly, Lord Edward's aunt, with whom Edward and Pamela continued intimate. Along with Francis Magan, Lady Louisa might help to trap her nephew.

Louisa prized law, order, authority and the status quo, and she and her husband refused to support reforming measures. Both suffered from the colonialist's fear of being attacked in the night by native servants. Lady Louisa had worked hard at being mistress of Castletown; in return for her benevolence she expected loyalty and affection. But despite nearly forty years of showing "the greatest goodwill to the different classes around [her]" and despite recent visits to tenants in an effort to persuade them to reject revolt—she seems to have talked rather than listened—she now learned that nineteen men from the estate had been arrested as rebels, most of them her own people, including the family baker. Their plan had been for one to open her mansion door at night and let the others in; then they would rob and possibly murder the owners.

When he heard of the arrests Lord Castlereagh declared himself aghast: Louisa had been famously bountiful to her underlings and "had been more like a parent than a mistress" to her servants. Yet under the influence of United Irish rhetoric these same people had been prepared

to butcher her and her husband. With this potent example he and Clare warned the upper orders that any of them might be murdered by Catholic servants if they did not have Castle protection.

Louisa appreciated Castlereagh's concern. Unhappily she had not had the benefit of reading Percy Bysshe Shelley's later verses on her slippery nephew:

> I met Murder on the way—
> He had a mask like Castlereagh—
> Very smooth he looked, yet grim
> Seven blood-hounds followed him.

So she enjoyed his company and stayed with him whenever she was in Dublin. She was extremely grateful that he offered her his personal protection.

The friendship with Lady Louisa gave both Clare and Castlereagh much opportunity for conversation; during their talks they learned a good deal about Edward and Pamela. Perhaps in this she was simply being naive or perhaps she was secretly appalled by her rebel nephew abetting her enemies and wanted him stopped. The closeness of Louisa with these powerful government men troubled her sister Sarah, who had little property to lose and was more contemptuous of the rebel threat than Louisa; she saw Edward less as a traitor and rebel than as an impractical romanticist. Shrewder and less fearful than Louisa, Sarah worried that Clare and Castlereagh were using her sister for their own ends.

She could only convey her suspicions codedly but she wrote to another nephew, "The Deception of the C. & C. will not easily be discovered by the Dear Angelic pure Friend it works on. Nor am I sure I wish it should." It would be of no use to the fugitives and simply wound Louisa. Less innocent but equally fearful, her husband knew what was going on and had no interest in stopping it, but "she would be terribly tormented by knowing the truth." It was best, concluded Sarah, that she not have her eyes opened. As a result, Louisa continued useful to Clare

and Castlereagh and gave them much information about activities among the nobility that they could not easily have obtained elsewhere. She was a constant visitor to Pamela, whom she counseled to keep her mouth shut in this volatile season.

In fact Louisa was rather less naive than her sister suggested. At the time of the Kingston trial she wrote to Lord Edward's stepfather claiming that the "kind" Lord Lieutenant and Clare had authorized her nephew Castlereagh to use her to liaise with Pamela. She was also deputed to tell the Fitzgerald family that Pamela was suspected of plotting with the French and that the Castle government was planning to arrest her. Louisa was to let her know that she had ten days to get out of Ireland before this happened. "I still retain the most sanguine hopes, that the Information may turn out false," Louisa wrote. Pamela was furious: "Lady Egality complains dreadfully about Castlereagh ordering a short passport," reported Magan to Higgins, who reported it to the Castle. To Lady Moira Louisa fed the information that Pamela's incriminating letters were to be published. Lady Moira was appalled and wrote at once to Sarah complaining of "this proof of despotism."

All this female maneuvering gave the Castle some sense of where loyalties lay, but the main source of immediate information on Lord Edward during these crucial days remained Francis Magan, desperate now to accomplish the capture of this valuable man. Every few nights Edward shifted his hiding place. Margaret was aware of where he was at any moment, for she commented with details on a later inaccurate account. For a while he had been staying at the Yellow Lion, a pub in Thomas Street parallel to Usher's Island. Having learned it was to be searched, on the evening of the day of the Kingston trial Edward decided to move. Soldiers were prowling around and it seemed best if he went to Magan's house close by; from there he would also be able to see Pamela at Lady Moira's. Magan, who could hardly believe his luck, informed the Castle that this would be an excellent moment to capture the rebel leader, not actually within his house, which would be dangerous to himself, but just outside.

Acting on this vital detailed information, Major Sirr was dispatched to

do the deed just as Edward arrived at Magan's stable door at dusk. Things did not go according to plan, however, and Sirr tangled with Edward's bodyguards. In the ensuing fracas somehow Edward managed to escape. Magan was aghast at the incompetence. Again he had to keep watch at his back gate, hoping that another similar opportunity would present itself.

Edward now moved back to Thomas Street to the feather merchant Nicholas Murphy's house, intending to await the great day of the rising on the twenty-third. Then he would slip out of Dublin and lead the country troops into the city.

On the following evening, 19 May, he was lying in bed with a sore throat and chill in Murphy's warehouse, contemplating the coming rebellion and reading a comic French novel. His new scarlet and green revolutionary uniform, which an amazed Nicholas Murphy had just seen a woman delivering in a bundle, was nearby waiting for use, along with a couple of fantastic outfits perhaps intended for his later role in government. Outside, the aristocracy, including Lord Camden and his entourage, were assembling for a gala performance at the Theatre Royal of a comic opera, *Robin Hood,* written by a government spy. Not suspecting immediate attack, Edward yet kept a dagger or stiletto in his bosom, while "a number of stilleto armed men who formed a kind of bodyguard for him" carried "daggers & pistols." Unhappily, they were not close enough on this evening but drinking in a house in Queen Street, toasting a vision of Clare and Camden's blood in puddles on the Castle pavement.

Tipped off again by Francis Magan, soldiers now broke into Murphy's house to make a second attempt at capture. This time they had their victim to themselves. They struggled with Edward, who used his dagger to wound Captain Ryan, one of his assailants. Edward himself was shot twice in the shoulder and had to drop his dagger. He was then captured and taken as a prisoner to the Castle. Some of his followers tried to mount a rescue but Castle reinforcements saw them off. When they heard the news, the butchers in St. Patrick's market snatched pikes to attempt another rescue, but they scattered when they learned a squadron of horse was on the way to deal with them.

To their Castle masters Higgins and Magan apologized for the wounding of British officers. Their excuse was that Lord Edward had been unexpectedly armed. Captain Ryan was an especially sad casualty but the action had on the whole been worthwhile, they said, for it had "saved the lives of thousands" from Lord Edward and his "murderous crew."

The Castle now held a man who was both a traitor and a member of Ireland's premier aristocratic family. As the latter, he was given "every possible attention" by the Lord Lieutenant's private secretary, who offered to write a letter to Pamela with an account of what had happened. Edward asked that he "only break it to her gently." The secretary went himself to Moira House, where Pamela was known to be; when he arrived, he was intercepted by Margaret, who told her servant to warn Pamela's servants not to tell the news to their mistress that night. She was not yet properly recovered from her lying-in and was still very weak. There was no point giving her a sleepless night.

Meanwhile, Lady Sarah's daughter had heard of the capture while she was at the theater with Lady Castlereagh, sitting in a box next to the Lord Lieutenant's. When the news was whispered, she avoided any gesture or exclamation that would declare her views, then escaped the company and went straight to Pamela; she too was warned to keep her news till the morning. She stayed the night and next day spoke to Pamela, who seemed dazed by what they were telling her.

The arrest of Lord Edward made the United Irishmen headless at a crucial moment. From 24 May groups of rebels did rise with vigor but not in a concerted action and their efforts served mainly to give the Castle free rein to oppose and oppress through the militias and their rough justice. Lord Shannon reported the state of the nation:

> Here, whipping goes on at a great rate, and by proper flagellation, quantities of arms have been given up; but the cat-o'nine-tails is laid on with uncommon severity. The town is in one uproar, the streets so crowded that one walks with difficulty. We have had a most providential

escape here. It was more than an even bet that the rebels had prevailed, nor is the attack considered as over yet, but I should think the steps that have been taken and the discoveries that have been made will prevent the intended general rising, though we may not be secure against efforts of particular vengeance. Every street is alive with yeomen, and one hears no tune but *Croppies Lie Down.*

This anti–United Irishmen ballad was attributed to a captain in George's North Cork regiment.

As a traitor, Lord Edward was next taken to Newgate jail, where, although he was given the best room, his guards were less impressed with his exalted lineage than the Castle hierarchy had been. Since the wound had at first appeared slight, many people expected him to recover and then be put on trial, a procedure that would embarrass the Castle. Clare and Castlereagh had no wish to execute the brother of the Duke of Leinster, cousin of Charles James Fox, and acquaintance of the Prince of Wales.

But now in Newgate Edward's condition worsened and it seemed unlikely they would have to follow this politically difficult route. Although he had surgeons around him, no one had extracted the bullets he had received and he had become feverish. He raved patriotically, shouting at intervals, "Dear Ireland, I die for you!" and damning the doctor. Soon he was violent and incoherent. Meanwhile Captain Ryan died of the wound he had received in the scuffle; if Edward lived on, he would have to be tried for murder as well as treason.

Lady Louisa was now informed that Edward was very ill and likely to die soon. In distress she went to see the Lord Lieutenant to gain permission to visit her nephew. She was refused, though she knelt to him; unused to such treatment when she had demeaned herself, she furiously called him a "brute." She then proceeded to Lord Clare in Ely Place. Like Castlereagh, Clare admired Lady Louisa—"that excellent and admirable woman," he called her—and was mindful of her aid. Also he had heard that Edward was certainly dying and had decided on a strategic show of

mercy. So he agreed to her request and himself accompanied her and one of her other nephews on the visit. When they arrived at the prison he discreetly walked away so that she could speak to Edward alone. Later, when Edward died on 4 June, Clare publicly remarked that "it is over, but he knew her, and that, I hope, will be a comfort hereafter." In his private letters he had contemplated the death more wryly, thinking for a time that "Ld Edward bids fair to make his exit on the scaffold." But now he had exited more privately and it was most convenient. Unlike the informer Reynolds, Magan was terrified of being unmasked and he had not been prepared to testify against rebels in open court, so the trial would have been difficult to conduct. Even Edward's English uncle agreed to look on the bright side: sooner or later Edward would have "brought on Misery and Disgrace to his family, which indeed his Death alone has I fear now prevented."

To avoid disturbances from loyalists and Edward's followers, Castlereagh arranged for a midnight funeral, but since the city was under strict curfew, it took till dawn to get the body to the church and the few mourners, including Lady Louisa, out of it. Only in the early hours of the morning would she return exhausted to her home in Castletown. From then on it was Louisa's business to spiritualize Lord Edward and sentimentalize his wife.

The death satisfied others beyond Lord Clare and Edward's uncle. Higgins got the reward of £1,000, which he seems not to have shared quite fairly with the true informer, Francis Magan. He also received a pension of £300, while Magan got one of £200. In London the various Fitzgerald ladies had hysteria, an appropriate and conventional behavior for the time. Some were even considered in danger of their lives, but all survived.

Rebellion

Oh, croppies ye'd better be quiet and still
Ye shan't have your liberty, do what you will;
As long as salt water is formed in the deep,
A foot on the neck of the croppy we'll keep.

— "CROPPIES LIE DOWN"

AFTER HIS ACQUITTAL ROBERT WENT BACK TO MITCHELSTOWN. The area was still disturbed but he took little further part in its pacifying. Throughout Ireland the revolutionary coalition that had brought together peers and peasantry, Catholics and Protestants, was fragmenting and the liberal nobility were growing afraid for their property more than their liberty. Many Catholics seceded from the United Irishmen; at the end of May a petition declared, "We the undersigned, his Majesty's most loyal subjects, the Roman Catholics of Ireland, think it is necessary at this moment publicly to declare our firm attachment to his Majesty's royal person."

Five days after Edward was taken and six days after Robert's trial Dublin was put under martial law, an act almost unthinkable in London; it was proclaimed by the sound of a trumpet at the bridges and squares of the city. House-to-house searches for arms and rebels were made and the Dublin yeomanry mobilized. The military buildup and the troops already there for the Kingston trial, including some of George's North Cork men, were now used to launch a counterattack on the rebels. Had Margaret looked out from her house in St. Stephen's Green she could have seen a number of her fiercer neighbors from Mitchelstown and Kilworth mustering in the square in place of the elderly gentlemen in sedan chairs. There should, said a Castle spokesman, be an "energy" of government and no more "false lenity." The disturbances were aimed at landowners just as much as the British government, so it was absurd for members of this class to tolerate rebels who wanted to dispossess them. From England Lord Moira told his sister Selina to avoid Dublin and watch out for banditti pillaging near her home. She should fear a French invasion and distrust the loyalty of those surrounding her. Echoing the snobbishness of his mother, he declared that her only defense was the "elevation of the soul and steadiness of resolution which comes from preeminence of birth," the something in the blood "which is not imaginary." Lady Moira went to the seaside. "In case of any general insurrection, were it requisite to go to England, no spot is better situated to make a retreat from," she noted.

The Lord Lieutenant declared, "Martial law is established—the sword is drawn—I have kept it within the scabbard as long as possible—it must not be returned until this most alarming conspiracy is put down."

Initially George's North Cork regiment was not helpful. On 23 May, the day for which Lord Edward's rising had been planned, part of it was in Prosperous, a small cotton town in County Kildare. The men were seizing rebel arms, using their usual methods of flogging and burning as persuasion. The people told the soldiers that they were afraid to comply openly but that they would do so in the dark if unchallenged. The troops believed them and went off to eat and drink. At two in the morning they were attacked, their barracks set alight, and they themselves either burned alive or, if they jumped, impaled on rebel pikes. Fifty or sixty of the militia were killed. One of the officers, famous for his pitch-capping, was shot, piked and trampled under a horse's hooves; his body was burned in a tar barrel. A tree of liberty was placed in the square opposite the barracks.

The United Irishmen loudly proclaimed their success but in most

skirmishes during the following weeks their dead far exceeded the gov-ernment's. The very next day another section of the North Cork defeated three times their number of pikemen; nineteen carts had to be employed to take the dead to the gravel pits. The rebels had every reason to fight to the death, since General Lake, now in overall charge of the army, had ordered his officers to take no prisoners. Lord Camden was less blood-thirsty but there was such public rage at rumours of atrocities that Lake's opinion prevailed and the official Castle attitude was that "nothing but terror" would pacify the rebellious country.

In such circumstances it is remarkable that any groups of United Irish-men managed to rise at all, but, lacking leadership from Dublin, they did so haphazardly. The most spectacular effort came where least expected: against the North Cork regiment and others in Wexford. It was a prelude to some startling days in this startlingly hot, rainless summer.

The county of Wexford was a prosperous farming area less pene-trated by Castle spies than Ulster or Dublin. Its tardy envoy to the execu-tive meeting that had been betrayed by Reynolds had given the Castle a mistaken notion of a peaceful region. Yet, holding the biggest Protestant population outside Ulster, together with a largish number of Catholic gentry, it was known for sectarian rifts and for its squabbling Ascendancy figures. The Kings' friend George Ogle—splenetic and raving, according to enemies; noble and stalwart, according to friends—was one of its lead-ing politicians: he had been furious when the Catholics received the right to vote and had abandoned his House of Commons seat. Now he again warned of terrorists roaming the land and opposed his hard-line Protes-tant faction to the liberal Protestants who sided against him with the wealthier Catholics. Many of these liberals had United Irish sympathies. According to Lady Louisa Conolly, the division among the landowning classes in Wexford was the engine "set to work for the purpose of rebel-lion." In the interstices of the disputes, the United Irishmen grew and flourished. They were aided by the arrival in April of six hundred of George's North Cork militia, who set up headquarters in the town and

immediately organized an "Orange Party." Over the next weeks these undisciplined forces added much to the chaos of the county.

While important members from other areas languished in prison following Reynolds's betrayal, the Wexford United Irishmen developed their own organization, bringing in Catholics and Protestants. As a result, at the end of May and in early June 1798 they did what neither Dublin nor Belfast had succeeded in doing: established a successful republic.

The prelude was spectacular. On 27 May a detachment of 110 North Cork was set on by several thousand United Irishmen at Oulart Hill. When the rebels retreated up the slope to where their women and children were assembled, the militia followed. The pikemen, who fought best at close quarters, then ambushed them. The untrained volley fire of the North Cork proved disastrous against a charge of pikes and scythes; the soldiers panicked and the rebels chased and killed them as they pleaded for their lives. Only six North Cork escaped alive. After the battle the bodies were stripped by the rebels, who amassed muskets, cartridge boxes, military jackets, swords and pistols. A soldier from another regiment later surveyed the result: "I saw a large pit where some of the brave but unfortunate North Cork were buried; their legs and arms were bare, and a few of the fingers and toes were eat by the pigs, but we covered them decently with earth." It was the first ever open victory for the rebels, a huge defeat for the North Cork.

The soldiers suffered further trouncing the next day at the town of Enniscorthy, where some seventy or so were garrisoned along with about two hundred other troops. George Ogle had been marching his infantry to help them when he was called away to more pressing conflict near Wexford town. So once again the North Cork bore the brunt of the "black cloud" of rebels. Losses were large on both sides and much of the town was reduced to ashes. One of those trying to escape the burning town was Mary Moore, George Ogle's sister-in-law, the lady who had so gaily accompanied Caroline and Mary Wollstonecraft *en masquerade* in Dublin a decade before. Frightened for her life in the burning town, she found herself suddenly rescued by a Captain Hay, who carried her

through the flames and the volleys of musket fire to safety—or so he pleaded afterward when accused of commanding the rebel troops. She was taken to join her sister in Wexford, a small town of about ten thousand inhabitants, made safe, many assumed, by the presence there of the North Cork headquarters. It would turn out no safer for loyalists than Enniscorthy.

From Dublin Castlereagh wrote, "The rebellion in Wexford has assumed a more serious shape than was to be apprehended from a peasantry, however well organised." In England George III was appalled: he declared that since the sword was now drawn, it should not return to the sheath "until the whole country has submitted without conditions. The making of any compromise would be perfect destruction."

By 29 May the Wexford garrison had been reinforced but morale was undermined by the panic-stricken loyalist refugees such as Mary Moore arriving from Enniscorthy and outlying villages, joined by fleeing North Cork militiamen. Meanwhile, the disaster at Oulart Hill was brought home vividly when the mangled corpses of loyalist officers were carried into Wexford. As one lady recorded:

> Every moment becomes more frightful. An account has just arrived that the North Cork are all put to death, in an engagement with the rebels. The unfortunate soldiers' wives are screaming through the streets of Wexford; every creature that appears is put under arms: and the thatch is stripped off all the cabins in the suburbs of the town. Enniscorthy is burned, and the inhabitants are pouring into Wexford. Women of fortune, half-dressed, some having neither shoes nor stockings, with their children on their backs and in their arms, are in this state endeavouring to get on board ship. I am told there never was a more dreadful scene than Wexford at this moment exhibits.

Even before the rebels attacked the town, the North Cork men, supposedly guarding the southern entrance, were deserting their posts. As

the United Irishmen approached, they simply fled. Their officers swiftly followed, many making their escape on ships in the harbor—although to their horror they discovered that some of these were captained by rebel sympathizers. For a while the garrison commander pretended to negotiate with the rebels, but while his emissaries rode toward the enemy, he quietly decamped with the rest of the garrison through the southern entrance of the town. He had abandoned the Wexford yeomen infantry, the refugees and loyalist townspeople, many now trapped on board the stationary ships. The town was soon in the hands of rebels, who marched in to find a mixture of green and white flags flying.

George Ogle's wife and sister-in-law were among those trying to escape during the last hours before Wexford fell. Their house had been targeted for plunder and George Ogle himself was on a blacklist of Protestants for assassination when the rebels caught up with him. It was essential for the ladies to quit the town.

So they joined other Protestant women who were embarking on a sloop called the *Lovely Kitty,* which they hoped would take them out of the harbor and along the coast to safety. But as it set off, the ship was surrounded by drunken rebel sailors, who pointed pistols at the ladies' breasts. The next day they were taken prisoner and brought back to Wexford, by now in rebel hands. Twenty-six of them, all women except six children, were kept in one small room with just one bed to share between them. As they watched men being murdered—captured soldiers were piked despite the relative discipline of the rebels—the ladies feared that any moment they themselves would be raped and killed. Neither side set much store by women as individuals and rape was used to slake lust and dishonor opponents.

Although Oulart Hill had been a fine victory, the United Irishmen were not usually triumphant in battle. At the beginning of June government troops, including George's great-uncle Henry King as well as more North Cork men, faced a large but undisciplined rebel force at New Ross near Waterford, a strategic town controlling the route to the western gar-

risons. The contest was going to the United Irish besiegers when the tired men lost energy and order in the narrow town streets and turned to drinking and looting; large numbers were slaughtered. The town was plundered by its defenders and, it was claimed, the rebel sick and wounded were burned in the hospital by orders of General Lake. Pigs and dogs preyed on the piled bodies of the militia and insurgents alike; one officer noted that pigs ate "the brains out of the cloven skulls and gnaw[ed] the flesh about the raw wounds." A civilian observed of this slaughtering summer, "For several months there was no sale for bacon cured in Ireland, from the well founded dread of the hogs having fed upon the flesh of men." Henry King was wounded in the contest but not fatally.

During the battle of New Ross a messenger bringing news of government butchery approached rebels guarding prisoners at a farm at Scullabogue. He insisted that, in revenge, they should kill their captives, among whom were wives and children of the North Cork militia as well as an old bagpiper accused of playing a loyal tune. After some demurring from their leader, the men agreed and set to killing with a will. First they shot thirty or so male prisoners, then they herded about eighty men, women and children into a barn and burned them alive. No one was allowed to escape, not even children; rebels hacked at the hands and fingers of those trying to force open a door. One child was said to have crept out, only to be piked and thrown back onto the bonfire.

In London the cartoonist Cruikshank made a picture of the Scullabogue massacre; it became powerful government propaganda. When he heard of the incident, George Ogle declared that his prophecies of Catholics "cleansing by the pike" had come true.

It was high time that George King, Lord Kingsborough, came to the rescue, although he remained unaware that Wexford had entirely fallen into the hands of rebels. Because the roads down the coast were surrounded by banditti he chose to go by sea with two officers and some trusted sailors. Some way south of Dublin he stopped for refreshments; a

United Irish informer noted him and tipped off the Wexford rebels. It was hard to believe: the almost mythical Orangeman, famed for raping women and torturing suspects, was about to be within their grasp.

On 2 June near the mouth of Wexford Harbor George and his followers saw armed men on a hill and fired. A boat apparently full of women—George's weakness was well known—approached; when it was close, the women threw off their disguise and became fifty armed men who hoisted a green flag with a harp. A terrified George was captured and taken to Wexford. When Lord Shannon heard the news he was elated—it made up for the acquittal of George's father. He is "probably murdered or kept as a hostage," he reported. In her Windsor cottage Caroline was also informed of her son's capture and imminent danger of death. Her private response is unrecorded, but she conveyed the proper maternal anxiety to the restrained Queen when she met her.

By now the United Irishmen had set about establishing their republic in Wexford. A directory of Protestants and Catholics governed and maintained order. They rationed food within the town and manufactured gunpowder for defense. To keep discipline they organized parades and patrols. When informers were caught, they were properly tried and ritually executed to the sound of muffled drums. A green rebel flag was hoisted on the town barracks; trees of liberty were planted and patriotic ceremonies held to raise morale.

The Castle was unimpressed and insisted on regarding the Wexford republicans as a drunken mob given to murdering government soldiers. Yet the rebels did maintain order in the town for three difficult weeks, and they succeeded against all odds in keeping George alive—an immense achievement considering the hatred so many felt for him and his ferocious troops.

Because of the high feeling he provoked, George was moved from house to house during his captivity. On one occasion a captor asked him how he thought loyalist forces would treat a rebel leader were he taken prisoner as George himself had been. George replied that they would hang him. "We know that we fight with halters round our necks," came

the reply. George remained understandably nervous and asked the wife of a captured captain in his regiment if she expected him to be killed. He was relieved at her reply: she thought not since he was too good a bargaining counter.

Nonetheless, to many George was simply a "bloody orangeman." The republican rank and file regarded the revolution as accomplished— it remained only to share out the land and goods of the gentry—and so they saw no need to bargain through Lord Kingsborough. Indeed, it was later claimed that the hatred felt for George saved other Protestant townspeople: "The great anxiety to kill his Lordship first was, I believe, one cause of our escape, for the mob wasted much time in endeavouring to get him," reported one inhabitant. At some point a group of "savage pikemen" did insist on dealing with George; a pitch-cap for torturing prisoners had apparently been discovered as an Orange relic in the town and the enraged citizens surrounded the inn where George was being held, then raised a pitch-cap on a pike to taunt him. The leaders had to intervene and hurry him to a half-waterlogged prison hulk in the harbor until the hysteria calmed. At another time a man took a shot at him but was killed by a loyalist.

It was as well for George Ogle that he had quit the town, since he was as locally hated as his friend. On one occasion a band of rebels burst in on a dinner some loyalists were attending and roughly demanded to know the whereabouts of George Ogle. His wife and sister-in-law remained alive but their cramped situation was "truly miserable." Probably both were near starving, since rebels constantly raided loyalist houses for food and not much remained for loyalist townspeople to eat. The result of this policy was recorded by a lady; she had no more food to give to rebels, so had to offer whiskey:

> one of the men advanced, and desired I would drink some myself; that
> they had got an order not to take any thing from *us* without our previ-
> ously tasting it. . . . It instantly occurred to me, that should this man or
> any of the party get sick, the rest might come and revenge it on me; I

therefore called for a glass of water and put some whiskey in it, took some myself, and made each of the children do so; they were then satisfied, and after finishing the bottle, rode off.

Others who had more reason to fear for their lives ran to religion. There is no record of either George or Mrs. Ogle becoming Catholic in extremity, but some Protestants tried the ruse—especially since, even before the taking of the town, Wexford inhabitants had worried they would be "surrounded by rebels at the communion table." Although the leaders wanted Protestant services performed to suggest the nonsectarian nature of their revolution, none occurred, and many Protestants were understandably seen in postures of piety within the Catholic chapel. Some went further and were rechristened.

Frightened for his life and urged by the other captives, George now tried a maneuver. He wrote a letter to the Lord Lieutenant declaring that he and other loyalists had been properly treated as prisoners of war and hoping that the government's captives would be dealt with in the same way. He sent the message by one of his North Cork officers, but the man was intercepted by rebels who disagreed with this pacific move.

Now George's alienated family became involved. A woman whose rebel husband had been caught by the Castle authorities went to Robert at Mitchelstown Castle. There she saw one of the daughters, just possibly Mary, to whom she made the proposition that if the Earl of Kingston would persuade the government to save her husband, she would see that his son George was let go. Robert consulted Stephen and Margaret in nearby Kilworth and together they relayed the idea to the Castle. For Castlereagh and Clare the trio of King and Mount Cashells—acquitted murderer, suspected rebel and nondescript nobleman—was not a winning combination, nor perhaps were their hearts entirely in the application, which was ineffectual. Lord Shannon, a Privy Counsellor, commented on the meeting at which the proposition was discussed, "The Cabinet that decided on the business was an inferior one, I was not at it. I know it's sup-

posed that, hemmed in as the rebels are, they will not venture to execute Kingsborough."

George was indeed too useful to the insurgents, especially now since matters were not going well outside Wexford. The French under Napoleon had lately had a string of victories and the London government had feared an invasion of England and Ireland, so in early 1798 they ordered more regular troops to be sent over, among them Henry Fitzgerald's old regiment, along with his predecessor Charles Asgill, now promoted to general. In fact, however, Napoleon persuaded the French not to capitalize on England's troubles in Ireland but to turn their attention to Egypt instead. With no help likely to come from France and cut off by new government troops from receiving aid from other parts of the country, the United Irishmen now saw that, although tempting, it had not been clever tactics to take Wexford and establish themselves in one indefensible, conspicuous place.

In Dublin General Lake was still superintending the overall campaign against rebels in the north as well as around Wexford. Once again the Moira tenants at Ballynahinch became suspect. An insurgent army had reached Lord Moira's model town and his tenants had prudently welcomed them. In their honor they had taken to wearing green, if only in a knot of ribbon. Later, when government troops arrived, they were unimpressed by the disloyal show and even more by the discovery of pikes on and around the estate. One Castle official sneered that "the countenances of his Lordship's tenants were beaming with loyalty" as they saw the troops coming. Fearing reprisals, both rebels and tenants fled, leaving the soldiers to burn down much of the town and kill those they could catch. Afterward, when the dead were calculated, it was noted that a large number of rebel corpses had been found in Lord Moira's woods and pleasure park.

The soldiers had damaged the mansion but the commanders prevented them from completely gutting it. Although she did not care for the family's country house—"I hate the North. I detest Ballynahinch,"

she wrote—nonetheless Lady Moira was alarmed by the destruction and suspected treachery: the pikes had been planted on the estate, she was sure, and she had even heard of plans to "find" "a Commission for Ld. Moira to have commanded the United Irishmen, or his orders for them to assemble"—a discovery that would have made her son a traitor. She was furious at what she saw as plotting against her illustrious family, but again could respond only socially:

> I have brake off not only intimacy, but being on speaking terms with . . . Lord Castlereagh their families, connections & Alliances, every Individual belonging to them, & I have expressed *to them* in the most explicit manner that decision—I wait for all that is to be said against me & Mine with the most perfect Composure, there are those of whom to be dispraised is no small praise.

Once the north was calmer General Lake himself traveled south to put an end to the Wexford outrage. He came with reinforcements of artillery and cavalry from Britain, poor, ill-disciplined men who had little respect for military honor or for their Irish enemies. In the contests that followed casualties among the pikemen mounted. By 16 June government troops were closing in on the town and the rebel leaders were growing desperate.

On 21 June at Vinegar Hill twenty miles north of Wexford the United Irish pikemen took their last major stand. They were opposed by twenty thousand government men, including some from the North Cork militia. All were urged by Castlereagh to "make the rebels there an example to the rest of the kingdom."

In the end pikes and enthusiasm were no match for superior forces, even these unruly government ones. The booming cannons could be heard as far away as Wexford. Lasting about two hours, the battle was decisive and the rebels lost. Some fled, some were betrayed, but most retreated in fairly decent order. "The rascals made a tolerable good fight

of it," wrote General Lake. "The carnage was dreadful." It was the last great open battle in Irish history.

The men commanded by Lord Roden, brother-in-law of Caroline's youngest half sister, Margaret Jocelyn, were particularly ferocious. A Scottish soldier reported one incident of many:

> After the battle some soldiers got hold of a croppie's wife whom they dragged into a house and shame to say four and twenty of the brutes (ambitious to disgrace a redcoat) had connection with her. Even the blind-eyed Michael Horgan . . . [was] meant to have been one of the number. As I passed, I saw him coming out at the door and exclaiming "blood and wounds I've lost my turn." I began to expostulate with him upon the impropriety of his conduct, knowing that he had a wife and six children in Dublin but he cut me off short with a "blood and wounds man, Kitty and I have made an agreement; she gives me liberty to do what I please and I give her the same when I'm from home." I could not help laughing.

As successful government troops moved closer and closer to the town of Wexford, small skirmishes continued. In one on 24 June the North Cork drove their enemy into the arms of the implacable Charles Asgill, who claimed a thousand rebels were killed.

Watching refugees pour into the town, many of the Wexford insurgents panicked, anticipating a final surrender. Civic control collapsed. Some rebels insisted on changing places with prison inmates to try to save themselves. Others made hasty tribunals and murdered almost a hundred unarmed loyalist captives on the wooden bridge across the Wexford estuary. Government informers and agents had been busy in the town and the ebullient signs of independence disappeared; the green sashes were torn off, the flags taken down.

Lord Shannon had heard that the Wexford rebels had "flogged [George] and asked how he liked *that*," but Shannon did not believe the

story. He was right not to do so for, instead of flogging him, his captors were now regarding George as their potential savior, hoping that his notorious Orangeism would give him power with the Castle. They knew they could not hold out without reinforcements and they wanted to ensure that the inhabitants of Wexford would be spared if they capitulated. So, after nineteen days of imprisoning him and keeping him alive with difficulty, they released Lord Kingsborough.

Then the leaders told him to write to General Lake, informing him how well he and other important loyalist prisoners had been treated and how he in particular had been saved from enemy pikes. They hoped that if Wexford fell, its people would be similarly dealt with. He agreed to do as they wished and concluded his letter with the belief that when all was over, the rebels would "return to their allegiance with the greatest satisfaction."

George put on his militia uniform and accepted the sword of surrender from the rebels on behalf of the King. Some leaders then requested that he be a delegate with them to General Lake, but this he refused to do. So they set off alone with his letter to the government camp; it declared that George had "pledged his honour in the most solemn manner" that the people of the town would be protected.

Left alone, he now found himself in a curious position. Some townspeople still wanted to kill him on account of his unsavory past, while others regarded him as the ruler of Wexford. He himself was uneasy at his prominence—he was a militia colonel treating with regular army generals.

Meanwhile, the delegation rode through the retreating rebel lines and arrived at Lake's camp just after the battle of Vinegar Hill. In dismay they saw bodies strewn far and wide. They handed in the letter and informed the General that they had surrendered Wexford to George Lord Kingsborough in return for the safety of the town. Lake was unimpressed, knowing the attitude of his rough soldiers after victory and distrusting George's judgment. He sent the letter on to Castlereagh with his comments: his soldiers, he wrote, had "behaved excessively well in action, but their determination to destroy every one they think a rebel is beyond description, and wants much correction. You will see, by the enclosed let-

ter and address from Wexford, what an unpleasant situation I am led into by Lord Kingsborough. My intention is at present to march near Wexford tomorrow," and he noted ominously that "the people of Wexford have done much mischief."

Knowing nothing of Lake's private determination, the rebel delegation waited through twelve alarming hours for an answer. Then they received a message that the General would not negotiate with men in arms and if any of the loyalist prisoners were harmed, he would annihilate the town. They were appalled. Their plan had failed and it was now too late to resist. A contingent of General Lake's army was already marching toward Wexford.

While the leaders had been away the remaining loyalist prisoners prepared to be massacred by the desperate townspeople and a mob surrounded George's lodgings. Then all changed; the rebels abandoned the defense and the fight and most simply left the town. When they arrived, the government forces marched in with ease, much as the rebels had done a few eventful weeks before. Once success seemed ensured, the victorious soldiers sought out George in his scarlet regimentals and carrying the sword of surrender.

Now released and among his own people again, he did not protest that his treaty had been met with contempt—indeed, his main annoyance was that General Lake had not had the safety of himself and Mrs. Ogle uppermost in his mind when he purposed the capture of Wexford. It was no thanks to the commander that he and the ladies had in the end escaped unharmed. Nor did he make much attempt to use his sudden power to influence the victors. Mindful of the rebel atrocities at Scullabogue and the slaughtering of prisoners on Wexford bridge, the triumphant soldiers were killing and plundering, although they largely spared the houses. George put up no resistance to their acts. Indeed, he had so far forgotten his recent experiences that the day after his liberation he joined in the plunder. During his captivity he had spied some fine coach horses; to these he now helped himself.

When he arrived in town General Lake offered some clemency to

lesser insurgents but the leaders, the men who had protected George for nearly three weeks, were executed and their heads stuck on spikes. Realizing how little they had gained through surrendering, many rebels wished they had gone out fighting and had sent George's mutilated body to General Lake rather than a letter of surrender. Remembering the tender treatment of their hated prisoner, one bitter rebel memoirist wrote, "If we had had a general commanding in Wexford on the 21st of June, of the stamp of the Greek generals . . . he would no doubt have dispatched Lord Kingsborough and his fellow English prisoners to the English headquarters with their ears and noses cut off." A Catholic United Irishman summed up the sense of betrayal:

> had he evinced any sympathy for the unfortunate sufferers—had he shown any position to mitigate, as far as his influence might have extended, the miseries in which an implicit reliance on his faith had involved men of rank, of fortune, and unquestionable truth; though his efforts might not, perhaps, have proved successful, his conduct would have been less exceptionable, and neither his honour nor humanity been compromised in the attempt. The protection of his life had been a task of no small difficulty, and often pregnant with danger. Yet he hourly beheld, with a cold-blooded complacency, those generous-minded men led to the scaffold, to whose humane interference he was solely indebted for his preservation from popular vengeance.

In England London society was incredulous that the United Irishmen had succeeded as far as they had and relieved that they had gone no further. In Windsor Caroline was gratified to find Queen Charlotte driving up to her cottage. "I have ventured to call upon your ladyship," she said, "to tell you that Lord Kingsborough is safe. I think the news we have at the castle may be earlier than what your ladyship may have received."

At the end of June, after much burning and flogging, in which the unchastened George once again took his part, Lord Castlereagh asserted

that the government had made the crushed rebels sensible of their
"crimes, as well as of the authority of government," and by mid-July he
declared the rebellion in Ireland over. It was—along with the fragile
unity of Catholics, Anglicans and Dissenters that had sustained it.

From the English point of view the whole episode of the rebellion
had been bungled by the Castle authorities. Ill and weary with the
French wars, Pitt decided to change the policy in Ireland and with it the
personnel. Just after the fall of Wexford he removed the Lord Lieutenant; Camden's letters had been increasingly shrill and he himself was
eager to leave his post—indeed, he had been so anxious during these
last turbulent months that he had sent his wife and children to England,
as Lady Castlereagh imprudently revealed. Pitt also removed General
Lake from supreme command, letting him revert to his former second-
ary position. The two functions of civil and military commander could
now be combined in one more capable and conciliatory man: Marquess
Cornwallis, the American veteran who had recently returned from command in India. He arrived in Dublin and was sworn in on 20 June 1798.
It was not a popular appointment with the sociable aristocracy: Cornwallis had no wife to preside at Drawing Rooms, drank little and did not
enjoy ceremony. "The life of a Lord Lieutenant in Ireland comes up to
my idea of perfect misery," he wrote after his appointment, "I wish I were
back in Bengal."

The new Lord Lieutenant was keen to distance himself from the attitudes of his predecessor. He saw his first priority not as crushing rebels
but as bringing them back to loyalty. He was particularly hostile to the
North Cork militia, which had been barbaric in safety and often contemptible in danger, and they in turn despised him and his policies,
especially his proclamation of pardon and amnesty to insurgents outside
the ringleaders. Despite martial law Cornwallis insisted that no more sentences should be summarily carried out by soldiers and militia gentry
without his approval. Indeed, he appeared so moderate that some loyalists thought he sympathized with the rebels and began calling him
"Cropwallis." To the amazement of many Lord Clare approved the

stance: he had always seen danger less from Catholics and rebels than from the misguided Ascendancy and principled revolutionaries. His alliance with the new Lord Lieutenant was crucial to success.

Lady Moira judged most military actions on the basis of their leaders' gallantry and their treatment of patrician ladies. She now praised Lord Cornwallis for his fairness and discipline as he mopped up the rebellion. "[H]e is a source of wonder by comparing him to former commanders in chief, & every one looks up to his worth as well as his exertions with a confidence of success," she wrote.

George disagreed. "His X thinks he may domineer here as in India," he sneered. In turn the Lord Lieutenant let it be known that he disliked George. His recent experiences had not changed Lord Kingsborough's enthusiasm for repression—he was seen throwing salt on the back of a man he was flogging, for instance—and he was keenly aware of loyalist casualties and sacrifices in the recent fighting: the 1,400 Protestants murdered at Wexford. He recalled how a girl who sang the antirebel song "Croppies Lie Down" was stripped naked, tied head and knees like a ball and kicked down a hill to her death. Such outrages should be met by more severity, he believed. "Ld. Cornwallis was in the wrong & he in the Right," he asserted. In England Caroline had at last found her family popular with the King and Queen and had milked the situation for all it was worth. Already in high favor with the Ascendancy after Wexford, George was now also "the first rate Court favorite," Lady Moira noted, adding, "The whole of the Kingston Race are enjoying & basking beneath the Sunshine of Royal Countenance." But even royal favor could not support George locally in Ireland and, to the satisfaction of Margaret and Lady Moira, Lord Cornwallis "gave him such a Lecture . . . as he never received before in his Life." Spurned by General Lake and now the Lord Lieutenant, George resigned as colonel of the North Cork militia in November.

The new regime made aristocratic liberals such as Lady Moira sigh for relief. They could be loyal again. In late August she wrote that "the rational and cool belief here is, that rebellion is extinguished . . . but [there is] much impatient censure against his Excellency for not permit-

ting country squires vested with a brief military authority to tyran-
nize . . . as they think proper." She might have been thinking of George.
Her daughter Selina was less sanguine about the new order, noting the
retention of Lord Castlereagh as Chief Secretary and Lord Clare as Lord
Chancellor: "As for Ld. Cornwallis, I hope he means well, & I believe wd.
act so if let alone, but as long as Lord Castlereagh is keeper of his Conscience & director of his Brains, what have honest people to hope for?"
Later it was supposed that Cornwallis was softening Catholic and liberal
opinion so that the country would more easily accept Pitt's favorite measure: the union of England, Scotland and Ireland. Yet to many Cornwallis
seemed genuinely eager to heal some of the self-inflicted wounds of the
strange land.

All during the weeks of the rebellion the United Irishmen had waited
impatiently for French help. Now the uprising was crushed, but, responding to news of the early success in Wexford, the French chose this moment
to act. General Hoche, who had led the disaster at Bantry Bay, was dead,
but Wolfe Tone had found a less charismatic yet still experienced successor in Joseph Humbert. It was decided that General Humbert would lead
one of three expeditions to invade Ireland for the second time.

At the end of August Humbert's army of just over one thousand men
arrived in Killala, a small town on the coast of County Mayo. Few government soldiers resisted their landing and they quickly took possession
of the surrounding countryside. The local Catholics enjoyed the excitement and eagerly put on the new uniforms the French had brought for
them. An early victory at Castlebar over General Lake and the militias
heartened them—and depressed Lord Granard, who was commanding
the Longford militia. According to his disgusted mother-in-law, his men
simply fled from the disciplined French infantry. Later Cornwallis tried
to make Granard feel better by praising his personal gallantry in rallying
his disaffected men.

Close to the path of the invasion Richard Lovell Edgeworth and his
daughter Maria felt increasingly British. The French success discom-

posed them and they left their house and took refuge at an inn in Longford. A man to whom they had once lent money when his wife was distressed guarded their property and it was not sacked. The circumstance was difficult to believe and rumors flew that the Edgeworths had colluded with the French and were signaling to them through Richard Lovell's experimental telegraph; they had an unhappy time among their Protestant neighbors in Longford.

The French success could not be sustained. No reinforcements came from France and General Humbert upset many of the Irish recruits by refusing to let them pillage the great houses—though Henry King's seat at Ballina was damaged. British forces were added to Lake's army and Cornwallis came from Dublin to hearten the troops. As the contest seemed increasingly hopeless, many of the Irish allies melted away.

On 8 September the two by now unequal sides met and briefly fought. For the French (and Lord Granard) honor was satisfied within half an hour. General Humbert surrendered to General Lake, mistaking him for Lord Cornwallis.

Then the French turned on their former allies, cursed the United Irishmen for inveigling them into a fruitless invasion and made matters worse by declaring the Irish treacherous and cowardly. Government troops distinguished between combatants: the remaining United Irishmen who had served with the French were killed, while the invaders were leniently treated. Released on parole, the officers rode back to Dublin with their British counterparts; the ordinary soldiers were packed into a string of turf boats and sent by canal. They were slowly towed along, singing the "Marseillaise" at the top of their voices as they floated through the bogs.

In Dublin the two armies, French and British, commingled and chatted, as Lady Moira described in a letter to Sarah Napier:

An Officer an Acquaintance of mine supped with the French Officers. . . . they were very free in their Conversation—Spoke highly of

Lord Cornwallis's Military Abilities laughed at Lake & said that he did not know even how to station his Men . . . —They said that they never met with in any Country such Savages as the Mayo Peasantry, yet capable of making excellent Soldiers.

Some weeks later, on 12 October, the second part of the invasion, an army of three thousand men accompanied by Wolfe Tone, arrived in County Donegal, unaware of the scale of the recent military disaster. The force was easily defeated by the British navy and Tone himself was captured wearing a French uniform. Refused a military execution, he slit his throat and died painfully and heroically from his wound—much to Lord Clare's chagrin since, unlike Lord Edward, Tone had no aristocratic family to thwart his hanging. Instead, he had accomplished the sort of classical suicide the early French Revolution encouraged.

Danger from France had underpinned the Castle's rigor; now it was gone through the recent bungled invasions and, more decisively, through a much-desired victory for Britain in Egypt. Admiral Nelson had ended a long series of British disasters and French triumphs by heavily defeating Napoleon at the Battle of the Nile in August 1798, destroying the French fleet and the threat of further invasion of Ireland or England through Ireland. It was little wonder that a most elaborate pillar was erected to him in Dublin.

Meanwhile, the remaining prominent United Irishmen such as Thomas Addis Emmet, in prison since their roundup in March 1798, were about to be outmaneuvered by Clare and Castlereagh. To save their necks sixty-four of them agreed to end rebellious activities and give full information about the last years of insurgency, especially concerning the treasonable dealings with France. In return they would receive a sentence of banishment from the British Empire.

Such an exchange pleased Clare and Castlereagh, as well as Cornwallis, who was weary of weeping wives and daughters and exasperated at the cost of keeping so many men in prison—"the expence of this regiment of

traitors exceeds five-fold that of the best regiment in the King's service,"
he remarked. Trials too were expensive and rebels could not easily be
convicted by juries without the involvement of reluctant informers.

The admission of treasonable plots with France was a propaganda
coup for the Castle. Retrospectively it justified their brutality toward dissidents through the 1790s and embarrassed moderate sympathizers like
Lord Moira, who had always insisted that the rebellion was homegrown,
a response to Irish conditions and government mismanagement rather
than to French encouragement.

More significantly, to their own followers who had been willing to
die for the United Irish cause, the imprisoned men laid themselves open
to a charge of cowardice. With their full confessions they were saving
themselves through selling the rebellion. Lord Clare aided the discomfort they must have felt by making public a cunningly altered version of
their evidence, which swung moderate opinion farther away from them.

Few in England had really appreciated the importance of Irish events in
1798. Castlereagh wrote to a friend there, "I understand . . . you are
rather inclined to hold the insurrection cheap. Rely upon it there never
was in any country so formidable an effort on the part of the people."
Margaret agreed. "However insignificant an unsuccessful rebellion may
appear in the eyes of British Ministers, it is by no means an unimportant
event in the contemplation of men, whose persons and properties are
exposed to destruction in the conflict." All in all the rebellion in the
1790s and the countermeasures used to deal with it killed over twenty
thousand people. The majority were slaughtered by government armies.

In the end the Irish rebellion failed through lack of organization,
inadequate military tactics and bad French timing. It also failed through
lack of support from Catholics. Most were too poor to be much interested in freedom and reform and, desiring peace and security above all,
sided with the government throughout—as the Catholic Church authorities had also done. Many of the Catholic propertied and mercantile
classes were also solidly conservative. The great loser through all the

effort was Ireland, which, as one traveler remarked, had been devastated by "the joint labours of rebellion and of loyalty, soldiers and insurgents."

Margaret left no clear assessment of what in her view had gone wrong but in her novel "The Chieftains of Erin" she presented an earlier Irish rebellion being defeated by some treachery, some collusion with the English, mistaken reliance on foreign aid, and much division between the proud and envious chieftains. The "eternal bane of Erin's liberty" was "dissention among her sons."

Now that the country was more or less pacified William Pitt could introduce the political measure he had long contemplated as the only solution to the island's problems: the union of the three kingdoms of England, Scotland and Ireland. It would mean the end of the Dublin Parliament—but not the Lord Lieutenant and his court—and he expected it would be heartily opposed by the Protestant elite not welded to Castle interest.

As usual, the landowning class responded sartorially when they felt the threat. By December garter blue ribbons were being worn in Dublin inscribed with the words "British Connection. Irish Independence. No Union." Margaret's husband, Stephen, sent one to his aunt Selina. Others such as Lord Shannon wanted to see what England would offer Irish peers for their support. For him the price was obviously right because, "after much coquetry," he decided to go in with the British government on the first vote.

For the only time in his adult life George agreed with his sister Margaret since both opposed the union. In so doing he voted against his friend George Ogle, who believed that the union was "proposed on Protestant principles" and might actually modify the baneful effects of Catholic suffrage. (In addition, Ogle enjoyed being courted by Lord Castlereagh for his support.) George's opposition was based on reasons very different from his sister's: with many in the Orange Order, he felt that the union would diminish rather than support the authority of the great landowners and, in taking away the independent Irish Parliament,

lessen their ability to control government by controlling MPs. It would not, as Ogle supposed, strengthen Protestant power but in reality deliver Ireland to the Catholics, who, George noticed, were much in favor of the measure. Pitt had implied that union would include complete emancipation for them, although Clare—and indeed George III—was opposed to this. Each group was therefore being persuaded that the measure would primarily defend their interests.

One close vote was taken in the Irish Parliament. Cornwallis held aloof from the discussion and Grattan thundered against the measure. Then Castlereagh set about wooing Lords and Commons alike with money, pensions and promises of patronage, as well as quick elevations to the peerage—forty-eight in all. In this time of largesse the more astute made sure that they actually had the money or the honors before the next vote occurred. Some of the great were paid as much as £15,000 for the patronage of parliamentary seats, although the more usual price was about £7,000. Stephen failed to achieve even this level and sold his borough influence at a cut-down price. The money for all this payment to already wealthy Irish owners was taken directly from taxes on the Irish and British people.

Many were shocked at the undenied and open venality of the Castle, and Grattan and Castlereagh came close to a duel over it. Castlereagh spoke of the union buying "the fee simple of Irish corruption" and Cornwallis despised himself for being at all involved in such "dirty work." Margaret was simply appalled at the strategies and the lack of resistance to them. She dashed off three pamphlets in which she proclaimed that Ireland was on the edge of an "unfathomable abyss." The great and good, who should, according to classic republican doctrine, have led a backward nation, had failed their country. Mary Wollstonecraft had recoiled from any appeals to nationalism, believing it simply an extension of family love heading toward glory and barbarity, but by now the United Irishmen with their belief in universal enlightenment had been defeated, and indiscriminate nationalism was the best counter against English imperialism: "My Countrymen!" exhorted Margaret, "Ye who first drew breath in

this persecuted land! Ye who inhale the native air of Ireland!" all "must speak out" and save their land from destruction.

She was close to admitting openly her involvement with the United Irishmen and recommending revolt once more—but now on quite other grounds: in support of a status quo and a Parliament she had earlier seen as venal and corrupt. But, however she exhorted, there was to be no revolt over union and the Bishop of Limerick remarked, "Union goes on swimmingly, and the case of the anti-Unionists is become almost Desperate, by legal measures; they give broad hints of Rebellion however, but they are very Little attended to, either within doors or without."

Four months after his first attempt Castlereagh moved the motion for Union again in Parliament. He was no orator and it was left to Lord Clare to make a somber supporting speech in which he eradicated the years of United Irish one-nation rhetoric by calling the Anglo-Irish landowners "adventurers" and "settlers" hemmed in on all sides by brooding discontented Catholic natives. Attacking the faction that included George rather than the one to which Margaret belonged, he called the anti-Unionists "a puny and rapacious oligarchy" who considered Ireland their political inheritance and were prepared to sacrifice "public peace and happiness to their insatiate love of patronage and power"; without their Parliament Ireland could be defended simply by the British army and Irish leaders could pursue the proper business of eradicating the "squalid misery" of the mass of the people.

This time the vote went decisively in favor of the Act of Union. For a variety of reasons—because they wished to hold on to a modicum of Irish independence, retain Ascendancy power against the English government, keep their own seats in a House of Lords or preserve Protestant authority over Catholics—the noble brothers-in-law, George and Stephen and the Earls of Moira and Granard, all signed the Peers' Protest, although Lord Moira withdrew his opposition in Westminster when he came to believe Catholics would be advantaged by a union. His mother, an Englishwoman, was in the end equally ambivalent, the first time her politics had clearly diverged from Margaret's, and when the pro-Union

Bishop of Limerick called on her about this time, he found her in an unusually reticent mood: "I do not clearly understand what are her Politicks whether union or no union," he wrote. The noblemen who signed the protest did so not because they expected to influence events but so as "to transmit to after-times our names in solemn protest" against the "basest means" used to bring the event about. In supporting the Union Lord Shannon had, as usual, avoided siding with the Kings.

On 1 January 1801 the Union came into force and ended the semi-independent kingdom of Ireland, bringing it into one United Kingdom of Great Britain and Ireland. Diminished Irish representation was transferred from Dublin to Westminster, where it would always be in the minority, and the Parliament building on College Green was sold to a bank company on condition that it was altered so thoroughly that it could never again be a debating chamber. In Valentine Lawless's words, Ireland from being a "nation" with corrupt governors but huge potential turned into "a miserable province, her social system a mass of rottenness and decay." For Barrington, an "independent country was thus degraded into a province—Ireland, as a nation, was EXTINGUISHED." Pitt's implied promise of Catholic emancipation was overruled by King George III, who declared, "I shall reckon any man my personal enemy who proposes any such measure." Pitt, Cornwallis and Castlereagh all resigned.

Despite her apparent ambivalence and the "in-between" status she never shared with Margaret, once the Union became fact Lady Moira joined Margaret in regarding it as a stain on England as well as Ireland. The venal habits used to bring the latter into line would mark and mar the British Parliament, Margaret believed. Lady Moira agreed and lamented the mutual contamination:

> Those who come after us will talk much of this past [century]—The which doesn't do much Credit to the Era of Philosophers. . . . "The Sun of England's Glory *is set*" & I no longer feel any satisfaction at Chance's having stamped me as an Englishwoman—As for Events past, or passing I am like the careless Irishman, who having been told that he must

hastily quit the dwelling which was falling upon his Head; Answered, what was that to him, who was but a Lodger in it.

The whole of Ireland would never again be a united, self-governing nation and the Earl of Kingston's trial had been the last great pageant in the Irish House of Lords. In retrospect Jonah Barrington, who had excitedly watched the event, realized its political significance: "The grand and awful solemnity of that trial made a deep impression on my memory: and, coupled with the recollection that it proclaimed indisputably the sovereignty of the Irish nation, its effect on a contemplative mind was of a penetrating nature." From then on, those Irishmen who wanted social reform and political change for the whole island had only two options. They could persuade the government in London to support their cause or fight for it through open rebellion and clandestine terror. Over the next two centuries—up to the present moment—they followed both methods.

Margaret declared that she was haunted for the rest of her life by the happenings of 1798. It was true for everyone.

Lord Clare learned that the Union sidelined him. He grew disillusioned with the English power he had so ably maintained, writing to a friend that now he would look forward to future rebellions, "new scenes of misery and confusion" in Ireland, "with very little feeling." When he died in 1802 after a fall from his horse, people threw dead cats on his coffin, an ironic comment on his earlier boast that he would make the seditious as tame as cats.

The Union also sidelined George Ogle. With a band playing "The Protestant Boys," he had won a parliamentary seat in Dublin in 1798, just after the Catholic massacres he had foretold, but he lost it again in 1802, when partisan passions had subsided. Lord Castlereagh moved to London, where he became Secretary of War, then Foreign Secretary, acting at the defeat of Napoleon and the close of the French wars as the arbiter of Europe; he cut his throat with a penknife in 1822.

Cornwallis was sent back to India as Viceroy and forced to take on General Lake as his military commander. He had not long to protest about Lake's forthright treatment of natives, for he died of a fever soon after arrival. Meanwhile, Lake achieved the curious title of Baron Lake of Delhi and Leswaree and Aston Clinton in Bucks. Lord Moira followed his mother's advice and became a powerful London politician. In 1795 he urged the Prince of Wales to forget his morganatic marriage and enter a royal union with Princess Caroline for the sake of the nation; he even accompanied the reluctant bridegroom on his carriage ride to his wedding at the Chapel Royal. It was fitting, then, that during the Prince's regency he had the delicate duty of investigating the sexual conduct of his master's unwanted wife. He ended as Governor-General of Bengal. The adaptable Lord Shannon lost most of the parliamentary seats he commanded before the Union but kept his other offices; he died in 1807, having helped Pitt to get back into office as prime minister in 1804.

In 1798 Pamela had not been allowed to see her dying husband. Instead, her request had been met by the order to quit Ireland within three days. She left for England, accompanied by John Murphy, an old friend of Margaret's and Lady Moira's; when Murphy returned, he found himself dismissed from his chaplaincy of Magdalen Church, Dublin, so Margaret employed him as tutor to her young boys, though he drew the line at following her into the country to teach them.

Both her Irish and English relatives were glad when Pamela moved from London to Hamburg, leaving two of her three children with Edward's family. None had offered her a home and her stepfather-in-law, Mr. Ogilvie, in particular was eager to be rid of her. Curran, who had narrowly escaped being arrested for his radical activities, spoke for Pamela against a bill of attainder on the dead Lord Edward, which, by making him a traitor, deprived his widow of his property. His oratory failed and Pamela lost even her annuity—although Clare and Cornwallis saw to it that the small estate could later be bought back by Edward's family to enrich his son. Meanwhile, the Leinsters clubbed together to provide the

penniless widow with the moderate income of £200; it was rarely paid and, perhaps for financial as well as emotional needs, eighteen months after arriving in Germany Pamela married the American consul in Hamburg. The marriage failed and she moved on to a lover in Paris. Her sister-in-law Lucy had dropped her long before but when she heard of her death she wrote: "Poor Pamela, she was better, after all, than most of her accusers."

Meanwhile, with the political threat defanged, Lord Edward no longer seemed a dangerous traitor; instead, he was mythologized into a romantic aristocrat. George III inquired how his family did without him and the Prince of Wales openly praised him. His memorabilia became valuable. Lucy received his waistcoat stained with blood, Lady Louisa his gray cloak, watch and chain and locket of hair, which she sent to his brother. His unused uniform went to his admirer, the Duke of York, while Lord Clare got his dagger; he gave it to someone else, who lost it. Lucy sent his picture to Tom Paine; she became the guardian of his memory—as did his aunt Lady Louisa.

With Margaret, John Philpot Curran fiercely opposed the Union, but once it was accomplished he turned into a creature of the Castle—perhaps in part blackmailed through his earlier involvement with the treasonable United Irishmen: "It is fortunate that Mr. Curran is completely in our power," remarked a spokesman. He refused to defend any more rebels and disowned his more radical daughter, Sarah, whom the British Home Secretary described as "a true pupil of Mary Woolstonecraft." With his compromise he expected to be Attorney-General but had to accept the second-best judicial appointment as Master of the Rolls. His perennial depression increased and he died in 1817.

. CHAPTER 13 .

Aftermath

Was it for this the wild geese spread
The grey wing upon every tide;
For this that all that blood was shed,
For this Edward Fitzgerald died,
And Robert Emmet and Wolfe Tone,
All that delirium of the brave?
Romantic Ireland's dead and gone . . .

—WILLIAM BUTLER YEATS, "SEPTEMBER 1913"

ROBERT DID NOT LONG SURVIVE HIS ACQUITTAL FOR MURDER. HE died at Mitchelstown Castle in April 1799, less than two years after his father; he was buried in the family vault at Kingston College. His debts amounted to £90,000.

Robert Edward, the son he preferred, was with him a few days before he died and took over the parliamentary seat of Boyle, now in the gift of his eldest son, George. He also inherited his father's Roscommon estates, delivering the fat income of £11,000 per annum. Often Irish aristocracy did split an inheritance to support their sons but, considering the enthusiasm of old Edward for uniting the King lands, it does seem that Robert was making a statement with his will in his second son's favor. Mindful of the disgrace of his daughter Mary, he left her an annuity of £300; it was modest but appropriate for a sullied woman who would not or could not marry. Mitchelstown and its revenues of about £30,000 reverted to Caro-

line, who had brought the estate into the family; after an initial flirtation with abandoning it to George, she realized she had no intention of disposing of it or even sharing it: George would have it only over her dead body. But at least he was now Earl of Kingston; he gave up his parliamentary seat in Roscommon and entered the Irish House of Lords just before its dissolution. Despite opposing the Union in 1800 he yet managed to grab £15,000 from the government in payment for his interest in Boyle.

Although she remained often an absentee and visited only when her health allowed, Caroline took over the running of the Mitchelstown estate, hiring modern gardeners and planting, copsing and pruning trees— indeed, the garden book indicates that she employed between one hundred and one hundred fifty men and boys in the grounds and nurseries of her demesne. She wanted to begin a silk manufactory, since silk was expensive during the war with France, the usual source of imports; to this end she planted four hundred thousand mulberry trees, the biggest plantation in Ireland. But the enterprise failed when imported silk became available again. The other industries were more flourishing, and every Whit Monday she gave a dinner and dance on her castle lawn for the women workers in the cotton mill she and Robert had established. She also continued her charities, building a new church for the rector of Mitchelstown and opening a circulating library to encourage the reading of useful books. She established a school for orphans to be taught habits of industry, as well as spinning and weaving schools where children were apprenticed at her expense, and a slop shop to sell their work. As it had done earlier in her life, her charitable activity annoyed high-placed Catholics, who saw it as a form of Protestant proselytizing, but the local Anglican clergyman declared she had done everything "which the happy wisdom of charity and affluence could suggest, to enlighten the minds of the rising generation, and ameliorate the condition of the people."

Her wealth and position gave her considerable influence in the county and after Robert's death she became a political patron to be courted for her interest in the new parliamentary system. She was known to be close to the royal family and, combined with her local importance,

this made her a figure of power in Ireland. Just after the Union, Lord Clare, wanting to secure the election of one of his candidates in Limerick to the new Westminster Parliament, considered using the Queen or one of the princesses to approach Caroline for her help.

To those who did not show proper deference she could now appear insufferably arrogant and grand. In 1809 she even snubbed the Lord Lieutenant, the Duke of Richmond (the rebellious Lord Edward's cousin). She had invited Baron and Lady Cahir of Blarney Castle, Cork, to a fête at Mountain Lodge near Mitchelstown. Perhaps her invitation was primarily duty, since Lady Cahir was the niece of Lord Clare, whom the Kings always regarded as an upstart, as his family regarded them as usurpers. The Cahirs happened to be entertaining the Lord Lieutenant, then on a vice-regal tour, and they assumed this august guest would be welcome to Caroline.

In fact she was furious at her event being used by others to entertain their visitors and when Lady Cahir's party arrived in state at her gates they found them locked and guards placed along the walls in case of forced entry. Lady Cahir "supplicates in vain," reported an observer, "and then resorts to that elegant style of language which she displayed some years ago at a Parisian theatre—the party stood aghast." Drizzle was falling and the wet Lord Lieutenant and his entourage retreated to "the humble cabin of an emaciated peasant," where they brought out their rich food and lavish silverware to share with the poor man's family. They left the area tired, wet and very offended.

Caroline was just as uncharitable toward her older children. She had little correspondence with Margaret, although Stephen and her abandoned grandchildren visited her in Windsor—presumably the idea of her cottage attracted the eldest boy, who later built a Swiss one for his Swiss wife in the grounds of Moore Park. Caroline's greatest torment was her son George, who, having failed to benefit from his father's will, was left with only £6,000 to keep himself and family and live up to his boast of being "the principal man of County Cork." For a quarter of a century after Robert's death he fought his mother in the courts for control of her estate.

To frighten and spy on her he took to climbing over the demesne walls and prowling around the grounds with a group of retainers. Caroline employed servants to try to eject him but when accosted he announced with bravado that he came "to keep down tyranny and oppression."

On the basis of his snooping and suborning of the family's old gardeners he accused Caroline of bad husbandry, of improper culling of trees and of ruining views from the house to spite him. Although wooed by George, his brother Robert Edward supported their mother and when the case came to court testified that Caroline's changes had simply made the house and lands more magnificent. The quarrel, lasting through many years, enriched the lawyers, since George could not get Mitchelstown Castle and Caroline could not disinherit her eldest son. He was the more irritated when their great-uncle Henry King also left Robert Edward rather than himself his part of the family estates.

Denied access to Mitchelstown Castle, George often established himself with Stephen in Kilworth, his wife's old home. When Caroline was in residence, the parties used elaborate strategies to annoy each other and avoid speaking. Caroline tried to communicate directly with her grandson, George's eldest son, a curious youth of nineteen now studying at Oxford, whom she invited in as future acceptable owner of the estate. George, meanwhile, addressed his mother intemperately through his wife or brother.

On 13 January 1823 Caroline died in Roehampton at the age of sixty-eight. She left nothing of her disposable estates to Margaret or George but made a special mention of the once "idolized" Mary, leaving her £3,000. It was a good sum for an errant girl, although not as much as the £5,000 received by the other younger daughters.

From the will it seems that, apart from her second son, Robert Edward, the younger sons and daughters pleased Caroline more than the oldest; personal jewelry, which would conventionally have gone to Margaret or George's wife, went to another daughter-in-law. Her two firstborn children were unforgiven. Caroline could come to terms with a daughter who disappointed her but not one who despised her.

She was buried in Putney cemetery in a showy grave near the bridge where Mary Wollstonecraft had tried to kill herself just before Mary's copycat deception. On her side Margaret never softened to her mother and her only comment on her death came in a letter to Wollstonecraft's daughter: "I expect you saw in the papers the death of an old lady."

Mary King's fate is more obscure. The romantic Adèle, Comtesse de Boigne, said she declined and died after the birth (and presumed death) of Henry's baby. Others had her rusticated for life to North Wales. The truth was less sensational. For a time she may have been bundled off to Wales to live under a feigned name in a clergyman's family. Then, while her sisters married counts and generals, she made a match in 1805 with plain George Galbraith Meares. Apart from her scandalous past, which detracted from her value, she was much diminished at that time by having no portion from the estates of father or mother; as the first Marquess of Bute remarked, "Ladies of quality without fortunes are perhaps worse off than any other class."

Again mystery surrounds Mary's new lover. Most accounts elevate him into George Meares of Mearescourt in central Ireland. But George Meares did not own or live at the mansion of Mearescourt and he is more likely to have been a Dublin lawyer or tenant of the Kings' estates in County Longford. Reports make it clear that Mary was not crushed by her experiences in 1797 (a bride over whom men had fought and died could be a prize more than a liability to an imaginative husband); she continued lively, outspoken and generally good company.

What is certain is that husband and wife lived for some time in Richmond Place, Clifton, Gloucestershire, near where she had stayed with her family and been tutored by Mary Wollstonecraft. They raised two daughters and two sons. The Meares girls did not reach the social level of their mother, for their uncle Robert Edward in his will of 1842 left a younger sister £2,000, but Mary's daughters £100 a year each, to be paid every six months.

Mary herself had achieved some respectability, and the brother who had dueled for her half a century before and ignominiously stood trial in

Cork referred to her as his "dear sister Mary," while years later Margaret could refute the cautionary versions of her sister's fate that killed her with unkindness or remorse by declaring that she had married "a very respectable man." She could not sanitize the past, however, and always she remembered the year of Mary's elopement, Henry's murder and her father's trial "with Horror." Mary died in Shirehampton, Gloucestershire, in 1819.

Margaret lived longer and more eventfully. For a time after 1798 she continued heavily involved in Irish politics. As the Union came nearer, she wrote more and more stridently about the oppression of her country, the crassness of its governing classes and the misery that must come to the land from its abandoning any pretense to rule itself. Her acute sense of the disgrace of the Anglo-Irish in England, including her deluded mother, reappeared:

> When the nominal nobility of this degraded kingdom shall find themselves despised and neglected in the capital of Great Britain; when they shall behold themselves the subjects of clumsy raillery, and the objects of chilling contempt; when their properties diminish, and their expences encrease; when they are unable to support their accustomed magnificence, and perceive that even the price of their own honour and their country's welfare, is insufficient to enable them to vie with the meanest merchant in London; they will then, perhaps, look back on the days of their prosperity, and sigh for the possession of those virtues they despised. Who will compassionate the unfeeling votary of narrow-minded aristocracy? Who will lament the voluntary victim of self-degradation?

Although she had never reencountered Mary Wollstonecraft, Margaret did now meet her widower, William Godwin, who, in the year of the Union, traveled with John Philpot Curran to Dublin. Godwin dined with

her on several occasions when Stephen was absent. He was unimpressed: he called her a democrat and a republican without much "understanding or good nature" and accused her of being insufficiently tender with her children. To him she appeared grotesque, dressed like Mary Wollstonecraft in her ascetic vindicating period: austerely in gray with no frills. Probably she followed the habit of other well-born Irish ladies who, according to one amazed listener, used "nauseous" expressions more suited to a drunkard or butcher, expressions that would "shock an ear of common delicacy in England," such as "stinking," "dirty," "nasty," "the fellow's carcase," "swim in blood," and "rotten." The listener ascribed the habit to bad education, but it may simply have reflected recent Irish reality. Yet for all Godwin's sense of Margaret's ludicrousness and indelicacy, the pair began to correspond amicably enough and they discussed how children ought to be raised.

Shortly after Godwin's visit the Mount Cashells began a three-month stay in England. Despite her rebellion against upper-class customs and her apocalyptic fears of society after the Union, Margaret's aristocratic life remained much as ever, oiled by servants, governesses and tutors; now they traveled with four attendants while leaving the boys to be brought along later by tutors. As she admitted, "when you are rich the road [is] . . . straight enough & nothing makes travelling so smooth as a good purse of money." In London Margaret and Stephen heard that the war with France was (temporarily) over and they decided on a grand tour, starting in Paris and moving on to Italy.

As her parents had discovered on their travels, the Irish aristocracy were more fêted on the Continent than in England. As well as meeting old English and Irish radicals, Margaret encountered Madame de Staël, whom her mother silenced in England, and the politician Talleyrand, to whom Mary Wollstonecraft had addressed her *Rights of Woman* in what now seemed a distant age. She dined with Napoleon Bonaparte; on this occasion a young friend was complimentary about her manner and appearance, "Lady Mount Cashell looking beautiful and dress'd in black

crape and diamonds." Far more splendid, Napoleon's wife, Josephine, "sat under a canopy blazing in Purple and diamonds." Margaret noted that the French had forgotten all about their revolution.

She did not remind them. She was also circumspect in Rome, where, despite her dislike of Catholicism, she met Pope Pius VII. He plucked a hyacinth from his garden and presented it to her, along with prayer beads of agate and jasper encased in gold. In Naples the Mount Cashells were received by the King and Queen; Stephen wore velvet, embroidery, ruffles and a sword for the occasion. Margaret was unimpressed by the appearance both of her husband and of royalty, and she found the place cold.

Occasionally, when Stephen was out of the way, Margaret put on poor clothes and went with a friend "poking our noses into every haunt of the lower order of people"—apparently facilitated by her ability to shut off her nose to avoid bad smells. She kept in touch with Godwin, who had provided a letter of introduction to an old friend of his and Mary Wollstonecraft's in Paris, the dramatist son of a shoemaker, Thomas Holcroft. Holcroft had been one of the defendants in the Treason Trials, whose acquittals Margaret had so enthusiastically applauded a decade before. She sought him out and, although Stephen was appalled at the man, turned to him when she needed a governess for her girls. He recommended his own daughter Fanny, whom he introduced as a serious, well-educated young woman.

Unhappily, the affected Fanny was no Mary Wollstonecraft, despite sharing her dislike of patronizing employers, and she paid scant attention to her charges. Instead, she spent all her time writing. Margaret reported:

> Did a great man enter the house she wrote Poetry—a little one?—she wrote poetry—was there a party to dinner she wrote poetry—Was there no party to dinner? still she wrote poetry—and such poetry! She was called down by one of the servants on the arrival of a party of strangers—she rushed into the room, breathless and with a pen in her hand. "Ah! My God!" said she—"have the kindness to excuse me I have left my hero-

ine in my hero's arms and I must fly to relieve them"—so saying she disappeared to the great astonishment of all the company.

Then Fanny Holcroft (temporarily) ran off with a gentleman whom she could later identify only as wearing a green coat. Stephen, who disliked Holcroft for himself and his lowly class position, was now warned about his radical past and trial for high treason; he insisted the daughter be ejected.

Hoping to soften the dismissal, Margaret invited Holcroft and Fanny to her soiree, where the latter could shine with her playing and singing; then she gave Holcroft a letter telling him that Stephen had learned of his political past and, to preserve domestic peace, she must part with Fanny. Holcroft was furious, declaring he would tell the world how a peeress treated a poet and punished an innocent girl for the sins of her father. Margaret was obliged to inform him of the more pressing reasons for the dismissal—Fanny's elopement, her "uncultivation of understanding, a want of polish of mind, and an entire absence of those numerous little delicacies easier to be imagined than expressed." Both parties sent their biased versions of the quarrel to Godwin in London, where he now ran a publishing house. Holcroft wanted his printed but Godwin declined.

Through all these years Margaret continued breeding. Edward had been born in 1798, just after the rebellion was crushed; then came Francis in October 1800, named perhaps for Lord Moira, whose sister Selina agreed to be godmother. The child proved weak and died young. In Paris in 1802 Margaret gave birth to another son and in Rome in 1804 to a final girl, making eight children in all.

Perhaps she felt she had had enough of bearing children for the Mount Cashells; perhaps she had come to the Continent with a hidden agenda. Or perhaps on the tour she had been thrown more on the company of her lord than formerly and, as they met new people—including Tom Paine and many from the United Irish circle now exiled from Dublin—as well as old friends such as Valentine Lawless, she found Stephen increasingly "contemptible." He had always been considered "a

very weak man"; now she felt "less regard for him every day." Yet she remained at his side until a replacement appeared. In Rome it seemed to have done so.

Back in Ireland Lady Moira heard disturbing rumors. One reported that when she traveled to Italy Margaret left all her children (except the new one she was breast-feeding) with a young tutor, one of the many former United Irishmen now wandering around France. According to Lady Moira, he was conceited, vulgar and absurd and quite inappropriate considering Margaret's resolve to bring her children up differently than her mother had. But there was soon much worse.

It was said that Lady Mount Cashell was seeing too much of George William Tighe, a friend of Stephen's whom they had met or remet in Rome. He was the son of a literary-minded barrister and parliamentarian of good family and modest estate in County Wicklow, a scholarly, well-educated bachelor who had formerly been at Eton with her brothers. Four years younger than Margaret, who was now thirty-one, he had moved in much the same Ascendancy circles in Ireland as the Kings and Mount Cashells. Most probably he had been known to her during the 1790s in Dublin, although possibly the kinship with Lord Shannon prevented intimacy. Tighe was considered "very handsome & a great Beau," while his poetry suggests he may have been more moved by male friends than by young women. He and Margaret shared an interest in literature and medicine, as well as a contempt for fashion, dress and equipage.

Margaret fell passionately in love with Tighe and he reciprocated in calmer fashion. It was not what she could have wished, any more than Mary Wollstonecraft's obsession with Imlay had been for her, and Margaret sighed in poetry, "Would thou couldst feel a passion strong as mine, / Or teach my heart the sentiments of thine!" Tighe was "Beloved beyond existence, health or fame." She was never that for him; indeed in some ways she was an interruption to his single life of study and congenial male friendship.

Society tolerated multiple adulteries but was appalled at a wife's

deserting a husband and children. Ostracism and poverty must follow, as Mary Wollstonecraft had known: if a woman had been

> practising insincerity, and neglecting her child to manage an intrigue, she would still have been visited and respected. If, instead of openly living with her lover, she could have condescended to call into play a thousand arts, which, degrading her own mind, might have allowed the people who were not deceived, to pretend to be so, she would have been caressed and treated like an honourable woman.

Undeterred, Margaret continued openly to see George Tighe. The rumors that had reached Lady Moira were true.

Although the Mount Cashells began their return to Ireland, they reached only Germany. There in 1805 Margaret and Stephen parted, and Stephen returned alone with the retinue of children, servants and tutors. The pair never met again. "The loss of my seven children was one of the severest punishments of my misconduct," Margaret wrote. She was shocked to find that she could not even retain the youngest as her own and that she could have no further input into her daughters' education, which she knew would be neglected without her.

Lady Moira was deeply saddened. "It is impossible to express what I feel concerning her," she wrote, "& I cannot bear to mention her to her enemies, or maligners." By now she felt herself dying and there would be no one to befriend Margaret in her disgrace. Both her mother and elder brothers, especially George, who should guard her reputation, were hostile—indeed, "her most worthless family has taken pains & pleasure to foment and publish [the scandal] with most exaggerated falsehood," she wrote. Valentine Lawless made things worse. Stephen, his old schoolfellow, had testified for him in court against his adulterous wife; presumably he and his family were reciprocating when they also became "the spreaders of much malice respecting her." Lady Moira execrated George Tighe as below Margaret in rank—an important consideration—as well

as character. "I am grieved to learn (by an indirect method of information) that Mr Tighe, once Ld M[ount] C[ashell]'s friend & favorite till
he assumed & professed a jealousy of him, is a man of insignificance in
every mental quality, & of a vanity to make a parade of being the cause of
such a disagreement." Yet although she believed her friend's conduct
erroneous, she accepted her "uprightness & real purity of mind" and
defended her when she could.

In 1812, four years after the death of his patroness, Lady Moira, and
seven years after Margaret's parting from Stephen, the lawyer Scully
drew up a deed of separation between the couple, by which Margaret
received £800 a year for a separate maintenance and the payment of
some debts. She did not yet live with Tighe, although she had borne him
a daughter in 1809, but friends feared she would soon take "the irre-
trievable false step." She did so the following year.

Her old governess had often come to mind for both her counsels
and example. In *Original Stories* the aristocratic child based on herself
concluded, "I wish to be a woman and to be like Mrs Mason," the stern
but kindly mentor of the tale and Wollstonecraft's own alter ego. George
Tighe wanted Margaret to avoid her married name and would not hide
her under his; so she assumed the style of Mrs. Mason, together with an
identity outside the Irish aristocracy she had so castigated. By doing so
she fulfilled in private part of the agenda of the failed Irish revolution.
She had moved into "that middle rank of life for which I always sighed."
In this capacity she would continue the educational writing for children
that Mary Wollstonecraft had begun; her Irish tales were published by
Godwin in 1807.

But she would not follow her governess's political path and reassert
Enlightenment political principles in a more conservative age. In later
life she sounded disillusioned, declaring she belonged to "no political
party" and once remarking of her life that "the political disturbances in
Ireland . . . augmented the number of my errors." She took up again the
novel "The Chieftains of Erin," which she had begun and abandoned
during her time with the United Irishmen, declaring that by now "that

restless patriotism which disturbed the peace of multitudes, & . . . the *ignis fatuus* of zeal which led so many individuals astray" had both dimmed in Ireland. Although she has a bard seeing "nobility hurled into oblivion by the whirlpool of time and the mud of the ocean thrown to the surface by the same power," her tale of the old times had become less a political statement than a response to the fashionable taste for romantic historical novels, like those of Sir Walter Scott and Sydney Owenson— although she had enough pride in authorship to declare she had begun her work long before the popular "Scotch novels" were thought of. In conversation too she had mellowed and she told a friend indignant about later British politics "to endeavour to turn his thoughts from what he cannot mend." In 1819 she wrote, "Since my country sunk never to rise again, I have been a cool politician, but I cannot forget how I once felt, & can still sympathize with those capable of similar feelings."

Late in life she felt herself tolerant through understanding that little good inhered in any nation or class:

> Perhaps the years of almost half a century & the ups & downs that I have had in life render me less prejudiced than my nature would incline to for I cannot boast of any of that cool good sense which is bestowed on some people at their birth—hard experience has beat into me the little I possess.

In 1814, to avoid further English and Irish winters, which were exacerbating the chest weakness Wollstonecraft had detected when she was a child, Margaret and George Tighe settled in Pisa, having obtained a passport out of England from Lord Castlereagh himself, the "selfish and crafty schemer," as she once termed him. In Pisa George, nicknamed "Tatty," experimented with growing potatoes in pots and in the ground, to the amazement of the Pisans, while Margaret compensated for deserting her and Stephen's children by running an informal clinic for poor children and writing advice on doctoring for more loyal mothers. Both were determined to avoid censorious English society.

Initially it was a serene life and George Tighe summed it up in one mellow moment: "Certain it is that after many storms we now enjoy as much happiness as falls to the lot of most people." Yet it came after years of "doubt and anxiety" and he remained convinced that in general "an illegitimate connection is as miserable as it is criminal."

On the day in July when Margaret's passport was issued Mary Wollstonecraft's daughter with Godwin emulated Mary King and eloped at sixteen with a married man, the poet Percy Bysshe Shelley. She took along her stepsister Claire Clairmont (London gossip declared that Godwin had sold both girls to Shelley, Mary for £800 and Claire for £700). Five years later, after the birth and death of several children, the publication of Mary's *Frankenstein* and Claire's affair with the poet Lord Byron, the trio arrived in Pisa. For these young, unconventional women Margaret made an exception to her rule that she received no English people and soon she became the surrogate mother Mary Wollstonecraft had been for her. She advised and schemed for them, helping to make contacts and keeping them away from compatriots who might despise them; in their turn, like daughters, they were sometimes grateful, sometimes a bit resentful.

She became especially close to Claire. For her she even overcame her dislike of Lord Byron and years later wrote asking him to send money to his destitute former mistress. Byron replied contemptuously to "Claire's Minerva." Still in the grip of her "Quixotic folly" Margaret wrote again, realizing she would probably be thought "a troublesome old Harridan." She was and, after a further haughty reply from Byron, resolved, "As to Lord B I have done with him . . . I will read no more of his poetry."

She found Mary Shelley more reserved than Claire but was useful to her in easing tension with her stepsister, in helping her dose her sick babies, in urging her briskly to look on the brightest side of things and in giving small sums of money when needed. Following her mother's example, Mary wrote a children's book called *Maurice*, which she intended for Margaret's daughter. Margaret reciprocated by sending a little child's reading book she had written; Mary was to use it with her baby son Percy.

Percy Bysshe Shelley was impressed by Margaret's intellect, scholar-ship and political grasp. The pair read Greek together and discussed Ire-land; a few years earlier the nineteen-year-old Shelley had gone to stir up Dublin with his pamphlets against the Union that she herself had so stren-uously opposed. Like Lady Moira contemplating Stephen, Shelley at one moment found Margaret unworthily matched—"her husband is . . . far inferior to her"—although at another he declared he prized Tighe as his friend while finding Margaret perverse. Mostly he was impressed, however, calling her "a superior and accomplished woman," unprejudiced, "ami-able and wise." It was alleged that she sat for the Lady in his poem "The Sensitive Plant":

> Whose form was upborne by a lovely mind
> Which, dilating, had moulded her mien and motion
> Like a sea-flower unfolded beneath the ocean . . .

Although Shelley rather admired the large physique that his father-in-law Godwin had ridiculed, it is unlikely that the stout, middle-aged Margaret was depicted in the light-footed Lady with trailing hair. Yet to his cousin Tom Medwin he claimed Margaret was indeed the source of some of the poem; probably she inspired the serenity and benevolence with which Shelley endowed his Lady.

In his turn the poet made a deep impression on his older friend. She was one of the last to see him alive—when, she noted, he had looked espe-cially healthy and vibrant. On the night of his drowning she dreamed he came to her, seeming ill and tired; she asked him to " 'sit down & eat.' 'No,' he replied, 'I shall never eat more.' " She awoke, then slept again and dreamed he was dead. Long after his death she still dreamed of him "in one of his most brilliant humours" and felt disappointed to wake up.

In 1826, four years after Stephen died, Margaret and George Tighe were married by the British chaplain of Leghorn, although Margaret retained the name Mrs. Mason. Their union was not enhanced by legal-ity. Over time their habits had diverged and they lived much apart, Tighe

increasingly sedentary and retired, privately writing that he longed to get away from "vulgar idle talk" and "Society," she still outgoing, interested, talkative and cheerful—at least in company and with her daughters. As she wrote sadly in a poem to rouse him, "Come then and though we are not what we've been / You'll find the friendship of the *friend* still '*green*.' " He found it hard to respond, instead declaring his love of solitude: "In the autumn of Love 'tis in vain / We look for the blossom of joy!" He was tired of being spurred into feeling and weary of Margaret's tears and reproaches, which had "wither'd this desolate heart." "Let us give o'er the unequal strife," he wrote. "Gay pleasure is for youth alone."

Both were intermittently homesick. Tighe wrote of Ireland and himself: "belov'd in vain! Exiled by Fate" and he longed for the fresh greenness of Wicklow, while Margaret called herself "a vagabond on the face of the earth." When she described her hero in the utopian world of her novel "Selene," she made him yet feel the pull of home: "so ardent was my desire to revisit my native country, I should readily resign all the moral & physical advantages enjoyed amongst the Selenians [moon people], to behold it once more." Both character and creator felt that "attachment to certain spots of ground which constitutes the *amor patriae* of many an exile." Yet Margaret also knew that "regret of all sorts is vain!"

About their relationship both were wry. Tighe wrote that, if he had his life again, he would look for a wife who was not of high rank; he would choose someone with health and mild temper, not a witty person who loved talking and was always sick. Concerned for her two young girls— who lamented they had been so well educated they would never manage to marry—Margaret looked for help not to her critical husband but to her "excellent and beloved daughter" Helena, from her first marriage.

Margaret and George Tighe quarreled fiercely, both at times declaring they had sacrificed their life for the other. She blamed him for her continual ill health as she had once blamed her mother and Stephen, while he lamented giving up friends and prospects to her passion for him, "my living with you separated me from the rest of mankind. . . . It was for your sake alone I came into this country and consented to establish

myself amongst people with whom I cannot associate." Both used the children as counters: Margaret insisted that Tighe failed to consider their interests properly—she had criticized Stephen in much the same way—and Tighe retorted that she had always been a "concealed enemy," poisoning his daughters' minds against him, making him "a cypher" in the family. His resentment grew so vast that he even thought of returning to Ireland and leaving her to support the girls—a threat she found "very shocking." Inevitably they disputed over money; he was penurious, she extravagant. He wanted to save for the children's future and bring them up properly; perhaps in reaction to her strictness with her first family, she desired only to be liked by them, so she laid out money on balls and assemblies that would also allow them to make advantageous marriages—acting just as Caroline had done for her girls.

Soon Margaret and Tighe decided to live separately, he privately in the country, she publicly in the center of Pisa about half an hour's drive away. She presided over what Tighe called "a slovenly House"—perhaps he knew how, years before, Mary Wollstonecraft had been pilloried for her unkempt appearance and housekeeping. Certainly it was an amusing establishment, since Margaret records people dancing there until after three in the morning at carnival time. The couple did not entirely part and the girls remained close to both parents.

In her last years Margaret held a fortnightly literary and philosophical salon at her house in Pisa, the "Academy of Lunatics," whose certificate of membership declared, "If you are not crazy we do not want you" but whose purpose was as serious as the earlier Lunar Society of Birmingham, in which so many of Mary Wollstonecraft's Dissenting scientific friends had participated. Among the Pisa "Lunatics" were many men and women, such as the poets Giuseppe Giusti and Giacomo Leopardi, who would play crucial parts in the patriotic revival of Italy, as their hostess had once done with Ireland. It was the latest flowering of Wollstonecraft's teaching.

By 1832 Claire Clairmont had returned from Russia and Germany to live with Margaret. "With her I am as her child," she wrote to Mary Shelley

and, along with her benefactor, she dreamed of a society of liberated women and children. Her happiness was marred only by Margaret's increasing ill health, exacerbated by her finally agreeing to the "mercurial treatment" she had formerly opposed. "It is too bitter, after a long life passed in unbroken misery, to find a good only that you may lose it," wrote Claire to Mary. Margaret died in January 1835. Two years later George Tighe was buried beside her in the Protestant cemetery in Leghorn.

The Mount Cashells' Dublin house on St. Stephen's Green had been deserted as soon as Stephen returned to Ireland without Margaret; it was bought by John Philpot Curran and now houses the Department of Foreign Affairs. After Stephen's death in 1822, the eldest son, whom Margaret had abandoned, duly inherited Moore Park, his father's title and his uncle George's politics. Margaret's poetic eulogist A. Maria had written, "Let each bright virtue, in her sons beam forth, / Their grand-sire's spirit, and their father's worth." That was before their "grand-sire" had been accused of murder and their father been abandoned by his wife as a hopeless reactionary snob.

The young man proved true to his male ancestors and was mocked in the Westminster House of Lords for revealing "the old Baronial prejudice against any change in the establishment." Although educated in Rome when his parents were abroad, he became evangelically Protestant and fiercely anti-Catholic and, when in 1829 the newly emancipated Catholics of Kilworth tried to build a chapel just outside his demesne wall, he closed the main path to his house so that his guests did not have to look at anything so offensive. For some years he bored the region with his personal interpretations of the Bible. At the close of one evangelical meeting in Fermoy, held to thank him for his zeal in promoting Protestantism, fighting broke out between Catholics and soldiers brought in to keep order; "the ruffian mob" even assaulted Lord Mount Cashell's carriage with mud. *The Freeholder* reported a Catholic response: "Let your tenants, my Lord, have their little holdings at a rate that may enable them to live like human beings. . . . Be no longer known as . . . the grinder of the faces of the poor."

After an agent had embezzled much of its income, Moore Park was sold to become a British army barracks. In 1908 it burned down during a riotous party—or was set on fire by officers covering up an embezzlement. The shell stood until the 1960s, when DairyGold, formerly the dairy cooperative of Mitchelstown, bought and demolished it. A piggery is built on part of the site.

George King's unsavory and licentious reputation increased with the title of Earl of Kingston. One story recounts that he spied a pretty girl, whom he finally tracked down. He asked her name: it was Katie Kingston. It is not known whether he added incest to his sins. Other stories include curses for which the Cork folk were famous: "The maledictions of the peasantry are very powerful, and embrace a climax of evils, gradually ascending to the most dreadful imprecations." The one targeting George was fairly prosaic. A priest was stopped while going across the Kingston land to give extreme unction to a tenant; he shouted, "I curse thee Kingsborough, pigs will live where you are standing"—not strictly true, perhaps, but close to the mark.

George now gave rein to fantasy, proving himself in a manner as romantic as his eloping sister Mary. While the power of the Ascendancy seeped away after the Union, he felt its glamour increase. He insisted he was the inheritor of the White Knight and demanded he be treated as such in all national ceremonies. He badgered the prime minister Robert Peel with his claim and, when Peel finally refused it, declared haughtily that his "people" recognized it nonetheless.

With or without exotic titles he was still a favorite of the Prince of Wales, now George IV. In 1821, en route to Ireland, the King learned that his hated wife Caroline was dead; he responded by arriving "dead DRUNK," according to the Countess of Glengall. Another witness added details: "The passage to Dublin was occupied in eating goose-pie and drinking whiskey in which his Majesty took most abundantly, singing many joyous songs, and being in a state, on his arrival, to double in number even the numbers of his gracious subjects assembled on the pier to

receive him." At his landing in Howth he greeted George, who had come to meet him, with the words "Kingston, Kingston, you black-whiskered, good-natured fellow! I am happy to see you in this friendly country"; then, with a ragged procession of farmers and gentlemen on horseback, he drove off to the vice-regal lodge, where he invited the crowds into the grounds, telling them not to worry about keeping off the grass. He promised to visit his old friend at Mitchelstown when he next came to Ireland.

After twenty-four years of fighting his mother for the estates George finally got his inheritance in 1823. Now his fantasy could be embodied in building. As the Anglo-Irish novelist Elizabeth Bowen put it, when he inherited he "came in with a roar." Influenced by the new century's enthusiasm for houses like neomedieval fortresses, he borrowed on a vast scale, then tore down the grand Palladian mansion Robert and Caroline had recently built and erected a Gothic castle in imitation of Windsor, thereby reverting to the style his parents' Palladian had replaced. The castle would have a new White Knight's Tower, bigger than anything around. When a manufacturer built a tall chimney nearby, George threatened to move himself and his patronage from Mitchelstown unless it disappeared; the townspeople obligingly visited the manufacturer during the night and he left town within three days.

Fired by the King's promise on his last visit to Ireland, George's aim was to entertain him lavishly in his new castle, the biggest in Ireland. To this end he insisted it be built in two years so as to be ready for the royal visit. He employed hundreds of workmen at a cost of between £100,000 and £220,000. He also ordered elaborate furnishings and tableware, including a set of Trafalgar commemorative napkins in finest damask linen; he stocked the best wines and employed the best chefs, among them as undercook William Claridge, later founder of the London hotel. The King never came, but others readily accepted George's formal, exotic hospitality, and parties and balls lit up the night around Mitchelstown. Meanwhile, his building mania unsated, he recast his parents' old Galtees hunting lodge in picturesque mode, adding an octagonal viewing tower.

Debts mounted. By the end of the 1820s George owed £400,000 and there was no chance of his ever repaying such a massive sum. Now the instability so salient in the brutalities of 1798 overwhelmed him. As he himself wrote of politics after the Union, "I know, as one large proprietor here, they have taken from me every power except that to do mischief," and he continued, "my influence among the people is such that I can defy the Irish government to weaken my influence. You may rest assured, we will take care of our properties and fight hard for them." But if he thought he could be a rebel like his sister, he was wrong. His father had been distraught when about to lose control over elections; the son went further. When the (finally) emancipated Catholic tenants did not vote for his candidate, George lost the little hold he had over himself. He summoned them into his magnificent gallery at Mitchelstown Castle to chastise them and lament the loss of his family's political power. As the tenants pressed forward on the floor and galleries, memories of the Wexford capture overwhelmed him. He leaped up shouting, "They are come to tear me in pieces!" He spent his last six years insane in England, believing alternately that he had no property in Ireland and that Ireland no longer existed. Elizabeth Bowen wrote his epitaph:

> [George] epitomises that rule by force of sheer fantasy that had, in great or small ways, become for his class the only possible one. From the big lord to the small country gentleman we were, about this time, being edged back upon a tract of clouds and obsessions that could each, from its nature, only be solitary. The sense of dislocation was everywhere. Property was still there, but power was going. It was democracy, facing him in his gallery, that sent Big George mad.

After his death George's body was taken back to Mitchelstown for burial in a fantastic medieval coffin complete with coronet and coat of arms. One of the chief mourners was Margaret's eldest son, the Earl of Mount Cashell.

The Henrietta Street house, such a bone of contention in the early

married life of Robert and Caroline, went to his brother Robert Edward, who sold it; then it began its descent into slum tenements, its marble, doors and banisters ripped out to adorn more gracious homes.

George's eldest son, Edward, was as fantastical as his father: he had glimpsed a Mexican manuscript in the Bodleian Library in Oxford and thereafter, while he paid for explorations in Mexico, shut himself up in the White Knight's Tower at Mitchelstown compiling a vastly annotated and sumptuously illustrated edition of ancient Mexican art, which would also prove the Mexicans were the lost tribe of Israel. It ran to nine heavy volumes with a tenth projected. He sent elaborate copies to the King of Prussia and the Tsar of Russia as well as to the Louvre and the British Museum. The edition cost £32,000, chargeable to the Mitchelstown estate.

No more than his father could Edward pay his debts and the paper merchant had him arrested. He was lodged in the sheriff's prison in Dublin and died of typhus in 1837, just a couple of years before George, whose death would have given him the liberating inheritance. He too was buried at Mitchelstown.

George was succeeded by his second son, Robert, who continued the tradition of lavish and indiscriminate entertaining. He was indicted for sodomy in 1848. In the following year the sheriff came to seize the castle treasures in payment for the family's huge debts; believing aristocrats invincible as his father had done, Robert barred the doors of his home, but after a fortnight's siege food began to run out and he was forced to surrender. His career climaxed in Chester in 1860: he had insisted on walking through the tunnel of the Holyhead railway, then he refused to remove his hat in Chester cathedral; the next morning he went into the street naked. Taken to court, he sat himself on the judge's bench. He was judged insane and confined to an asylum. He left no heir and his next brother died shortly after. Much of the Mitchelstown land was then sold off. The aristocracy rarely loses all its money but in this case within two generations the great King inheritance had been reduced to not much more than a gentleman's estate.

Once George's line had died out the title went to his brother Robert Edward's line. They too proved eccentric, financially feckless and litigious. In the end all the family discovered that the notion of feudal loyalty on which they had set such store was outdated. When the chance of destroying their power came in the Irish civil war of 1922, the farmers, descendants of the peasants so long at the mercy of the Kings, turned into the local Irish Republican Army. George's Gothic extravaganza was seized and its treasures looted. The castle was burned, becoming a ruin less than a century after it was built. Some of the stones were used to construct a local Catholic church.

When the ruins were later demolished, the site was taken by those who had burned and looted the castle. They established their dairy cooperative in the grounds, building an ugly square factory on the elegant demesne, a pitch-and-putt club in the old walled garden and a sewage works in the ornamental lakes.

Notes

p. 3 **a fairly typical, ethnically diverse Anglo-Irish clan:** The destruction of
so many Irish archives during the 1922 civil war makes Irish family
history difficult. In the case of the Kings the destruction of the Rockingham mansion and total loss of the contents of Mitchelstown Castle add to the difficulty.

p. 4 **in the marriage market wealth far outweighed rank:** See A. P. W. Malcomson, *The Pursuit of the Heiress: Aristocratic Marriage in Ireland
1750–1820.*

p. 5 **They lived at Richard's estate . . . Merrion Square in Dublin:** There is
some confusion over these addresses. In *White Knights, Dark Earls* Bill
Power gives the Kingsboroughs' new address as 15 Merrion Square,
but this seems based on a letter in which Mary Wollstonecraft wants
her correspondence placed there for forwarding; in fact she makes it
clear that it is Mrs. Fitzgerald's house; see *The Letters of Mary Wollstonecraft,* 4 December 1786. *A List of the Proprietors of Licenses on Private Sedan Chairs, At 25th March, 1787, Alphabetically ranged, with their
respective residences . . .* describes Viscountess Kingsborough as resid-
ing in Henrietta Street, and the parliamentary lists give the same
address for Viscount Kingsborough.

p. 6 **"before she was aware of what man or money was":** Malcomson, *Pursuit of the Heiress,* 16.

p. 9 **William wrote from Florence to his mother:** *Correspondence of Emily,
Duchess of Leinster (1731–1814),* 3:480.

p. 10 **"I believe to make up . . . whenever they see her":** Ibid., 3:494.

p. 10 **"I like the description . . . married to her and settled":** Ibid., 3:501.

p. 10 **"most exceedingly for the match because William himself is":** Ibid.,
1:531.

pp. 10–11 **"how far it may be necessary . . . get Miss from the Marquess":** Ibid.,
1:542.

pp. 11–12 **There surely must be something in it . . . disagreeable person:** Ibid.,
3:552.

p. 13 **the rent roll of the Mitchelstown estates was £42,000 a year:** James S. Donnelly Jr., *The Land and the People of Nineteenth-Century Cork*, 70.

p. 13 **the letter containing the offer . . . four years after the wedding:** The letters of Robert and Edward King in the 1760s and 1770s quoted in the following pages are owned by Colonel Anthony Lawrence King-Harman. They have been deposited in the Public Record Office of Northern Ireland (PRONI) and listed as D/4168.

pp. 17–18 **"very near as good as Button . . . *lie*:** National Library of Ireland, Dublin, MS 8810(3).

p. 19 **Other critics . . . repartee replace wisdom:** *The Life and Correspondence of the Late Robert Southey*, 1:149.

p. 20 **"drink as much whiskey . . . demons of disease":** 23 October 1786, Darwin Papers, Cambridge University Library, DAR 216 B9. Future quotations from Richard Lovell Edgeworth are taken from these papers.

pp. 20–21 **According to the German Prince Pückler-Muskau . . . vigilance":** [Hermann Ludwig Heinrich von Pückler-Muskau], *Tour in England, Ireland, and France, in the Years 1828 & 1829 by a German Prince*, 2:21–27.

p. 21 **the combined ages . . . thirty-two:** The birth dates of Caroline's children are extremely difficult to work out since the dates on the letters appear at odds with the official birth dates in other records. In *The Kings, Earls of Kingston*, 36, R. D. King-Harman has 28 April 1771 for George, as does *The Eton College Register 1753–1790*. *Present Peerage for the Year 1817* has 3 April 1771. Given the mention of Caroline's next pregnancy, however, George seems to have been born rather earlier than this.

p. 21 **By July 1771 Caroline was pregnant again:** The memorial plaque at Livorno gives the date of Margaret's birth as 1773. Edward C. McAleer in *The Sensitive Plant: A Life of Lady Mount Cashell* follows *Exshaw Gentleman's and London Magazine* of November 1772 and states it as 24 October 1772. Counting backward from 1786, Mary Wollstonecraft also put it as 1772, as does Margaret herself when she married in 1791. Against this are letters written from Kingston by Robert to his father in Dublin and dated 9 and 15 October 1772 reporting Margaret's vaccination by a local doctor. This evidence seems the most persuasive and suggests that the pregnancy referred to in July 1771 resulted in Margaret's birth.

p. 22 **"They agree extremely well . . . not to do so":** 16 November 1771.

p. 22 **"hurly-burly . . . trod upon":** *The Autobiography and Correspondence of Mary Granville, Mrs Delany*.

pp. 22–23 **I told you in my last . . . three Guineas:** 23 November 1771.

p. 25 **"They are both taking the disorder very well":** 9 October 1772.

p. 25 **Mr. Tickell reported . . . five or six pairs each week:** 6 November 1772.

p. 26 **"I am convinc'd it is impossible . . . ever to agree":** 29 January 1773.

p. 28 **"genteel" and "more Proper than a Jobb Coach":** 4 January 1773.

p. 28 **"bought a very fine sallad Lettice . . . 18d":** *Betsy Sheridan's Journal: Letters from Sheridan's Sister 1784–1786 and 1788–1790*, 36.

pp. 28–29 **the dresses were splendid . . . flowed into the room:** Lord Moira to his mother, 28 March 1789. Copies of the Moira letters are held in PRONI as the Granard Papers (T/3765).

p. 29 **"Lord Kingsborough . . . till after her lying-in":** 21 January 1773.

p. 29 **"no people cou'd have lived . . . propose to do so":** 29 January 1773.

p. 30 **"I am in truth . . . never can be happy":** 23 February 1773.

p. 30 **"You will excuse me . . . ask forgiveness of":** 4 April and 30 April 1773.

p. 31 **In the face of this . . . act properly to his parents:** 15 June 1773.

p. 32 **"that, and that only . . . in the way you have it":** 23 November 1773.

p. 34 **"cormorants . . . breaking the spirit of the nation":** *The Works of Mary Wollstonecraft*, 4:28.

p. 35 **"have their excellencies . . . I have seen in England":** 4 September 1774.

p. 38 **A more mature and liberal landowner . . . for their own purposes:** 23 October 1786.

p. 39 **"illegally entailed . . . *Surplice Fees*":** William Bingley, *An Examination into the Origin and Continuance of the Discontents in Ireland, and the True Cause of the Rebellion*, iv.

p. 39 **"petty and despicable . . . proprietor":** John Bush in *The English Traveller in Ireland: Accounts of Ireland and the Irish Through Five Centuries*, 158.

p. 39 **on long leases . . . most humble tone and posture:** Maria Edgeworth, *Castle Rackrent and Ennui*, 73.

pp. 39–40 **For landowners . . . on similar land:** W. E. H. Lecky, *A History of Ireland in the Eighteenth Century*, 2:6f.

p. 40 **"air of neatness, order, dress and *properté*":** Arthur Young, *A Tour in Ireland 1776–1779*, 2:151.

p. 40 **"I long much . . . wait on you at Kingston":** 5 October 1775.

p. 41 **Lord Townshend went so far . . . withheld the royal letter:** Edith Mary Johnston-Liik, *History of the Irish Parliament, 1692–1800,* 4:155.

p. 41 **"a patern of the silk . . . quite new":** 21 December 1775.

p. 42 **"an uncouth mass, at war with every rule of architecture":** Sir Jonah Barrington, *Personal Sketches of His Own Times,* 1:1.

p. 42 **"a knowledge of the world corrects old manners":** Young, *A Tour in Ireland,* 2:155.

p. 43 **"In a country changing . . . even in the uncultivated mind:** Ibid., 1:463.

p. 44 **Magnificence o'er all the structure shines . . . woo the blushing fair":** *Carton* (1780).

p. 45 **A traveler now had to approach . . . gateways:** Power, *White Knights,* 24f.

p. 45 **When this style of landscape . . . community that served it:** See Uvedale Price, *A letter to H. Repton, Esq., on the application of the practice as well as the principles of landscape-painting to landscape-gardening.*

p. 46 **"at the hazard of our lives and fortunes":** James S. Donnelly Jr., "Irish Agrarian Rebellion: The Whiteboys of 1769–76," in *R.I.A. Proc.,* 85 section C, xii (1983), 330.

p. 46 **"I have blooded my young dog . . . bloodhound":** Lecky, *History of Ireland,* 2:40n.

p. 46 **"Few of the nobility . . . agreeableness of conversation":** R. D. King-Harman, *The Kings,* 9.

p. 46 **To retain the inheritance . . . few believed him sincere:** Power, *White Knights,* 6.

p. 47 **When they had pulled down . . . marketplace on an incline:** Robert and Caroline were more eager to use Kingston College architecturally than to support it. Consequently, the college had to sue Robert to get payment of its installments, which came from the estate. See *Mitchelstown Charity Minute Book,* in the possession of Bill Power.

p. 47 **"mud-wall houses . . . wretched habitations":** 16 May 1796, Darwin papers. The Kingsboroughs also improved the villages of Kildorrery, Ballyporeen and Ballylanders.

p. 48 **all over Ireland . . . middlemen and head tenants:** William J. Smyth, "Social, Economic and Landscape Transformations in County Cork from the Mid-Eighteenth to the Mid-Nineteenth Century" in *Cork: History and Society: Interdisciplinary Essays on the History of an Irish County,* 674.

p. 51 **"class of little country gentlemen . . . native soil":** Young, *A Tour in Ireland*, 2:155.

p. 52 **gossip made him a libertine . . . redress:** Bingley, *Examination*, 5n.

p. 54 **A landlord in Ireland . . . taken in patience:** Young, *A Tour in Ireland*, 2:54.

p. 55 **"there is no family . . . religious prejudice":** *Correspondence Etc. of Dr Hugh MacDermot M.D. 1754–1824*, 131.

p. 55 **Writing in the early nineteenth century . . . Protestant clergymen:** Barrington, *Personal Sketches*, 1:25f.

p. 57 **The Earl of Mount Cashell . . . yellow buttons:** Allan Blackstock, *An Ascendancy Army: The Irish Yeomanry, 1796–1834*, 108; *Journal of the Cork Historical and Archaeological Society* (1894), 2.

p. 57 **"What a glorious and pleasing sight . . . property of the nation":** *Exshaw Magazine* for 1789; Elizabeth Bowen, *Bowen's Court*, 120.

p. 58 **"a most bungling imperfect business . . . interests of their country":** Thomas Bartlett, "The Burden of the Present: Theobald Wolfe Tone, Republican and Separatist" in *The United Irishmen: Republicanism, Radicalism and Rebellion*, 11.

p. 59 **"Can poverty from Gold withdraw his hand?":** Marilyn Butler, *Maria Edgeworth: A Literary Biography*, 20.

p. 59 **Given the tempers aroused . . . no hits made:** James Kelly, *"That Damn'd Thing Called Honour": Duelling in Ireland 1570–1860*, 143f.

p. 59 **"the dignity of the Shannon family . . . so great a country":** Edith M. Johnston, *Great Britain and Ireland 1760–1800: A Study in Political Administration*, 130.

p. 59 **"first and highest ambition . . . *free*":** *Lord Shannon's Letters to his Son. A Calendar of the Letters Written by the 2nd Earl of Shannon to his Son, Viscount Boyle, 1790–1802*, lxii.

p. 60 **"*extortion* assume the *power* of legislation":** Grattan gave many graphic instances, e.g., one man was obliged to pay 24s for 2 acres of wheat and 17s for the potatoes grown to feed cattle. Another landlord charged 40s for an acre of potatoes. When the farmer refused to pay he was taken to court and this cost him £16.

p. 60 **"The people who cultivate . . . demanded from them":** Bingley, *Examination*, 27.

p. 61 **"to delight in searching . . . pebbles":** Some originals of the letters by Margaret, Countess of Mount Cashell, are kept in the Pforzheimer Collection of the New York Public Library; these will be referred to as the Cini Papers.

p. 62 **"The rich have all the intolerancy . . . piety":** George Cooper in *The English Traveller in Ireland*, 188.

p. 62 **"to subvert the Protestant religion . . . hands of papists":** Quoted in James Kelly, "The Genesis of 'Protestant Ascendancy': The Rightboy Disturbances of the 1780s and Their Impact upon Protestant Opinion" in *Parliament, Politics and People: Essays in Eighteenth-Century Irish History*, 96.

p. 63 **Ogle claimed . . . "rebels," not "papists," he said:** *Dictionary of National Biography.*

p. 63 **"the patriotic Mr. Ogle . . . mouthpiece of the court":** James Kelly, "Eighteenth-century Ascendancy: A Commentary" in *Eighteenth-Century Ireland*, 5:181; Kevin Whelan, "Politicisation in County Wexford and the Origins of the 1798 Rebellion," in *Ireland and the French Revolution*, 159.

p. 63 **It was fashionable . . . hear herself talk:** Henry MacDougall, *Sketches of Irish Political Characters*, 199f.

p. 64 **"to the shame of Ireland . . . ought to love":** [Margaret Countess of Mount Cashell], *Reply to a Ministerial Pamphlet intitled "Considerations upon the State of Public Affairs in the year 1799, in Ireland." By a Philanthropist* (1799), 18f. Margaret wrote three political pamphlets on Ireland in 1799 and 1800, all published anonymously. A penciled note on the front page of the pamphlets held in the National Library in Dublin ascribes them to her; firmer evidence comes from the fact that Bartolomeo Cini ("B.C."), Margaret's son-in-law, lists them as hers in the 1840 Italian version of *Advice to Young Mothers.*

p. 64 **They may occasionally . . . language":** See Diarmaid Ó Catháin, "An Irish Scholar Abroad: Bishop John O'Brien of Cloyne and the Macpherson Controversy," in *Cork*, ed. O'Flanagan and Buttimer, 502; John Bush in *The English Traveller*, 160.

p. 65 **"It is the misfortune . . . their interests are distinct":** George Knox to Abercorn, 16 March 1793, Abercorn Papers, PRONI T 2541/IBI/4/17.

p. 66 **"eaten by way of bread . . . peeling them":** Richard Twiss in *The English Traveller*, 170.

p. 66 **her aristocratic friend . . . fifty different ways:** *An Irish Peer on the Continent (1801–1803): being a narrative of the tour of Stephen, 2nd Earl Mountcashell . . . as related by Catherine Wilmot*, 81.

p. 67 **"It is a prison . . . ruin":** John Scott, 1st Earl of Llonmell, "Life in the Irish Country House," in *Quarterly Bulletin of the Irish Georgian Society* 7 (April-December 1964), 68f.

p. 67 **She wrote about the effect . . . wicked or obstinate:** Paper c. 1830 for a meeting of the Arezzo Academy, Dazzi-Cini Archive, San Marcello-Pistoiese.

p. 68 **"their liberty . . . with rights valid against their parents":** Francis Hutcheson, *A Short Introduction to Moral Philosophy,* 248; *A System of Moral Philosophy,* 1:192.

p. 72 **The very idea . . . as cheerful as possible:** Margaret Moore, Countess of Mount Cashell, *Advice to Young Mothers on the Physical Education of Children, by a Grandmother,* 170.

p. 72 **"*ses Ordinaires* . . . the force of Custom":** *The Synge Letters: Bishop Edward Synge to His Daughter Alicia, Roscommon to Dublin, 1746–1752,* 284.

p. 74 **"flounces and trimmings, and lace and trumpery of all sorts":** Moore, *Advice to Young Mothers,* 307.

p. 75 **"I have very good reason . . . as small as her arms":** Ibid., 309.

p. 80 **"I by no means like the proposal . . . surrounded by *unequals*":** *Letters of Mary Wollstonecraft,* 6 July 1786.

p. 81 **"I could not live the life . . . going forward":** Ibid., 9 October 1786.

p. 82 **"There was such a solemn kind . . . the Bastille":** Ibid., 30 October 1786.

p. 84 **Her three daughters . . . dresses and balls:** The description in *A Vindication of the Rights of Woman* of three vain, trivial girls, daughters of a widow, "a very good woman" of fortune and fashion and "narrow mind," may be based on these girls. *Works of Mary Wollstonecraft,* 5:256.

p. 85 **"shamefully ignorant . . . even at that early age, affected:** Ibid., 4:361.

p. 85 **"In due time . . . played with her dogs":** Ibid., 1:10.

p. 88 **Probably the doctor . . . soft linen and flannel:** Moore, *Advice to Young Mothers,* 178f.

p. 90 **a very "handsome" woman . . . selfish vanity of beauty had produced":** *Works of Mary Wollstonecraft,* 5:244f.

p. 90 **"besides the advantages . . . want of intelligence":** Ibid., 6:72f.

p. 92 **Of the Dublin poor . . . son and daughters:** Henry Ingliss contrasted the ragged wretches sitting on the steps of grand houses with the splendor of carriages waiting alongside, quoted in Liam de Paor, *The Peoples of Ireland,* 224f.

p. 92 **In response to the enclosure . . . artisans and tradesmen:** *The Gorgeous Mask: Dublin 1700–1850,* vii.

p. 92 **Entertainments for the wealthy . . . figures of wisdom and the arts:** John T. Gilbert, *A History of the City of Dublin,* 2:110.

p. 93 **One dramatic moment . . . seriously wounded:** *The Life and Letters of Lady Sarah Lennox 1745–1826,* 2:63.

p. 93 **Outside the theater . . . two more assembly rooms were added:** Desmond Guiness, *Georgian Dublin,* 90.

pp. 93–94 **In winter fashionable people . . . appear in the mode:** Constantia Maxwell, *Dublin Under the Georges 1714–1830,* 115.

p. 94 **"preferred a Life . . . Prostitution":** *Gentleman's Almanack* for 1799.

pp. 95–96 **Lady Clare at a Drawing Room . . . black flowers:** Mairead Dunlevy, *Dress in Ireland,* 117.

p. 96 **"a premature disgust to the follies of dress . . . female vanity":** "Autobiography for her daughters" by Margaret, Countess of Mount Cashell, in Cini Papers, reprinted in McAleer, *The Sensitive Plant,* 5. Dress was used for political and national purposes, e.g., many ladies wore Irish linen to support Irish industry.

p. 97 **"generally speaking, the despised part of the community . . . scandal & contempt":** Cini Papers.

p. 98 **"[They] only dress to gratify men . . . rebuffs affection":** *Works of Mary Wollstonecraft,* 5:199.

p. 99 **"I think him an eloquent madman . . . extraordinary selfishness":** Margaret, Countess of Mount Cashell [signed Mrs. Mason] to Mary Shelley, Abinger MSS Dep.c.517/2. Future quotations from the correspondence between Margaret and the Shelleys will be referred to as Abinger MSS.

p. 100 **He was *the* Protestant musician . . . chosen Israelites:** See Linda Colley, *Britons: Forging the Nation 1707–1837,* 31f.

p. 100 **"A more elegant or brilliant auditory . . . accommodate the numbers":** *Daily Universal Register* for Saturday, 12 May 1787.

pp. 100–1 **[N]ever was I more truly delighted . . . I had ever heard offer'd up:** *Betsy Sheridan's Journal,* 50.

p. 102 **"a *lilly* drooping . . . thin and lean, pale and wan' ":** *Letters of Mary Wollstonecraft,* 24 March 1787.

p. 103 **"balsamic air & charming Scenery":** *Dear Miss Heber: An Eighteenth-Century Correspondence,* 46.

pp. 103–4 **"like regular birds of passage . . . hottest months in summer":** Edgeworth, *Ennui,* 146.

p. 105 **"peculiar good fortune . . . whatever virtues I possess":** Margaret to William Godwin, 8 September 1800, in *Shelley and His Circle 1773–1822,* ed. Kenneth Neill Cameron, 1:84.

p. 105 **"almost the only person of superior merit . . . my governess":** Cini Papers.

p. 106 **"To this excellent man I am indebted . . . parental affection":** MS "Selene" in Cini Papers.

p. 108 **"[Clare] has no god but English government":** Ann C. Kavanaugh, "John Fitzgibbon, Earl of Clare" in *The United Irishmen*, 120.

p. 109 **"So long as the nature of men . . . the Protestant Empire of Great Britain":** Patrick Heffernan, *The Heffernans and Their Time*, 138f.

pp. 109–10 **"Civil governors are properly the servants . . . responsible to it":** Richard Price, *A Discourse on the Love of Our Country*, 23.

p. 110 **the want of sufficient power and patronage . . . county and city of Cork:** Johnston-Liik, *History of the Irish Parliament*, 3:249.

p. 110 **"distressed and distracted . . . lost his temper":** *Shannon's Letters*, 6.

p. 110 **A contested election . . . used to political obedience:** Frank O'Gorman, *Voters, Patrons and Parties: The Unreformed Electoral System of Hanoverian England 1734–1832*, 61.

p. 111 **one of Caroline's relatives:** Hewitt in *Shannon's Letters* identified this man as possibly Colonel Henry Gerald Fitz-Gerald and describes him as the "illegitimate son of Lady Kingston's brother-in-law," 2n, 87n. He is more likely to have been Colonel Robert Uniacke Fitzgerald, a more distant relative.

p. 111 **Robert lost the election . . . in these difficult times:** Kevin Whelan, "Politicisation in County Wexford" in *Ireland and the French Revolution*, 158.

p. 112 **Aimed at the protection . . . Protestant anxiety:** See Act of Parliament 33rd Geo.III., sub-sec. xv., c. 22.

p. 112 **"encouragement to protestant volunteers . . . fraternity of his people":** Sir Henry McAnally, *The Irish Militia: A Social and Military Study*, 48, 57f.

pp. 112–13 **In Cork the mayor . . . dinner and card party for him:** *The Council Book of the Corporation of the City of Cork*, ed. Richard Caulfield, entry for 30 November 1790.

p. 113 **"Cork is a very popish . . . tittle-tattle of the town":** *Shannon's Letters*, 38.

p. 113 **"afraid of drinking himself . . . Miss Farren":** *Betsy Sheridan's Journal*, 139.

p. 115 **"she did not wish . . . notice as her daughter":** *Works of Mary Wollstonecraft*, 1:10.

p. 115 **"Without having any seeds sown . . . to captivate Lords":** Ibid., 1:30.

p. 117 **To honor her friend Caroline . . . amazing sum of £500:** *Walker's Hibernian Magazine* for April 1790.

p. 119 **He was a distinguished classical scholar . . . King's Bench in Ireland:** *Memoirs of the Life and Times of the Right Honourable Henry Grattan,* 5:113f.

p. 120 **The Moores were not equal . . . Moore Park in Kilworth:** Catharine Anne Wilson, *A New Lease on Life: Landlords, Tenants, and Immigrants in Ireland and Canada,* 15f.

p. 121 **In Dublin the Moores also owned . . . save the cost of repairs:** *Dublin Chronicle* for 19 January 1788; *The Georgian Society Records of Eighteenth-Century Domestic Architecture,* 2:83.

p. 122 **"the rage for Sunday Schools . . . their natural effects":** [Margaret Moore, Countess of Mount Cashell], *A Few Words in favour of Ireland by Way of Reply to a Pamphlet Called "An Impartial View of the Causes leading this country to the Necessity of an UNION" by No Lawyer* (Dublin, 1799), 18.

p. 123 **"Guilty of numerous errors . . . a woman's mind":** Cini Papers.

p. 124 **"What merely wounds . . . legal cruelty":** Laurence Stone, *Road to Divorce: England 1530–1987,* 203.

p. 125 **"was famed . . . for each of his seats":** [Pückler-Muskau], *Tour in England,* 2:26.

p. 126 **On Sunday evenings at seven . . . another band was playing:** Olwen Hedley, *Windsor Castle,* 148.

p. 126 **"Lack of principle . . . distresses amongst our neighbours":** Letter in French, RA Georgian Add. MSS 21/121, Letter of Queen Charlotte to Prince Charles of Mecklenburg-Strelitz, 23 December 1789.

p. 127 **"contribute[d] to reconcile the lower class . . . God to place them":** Hannah More, *Strictures on Female Education,* 148n.

p. 127 **"seek for refuge . . . smiles of Majesty":** *A Few Words in favour of Ireland,* vii.

p. 127 **"chaste . . . did not make any actual *faux pas*":** *Works of Mary Wollstonecraft,* 1:9.

p. 128 **Margaret, who shared her father's dislike . . . more income from the tenants:** [Moore], *A Few Words in favour of Ireland,* 24.

p. 129 **"a patriotic if not democratic nobleman":** *The Drennan Letters,* 2, 556.

p. 130 **Abroad she attended medical lectures . . . more advanced courses:** *Clairmont Correspondence,* 135.

p. 131 **Mount Cashell! . . . sweetly are combined:** *Walker's Hibernian Magazine* for June 1795.

p. 133 **She probably received . . . *Anthologia Hibernica*, since it suited her serious and curious temperament:** Unlike Lady Moira, her daughter and Wolfe Tone, Margaret was not among the initial subscribers.

p. 134 **"My greatest object is to make my children happy and virtuous":** Margaret to William Godwin, 8 September 1800, in *Shelley and His Circle 1773–1822*, 1:84.

p. 134 **"Lord M. never considered education . . . most trifling advantage of this sort":** *The Catholic Question in Ireland & England 1798–1822: The Papers of Denys Scully*, 132f.; hereafter called Scully Papers.

p. 135 **"rather of French *Equality and Fraternity* . . . proper subordinate Distance":** Bishop Thomas Percy to his wife, 1 July 1799, British Library Add. MSS 32.335.

pp. 135–36 **A friend later remembered . . . "good severe mistress":** Abinger MSS.

p. 136 **a moody retainer . . . make the other speak to him:** Granard Papers.

p. 136 **her father's old enemy Lord Shannon . . . lay in a separate bed so as not to be disturbed:** NAI, Dublin, MS 13, 303.

p. 138 **Lady Sarah Napier thought Lord Moira a "toad-eater" in his desire to advance himself:** 1 August 1782, Granard Papers; Fitzgerald, *Correspondence of Duchess of Leinster*, 2:358.

pp. 138–39 **A close friendship developed . . . when unwanted company arrived:** [?9 April 1798], Napier Papers, British Library MSS Add. 49089, and Granard Papers.

p. 139 **"Recesses where you may sit . . . yet of regularity":** *Correspondence of Mrs Delany*, 3:526.

p. 139 **"[H]e is not willing . . . a greater Share of Opinion & free Will":** 15 January 1797, Napier Papers.

p. 139 **"Her attachment to me . . . chilly propriety":** Scully Papers, 146.

p. 139 **"sensible, rational & good natured . . . Providence did not endow *him* with":** 4 December 1800 and 8 May 1806, Granard Papers.

p. 140 **"an old basket-woman":** *Letters of Horace Walpole*, 5:504.

p. 140 **the bounty and beneficence . . . cultivated in an eminent degree:** Henry Nugent Bell, *The Huntingdon Peerage*, 146.

p. 140 **"grace upon every beneficial fashion":** Obituary in *Walker's Hibernian Magazine* for May 1808.

p. 140 **"nurse of Beauty—Isle of Saints":** [Henrietta Battier], *The Protected Fugitives: A Collection of Miscellaneous Poems.*

pp. 140–41 **"some alleviation to the miseries . . . it would not be imagined to exist":** Looking from farther down the social scale, Richard Lovell Edgeworth made the opposite point. Irish poverty just seemed worse than the English sort.

p. 143 **"the man who has now the best title . . . *the independence of Ireland*":** *Reply to a Ministerial Pamphlet,* 10.

p. 143 **An Aristocrat of the genuine Brand . . . to protect & serve are unknown:** 2 July 1782? and 11 March 1797, Granard Papers.

p. 144 **Stephen's crude pride in lineage . . . take the coronet off his carriage:** Wilmot, *An Irish Peer on the Continent,* 20.

p. 144 **she "sighed" for the "middle rank of life" though born noble:** Cini Papers.

p. 145 **Mary Anne McCracken . . . in Lady Moira's circle:** Letter to brother, quoted in Kevin Whelan, *Fellowship of Freedom: The United Irishmen and 1798,* 36.

p. 145 **"that proud plebeian . . . evil counsellor":** [Henrietta Battier], *The Gibbonade: or, Political Reviewer.*

p. 145 **Poetry did not bring her affluence . . . friends to tea:** *Memoirs, Journal, and Correspondence of Thomas Moore,* 1:40f.

p. 146 **One of his first cases . . . nailed up:** L. M. Cullen, "Blackwater Catholics and County Cork Society and Politics in the Eighteenth Century" in Cork, 573.

p. 146 **"He animated every debate . . . life and ardour":** *Dictionary of National Biography.*

p. 148 **"do not mix with the shallow herd . . . too sharp":** *Letters of Mary Wollstonecraft,* 12 November 1792.

p. 148 **After Eton and Oxford . . . It was claimed that he married her:** *The Journals of Claire Clairmont,* 145.

p. 149 **"amiable & accomplished":** *Hibernian Chronicle* for May 1794.

p. 149 **There were rumors that George . . . rents from Mitchelstown:** [Pückler-Muskau], *Tour in Ireland,* 2, 26.

p. 149 **"His majesty has the fullest reliance . . . on the ruins of law and order":** *Anthologia Hibernica* for January 1794.

p. 149 **"These are terrible times . . . at least very unfeeling":** Cini Papers.

p. 150 **"may the example of its citizen soldiers . . . extinct":** Stella Tillyard, *Citizen Lord: Edward Fitzgerald 1763–1798,* 139.

p. 150 **"Seek French co-operation . . . You will be swopped for some sugar island":** Denis Taaffe in Andrew O'Reilly, *Reminiscences of an Emigrant Milesian,* 2:227.

p. 150 **"the women, even in the highest ranks . . . "Grecian" style:** C. J. Woods, "The Secret Mission to Ireland of Captain Bernard Mac-Sheehy, an Irishman in French Service, 1796," *Journal of the Cork Historical and Archaeological Society* (July–December 1973), 94.

p. 151 **Like the Duchess of Devonshire . . . the transaction of condescension and gratitude pleased both:** *Journals of Claire Clairmont,* 125. Two years earlier in Dublin there had been a successful strike for better wages by journeymen shoemakers but there is no record of Margaret's support.

p. 153 **Sorry am I to say . . . *not* considerable:** *A Few Words in favour of Ireland,* 19.

p. 155 **she joined . . . the United Irishmen:** *Journals of Claire Clairmont,* 124. It is impossible to know for sure whether Margaret actually took the oath of the United Irishmen, a capital offense, but it seems likely that she did.

pp. 156 **"The present is an age of revolution . . . truth and reason":** *Northern Star* for 1 June 1795.

pp. 156–57 **In 1792 Wolfe Tone took part . . . "the best of kings":** Frank MacDermot, *Theobald Wolfe Tone: A Biographical Study,* 100.

p. 158 **"By liberty we never understood . . . the destruction of subordination":** *Society of United Irishmen of Dublin,* 8, 45, 55f.

p. 159 **"used with signal success . . . political manifestos":** Clare's speech 19 February 1798, quoted in Whelan, "The United Irishmen, the Establishment and Popular Culture" in *The United Irishmen,* 277.

p. 159 **Secret signs and words . . . *united*:** Nancy J. Curtin, "Symbols and Rituals of United Irish Mobilisation" in *Ireland and the French Revolution,* 74.

p. 160 **"a deluded peasantry aided by more intelligent treason":** Whelan, "The United Irishmen," in *The United Irishmen,* 278.

p. 160 **"desperate body of men . . . government terror":** *A Letter to the Earl of Moira, in Defence of the Conduct of His Majesty's Ministers and of the Army in Ireland* (1797).

p. 161 **"boys of the ascendancy . . . bondage of our hundred years":** [Henrietta Battier], *The Lemon, A Poem by Pat. Pindar, in Answer to a Scandalous Libel, entitled, The Orange* (1797).

pp. 161–62 **"Government . . . considering the Orange party . . . Papist mob":** *Reply to a Ministerial Pamphlet,* 40.

p. 162 **"dull cipher of a Lord Lieutenant":** *Correspondence of Duchess of Leinster,* 2:335.

p. 163 **Its being so completely aristocratical . . . fellow feeling for the low:** F. A. Smith, *Whig Principles and Party Politics: Earl Fitzwilliam and the Whig Party 1748–1833,* 231.

p. 163 **"To reform all these flagrant abuses:** *Life and Letters of Lady Sarah Lennox,* 2:119.

p. 163 **They formed a committee . . . Westminster government:** Deirdre Lindsay, "The Fitzwilliam Episode Revisited" in *The United Irishmen,* 200f.

p. 164 **"They will extinguish Ireland, or Ireland must remove them":** James Smyth, "Dublin's Political Underground in the 1790s" in *Parliament, Politics and People,* 138.

p. 164 **"on the brink of civil war":** Bishop Thomas Hussey in Whelan, *Fellowship of Freedom,* 39.

p. 164 **Camden . . . acting chief secretary for Ireland:** *The Times* (London) for 22 February 1797.

p. 164 **Great classes . . . a most dangerous revulsion:** Lecky, *History of Ireland,* 3:323.

p. 165 **the one brought intelligence . . . numerical force:** Moore, *The Life and Death of Lord Edward Fitzgerald,* 1:192. For reasons of brevity from now onward I use "United Irishmen" to refer to the two societies when acting in concert.

pp. 165–66 **[N]ow the sans culottes of Ireland . . . most horrid calamities may ensue:** 7 September and 11 December 1794, Darwin Papers.

p. 166 **"The monied & landed Interest . . . as if by accident":** Quoted in Butler, *Maria Edgeworth,* 112.

p. 166 **"I am not the least afraid . . . mob in all places":** *Life and Letters of Lady Sarah Lennox,* 2:128. Ironically, in 1797 Ogle himself fell afoul of the ill-disciplined troops when he was made a prisoner by the Welsh regiment, the Ancient British Fencible Cavalry, and imprisoned for two nights in Newry. See his indignant letter in *The Press,* 26 October 1797.

pp. 166–67 **If you have a mind . . . crying come eat me:** *Barnard Letters 1778–1824,* 87.

p. 167 **"We should put to death ten for every one":** "Lawless is just laying down the law . . . that all culprits should be executed on the instant, and that we should put to death 10 for every 1. This the Chancellor approves." *Shannon's Letters,* 80.

p. 167 **"second Lady Bountiful . . . happy in situation":** *Correspondence of Dr Hugh MacDermot*, 121.

p. 167 **"it becomes the duty . . . the national fund":** [Margaret Moore, Countess of Mount Cashell], *A Hint to the Inhabitants of Ireland by a Native*, 3.

p. 168 **"In political changes . . . the *mighty crisis which awaits her*":** *The Press*, 26 December 1797, no. 39 (ccxxxi).

p. 168 **"*All that Matter* . . . write upon":** 24 September 1798, Napier Papers.

p. 168 **They could take secret messages . . . hidden on their bodies:** NAI, Dublin, Rebellion Papers 620/60/18. Future quotations from this holding will be listed as Rebellion Papers.

p. 169 **middle size woman . . . Castle-street:** Whelan, *Fellowship of Freedom*, 35.

p. 170 **Margaret began to study the Irish language in earnest:** Later Margaret possessed Charles Vallancey's *Grammar of the Iberno-Celtic or Irish Language* (1773). Claire Clairmont may have borrowed it from her since she was reading it in Pisa. *Journals of Claire Clairmont*, 176.

p. 172 **"Edward Fitzgerald has acted . . . arms round his neck":** Tillyard, *Citizen Lord*, 152; *Correspondence of Duchess of Leinster*, 2:341.

p. 173 **"[Edward] and his elegant wife . . . in a short time":** Marianne Elliott, *Partners in Revolution*, 26.

p. 173 **"candour and sensibility":** Mrs. Thomas Concannon, *Women of 'Ninety-Eight*, 198.

p. 173 **On one occasion . . . He heard no more of the matter:** Moore, *Lord Edward Fitzgerald*, 1:267f.

p. 173 **At the theater in Smock Alley . . . some untimely end":** Tillyard, *Citizen Lord*, 158.

p. 174 **"When I am with Pam . . . as happy as possible":** The Duchess of Sermoneta, *The Locks of Norbury: The Story of a Remarkable Family in the XVIIIth and XIXth Centuries*, 102, 112.

p. 174 **"a sweet little, engaging, bewitching creature":** Concannon, *Women of 'Ninety-Eight*, 201.

p. 175 **"grossest libertine . . . jaundiced caprices of satiety":** *Works of Mary Wollstonecraft*, 4:207.

p. 175 **"too much connected with the aristocracy, to be really the friends of the people":** Rebellion Papers.

p. 176 **"Nothing in the world . . . cultivation or population":** Marianne Elliott, *Wolfe Tone: Prophet of Irish Independence*, 316; Elliott, *Partners in Revolution*, 113.

p. 177 **"the wind has saved us the trouble of driving the French away"**: Marchioness of Londonderry, *Robert Stewart Viscount Castlereagh*, 14.

p. 177 **"Hoche and his Banditti"**: 11 March 1797, Granard Papers.

p. 177 **The nobleman was preparing a speech . . . all were United Irishmen**: Rebellion Papers.

p. 177 **"at full length . . . a deeper designing one"**: Sir Richard Musgrave, *Memoirs of the Different Rebellions in Ireland*, 199.

p. 178 **"he terrifies dearest Louisa . . . if they succeeded"**: *Correspondence of Duchess of Leinster*, 2:343; Sermoneta, *Locks of Norbury*, 122f.

p. 179 **One officer reported . . . demanding services**: Major R. T. Wilson to Lord William Bentinck, July 1798, quoted in *Eighteenth-Century Irish Official Papers in Great Britain*, 1:187.

pp. 179–80 **One such incident . . . how they liked it"**: Power, *White Knights*, 54.

p. 180 **the appointed government interceptor of mail . . . United Irishman**: 16 March 1796, Rebellion Papers.

p. 181 **Yesterday, rather a genteel looking man . . . "Paine's Age of Reason"**: The diary of Jane Adams in T. Crofton Croker, *Researches in the South of Ireland*, 347.

p. 181 **on her way from Dublin . . . murdered by the rebels"**: 5 July 1797, Darwin Papers.

pp. 181–82 **"corrupted and enslaved . . . ruinous expence"**: "Letters from the Mountains," *The Press*, Letter II (signed Montanus), 7 October 1797.

p. 184 **Attracted rather than deterred . . . down through dukes and earls**: *Shannon's Letters*, 67f.

p. 184 **"arrive[d] to take possession . . . discontented at his fare"**: Ibid., 58.

p. 185 **"How [she] does talk!" . . . Madame de Staël**: Mrs. Warrenne Blake, *An Irish Beauty of the Regency. Compiled from "Mes Souvenirs"—The Unpublished Journals of the Hon. Mrs. Calvert 1789–1822*, 59, 208f.

p. 186 **When Mary shifted her own life . . . on hand to record it**: *Memoirs of the Comtesse de Boigne (1781–1814)*, 1:120f.

pp. 187–88 **To bring together these two disparate men . . . greatest kindness**: *Walker's Hibernian Magazine* for November 1800. A letter to the editor identifies Colonel Fitzgerald as "natural brother of his countess." See also R. D. King-Harman, *The Kings*, 73; A. L. King-Harman, *The Kings of King House*, 26.

p. 188 **Another story is more extreme . . . young orphan"**: *Memoirs of the Comtesse de Boigne*, 1:120.

p. 189 **In his description of the Kings . . . did not refute this part of it:** *The Annual Register* for 1797, 68, and *Hibernian Chronicle* for 12 October 1797; both called him "second cousin to Miss King."

p. 189 **Of all the professions . . . over £4,000:** Malcomson, *Pursuit of the Heiress*, 6.

p. 190 **They set up home . . . belonging to the Kings:** J. Roderick O'Flanagan, *The Lives of the Lord Chancellors*, 2:236.

p. 191 **After a lengthy and fraught march . . . returned to England:** *Walker's Hibernian Magazine* for April 1799; *Anthologia Hibernica* for July 1794.

pp. 191–92 **"I build little on any of Pitt's expeditions . . . Military Manoeuvres":** 30 July [1799], Napier Papers.

p. 192 **he had taken over from Charles Asgill as lieutenant colonel of the King's Company:** F. W. Hamilton, *The Origin and History of the First or Grenadier Guards*, 2:322; Steven T. Ross, *Historical Dictionary of the Wars of the French Revolution; Walker's Hibernian Magazine* for April 1799; *Anthologia Hibernica* for July 1794.

p. 193 **Bury Street, St James's:** Mrs. Fitzgerald gives this as her address the following year. *Journals of the Irish House of Lords for 1798*, 8:89.

p. 193 **Now they enjoyed walking and riding together . . . dogcart:** *The Gentleman's Magazine* wrote that Henry was a "constant visitor" to the household.

p. 193 **"more uninformed of the vicious habits . . . that early age":** *The Hibernian Chronicle* for 12 October 1797.

pp. 193–94 **For some time Adèle watched . . . her father and mother were present:** Another version (PRONI D/20/1 De Vere) rewrites events to make Mary the innocent and Henry the villain. In this account Mary was living with the Colonel's wife to finish her education. Henry took base and unmanly advantage of their guest.

p. 195 **During her friend's absence . . . withdrawal from opium:** Desmond Young, *Fountain of the Elephants*, 156.

p. 203 **"reproaching Herself with having Idolized Her Mary too much":** Queen Charlotte to Lady Harcourt, 30 October 1797, quoted in *the Harcourt Papers*, 5:56.

p. 203 **According to the Dublin *Press* . . . what had happened:** *The Press*, 7 October 1797.

p. 204 **The newspaper declared . . . at least far from scandalmongers:** *The Times* (London) for 30 December 1797.

p. 204 **"The family have an asylum . . . would prove her ruin":** *The Drennan-McTier Letters*, 2:354.

p. 205 **They all listened to the "tragedy" and found it very "shocking":** Ibid., 2:354.

p. 206 **I shall be obliged to any of your numerous correspondents . . . to a long oblivion the better":** *The Gentleman's Magazine* for May 1798.

p. 206 **their living apart . . . excite general and sincere concern":** *The Press* for 10 October 1797.

p. 209 **"with tears congratulated him on his safety":** *Betsy Sheridan's Journal,* 162.

p. 210 **"a most melancholy sight . . . Mild about every body":** Queen Charlotte to Lady Harcourt, 30 October 1797, quoted in *The Harcourt Papers,* 5:56.

p. 213 **Dr. MacDermot was amazed to report . . . of the finest kind for supper:** *Correspondence of Dr Hugh MacDermot,* 120f.

p. 214 **"I believe it to be absolutely necessary":** 11 November 1797, Rebellion Papers.

p. 214 **Others openly blamed . . . that in Kildare:** Rebellion Papers. On 9 December 1797 Lord Shannon wanted the county proclaimed because of the "lawlessness of the people."

p. 214 **"It is generally thought . . . country of Kildare":** 24 March 1798, Rebellion Papers.

p. 214 **His heart had never been in politics . . . Stephen had been:** see Richard Aylmer, "The Duke of Leinster Withdraws from Ireland: October 1797," *Journal of Kildare Archaeological Society* 19, 1 (2000–2001) 161–83.

p. 215 **Like the rest of his male relatives . . . region he represented:** *Shannon's Letters,* 89.

p. 215 **"the revolution has commenced":** J. M. Barry, *Pitchcap and Triangle: The Cork Militia in the Wexford Rising,* 60.

p. 216 **"so atrocious that humanity . . . without process or accusation":** William Sampson, *Memoirs,* 4.

p. 216 **"dreadful outrages" . . . "ferocious spirit":** Rebellion Papers.

p. 216 **"redundancy of victualling":** *Report from the Committee of Secrecy Appointed to take into consideration the Treasonable Papers presented to the House of Commons in Ireland, reported 10 May 1797,* 23.

p. 216 **"country to be ravaged by a popish banditti":** Rebellion Papers.

pp. 217–18 **"stranger of noble stature . . . considered him with fear":** Sydney Owenson in *The Wild Irish Girl: A National Tale,* 207f.

p. 221 **"God! I don't know how I did it . . . are better told at once":** Abinger
MSS.

pp. 221–22 **In "Selene" she portrayed a man . . . for my strange conduct, I
retired":** MS "Selene," Cini Papers.

p. 222 **"A great man talks . . . and the jury makes the law":** Edgeworth,
Ennui, 198.

p. 223 **Colonel Henry Fitzgerald was buried . . . a corporal and five privates:** *The Times* (London) for 25 December 1798.

p. 224 **"My tenants and my servants . . . confusion of public vengeance":** 21
September 1797, Napier Papers.

p. 224 **Lord Moira brought a motion . . . an emotive image for Protestants:**
See *Speech of Earl Moira, on the present alarming and dreadful state of Ireland in the House of Lords, On Wednesday, November 22, 1797.*

p. 224 **"[T]he noble lord, secure in another kingdom" . . . the French to
invade:** *The Anti-Jacobin Review and Magazine* for September 1798.

p. 225 **"[T]hey are all off . . . as she gets in and out of her Carriage":** Bishop
Percy to his wife, British Library Add. MSS 32.335.

p. 225 **the Bishop of Ossory preached a sermon . . . that virgin hope of the
state":** I am assuming that this sermon was the one referred to by Margaret and that the reference was to the second preaching: *A Sermon
preached before his Excellency John Jeffries, Earl Camden, Lord Lieutenant, . . . by the Rev. Thomas Lewis O'Beirne, D. D. Lord Bishop of Ossory.*

p. 226 **"The late Mr. Thomas Geoghegan . . . precautions taken by Lady
Moira":** W. J. Fitzpatrick, *Secret Service Under Pitt,* 139.

p. 226 **"did not confine himself to the strict rules of law":** Lecky, *History of
Ireland,* 3:419.

p. 227 **"the prey of the Orange and Castle bloodhounds":** Whelan, *Fellowship of Freedom,* 61.

p. 228 **After the multiple arrests . . . visit his men in disguise:** Fitzpatrick,
Secret Service Under Pitt, 137n.

p. 228 **For Edward the safest house . . . where Lord Edward was hiding:**
"The Gentlewoman of Moore Park," *The Avondhu* for 23 December
1999.

p. 228 **Lady Moira was especially impressed by the attentive doctor:** 11 April
1798, Napier Papers.

p. 229 **"Your husband has not been taken":** Sermoneta, *Locks of Norbury,*
130.

p. 230 **"I warn ministers . . . upon the heads of their oppressors":** *The Press*
for 6 January 1798.

p. 230 **He was famous for bullying witnesses . . . vomited before the verdict:** See the trial of William Orr in September 1797, Lecky, *History of Ireland,* 4:106.

pp. 231–32 **The plan demanded little initial force . . . once an open uprising began:** Blackstock, *Ascendancy Army,* 137; see also James Smyth, "Dublin's Political Underground in the 1790s" in *Parliament, Politics and People,* 129.

p. 234 **As a result of such information . . . move his North Cork troops to Dublin:** *Shannon's Letters,* 72.

p. 239 **"The eyes of every body . . . some accuser":** Barrington, *Personal Sketches,* 1:109.

p. 240 **I am in Dublin . . . I am going Home again on Saturday:** *Barnard Letters,* 85.

p. 240 **Yet Curran testified . . . Bury Street, London:** *Journals of the Irish House of Lords for 1798,* 8:89.

p. 242 **The meeting over . . . before or after Robert's trial:** Six days after the trial, Higgins mentioned the plan. No doubt he wrote in part to incriminate Lord Edward and make Magan, his particular agent, more important.

pp. 242–43 **After abandoning their plan . . . exterminate the Catholics:** NAI 2198.

p. 243 **But despite nearly forty years . . . the family baker:** Stella Tillyard, *Aristocrats,* 377f.

p. 244 **I met Murder . . . Seven blood-hounds followed him:** Percy Bysshe Shelley, *The Mask of Anarchy* (wr. 1819, pub. 1832).

p. 244 **She could only convey her suspicions . . . not have her eyes opened:** PRONI Mic 57-3/10/105-7.

p. 245 **"I still retain the most sanguine hopes, that the Information may turn out false":** F transcripts at Tarling place, PRONI.

p. 245 **"this proof of despotism":** [?24 May 1798], Napier Papers.

p. 247 **Lady Sarah's daughter . . . they were telling her:** Lady Louisa Conolly, 21 May 1798, in Moore, *Lord Edward Fitzgerald,* 2:98; Katharine Tynan, *Lord Edward: A Study in Romance,* 273f.

pp. 247–48 **Here, whipping goes on at a great rate . . . *Croppies Lie Down:*** *Shannon's Letters,* 101f.

p. 249 **Later, when Edward died . . . most convenient:** Sermoneta, *Locks of Norbury,* 135; *The Journal and Correspondence of William, Lord Auckland,* 21 May 1798, 3:422.

p. 249 **"brought on Misery and Disgrace . . . now prevented":** Thomas Pakenham, *The Year of Liberty: The Story of the Great Irish Rebellion of 1798,*
238.

p. 251 **"We the undersigned . . . his Majesty's royal person":** Whelan, *Fellowship of Freedom,* 66.

p. 252 **"elevation of the soul . . . which is not imaginary":** 24 September
1798, Granard Papers.

p. 252 **"Martial law is established . . . conspiracy is put down":** Thomas
Bartlett, Kevin Dawson and Daire Keogh, *Rebellion: A Television History
of 1798,* 101.

p. 253 **"set to work for the purpose of rebellion":** Ibid., 110.

p. 254 **On 27 May a detachment of 110 North Cork . . . a huge defeat for
the North Cork:** Archibald M'Laren, *A minute description of the battles
of Gorey, Arklow and Vinegar Hill together with the movements of the army
through the Wicklow mountains in quest of the rebels,* 32; Musgrave, *Memoirs of the Different Rebellions,* 341f.; Daniel Gahan, *The People's Rising:
Wexford 1798,* 38f.

pp. 254–55 **Frightened for her life . . . accused of commanding the rebel troops:**
Sir Jonah Barrington, *Historic Memoirs of Ireland,* 2:262.

p. 255 **From Dublin Castlereagh wrote . . . perfect destruction":** Pakenham, *Year of Liberty,* 241.

p. 255 **Every moment becomes more frightful . . . than Wexford at this
moment exhibits:** Jane Adams in Croker, *Researches in the South of Ireland,* 348.

p. 256 **So they joined . . . opponents:** Gahan, *People's Rising,* 62f.; Musgrave,
Memoirs of the Different Rebellions, 449f.; Pakenham, *Year of Liberty,*
170f.; Charles Dickson, *The Wexford Rising in 1798,* 86f., Appendix
IIIA.

p. 257 **The town was plundered . . . the flesh of men":** Pakenham, *Year of
Liberty,* 209; Terence Folley, *Eyewitness to 1798,* 89.

p. 258 **"probably murdered or kept as a hostage":** *Shannon's Letters,* 116.

p. 259 **"The great anxiety to kill his Lordship . . . endeavouring to get him":**
"A Three Weeks' Terror: Mrs Brownrigg's Journal at Wexford, 26th
May–21st June," quoted in *The War in Wexford: An Account of the Rebel-
lion in the South of Ireland in 1798 Told from Original Documents by
H. F. B. Wheeler and A. M. Broadley,* 191.

p. 259 **On one occasion a band of rebels . . . whereabouts of George Ogle:**
The Diary of Elizabeth Richards (1798–1823), 43f.

p. 259 **"truly miserable":** "Mrs Brownrigg's Journal" in *The War in Wexford,*
179.

pp. 259–60 **one of the men advanced . . . rode off:** Jane Adams in Croker, *Researches in the South of Ireland*, 360.

p. 260 **"surrounded by rebels at the communion table":** Ibid., 348.

p. 260 **Although the leaders wanted Protestant services . . . rechristened:** James S. Donnelly Jr., "Sectarianism in 1798 and in Catholic Nationalist Memory," in *Rebellion and Remembrance in Modern Ireland*, ed. Laurence M. Geary, 30f.

p. 260 **Frightened for his life . . . pacific move:** Pakenham, *Year of Liberty*, 253.

pp. 260–61 **"The Cabinet that decided . . . venture to execute Kingsborough":** *Shannon's Letters*, 123.

p. 261 **Once again the Moira tenants . . . knot of ribbon:** "Recollections of the Battle of Ballynahinch by an Eye-Witness" in *The Belfast Magazine and Literary Journal* no. 1 (1825), 1.

p. 261 **Later, when government troops arrived . . . pleasure park:** Thomas Bartlett, "Defence, Counter-insurgency and Rebellion: Ireland, 1793–1803" in *A Military History of Ireland*, 282.

pp. 261–62 **Although she did not care . . . made her son a traitor:** 11 May 1782, Granard Papers; [?c. end July 1798], Napier Papers.

p. 262 **I have brake off not only intimacy . . . no small praise:** Lady Moira to Lady Sarah Napier [?c. end July 1798], Napier Papers.

pp. 262–63 **"The rascals made a tolerable good fight of it . . . The carnage was dreadful":** Bartlett et al., *Rebellion*, 131.

p. 263 **After the battle . . . I could not help laughing:** M'Laren, *Battles of Gorey, Arklow and Vinegar Hill*, 39; NLI P 5329.

p. 263 **As successful government troops . . . a thousand rebels were killed:** Bartlett et al., *Rebellion*, 133; *Cork Journal* 4 (1898), 236.

pp. 263–64 **Lord Shannon had heard . . . did not believe the story:** *Shannon's Letters*, 118f.

pp. 264–65 **"behaved excessively well . . . have done much mischief":** Lake to Castlereagh, 21 June 1798, quoted in Folley, *Eyewitness to 1798*, 58.

p. 265 **George put up no resistance . . . helped himself:** James Bentley Gordon, *History of the Rebellion in Ireland in 1798*, 239f.

p. 266 **"If we had had a general . . . ears and noses cut off":** *Memoirs of Miles Byrne edited by his widow*, 198.

p. 266 **had he evinced any sympathy . . . preservation from popular vengeance:** Charles Hamilton Teeling, *History of the Irish Rebellion 1798: A Personal Narrative*, 275f. See also *Musgrave's Memoirs*, 462f.; and *Who Fears to Speak of '98?*

pp. 266–67 **Lord Castlereagh asserted . . . declared the rebellion in Ireland over:** *Memoirs and Correspondence of Viscount Castlereagh,* 1:223f.

p. 268 **"[H]e is a source of wonder . . . confidence of success":** *Scully Papers,* 10.

p. 268 **In turn the Lord Lieutenant let it be known that he disliked George:** Pakenham, *Year of Liberty,* 272.

p. 268 **"Ld. Cornwallis was in the wrong & he in the Right":** 12 June 1799, Napier Papers.

pp. 268–69 **"the rational and cool belief . . . as they think proper":** *Scully Papers,* 8.

p. 269 **"As for Ld. Cornwallis . . . what have honest people to hope for?":** 28 August 1799, Napier Papers.

p. 270 **though Henry King's seat at Ballina was damaged:** Later compensation was paid both to Henry King and to George Ogle for the earlier damaging of his estate at Bellevue. *Journals of the Irish House of Commons* 19, (7 February 1800), cclxxii and cccxcix.

pp. 270–71 **An Officer an Acquaintance . . . capable of making excellent Soldiers:** 24 September 1798, Napier Papers.

p. 272 **Lord Clare aided the discomfort . . . swung moderate opinion farther away from them:** See Michael Durey, "The United Irishmen and the Politics of Banishment 1798–1807" in *Radicalism and Revolution in Britain, 1775–1848,* 96–109.

p. 272 **"However insignificant an unsuccessful rebellion . . . exposed to destruction in the conflict":** *Reply to a Ministerial Pamphlet,* 9.

p. 273 **"the joint labours of rebellion and of loyalty, soldiers and insurgents":** Bartlett et al., *Rebellion,* 144.

p. 273 **For him the price was obviously right . . . on the first vote:** Barrington, *Historic Memoirs,* 2:342.

p. 273 **Ogle enjoyed being courted by Lord Castlereagh for his support:** G. C. Bolton, *The Passing of the Irish Act of Union: A Study in Parliamentary Politics,* 73.

p. 275 **"Union goes on swimmingly . . . either within doors or without":** Barnard, *Barnard Letters,* 117.

p. 276 **"a miserable province, her social system a mass of rottenness and decay":** *Personal Recollections of the Life and Times of Valentine, Lord Cloncurry,* 150.

p. 276 **"independent country was thus degraded . . . EXTINGUISHED":** Barrington, *Historic Memoirs,* 2:251.

p. 276 **"I shall reckon any man my personal enemy who proposes any such measure":** Steven J. Watson, *The Reign of George III*, 401.

pp. 276–77 **Those who come after us . . . who was but a Lodger in it:** *Reply to a Ministerial Pamphlet*, 33f; 2 January 1801, Napier Papers.

p. 277 **"The grand and awful solemnity of that trial . . . of a penetrating nature":** Barrington, *Personal Sketches*, 1:106.

p. 277 **"new scenes of misery and confusion . . . with very little feeling":** Kavanaugh, "Earl of Clare" in *The United Irishmen*, 123.

p. 278 **His oratory failed . . . to enrich his son:** Moore, *Lord Edward Fitzgerald*, 2:201.

p. 279 **"Poor Pamela, she was better, after all, than most of her accusers":** Sermoneta, *Locks of Norbury*, 140.

p. 279 **"It is fortunate that Mr Curran is completely in our power":** Leslie Hale, *John Philpot Curran: His Life and Times*, 233.

p. 279 **"a true pupil of Mary Woolstonecraft":** Ibid., 222f. Two letters by Sarah Curran to her lover, Robert Emmet, were found on him after his arrest following his failed rebellion in 1803; they implicated Sarah and her siblings.

p. 281 **Robert did not long survive . . . family vault at Kingston College:** *The Gentleman's Magazine* for May 1799; *Hibernian Chronicle* for 11 April 1797.

p. 282 **every Whit Monday . . . the cotton mill she and Robert had established:** R. B. McDowell, "Ireland in 1800" in *A New History of Ireland*, ed. T. W. Moody and W. E. Vaughan, 4:667.

p. 283 **Just after the Union, Lord Clare . . . approach Caroline for her help:** Hobart Papers, Buckinghamshire Record Office, I/30.

p. 284 **"to keep down tyranny and oppression":** Records of disputes, Public Record Office, Kew.

p. 285 **"I expect you saw in the papers the death of an old lady":** Abinger MSS.

p. 285 **"Ladies of quality without fortunes are perhaps worse off than any other class":** Malcomson, *Pursuit of the Heiress*, 4.

p. 285 **Most accounts elevate him . . . the Kings' estates in County Longford:** A Dublin lawyer called George Meares was an executor for one of the more highly placed Meares. R. D. King-Harman states that Mary's husband was from New Castle. *The Kings*, 77.

p. 286 **"a very respectable man":** R. D. King-Harman, *The Kings*, 291.

p. 286 **"with Horror":** Marginalia to [Pückler-Muskau's] *Tour in Ireland*, Cini Papers.

p. 286 **When the nominal nobility of this degraded kingdom . . . self-degradation:** [Moore], *A Hint to the Inhabitants of Ireland*, 8f.

p. 287 **used "nauseous" expressions . . . "rotten":** *Scully Papers*, 43.

p. 287 **"when you are rich . . . a good purse of money":** Margaret, to Mary Shelley, 22 August 1824, Abinger MSS.

pp. 288–89 **Did a great man . . . Godwin declined:** *Journals of Claire Clairmont*, 125f.; Charles Kegan Paul, *William Godwin: His Friends and Contemporaries*, 2:110f.

p. 290 **"Would thou couldst feel . . . Beloved beyond existence, health or fame":** The MS poetry of Margaret and George Tighe, Dazzi-Cini Archive.

p. 291 **practising insincerity . . . treated like an honourable woman:** *Works of Mary Wollstonecraft*, 1:176.

p. 292 **"I am grieved to learn . . . the cause of such a disagreement":** *Scully Papers*, 144.

p. 293 **"Since my country sunk . . . those capable of similar feelings":** Margaret to Mary Shelley, 1819, Abinger MSS. Yet Margaret retained her hatred of Castlereagh as a renegade Irishman who had taken his corrupt parliamentary methods to Westminster: "I always foresaw that the Union with Ireland would be fatal to the British Constitution," she wrote to Mary Shelley.

p. 293 **"Perhaps the years of almost half a century . . . the little I possess":** Margaret to Mary Shelley, Abinger MSS.

p. 295 **"her husband is . . . amiable and wise":** *The Letters of Percy Bysshe Shelley*, 180, 186, 339.

p. 295 **Yet to his cousin Tom Medwin . . . Shelley endowed his Lady:** Edmund Gosse, introduction to Shelley's *The Sensitive Plant*, xi.

p. 295 **"in one of his most brilliant humours":** *The Letters of Mary Wollstonecraft Shelley*, 1:250.

p. 296 **"Come then and though we are not . . . *friend* still *'green'* ":** Cini Papers.

p. 296 **"In the autumn of Love . . . Gay pleasure is for youth alone":** Dazzi-Cini Archive.

p. 296 **"a vagabond on the face of the earth . . . regret of all sorts is vain!":** Margaret to Mary Shelley, 29 November 1824, Abinger MSS.

p. 296 **"excellent and beloved daughter":** Will of Margaret, Countess of Mount Cashell, 1824, Cini Papers; see also *Clairmont Correspondence*, 312f.

p. 297 **"very shocking":** 16 November 1828, Dazzi-Cini Archive.

p. 298 **"It is too bitter . . . only that you may lose it":** *Clairmont Correspondence*, 291.

p. 298 **"the old Baronial prejudice against any change in the establishment":** *Correspondence between the Lord Bishop of Ferns, and the Right Honourable the Earl of Mountcashel in the Church Establishment.*

p. 298 **"Let your tenants, my Lord . . . faces of the poor":** Wilson, *New Lease on Life*, 43f.

p. 299 **"The maledictions of the peasantry . . . the most dreadful imprecations":** Croker, *Researches in the South of Ireland*, 233.

pp. 299–300 **With or without exotic titles . . . keeping off the grass:** Christopher Hibbert, *George IV*, 62f.

p. 300 **Fired by the King's promise . . . £220,000:** Donnelly, *Land and People of Nineteenth-Century Cork*, 70.

p. 301 **Debts mounted . . . such a massive sum:** Alexis de Tocqueville, *Journeys to England and Ireland*, 158.

p. 301 **"I know, as one large proprietor here . . . fight hard for them":** 3rd Earl of Kingston, to Redesdale, 21 December 1824 in *Eighteenth-Century Irish Official Papers*, 2:443–45.

p. 301 **He spent his last six years . . . Ireland no longer existed:** *Constitution; or Cork Advertiser* for 27 July 1833.

p. 301 **[George] epitomises that rule by force of sheer fantasy . . . that sent Big George mad:** Bowen, *Bowen's Court*, 190.

pp. 301–2 **The Henrietta Street house . . . to adorn more gracious homes:** Two plaques on the houses lament the gutting of these elegant mansions.

p. 302 **It ran to nine heavy volumes . . . chargeable to the Mitchelstown estate:** Volume 8 in the British Library reprints James Adair's "History of the North-American Indians," which includes a lengthy chapter titled "Observations and Arguments, in proof of the American Indians being descended from the Jews." The notes accompanying the illustrations also devote much space to this argument.

p. 302 **He was judged insane and confined to an asylum:** R. D. King-Harman, *The Kings*, Appendix X.

Bibliography

Archival Sources

Abinger MSS, Dep.c.517/2, Bodleian Library, Oxford.
Abercorn Papers, T 2541, Public Record Office of Northern Ireland.
Bishop Percy Correspondence, Add. MSS 32.335, British Library.
Cini Papers, Pforzheimer Collection, New York Public Library.
Darwin Papers, DAR 216 B9, Cambridge University Library.
Dazzi-Cini Archive, San Marcello–Pistoiese.
Granard Papers T/3765, Public Record Office of Northern Ireland.
Hobart Papers, Buckinghamshire Record Office.
King-Harman papers, D/4168, Public Record Office of Northern Ireland.
Napier Papers, MSS Add. 49089, British Library.
Rebellion Papers, 620, National Archives of Ireland.

Journals, Magazines and Newspapers (1760–1840)

The Annual Register
Anthologia Hibernica
The Anti-Jacobin Review and Magazine
The Belfast Magazine and Literary Journal
Constitution; or Cork Advertiser
Daily Universal Register
Dublin Chronicle
Exshaw Gentleman's and London Magazine
Gentleman's Almanack
The Gentleman's Magazine
Hibernian Chronicle
Northern Star
The Press (Dublin)
The Times (London)
Walker's Hibernian Magazine

Primary Works

Auckland, Lord, *see* Eden, William.
Barnard, Thomas, *Barnard Letters 1778–1824*, ed. Anthony Powell (London: Duckworth, 1928).
Barrington, Sir Jonah, *Historic Memoirs of Ireland; Comprising Secret Records of the*

National Convention, the Rebellion, and the Union; with Delineations of the Principal Characters Connected with these Transactions (London, 1833).

[Battier, Henrietta], *The Gibbonade: or, Politcal Reviewer* (Dublin, 1793).

———, *The Lemon, A Poem by Pat. Pindar, in Answer to a Scandalous Libel, entitled, The Orange* (Dublin, 1797)

———, *The Protected Fugitives: A Collection of Miscellaneous Poems* (Dublin, 1797).

Bell, Henry Nugent, *The Huntingdon Peerage* (London, 1820).

Bingley, William, *An Examination into the Origin and Continuance of the Discontents in Ireland, and the True Cause of the Rebellion* (London, 1799).

Blake, Mrs. Warrenne, *An Irish Beauty of the Regency. Compiled from "Mes Souvenirs"—The Unpublished Journals of the Hon. Mrs. Calvert 1789–1822* (London, 1911).

Boigne, Louise-Eleonore-Charlotte-Adelaide d'Osmond, *Memoirs of the Comtesse de Boigne (1781–1814)*, ed. M. Charles Nicoullaud (London, 1907).

Boyle, Richard, *Lord Shannon's Letters to his Son. A calendar of the letters written by the 2nd Earl of Shannon to his son, Viscount Boyle, 1790–1802*, ed. Esther Hewitt (Belfast: PRONI, 1982).

Byrne, Miles, *Memoirs of Miles Byrne edited by his widow* (New York, 1863).

Carton (Dublin, 1780).

Castlereagh, Viscount, *see* Stewart, Robert.

Clairmont, Claire, *The Clairmont Correspondence*, ed. Marion Kingston Stocking (Baltimore: Johns Hopkins University Press, 1995).

———, *The Journals of Claire Clairmont*, ed. Marion Kingston Stocking (Cambridge, Mass.: Harvard University Press, 1968).

Cloncurry, Lord, *see* Lawless, Valentine.

Clonmell, 1st Earl of, *see* Scott, John.

Concannon, Mrs. Thomas, *Women of 'Ninety-Eight* (Dublin: M. H. Gill and Son, 1919).

The Council Book of the Corporation of the City of Cork, ed. Richard Caufield (Guildford, 1876).

Croker, T. Crofton, *Researches in the South of Ireland with an Appendix, Containing a Private Narrative of the Rebellion of 1798* (London, 1824).

Dear Miss Heber: An Eighteenth-Century Correspondence, ed. Francis Bamford (London: Constable, 1936).

Delany, Mary, *The Autobiography and Correspondence of Mary Granville, Mrs. Delany*, ed. Lady Llanover (London, 1861).

Drennan, William, *The Drennan Letters*, ed. D. A. Chart (Belfast, 1931).

———, *The Drennan-McTier Letters*, ed. Jean Agnes (Dublin: Women's Historical Project, 1998–99).

Eden, William, *The Journal and Correspondence of William, Lord Auckland* (London, 1862).

Edgeworth, Maria, *Castle Rackrent and Ennui*, ed. Marilyn Butler (London: Penguin, 1992).

———, *The Novels and Selected Works of Maria Edgeworth*, ed. Jane Desmarais, Tim McLoughlin and Marilyn Butler (London: Pickering & Chatto, 1999).

Eighteenth-Century Irish Official Papers in Great Britain, ed. A. P. W. Malcomson (Belfast: PRONI, 1973).

Eighteenth-Century Irish Official Papers in Great Britain—Private Collection, Volume 2, ed. A. P. W. Malcomson (Belfast: PRONI, 1990).

Elrington, Thomas, *Correspondence between the Lord Bishop of Ferns, and the Right*

Honourable the Earl of Mountcashel in the Church Establishment (Dublin, 1830).

The Eton College Register 1753–1790, ed. Richard Arthur Austen-Leigh (Eton, 1927).

Ferns, Bishop of, *see* Elrington, Thomas.

Fitzgerald, Emily, *Correspondence of Emily, Duchess of Leinster (1731–1814),* ed. Brian Fitzgerald (Dublin, 1953).

Gilbert, John T., *A History of the City of Dublin* (Shannon: Irish University Press, 1972).

Gordon, James Bentley, *History of the Rebellion in Ireland in 1798* (London, 1803).

Gosse, Edmund, introduction to Shelley, *The Sensitive Plant* (London: William Heinemann, 1911).

Grattan, Henry, *Memoirs of the Life and Times of the Right Honourable Henry Grattan* (London, 1846).

The Harcourt Papers, ed. Edward William Harcourt (Oxford, 1888–1905).

Hutcheson, Francis, *A Short Introduction to Moral Philosophy* (Glasgow, 1753).

———, *A System of Moral Philosophy* (London, 1755).

Journals of the House of Commons of the Kingdom of Ireland (Dublin, 1796–1800).

Journals of the House of Lords (Dublin, 1779–1800).

Lawless, Valentine, *Personal Recollections of the Life and Times of Valentine, Lord Cloncurry* (Dublin, 1849).

Lecky, W. E. H., *A History of Ireland in the Eighteenth Century* (London, 1892).

Leinster, Duchess of, *see* Fitzgerald, Emily.

Lennox, Sarah, *The Life and Letters of Lady Sarah Lennox 1745–1826,* ed. Countess of Ilchester and Lord Staverdale (London, 1901).

A Letter to the Earl of Moira, in Defence of the Conduct of His Majesty's Ministers and of the Army in Ireland (London, 1797).

A List of the Proprietors of Licenses on Private Sedan Chairs, At 25th March, 1787, Alphabetically ranged, with their respective residences . . . (Dublin, 1787).

MacDermot, Hugh, *Correspondence Etc. of Dr Hugh MacDermot M.D. 1754–1824,* ed. B. C. MacDermot (printed for the editor, 1996).

MacDougall, Henry, *Sketches of Irish Political Characters* (London, 1799).

M'Laren, Archibald, *A minute description of the battles of Gorey, Arklow and Vinegar Hill together with the movements of the army through the Wicklow mountains in quest of the rebels* (Dublin, 1798).

Moira, Earl of, *see* Rawdon-Hastings, Francis.

Moore, Margaret, Countess of Mount Cashell, *Advice to Young Mothers on the Physical Education of Children. By a Grandmother* (London, 1823).

[Moore, Margaret, Countess of Mount Cashell], *A Few Words in favour of Ireland by Way of Reply to a Pamphlet Called "An Impartial View of the Causes leading this country to the Necessity of an UNION" by No Lawyer* (Dublin, 1799).

———, *A Hint to the Inhabitants of Ireland by a Native* (Dublin, 1800).

———, *Reply to a Ministerial Pamphlet intitled "Considerations upon the State of Public Affairs in the year 1799, in Ireland." By a Philanthropist* (Dublin, 1799).

Moore, Thomas, *The Life and Death of Lord Edward Fitzgerald* (London, 1831).

———, *Memoirs, Journal, and Correspondence of Thomas Moore* (London, 1853).

More, Hannah, *Strictures on Female Education* (London, 1799).

Mount Cashell, Margaret Countess of, *see* Moore, Margaret.

Musgrave, Sir Richard, *Memoirs of the Different Rebellions in Ireland* (Dublin, 1801).

O'Beirne, Thomas Lewis, *A Sermon preached before his Excellency John Jeffries, Earl*

Camden, Lord Lieutenant, President, and the Members of the Association for Dis-
countenancing Vice, and Promoting the Practice of Virtue and Religion in St. Peter's
Church, on Tuesday 22d May, 1798 by the Rev. Thomas Lewis O'Beirne, D.D. Lord
Bishop of Ossory (Dublin, 1798).

O'Reilly, Andrew, Reminiscences of an Emigrant Milesian (London, 1853).

Owenson, Sydney, The Wild Irish Girl: A National Tale, ed. Claire Connolly and
Stephen Copley (London: Pickering and Chatto, 2000).

Paul, Charles Kegan, William Godwin: His Friends and Contemporaries (London,
1876).

Present Peerage of the United Kingdom (London, 1817).

Price, Richard, A Discourse on the Love of Our Country (London, 1789).

Price, Uvedale, A letter to H. Repton, Esq., on the application of the practice as well as
the principles of landscape-painting to landscape-gardening (Hereford, 1798).

[Pückler-Muskau, Hermann Ludwig Heinrich von, Prince], Tour in England, Ireland, and France, in the Years 1828 & 1829 by a German Prince (London, 1832).

Rawdon-Hastings, Francis, Speech of Earl Moira, on the present alarming and dreadful state of Ireland in the House of Lords, On Wednesday, November 22, 1797
(London, n.d.).

Report from the Committee of Secrecy Appointed to take into consideration the Treasonable
Papers presented to the House of Commons in Ireland (London, 1797).

Richards, Elizabeth, The Diary of Elizabeth Richards (1798–1823), ed. Marie de
Jong-Ijsselstein (Hilversum: Verloren, 1999).

Sampson, William, Memoirs (New York, 1807).

Scott, John, "Life in the Irish Country House," in Quarterly Bulletin of the Irish
Georgian Society, 7 (April–December 1964), 68–70.

Scully, Denys, The Catholic Question in Ireland & England 1798–1822: The Papers
of Denys Scully, ed. Brian MacDermot (Dublin: Irish Academic Press, 1988).

Sermoneta, Duchess of, The Locks of Norbury: The Story of a Remarkable Family in the
XVIIIth and XIXth centuries (London: John Murray, 1940).

Shannon, Lord, see Boyle, Richard.

Shelley and His Circle 1773–1822, ed. Kenneth Neill Cameron (Cambridge,
Mass.: Harvard University Press, 1961–67).

Shelley, Mary Wollstonecraft, The Letters of Mary Wollstonecraft Shelley, ed. Betty T.
Bennett (Baltimore: Johns Hopkins University Press, 1980).

Shelley, Percy Bysshe, The Letters of Percy Bysshe Shelley, ed. Frederick L. Jones
(Oxford: Clarendon Press, 1964).

———, The Mask of Anarchy (wr. 1819, pub. 1832).

Sheridan, Betsy, Betsy Sheridan's Journal: Letters from Sheridan's Sister 1784–1786
and 1788–1790, ed. William LeFanu (New Brunswick: Rutgers University
Press, 1960).

Society of United Irishmen of Dublin (Dublin, 1794).

Southey, Robert, The Life and Correspondence of the Late Robert Southey, ed. C. C.
Southey (London, 1849).

Stewart, Robert, Memoirs and Correspondence of Viscount Castlereagh by his brother
Charles Vane, Marquess of Londonderry (London, 1848).

Swift, Jonathan, A Short View of the State of Ireland (Dublin, 1727–28).

Synge, Edward, The Synge Letters: Bishop Edward Synge to His Daughter Alicia, Roscommon to Dublin, 1746–1752, ed. Maria Louise Legg (Dublin: Lilliput Press,
1996).

Teeling, Charles Hamilton, *History of the Irish Rebellion 1798: A Personal Narrative* (Glasgow, 1876).

Tocqueville, Alexis de, *Journeys to England and Ireland* (London: Faber and Faber, 1958).

Unpublished Geraldine Documents, ed. James Graves (Dublin, 1881).

Walpole, Horace, *The Letters of Horace Walpole*, ed. Peter Cunningham (London: Bohn, 1861).

The War in Wexford, An Account of the Rebellion in the South of Ireland in 1798 told from Original Documents by H. F. B. Wheeler and A. M. Broadley (London, 1910).

Who Fears to Speak of '98?, pamphlet (London: Joseph H. Fowler, 1938).

Wilmot, Catherine, An Irish Peer on the Continent (1801–1803): being a narrative of the tour of Stephen, 2nd Earl Mountcashell . . . as related by Catherine Wilmot, ed. Thomas U. Sadleir (London, 1924).

Wollstonecraft, Mary, *Letters of Mary Wollstonecraft*, ed. Janet Todd (London: Penguin, 2003).

———, *Works of Mary Wollstonecraft*, ed. Janet Todd and Marilyn Butler (London: William Pickering, 1989).

Young, Arthur, *A Tour in Ireland 1776–1779* (Shannon: Irish University Press, 1970).

———, *The Autobiography of Arthur Young*, ed. M. Betham-Edwards (London, 1898).

SECONDARY WORKS

Aylmer, Richard, "The Duke of Leinster Withdraws from Ireland: October 1797," *Journal of Kildare Archaeological Society* 19, 1 (2000–2001), 161–83.

Barry, J. M., *Pitchcap and Triangle: The Cork Militia in the Wexford Rising* (Cork: private printing, 1998).

Bartlett, Thomas, "The Burden of the Present: Theobald Wolfe Tone, Republican and Separatist," in *The United Irishmen: Republicanism, Radicalism and Rebellion*, ed. David Dickson, Dáire Keogh and Kevin Whelan (Dublin: Lilliput Press, 1993), 1–15.

———, "Defence, Counter-insurgency and Rebellion: Ireland, 1793–1803," in *A Military History of Ireland*, ed. Thomas Bartlett and Keith Jeffery (Cambridge: Cambridge University Press, 1996), 247–93.

Bartlett, Thomas, Kevin Dawson and Daire Keogh, *Rebellion: A Television History of 1798* (Dublin: Gill & Macmillan, 1998).

Blackstock, Allan, *An Ascendancy Army: The Irish Yeomanry, 1796–1834* (Dublin: Four Courts Press, 1998).

Bolton, G. C., *The Passing of the Irish Act of Union: A Study in Parliamentary Politics* (Oxford: Oxford University Press, 1966).

Bowen, Elizabeth, *Bowen's Court* (London: Longmans and Co., 1942).

Butler, Marilyn, *Maria Edgeworth: A Literary Biography* (Oxford: Clarendon Press, 1972).

Colley, Linda, *Britons: Forging the Nation 1707–1837* (New Haven: Yale University Press, 1992).

Cullen, L. M., "Blackwater Catholics and County Cork: Society and Politics in the Eighteenth Century," in *Cork: History and Society: Interdisciplinary Essays on the History of an Irish County,* ed. Patrick O'Flanagan and Cornelius G. Buttimer (Dublin: Geography Publication, 1993), 535–84.

Curtin, Nancy J., "Symbols and Rituals of United Irish Mobilisation," in *Ireland and the French Revolution,* ed. Hugh Gough and David Dickson (Dublin: Irish Academic Press, 1990), 68–82.

Dickson, Charles, *The Wexford Rising in 1798* (London: Constable, 1997).

Dickson, David, ed., *The Gorgeous Mask: Dublin 1700–1850* (Dublin: Trinity History Workshop, 1987).

Donnelly, James S. Jr., "Irish Agrarian Revolution: The Whiteboys of 1769–76," in *R.I.A. Proc.,* Section C, xii (1983).

———, *The Land and the People of Nineteenth-Century Cork: The Rural Economy and the Land Question* (London: Routledge & Kegan Paul, 1975).

———, "Sectarianism in 1798 and in Catholic Nationalist Memory," in *Rebellion and Remembrance in Modern Ireland,* ed. Laurence M. Geary (Dublin: Four Courts Press, 2001), 15–37.

Dunlevy, Mairead, *Dress in Ireland* (London: B. T. Batsford, 1989).

Durey, Michael, "The United Irishmen and the Politics of Banishment 1798–1807," in *Radicalism and Revolution in Britain, 1775–1848,* ed. Michael T. Davis (London: Macmillan, 2000), 96–109.

Elliott, Marianne, *Partners in Revolution: The United Irishmen and France* (New Haven: Yale University Press, 1982).

———, *Wolfe Tone: Prophet of Irish Independence* (New Haven: Yale University Press, 1989).

Fitzpatrick, W. J., *Secret Service Under Pitt* (London: Longmans, 1892).

Folley, Terence, *Eyewitness to 1798* (Cork: Mercier Press, 1996).

Gahan, Daniel, *The People's Rising: Wexford 1798* (Dublin: Gill & Macmillan, 1995).

"The Gentlewomen of Moore Park," *The Avondhu,* 23 December 1999.

The Georgian Society Records of Eighteenth-Century Domestic Architecture (Dublin, 1910).

Guiness, Desmond, *Georgian Dublin* (London: Batsford, 1979).

Hale, Leslie, *John Philpot Curran: His Life and Times* (London: Jonathan Cape, 1958).

Hamilton, F. W., *The Origin and History of the First or Grenadier Guards* (London, 1874).

Hedley, Olwen, *Windsor Castle* (London: Robert Hale, 1994).

Heffernan, Patrick, *The Heffernans and Their Time* (London: J. Clarke & Co., 1940).

Hibbert, Christopher, *George IV* (London: Penguin, 1972).

Johnston, Edith M., *Great Britain and Ireland 1760–1800: A Study in Political Administration* (Edinburgh: Oliver & Boyd, 1963).

Johnston-Liik, Edith M., *History of the Irish Parliament, 1692–1800* (Belfast: Ulster Historical Foundation, 2002).

Kavanaugh, Ann C., "John Fitzgibbon, Earl of Clare," in *The United Irishmen: Republicanism, Radicalism and Rebellion,* ed. David Dickson, Dáire Keogh and Keven Whelan (Dublin: Lilliput Press, 1993), 115–23.

Kelly, James, "Eighteenth-century Ascendancy: A Commentary," *Eighteenth-Century Ireland* 5 (1990).

———, "The Genesis of 'Protestant Ascendancy': The Rightboy Disturbances of the 1780s and Their Impact upon Protestant Opinion," in *Parliament, Politics and People: Essays in Eighteenth-Century Irish History,* ed. Gerard O'Brien (Dublin: Irish Academic Press, 1989), 93–127.

——, *"That Damn'd Thing Called Honour": Duelling in Ireland 1570–1860* (Cork: University Press, 1995).

King-Harman, Anthony Lawrence, *The Kings of King House* (Bedford: privately printed, 1996).

King-Harman, Robert Douglas, *The Kings, Earls of Kingston* (Cambridge: printed privately by W. Heffer & Sons, 1959).

Lindsay, Deirdre, "The Fitzwilliam Episode Revisited," in *The United Irishmen: Republicanism, Radicalism and Rebellion,* ed. David Dickson, Dáire Keogh and Kevin Whelan (Dublin: Lilliput Press, 1993), 197–208.

Londonderry, Marchioness of, *Robert Stewart Viscount Castlereagh* (London, 1904).

MacDermot, Frank, *Theobald Wolfe Tone: A Biographical Study* (London: Macmillan & Co., 1939).

Malcomson, A. P. W., *The Pursuit of the Heiress: Aristocratic Marriage in Ireland 1750–1820* (Belfast: Ulster Historical Foundation, 1982).

Maxwell, Constantia, *Dublin Under the Georges 1714–1830* (London: Faber and Faber, 1956).

McAleer, Edward C., *The Sensitive Plant: A Life of Lady Mount Cashell* (Chapel Hill: University of North Carolina Press, 1958).

McAnally, Henry, *The Irish Militia: A Social and Military Study* (Dublin: Clonmore & Reynolds, 1949).

McDowell, R. B., "Ireland in 1800," in *A New History of Ireland,* ed. T. W. Moody and W. E. Vaughan (Oxford: Clarendon Press, 1986), 657–712.

Ó Catháin, Diarmaid, "An Irish Scholar Abroad: Bishop John O'Brien of Cloyne and the Macpherson Controversy," in *Cork: History and Society: Interdisciplinary Essays on the History of an Irish County,* ed. Patrick O'Flanagan and Cornelius G. Buttimer (Dublin: Geography Publication, 1993), 499–534.

O'Flanagan, J. Roderick, *The Lives of the Lord Chancellors* (London, 1870).

O'Gorman, Frank, *Voters, Patrons and Parties: The Unreformed Electoral System of Hanoverian England 1734–1832* (Oxford: University Press, 1989).

Pakenham, Thomas, *The Year of Liberty: The Story of the Great Irish Rebellion of 1798* (London: Weidenfeld & Nicolson, 1998).

Paor, Liam de, *The Peoples of Ireland* (London: Hutchinson and Co., 1986).

Power, Bill, *White Knights, Dark Earls* (Cork: The Collins Press, 2000).

Ross, Steven T., *Historical Dictionary of the Wars of the French Revolution* (London: Scarecrow, 1998).

Smith, F. A., *Whig Principles and Party Politics: Earl Fitzwilliam and the Whig Party 1748–1833* (Manchester: Manchester University Press, 1975).

Smyth, James, "Dublin's Political Underground in the 1790s," in *Parliament, Politics and People: Essays in Eighteenth-Century Irish History,* ed. Gerard O'Brien (Dublin: Irish Academic Press, 1989), 129–48.

Smyth, William J., "Social, Economic and Landscape Transformations in County Cork from the Mid-Eighteenth to the Mid-Nineteenth Century," in *Cork: History and Society: Interdisciplinary Essays on the History of an Irish County,* ed. Patrick O'Flanagan and Cornelius G. Buttimer (Dublin: Geography Publication, 1993), 655–98.

Stone, Laurence, *Road to Divorce: England 1530–1987* (Oxford: University Press, 1990).

Tillyard, Stella, *Aristocrats* (London: Chatto & Windus, 1994).

———, *Citizen Lord: Edward Fitzgerald 1763–1798* (London: Chatto & Windus, 1997).

Tynan, Katharine, *Lord Edward: A Study in Romance* (London: Smith, Elder & Co., 1916).

Watson, Steven J., *The Reign of George III* (Oxford: Clarendon Press, 1981).

Whelan, Kevin, *Fellowship of Freedom: The United Irishmen and 1798* (Cork: University Press, 1998).

———, "Politicisation in County Wexford and the Origins of the 1798 Rebellion," in *Ireland and the French Revolution*, ed. Hugh Gough and David Dickson (Dublin: Irish Academic Press, 1990), 156–78.

———, "The United Irishmen, the Enlightenment and Popular Culture," in *The United Irishmen: Republicanism, Radicalism and Rebellion*, ed. David Dickson, Dáire Keogh and Kevin Whelan (Dublin: Lilliput Press, 1993), 269–96.

Wilson, Catharine Anne, *A New Lease on Life: Landlords, Tenants, and Immigrants in Ireland and Canada* (Montreal: McGill-Queen's University Press, 1994).

Woods, C. J. "The Secret Mission to Ireland of Captain Bernard MacSheehy, an Irishman in French Service, 1796," *Journal of the Cork Historical and Archaeological Society*, July–December 1973.

Young, Desmond, *Fountain of the Elephants* (London: Collins, 1959).

Index

favors Union, 273
loses parliamentary seat, 277
and Mary Wollstonecraft, 84, 94, 101,
    102, 104
personality, 63
and Rebellion, 256–259
supports Protestant rule, 62–63, 107
Orange Order
    founded, 161
    George King's involvement in, 178–179,
        229–230, 264, 273
    membership, 161
    used by Dublin Castle, 161–162
Orleans, Philippe Egalité, Duke of, 172,
    174, 175, 185
Orr, Robert, 144
Ossory, Bishop of, 225
Owenson, Sydney, 293
    The Wild Irish Girl, 217–218

Paddy's Resource, 235
Paine, Thomas, 142, 147, 148, 150, 157,
    174, 279, 289
    The Age of Reason, 181
    The Rights of Man, 122, 123
Paris, 34–35, 65, 117, 289
Peel, Robert, 299
Peep O'Day Boys, 160
Percy, Bishop, 205, 223, 225, 226, 240
Pisa, 293, 297
Pisa "Lunatics," 297
Pitt, William, the Younger, 107, 110, 137,
    147, 151, 158, 160, 162–164, 183,
    226, 267, 269, 274, 276, 278
Pius VII, Pope, 288
Ponsonby, John, 8, 18
Pratt, John Jeffreys, Earl Camden, 164, 227,
    246, 252, 253, 267
Press, The (Dublin), 168, 181–182, 184, 203
Price, Dr. Richard, 77
Prior, Mr. and Mrs. John, 76–77, 81–82
Protestantism
    and Defenders, 160
    and George Ogle, 62–63
    grants to, 55
    and the Kings, 46, 47, 55, 107–108
    and Mary Wollstonecraft, 81
Pückler-Muskau, Hermann Ludwig
    Heinrich von, Prince, 20–21, 187, 189,
    204, 240

Rawdon, John, 1st Earl of Moira, 137, 140
Rawdon-Hastings, Elizabeth, Countess of
    Moira (wife of 1st Earl of Moira), 53,
    94, 122n, 129, 138, 155, 163, 165,
    168, 169, 228, 229, 232, 243, 245,
    252, 295
    on Cornwallis, 268
    death, 292
    defends son, 225
    and destruction at Ballynahinch, 262
    and French invasions, 177, 270–271
    and Irish culture, 140–141
    personality, 139–141

relationship with Margaret King,
    138–139, 143, 175, 290–292
and Union, 276–277
and United Irishmen, 155
Rawdon-Hastings, Francis, 2nd Earl of
    Moira, 137–138, 160, 162, 175, 177,
    191–192, 209, 223–225, 252, 261,
    262, 275, 278, 289
Regency Crisis, 107, 110
Republicanism, 142–145, 157–158, 171
Reynolds, Thomas, 227, 249, 253, 254
Robespierre, Maximilien de, 147, 178
Roden, Lord, 263
Roman Catholics
    attitude of Lord Clare to, 108–109
    education of, 47
    emancipation issue, 56, 58, 162
    and failure of Rebellion, 272
    firearms laws, 45–46
    Protestant fear of, 56
Romney, George, 67
Roscommon, County, 4, 8, 12, 45, 54, 215,
    267, 281–282
Roscommon militia, 218
Rousseau, Jean-Jacques, 99–100, 134, 172,
    196
Rowan, Archibald Hamilton, 171
Ryan, Captain, 246–247

St John, William, 180n
Scott, John, Earl of Clonmell, 67
Scott, Sir Walter, 293
Scott, Sir William, 124
Scully, Denys, 144, 292
Sedition Acts, 183
Shakespeare, William, 27, 147
Shannon, 2nd Earl of, *see* Boyle, Richard
Shelley, Mary (*née* Godwin), 294, 297
    Frankenstein, 294
    Maurice, 294
Shelley, Percy Bysshe, 75, 244, 294–295
    "The Sensitive Plant," 295
Sheridan, Betsy, 74–75, 100–101, 113, 118
Sheridan, Elizabeth, 118, 172
Siddons, Sarah, 149
Sirr, Major, 245–246
Skeffington, Lady Harriet, 204, 205
Smith, Charlotte, 198
    Emmeline, 107
Staël, Madame de, 185, 287
Stewart, Emily Anne, Lady Castlereagh, 247,
    267
Stewart, Robert, Viscount Castlereagh, 164,
    262, 277, 293
    and Cornwallis, 269, 271
    and Kingston trial plot, 237, 242
    and Lady Louisa Conolly, 178, 243–244,
        248, 249
    military involvement, 167, 214, 224,
        227
    and Rebellion, 260, 262, 264, 266–267,
        272
    and Union, 274–276
Synge, Bishop Edward, 68, 69, 72

About the Author

JANET TODD is the author of many books on early women writers. Her best-known recent books are the biographies *Mary Wollstonecraft* and *The Secret Life of Aphra Behn*. She lives in Glasgow and Cambridge.